For the People

Ronald P. Formisano

# For the People

AMERICAN POPULIST MOVEMENTS

from the REVOLUTION to the 1850s

The University of North Carolina Press    Chapel Hill

This book was published with the assistance of the Anniversary
Endowment Fund of the University of North Carolina Press.

The paper in this book meets the guidelines for permanence
and durability of the Committee on Production Guidelines for
Book Longevity of the Council on Library Resources.

Library of Congress Cataloging-in-Publication Data
Formisano, Ronald P., 1939–
For the people : American populist movements from the
Revolution to the 1850s / Ronald P. Formisano.
p. cm.
Includes bibliographical references and index.
ISBN-13: 978-0-8078-3172-4 (cloth : alk. paper)
1. United States—Politics and government—1775–1783.
2. United States—Politics and government—1783–1865—
Congress. 3. Populism—United States—History—18th century.
4. Populism—United States—History—19th century. 5. Social
movements—United States—History—18th century. 6. Social
movements—United States—History—19th century. 7. United
States—Social conditions—To 1865. 8. Political culture—
United States—History—18th century. 9. Political culture—
United States—History—19th century. 10. Anti-Masonic
movements—United States—History. I. Title.
E302.1.F67 2008
973.3—dc22 2007027976

A Caravan book. For more information, visit
www.caravanbooks.org.

12 11 10 09 08   5 4 3 2 1

# Contents

# Acknowledgments

I began to consider writing about populisms during a five-month stint in 1994 as Fulbright Chair of Political Science at the University of Bologna, where I offered a course on comparative populist movements to a group of Italian and European students. As it happened it was an election year, and populist movements such as the Northern League and La Rete, as well as Silvio Berlusconi's pseudopopulist Forza Italia, were sweeping Italy. My host at Bologna, Tiziano Bonazzi, provided a stimulating intellectual environment by engaging me with his conversation, his colleagues, and conferences. Before that, of course, populist impulses had engulfed U.S. politics too, in the form of Ross Perot's presidential candidacy, the term limits movement, single-issue enthusiasms, and various independent candidacies.

The framework that informs the first chapter of this book took shape about that time and evolved as a talk, essay, or lecture through the years to various groups of colleagues and students, some of whom no doubt I have forgotten. But I want to thank colleagues at the University of Genoa, notably Ferdinando Fasce, and at the Universities of Florida and Kentucky for their critical responses to one or another version. The undergraduate and graduate students in seminars at Florida and Kentucky who sat through lectures or discussions also deserve thanks for aiding my continuing education about the populist dimension of American political culture and populist movements from the Revolution to the present.

In January 2003 the Liguria Study Center for Arts and Letters, Bogliasco, Italy, hosted an international conference on populism that explored populism in various countries in historical and comparative perspective. That greatly aided my thinking in the process of writing this book.

Kathleen Smith Kutolowski, SUNY Brockport, read early versions of chapters 5, 6, and 7, and since she knows more about Anti-Masonry than perhaps anyone on the planet, she gave them an exceptionally critical read. If the compliment to her regarding "the blessed spirit" seems left-handed, one aim of this book is to deepen nineteenth-century historians' understanding of that significant transitional movement.

John L. Brooke and Bruce Laurie, who read the manuscript at the request of University of North Carolina Press editor Chuck Grench, shared their extensive critical, as well as appreciative, responses with me, and it is difficult to imagine two better-qualified scholars to assess this project. Understanding so well my aims, they clarified, suggested, and prompted important revisions. Thanks to John, Bruce, and Chuck for all their help.

Michael F. Holt read the manuscript as a favor and saved me from making more errors than those that may remain, particularly in the later chapters.

The research fund provided by the University of Kentucky since 2001 has helped bring to a conclusion this part of my populism project, which has otherwise seen so many interruptions since 1994. Joanna Pollard Lile has served as an exceptionally able, and patient, research assistant.

Having worked before with UNC Press, I know it to have an excellent staff, two of whom deserve special thanks: associate managing editor Paula Wald and copyeditor Bethany Johnson. Thanks also to the staff of the University of Kentucky history department for help with logistics: Rachelle Green, Tina Hagee, and Carol O'Reilly.

My family, Erica, Laura, and Matthew, seemingly part of the distractions from scholarly "work," have helped me do this in ways as difficult to measure as they are invaluable.

For the People

# Chapter 1

# INTRODUCTION
## Populisms, Progressive and Reactionary

*Government of the people, by the people, for the people.*
—*Abraham Lincoln, Gettysburg Address, 1863*

"A spectre is haunting the world—populism": That ominous observation could have been uttered at various times in recent years, but it opened a now classic 1969 book of essays by an international group of scholars seeking to define populism and to identify its specific national, as well as cross-cultural, features. While the authors of *Populism: Its Meaning and National Characteristics* generally viewed their subject negatively, through lenses shaped by the excesses of anticommunist hysteria in the 1950s or of the New Left in the 1960s, their critiques of populist social movements and political parties now appear tame compared to the widespread and intense association of populism, over the past two decades and more, with extremism, specifically extreme right radicalism.[1] This association has been particularly intense in Europe since the 1980s, while in the United States populism possesses a more mixed history and legacy. Although North American populism emerged most prominently as an expression of reformist and progressive farmers' movements, recently populist impulses in the United States have tended more often to promote the ascendancy of conservative and reactionary leaders and policies.

Yet across the globe during the last two decades of the twentieth century a bewildering variety of new populist protest movements and political parties emerged to challenge traditional parties, ruling elites, and accepted social norms. They sprang from many kinds of social groupings and from diverse points on the political spectrum. In Western and Eastern Europe, Latin America, Africa, Asia, and North America, populist discontent has erupted intermittently. The end of the Cold War, notably, unleashed a torrent of popular movements opposed to politics-as-usual. Some promoted more democracy, pluralism, and economic opportunity; some unleashed intolerance, bigotry, and xenophobic nationalism; and others mixed together some combination of these impulses.[2] Indeed, a central argument of this book is that populist movements usually tend to be amalgams of contradictory tendencies.

In the United States in the 1990s the angry voter, especially the angry white male, became a cliché of media commentary and subject of scholarly inquiry. Citizens disgusted with the two major political parties mobilized behind "billionaire populist" Ross Perot's independent presidential candidacy in 1992 and rallied to an anti–professional politician term limits movement that succeeded in close to half the states by 1994, a year in which the angry white males helped to end forty years of Democratic control of Congress. Minnesotans' elevation to governor of independent candidate, exprofessional wrestler, and antipolitician Jesse Ventura typified many state and local episodes of populist rebellion during the late 1990s, while countless referenda appeared on state and city ballots as a result of single-issue, "direct democracy" crusades.[3]

By the early years of the new century a populist style and posture on the part of all politicians to speak for common ordinary people had come to permeate American politics. As one columnist aptly observed, "Almost every politician in modern America pretends to be a populist; indeed, it's a general rule that the more slavishly a politician supports the interests of wealthy individuals and big corporations, the folksier his manner."[4]

Clearly the populist style has been a central element of the American political tradition, and just as obviously style and rhetoric can be appropriated by just about anybody. Michael Kazin's valuable book *The Populist Persuasion* (1995) argued that before World War II populist rhetoric had been employed by movements and political leaders generally seeking progressive reform and social justice, or challenging the status quo on behalf of the dispossessed. It was also true, Kazin noted, that populist appeals had been used to buttress racial discrimination. Kazin and others have shown, too, that after World War II populist rhetoric gradually became appropriated by conservative champions of big business, the free market, the religious right, and the white backlash against the civil rights movement. Kazin's study focused on populism as a language and rhetorical style, and thus he conceded that he did not necessarily regard his subjects *as* populists, but rather as political actors using a language.[5]

The process of populist rhetoric coming to dominate political discourse, and its use often by charismatic leaders, without necessarily entailing a populist agenda, has been observed in other countries — in Italy, for example, with the rise of media magnate Silvio Berlusconi, and even in the formerly staid English political arena. The problem with a strategy of studying populism as rhetoric and style is, as Alan Ware has observed, that "populism is everywhere, and nowhere."[6] The study of populist social *movements*, my concern here, is difficult enough without opening the door to all the pretenders and free riders.

Authentically populist social movements and parties have played important roles at critical times in U.S. history. Moreover, since at least the early nineteenth century, populism has been a central element of, if not *the* dominant theme of, the political culture of the United States. Since the 1820s and 1830s, when electoral politics became permeated with an egalitarian ethos, even candidates for office born on plantations have preferred to present themselves to the electorate as born in rude log cabins and have played upon their ties to and sympathies for the common man. But movements mobilizing masses of ordinary people, arising at least initially from the grass roots and invoking the name of "the people" against established or corrupt elites, can be distinguished from the many political leaders and officials who have used populist rhetoric or adopted a populist style as a political strategy. And some of those populist movements should be regarded as predominantly *progressive* in nature.

Attempts to define populism as a general phenomenon according to some essential features that can be found in populist expressions across time and cultures have met with little success. As with similar terms such as "democracy," "ideology," or "the people," the concept is indeterminate and susceptible to many meanings.[7] This is another reason for my preference to concentrate on populist *movements* rather than the much more inclusive entity of *populism*. If the difficulty with populism as an object of study tends to be its expansiveness, the problem posed by populist movements comes in their variety and capacity to express both right-wing (reactionary) and left-wing (progressive) tendencies. In this introduction I shall try to construct an analytical framework with which to analyze populist movements of two basic, but not necessarily homogeneous, types: reactionary and progressive.

My approach to populist movements seeks to avoid romanticizing champions of "the people" as paragons of grassroots innocence and goodness, and to avoid also a tendency to dismiss such movements as unrealistic, impractical, or worse—for example, irrational and destructive. While the impulses to dismiss and to lionize have been present both in popular discussions and in academic circles, I have been more impressed with the persistence of an antipopulist mentality in scholarly discussions of what makes democracy work best. Since World War II a strong current of thinking among political theorists has demoted the desirability of popular participation by ordinary people in favor of minority elites who are said, above all, to lend stability to democratic systems.[8]

This line of thinking, and the debate in which it engages, is as old as democracy itself. In classical Athens there were those who, on the one hand, held that the freedom Athenians enjoyed "was the product of the day-to-day activities of a mass of ordinary men." On the other hand, although that "mass" was in fact only part of the population, it was too large for elite critics who argued that the extension of participation to the many was a mistake and that governing was best left to men of superior learning and status. Contemporary theories of democratic elitism similarly assume that the masses are "inherently incompetent, and . . . that they are, at best, pliable, inert stuff or, at worst, aroused unruly creatures possessing an insatiable proclivity to undermine both culture and liberty."[9]

A corollary to this perspective leads to critiques of populist movements as impractical in that they make demands on democracy that are unobtainable.[10] There is some truth to this view, but too often it is associated with a reflexive denigration of popular engagement that entails a dichotomy between the unrealism and impatience of ordinary people, on one hand, and the pragmatism and patience of elites on the other. To either side of the dichotomy might be added a long list of such invidious antonyms, as Richard D. Parker has done in a little-noticed book that tries to reconcile constitutional democracy and populist democracy. According to Parker, the "anti-populist sensibility" sees the "political energy of ordinary people" as "qualitatively inferior to more 'refined' sources of political participation." Ordinary energy thus is "emotional as opposed to reasonable, ignorant as opposed to informed, fuzzy-minded as opposed to clear-headed, simple-minded as opposed to complex." The dualities go on: short-sighted/reasonable, narrow-minded/broad-minded, self-centered/public-spirited, arbitrary/principled, low standards/high standards, and so forth.[11]

In contrast, a populist sensibility "measures *how much* political energy is being expressed—how widespread is its expression, to what extent individuals are engaging one another politically," and assumes that "expression of such energy is better than passivity or insulation." The populist sensibility ideally encourages the development of the individual political capacities of ordinary individuals and recognizes that "disdain" for the political energy of ordinary people fosters the erosion of self-confidence, passivity, and withdrawal.[12] It should be clear by now that my sympathies are with Parker and the populist sensibility, but the reader may judge, eventually, whether that means that the treatment of populist movements in this book has been uncritical.

The study of populist movements in U.S. history writing can hardly be said to constitute a "field." Thus, historians concerned with, for example, rural insurgencies of the late eighteenth century, or the Anti-Masons of the 1820s, or the People's Party of the 1890s, or, still further apart, progressive or reactionary movements in the twentieth century do not usually regard their works as connected or sharing similar questions and explanations. In any case, the study of populist movements has been obstructed by the impulse to categorize them as either/or, progressive or reactionary, as well as by the prevailing association of populism generally with antidemocratic tendencies.[13]

It is instructive to recall that the political party that gave the language the word "populist" has itself gone through cycles of interpretation that have swung from progressive to reactionary to progressive again. The People's Party of the 1890s was viewed originally as a precursor of the Progressive Era and its democratic reforms, but forty years ago, many historians viewed "capital P" Populists as illiberal nativists and intolerant precursors of Mc-Carthyism. Since the 1970s, however, interpretations of the Populists have brought them into line with Parker's definition of a populist sensibility: a widespread movement of ordinary people, men and women, encouraging political engagement and energized by what political scientists would call a sense of efficacy, or hope. While points of contention inevitably persist, recent books of synthesis by Norman Pollack, Gene Clanton, Robert C. Mc-Math Jr., and Elizabeth Sanders, as well as several influential monographs, indicate that the discussion proceeds within an understanding of the basically humane, republican, and progressive nature of Populism.[14]

A similar shift has taken place in the last generation in interpretations of the Anti-Federalist critics and opponents of the federal constitution in the 1780s. Historians and commentators from left to right on the political spectrum have looked with increasing appreciation at the Anti-Federalists' giving voice to fears of centralized power and the threat they perceived from a too powerful national government to states, local communities, and individual rights. The "historical fortunes" of other late eighteenth-century defenders of community and individual rights, those who engaged in mob and crowd actions and who often took the law into their own hands by force or the threat of force from assembled numbers ("the people out of doors"), also have improved in recent decades. Yet historians have seldom judged traditionalist or "primitive rebels" as harshly as the 1890s Populists were assessed during the 1950s and 1960s heyday of reaction against mass behavior.[15]

But the contemporary study of modern "small p" populism has lacked the perspective that could be afforded by a long historical view that reaches back well before the 1890s Populists to eighteenth-century forerunners of later popular movements, protests, and discontents. Some historians are impressed with the differences between traditional popular insurgencies of rural rebels, crowds, and mobs characteristic of the eighteenth century and the later mass social movements that arose in a different economic, communications, and political environment after the War of 1812. The latter usually turned to political organizing and electioneering and away from violence, the threat of violence, or extralegal methods. But granting those and other departures, this narrative will focus more on their similarities and, particularly, on the mixture of progressive and reactionary features that existed on both sides of the traditional-modern divide.[16]

Eighteenth-century insurgencies often aimed at the restoration of a social order that provided economic security, fair treatment, and equality before the law. "They were firmly convinced," one historian argues, "that justice—and even the law—was on their side." Thus, traditional populisms tended to be "'backward' rather than 'forward-looking,'" but some could also graft new beliefs onto the old, creating a new popular ideology.[17] The populist movements to be encountered in the chapters that follow, from the Revolutionary era to the 1850s, were not "revolutionary" or even "radical," including those that resorted to mobilizing under arms large numbers of aggrieved protesters. Of course, many of their elite opponents resorted to hyperbole to exaggerate the threat posed by unwanted challenges to the social order or to political routine, but the goals of populist insurgents were usually limited and, in their minds, constitutional within the bounds of the social contract.

Over two decades ago Alan Brinkley's *Voices of Protest: Huey Long, Father Coughlin, and the Great Depression* (1982) constituted a breakthrough in the general study of populism by taking seriously the main populist demagogues of the 1930s. Avoiding scholars' tendency to disparage or to marginalize such figures as Long and Coughlin, Brinkley sought to discover what their popularity revealed about popular protest in American culture. He looked beyond the mesmerizing, charismatic, and flawed personalities and leadership of Long and Coughlin to connect them to long-standing populist traditions embodying a deep-seated fear of centralized power and a concern for the autonomy of local communities: "some of the oldest and deepest impulses in American political life."[18] Brinkley's theme resonated with historians of the American Revolution, who had maintained that resistance to an aggressive central power that threatened the very existence of "liberty" constituted a driving force of the rebellion against Great Britain.[19] Further, during the decades after the Revolution, and particularly after the establishment of a federal government in 1789, the efforts of local communities to preserve local autonomy and preserve threatened individual rights propelled populist insurgencies against the Americans' own central and state governments. The present study is an attempt to show the bedrock of those old and deep impulses.

A different approach to reconceptualizing populism came from Christopher Lasch, who, in several works before his untimely death, focused on the tensions between classical liberalism (broadly conceived) and populism. His major work in this vein, *The True and Only Heaven: Progress and Its Critics* (1991), argued that positing republicanism as the major radical alternative tradition to liberalism—a recent fad in U.S. history writing—had been exaggerated. Radical challenges to an unbridled capitalist political economy stemmed not just from the Revolutionary generation's republican ideology but also from "a populist tradition that drew on republicanism and liberalism alike but mixed these ingredients into something new." In related essays Lasch described populism as hostile both to the free market and to the welfare state, emphasizing that populists took responsibility for themselves. He credited the Populists of the 1890s and their subtreasury proposal to gain low-cost government credit as a way to get government help to help themselves. Although Lasch's writings were filled with scathing critiques of the materialism of liberal society, nowhere did he reject "constitutional restraints" or "constitutional democracy."[20]

Lasch understood well that populist movements often expressed anger, resentment, and even intolerance, and thus he believed that they needed to embrace a "spiritual discipline against resentment," which he found admirably present in the post-1945 southern civil rights movement. Otherwise, Lasch saw populist movements as emanating from the lower middle class, a social sector prone to narrowness, provincialism, nativism, anti-intellectualism, and racism. Lasch erred, I believe, in allocating populism (and intolerance) largely to the lower middle class. In doing so he followed a long tradition dating back to Lenin's analysis of the late nineteenth-century Russian *narodniki*, or people's movement, as a petit-bourgeois effusion.[21]

Giving the lower classes a monopoly on intolerance is an all too common fallacy.[22] But Lasch did confront realistically what I call "populism's chronic illiberalism"—chronic, but not universal or inevitable. His critique of liberalism, meanwhile, contained some harsh diagnoses of a pathologically materialistic culture. Whatever one's attitude to his rather pessimistic view of liberal culture, his analysis of populism hardly romanticized it and provides an additional basis for comprehending its complex variations in American society.

Although ignored by historians, political scientist Allen D. Hertzke's examination of two different protest movements of the 1980s reinforced Lasch's connection of populist movements as reactions to the excesses of liberalism. Hertzke proposed that cultural and economic populism were once joined together, in William Jennings Bryan, for example, but by the late twentieth century were split into two branches. Hertzke devoted most of his book to an analysis of Jesse Jackson's left-wing economic populism, on one hand, and Christian right-wing preacher Pat Robertson's cultural populism on the other, arguing that both left and right variants of populism were reacting to the same "ascendent liberalism in economics and culture." Like Lasch, Hertzke pitted both populisms against liberal ideology "in its broad classical meaning," that is, "a blend of free-market economics and protection of individual liberty—a position embraced by most Democrats and Republicans today."[23] More important, however, Hertzke also found the classical republican tradition of the Founders alone insufficient as a source of opposition to unfettered individualist liberalism and its nurture of "a democracy of cupidity." Rather, a synthesis of republicanism, liberalism, and a heritage of Christian communalism also helped to shape regard for the public good and social justice. While Hertzke perhaps attributed more influence to "communitarian republican and Christian notions of virtue" in shaping Anti-Federalist opposition to the Constitution than most historians of the nation's founding would accept, he did call attention to the strong strain of local communalism (and defense of local autonomy) rooted in the colonial and Revolutionary heritage that, implicitly or explicitly, Brinkley and Lasch had emphasized.[24]

While a number of general works and monographs in U.S. history writing point to new directions in the understanding of populist movements, surprisingly little if any attention has been paid by North Americanists to the substantial literature dealing with Latin American populist movements, which have played so prominent a role in South and Central American countries since the late nineteenth century. Indeed, from a transatlantic perspective, the study of both North American and contemporary European populist movements and parties, past and present, proceeds without reference to Latin America. Yet in Europe during the last two decades so-called new right populist parties have attracted enormous attention as they have challenged and even helped to displace more traditional parties of left and right. Since the neopopulist parties have mobilized voters reacting negatively to new immigration and related issues, such as fear of crime, European scholars overwhelmingly have tended to see the new parties as "extreme right" or "radical right" and, often, as threats to "destabilize" democratic systems.[25]

Studies of populist movements on the other side of the Atlantic differ greatly, especially those of Latin American populisms. In South America, not only have populist movements, leaders, and regimes constituted the most impressive political forces from the 1920s to the 1960s, with neopopulism emerging in several countries in the 1990s, but also the great majority of Latin Americanists associate such populist impulses with progressive reform to the degree that European scholars now associate populism with reactionary extremism. Considering that European neopopulist right-wing parties are thought to be xenophobic or even racist because of anti-immigrant postures, it is worth observing that in Latin America populist movements and leaders have promoted the extension of not only "symbolic dignity" to social groups previously excluded or marginalized by poverty or color but also political participation and economic opportunity.[26]

Latin American populist studies appear especially useful because they tend to distinguish clearly between populist discourse or rhetoric, regimes in power, strategies of mobilization, social and electoral movements, and political parties. This is not to say that Latin Americanists have found "populism" without ambiguity or excessive malleability, yet even for a scholar who remarked on the concept's "perverse perdurability," its political expression should not be set "apart from mainstream politics." Indeed, "populist movements—not to mention regimes—are thoroughly mundane, even conventional."[27]

Thus, while ostensibly dealing with very different cultures and concerns, and with infrequent if not rare attention to one another, North American and Latin American studies of populisms are converging in emphasizing the variety and contradictions of such movements and parties, as well as their centrality to their political cultures. Yet the United States does offer a more mixed spectrum of populisms, and right-wing populist impulses and movements have tended to be more important there than in Latin America, especially in recent decades. Even in Latin America, however, and especially in the United States, populist movements sometimes fuse together left *and* right, progressive *and* reactionary, tendencies in an amalgam that may defy traditional left-right categories.[28]

North American populism, at least from the Anti-Federalists of the 1780s, has often been generated from fear of centralized power on the part of local communities resisting external forces that are perceived to threaten their autonomy, political rights, or economic security. Ordinary people defending local communities can be found in episodes of both progressive and reactionary populism, with the former represented by various "Regulators" in the late eighteenth and early nineteenth centuries and the latter represented by the second Ku Klux Klan or, say, resistance to school desegregation in the 1970s. It has been clear for some time that localist defense or the fear of outside concentrated power can lead left or right, or "to both simultaneously."[29]

This last point cannot be emphasized too much. Entirely progressive or wholly reactionary movements seldom exist in reality but tend to be fabricated through reification or transforming processes of idealizing or demonizing. Both progressive and reactionary populist movements will usually possess features shared by the other. The point is illustrated well by Hertzke's analysis of Jesse Jackson's economic populism and Pat Robertson's cultural populism. Not only did the two branches of populism react to a liberalism that they saw as taking society in the wrong direction, but Jackson's outlook also possessed a strong cultural component, indeed, "a cultural and moral conservatism suggestive of [William Jennings] Bryan's crusades against alcohol and libertine morality." Jackson regarded freedom without limits as destructive, and he denounced the counterculture's indulgence in sex and drugs. His ten-point urban policy was one, he said, that "Moses brought from the mountain." Similarly, Robertson expressed themes of economic populism, some of which hearkened back to midwestern Populism, as Robertson denounced "profligate banks, the savings and loan bailout, and the Trilateral Commission's domination of U.S. foreign policy."[30]

Populist movements need to be positioned on a spectrum bounded by ideal types of progressive and reactionary, recognizing that the prototypes are unlikely to be found in reality. Yet both progressive and reactionary movements share the common energizing sense, in Margaret Canovan's words, "that politics has escaped popular control. The message is, 'this is our polity, in which we, the democratic sovereign, have a right to practice government by the people; but we have been shut out of power by corrupt politicians and an unrepresentative elite who betray our interests, ignore our opinions, and treat us with contempt.'"[31]

Progressive populist movements in the United States show a concern for the redistribution of political or economic power downward. They tend to be egalitarian and suffused with an ethic of "producerism" that has drawn energy less from class conflict and more from resentment of those privileged economic interests that are able to manipulate capital, law, and politics to their profit. At the crudest level they protest that too few have too much; or they voice resentment against specific targets—the wealthy, corporations, professional politicians, professional elites or experts, social engineers, bureaucrats, or as a Kansas Populist once put it, "the aristocrats, plutocrats, and all the other rats."

Progressive movements also have tended to lift women out of traditional gender roles and to promote at least an incipient feminism and decidedly an expanded role for women in the public sphere. In progressive populist movements women have held leadership positions, and their concerns often have influenced the agenda of the movement.[32] This has sometimes been true even in reactionary populist movements, though, as will be noted shortly, their overall tendency is different. The gendered appeals of populist movements and gender relations within them are underexamined areas, a situation that this study hopes to redress.

Progressive movements also may possess the following features:

They arise from the grass roots and gain a wide popular base of "ordinary people," and they may attract cross-class support.

While concentrated in the middle and lower classes, they may also spring from communal or subcultural groups.

In the early stages their leaders tend to be indigenous or "homegrown," with many who were not previously involved politically, though they usually include men and women active in community or neighborhood organizations.

They seek greater opportunity because they see society as tilted out of balance. They are not necessarily anti-institutional (as often depicted) but have concluded that political and other institutions are not functioning fairly and, hence, ordinary citizens are disadvantaged; oppressive conditions exist and must be removed and fairness restored.

Their supporters believe that they have lost control over their lives, and so they seek to regain some management of their own destiny, a con-

trol or autonomy they once experienced or, if not, that democratic
ideology tells them they ought to have.

They can be, in the manner of reformers, restorationist and innovative
at the same time. The People's Party, for example, wanted to restore
the traditional independence of farmers through the novel means of
the subtreasury plan.

Progressive movements exhibit a healthy distrust of conventional
politics, which sometimes can run to excessive fears or unrealistic
visions of conspiracies arrayed against them. Much has been made
of the "paranoid" tendencies of populist movements generally, a
judgment which itself might be regarded as rhetorical overkill. Indeed, it often goes unremarked that a high degree of exaggeration,
hysterical rhetoric, or hyperbole routinely exists in mainstream politics among major party politicians. As Mark Summers has observed
regarding Republican and Democratic excesses in the 1884 campaign, "The paranoid style for which Populists would be pilloried by
later historians was the natural child of the mainstream parties."[33]

Reactionary populist movements may possess features of progressive
movements (as the latter may also possess features of the former):

Reactionary movements project a masculine if not macho appeal that
results in a significant gender gap, that is, disproportionate male
support for the movement or party. Though my concern is primarily
with the United States, this disparity appears strikingly in the case
of several of the contemporary new right populist parties in Europe.
Despite this strong relationship between reactionary populist parties
and a specifically gendered masculine/macho appeal, such movements may nevertheless push women into the public sphere and
beyond traditional gender boundaries. They usually do so under
cover of traditional gender ideology and accompanied by antifemi-
nist protestations, as in the case of nativist women in the 1850s who
supported the anti-Catholic Know-Nothing movement or the women
auxiliaries of the second Klan.[34]

They usually express culturally illiberal tendencies, or intolerance, denying equal opportunity or equal rights to groups to which the movement or party is hostile, groups regarded as not of the true people.
As a corollary, much has been made of the ethnic nationalism of

reactionary populisms, and they do tend to advocate more exclusive forms of nationalism.[35] Progressive populisms, in contrast, tend to advocate a form of civic nationalism (contrast, for example, the second Klan with the civil rights movement of the 1960s).

Reactionary populisms may use methods that violate norms of civility essential to a democratic society, for example, by denying opponents the ability to assemble or speak or by engaging in harsher persecutions or silencing through violence.

They tend to scapegoat vulnerable groups, especially minority cultural or racial groups, and attack them rhetorically. Sometimes these verbal aggressions are displacements of anger against more powerful groups, and sometimes groups that are the target of populist resentment may in fact bear some responsibility for the conditions of which protesters complain, and hence this is not true scapegoating (though it is frequently alleged).

Reactionary populisms more easily slide into exaggerated fear regarding their enemies and the causes of social ills, while some of the most extreme and marginal entertain the desperate conviction, as Richard Hofstadter put it some time ago, that history itself is a conspiracy.

In an excess of psychobabble, critics of populist movements often label them "paranoid." Liberal ideologues tend to use the term or its cognates as a stick to beat all populisms. Many political actors and groups engage in exaggeration and hyperbole. The well-educated gentry of the founding generation, as they divided into two extremely distrustful camps, began to believe the worst of one another: the centralizing "Court" party of the Washington administration saw the opposition developing around Thomas Jefferson and James Madison as a French Jacobinite conspiracy of radicals and unbelievers out to undermine government and religion, while Jeffersonians of the "Country" party believed that "aristocrats" allied with Treasury Secretary Alexander Hamilton were conspiring to establish a monarchy in place of the republic. For twelve years "[Jeffersonian] Republican publishers' favorite epithet for their adversaries" was "monarchist." In the late 1790s Federalist clergymen and pamphleteers appropriated a theory that originated in Europe that a secret Masonic lodge known as the Bavarian Illuminati had plotted the French Revolution and now had infiltrated the United States through the Democratic societies and other "Jacobinical" influences associated with the Republicans. Both sides believed that their political opponents were conspirators who posed a mortal danger to republican principles and government.[36]

As heirs of the Revolutionary ideology it could hardly be surprising that Federalists and Republicans in the 1790s perceived one another as necessarily conspiratorial. For a half century before the Revolution the dominant elements in colonial thinking about relations with imperial Britain "were a fear of corruption—of its anticonstitutional destructiveness—and of the menace of a ministerial conspiracy." After 1763 the Whig colonists perceived "overwhelming evidence . . . that they were faced with conspirators against liberty. . . . And it was this above all else that in the end propelled them into Revolution." Not just Whig leaders and pamphleteers came to this conviction; the "ever present danger of an active conspiracy of power against liberty . . . rose in the consciousness of a large segment of the American population before any of the famous political events of the struggle with England took place." Moreover, the patriots' opponents, royal officials in the colonies and their superiors in London, became increasingly persuaded that they were confronted by a conspiracy "of intriguing men whose professions masked their true intentions."[37]

This provocative argument of noted historian Bernard Bailyn raised questions among some other historians as to whether the American revolutionaries were paranoid—either metaphorically (the soft view) or literally, "clinically" (the hard view). Gordon Wood directly confronted the possibility that Revolutionary leaders suffered "from actual delusions of persecution and were unable to assess reality in a rational fashion" by exploring the "general presuppositions and conventions . . . the underlying metaphysics—of eighteenth-century culture." Wood concluded that this was the "great era" of conspiratorial fears, and "all manner of people . . . resorted readily to conspiratorial modes of explanation." Indeed, such approaches resulted from the Enlightenment and the advance of science. Perceiving conspiracies "became a major means by which educated men in the early modern period ordered and gave meaning to their political world. Far from being symptomatic of irrationality, this conspiratorial mode of explanation represented an enlightened stage in Western man's long struggle to comprehend his social reality."[38] But many historians who might accept Wood's argument for Revolutionary leaders do not regard it as applicable to the populist movements that arose after the 1820s, notably the Anti-Masons and Know-Nothings. Those movements, along with abolitionism, are still regarded by many observers as exhibiting the "paranoid style" if not a paranoid mentality.[39] One leading scholar of Anti-Masonry has described it as a "social paranoia" with "roots in reality." This psychologizing of populist movements springs from various causes, some of which have been suggested above. They include the marginalizing of the "political energy of ordinary people," the tendency to minimize the actual grievances of protesters, the lack of attention to the varied composition of movements (unstable individuals can be found practically anywhere), and, as well, a failure to probe deeply enough into the social and political reality confronting movement leaders and participants.

In assessing grassroots populist leaders who tend to use blunt and hyperbolic language, perhaps perspective can be gained by considering the tsunamis of negative television advertising that inundate every U.S. election cycle, and in particular the recent spot that suggested that a U.S. senator and veteran who lost his limbs in Vietnam was an ally of Osama bin Laden. Only in America, as they say, nothing succeeds like excess. Conventional politicians often make fantastic charges against one another. Populists often do, too, and are especially known for blunt, politically incorrect speech. Is the difference that those in the mainstream do not mean what they say and populists do? That populists of whatever kind are sincere and stupid while traditional politicians are cynical and smart? Rather, political leaders of various kinds use language directed to particular constituencies, and all routinely engage in exaggeration. Sometimes they believe what they say; sometimes they do not.

In any case, historians and social scientists should not expect social movements to maintain the purity of what Lasch has called a "spiritual discipline against resentment." Richard Rorty has recently criticized the need to idealize popular movements, which too often results in overreaction when they do not turn out to be "flawless." "Bottom-up leftist initiatives," he writes, "come from people who have little security, money, or power and who rebel against the unfair treatment which they or others like them, are receiving." Of the now favorably viewed agrarian protesters of the late nineteenth century he contends: "Those dispossessed farmers were often racist, nativist and sadistic. . . . We need to get rid of the Marxist idea that only bottom-up initiatives, conducted by workers and peasants who have somehow been so freed from resentment as to show no trace of prejudice, can achieve our country."[40] The point is not the accuracy of Rorty's description of Greenbackers and Populists, but rather his injunction to resist imposing impossible standards of purity on those disadvantaged groups who have sought social justice.

Two points bear repeating: First, the distinction between progressive and reactionary populist movements is not an absolute dichotomy; each may, and usually does, possess features of the other; few progressive movements are "flawless." Thus, the complexities of populist movements should not be underestimated. Many contemporary and earlier populist movements in Europe and North America, progressive and reactionary, often have defied traditional left-right categories and classic liberal-conservative dichotomies.

Second, populist movements and parties should not be described, explained, or evaluated any differently from mainstream, conventional movements and parties. Thus, psychological reductionism should be avoided as it normally is with, say, Republican and Democratic voters and political leaders. Although populist movements in the United States historically often expressed antipolitical and antipartisan impulses, they drew on attitudes and predispositions embedded deep in American political culture and reaching back at least to the nation's founding.

In the pages that follow, I shall argue that the history of populist movements in the United States, from the era of the American Revolution to the 1850s, presents a record that similarly defies and contradicts attempts to impose rigid categorization. I originally intended to write a history that focused on populist movements from the mid-nineteenth century to the present, but in considering the ideological and (even) constitutional background, it became clear that understanding the populist strain in American political culture must begin with the American Revolution and its aftermath, when the principle of the people's sovereignty was widely held by a substantial number of Americans throughout the country.

In a subsequent book I plan to carry the argument forward through the nineteenth century. Before then, it should become evident that the ambiguities of some recent populist movements share much in common with those from the past. Further, populist insurgencies of the late eighteenth and early nineteenth centuries, which drew so obviously on Revolutionary ideas and crowd strategies, differed in kind from the populist movements that followed the rise of popular politics and the commercial and communications revolutions. But the late eighteenth-century popular disturbances shared with the social movements of the antebellum era the often-expressed republican ideal of realizing the egalitarian promise of the American Revolution.

## THE PEOPLE'S SOVEREIGNTY

*The sovereignty of the people, emphasizing the popular character of governmental authority, rested on supposed acts of the people, both past and present, that were almost as difficult to examine as acts of God. The very existence of such a thing as the people, capable of acting to empower, define, and limit a previously nonexistent government required a suspension of disbelief. History recorded no such action.*
— Edmund Morgan, Inventing the People: The Rise of Popular Sovereignty in England and America (1988)

Populist currents ran through the politics of the British American colonies well before the American Revolution, but populist expectations became endemic to American political culture in large part because the leaders of the movement for independence from Britain necessarily appealed to natural rights and popular sovereignty as their source of authority—to the rights of the "people" or "peoples"—both terms were used—of the several colonies and then states. As Edmund Morgan has explained so well, the very concept of popular sovereignty originated over the course of the preceding century and a half in England and the colonies as a "fiction" created by elites to justify government by the few.[41] It was first used to limit the king and empower Parliament. Popular sovereignty is a fiction because while the people may be the source of legitimacy, they themselves cannot rule; through the mechanism of representative government elites rule in the name of the people.[42]

Morgan's shrewd observation in effect explains the inevitability of populist protest and progressive reform movements in a political culture in which "democracy" is realized indirectly through representative institutions. "The history of popular sovereignty in both England and America after 1689," he writes, "can be read as a history of the successive efforts of different generations to bring the facts into closer conformity with the fiction, efforts that have gradually transformed the very structure of society." As early as the mid-seventeenth century, when the concept of popular sovereignty emerged, a movement arose that took literally the idea (or fiction) of popular sovereignty. The reformers known as the Levellers, who sought not social upheaval as their opponents who named them suggested but rather political reform, were early populists who wanted to set limits on parliamentary power and to give the people a more direct way of exercising their sovereignty. "Whereas all power is originally and essentially in the whole body of the people of this Nation, and whereas their free choice or consent by their Representors is the only originall [sic] of foundation of all just government," then those representatives must be held accountable, with the people able "to continue or displace and remove [Representors] from their offices."[43] The Levellers, in the manner of populists after them, combined practical suggestions—annual elections, geographic districts according to population, an expanded suffrage—with the idealistic vision "of the people acting apart from their representatives in Parliament."[44]

The canon that sovereignty comes from the people, to put it differently, raises the temptation that authority should be exercised directly by the people, which is hardly feasible. Thus the populist ideal of the people's sovereignty, in promising more than it could deliver, led to instability and challenges to authority during the early years of the republic and well into the nineteenth century.[45] From this perspective, the history of protest and challenging movements after the establishment of a federal government can be looked on as efforts to bring the reality into line with the fiction.

# Chapter 2

# The American Revolution and the Anti-Federalist Legacy

*It is vain to expect or hope to carry on government against the universal bent and opinion of the people.*
—John Adams

*The people are now contending for freedom; and would to God they might not only obtain, but likewise keep it in their own hands.*
—Anonymous, The People the Best Gove[r]nors (1776)

## THE AMERICAN REVOLUTION'S POPULIST LEGACY

In the colonies and then states during the 1760s and 1770s Americans drew repeatedly on the notion of popular sovereignty to justify crowd actions and riots and then armed resistance to British authority. During the eighteenth century, in England and America, traditions of popular insurgency were already "quasi-legitimate," even regarded as part of the "natural order." Routinely, popular disturbances broke out in defense of local communities when authorities failed to act or acted unlawfully. Though common, crowds and mob actions showed remarkable restraint and sought to avoid violence, and especially bloodshed, whenever possible. After 1765 the conflict with British officials called into play an extraordinary outburst of crowd activity, and popular protests, inside and outside the law, gained further legitimacy. The patriot cause entrenched a template for later movements that would attempt, in the name of "the people," to end social injustice or the corrupt sway of powerful elites. This was a complicated, many-sided process because the American Revolution expressed conservative, even reactionary, elements, as well as populist, reformist, and egalitarian impulses. The Revolution, in short, both "extended *and contained* liberty."[1]

Thus, claims regarding the "radicalism" of the American Revolution need to be tempered with a recognition of the conflicting currents it drew on and set loose, radical and conservative, populist and antipopulist. The contention that the Revolution brought not only respectability but "even dominance to ordinary people" has overstated the case for change.[2] While many "ordinary people's" lives were elevated in the course and consequence of independence, nevertheless propertied white men tended to retain social and political hegemony, while many ordinary people felt excluded from the revolutionary settlement in the newly independent states. Indeed, popular movements of protest undertaken by those seeking redress of grievances *after* the Revolution ran into unexpectedly stiff elite resistance.

The American Revolution was made more in the name of "the people," conceptualized in the plural, than for a collective entity or for an American "nation." To understand that claim, the evolution of the meaning of those terms during the eighteenth century requires examination. In sixteenth-century England the words "nation" and "people" became synonymous, signaling "the emergence of the first nation in the world, in the sense in which the word is understood today, and launch[ing] the era of national-ism." In France, too, by the eighteenth century "people" and "nation" could be synonymous, although "people" could have several, divergent meanings, referring to "everyone other than the king and his ministers," or the entire Third Estate, or the lower classes. While many possible referents and con-fusion existed, nevertheless the increasing positive use of "public opinion," "nation," and "people" became part of the movement against absolutism and for democracy.[3]

But in the late eighteenth century the leaders of the American colonies, as they moved toward independence, did not conceive of themselves as a unified people or nation. "People" appears several times in the Declaration of Independence, in one instance to refer to the colonists as "one people" distinct from their "British brethren," and in another in the plural, as in the assertion of "the People" having a right to institute a new government "to affect *their* Safety and Happiness." The "Representatives of the United States of America" in one breath invoked the "Authority of the good People of these Colonies," and in the next breath the United States became "these United Colonies . . . of . . . FREE AND INDEPENDENT STATES." The word "nation" was entirely absent from the Declaration.[4]

The Declaration's author, Thomas Jefferson, would become an inspira-tion to champions of the people during the nineteenth century and later. Jefferson and his fellow gentry who led the patriot cause in their various regions and colonies certainly did appeal to "the people" as their source of power and legitimacy against Crown and Parliament. Indeed, the Whig leaders had little choice but to emphasize that sovereignty came from the people. But notions of "the people" varied among American elites as they had in Britain and France, and gentlemen assumed that after the *few* debated to formulate policy, the *many* would participate by way of granting consent. With regard to the lower orders of white men, not to mention women and nonwhites, the American gentry espoused largely a populism without egalitarianism.[5]

None of this mattered, however, because notions of popular sovereignty and "the people" were abroad and widening their influence within the political culture. In addition, the ideology of the American Revolution deepened the populist strain of political culture by drawing on English "Country" thought, which set itself in opposition to centralized power (and the inevitable corruption) accruing to the king and his ministers. Colonists at odds with royal officials came to believe increasingly in a ministerial conspiracy to deprive American Britons of their rights as Englishmen. The conviction of an inherent conflict between liberty and power became embedded in the American grain and, throughout U.S. history, would energize countless popular movements arrayed against corrupt elites to reclaim the liberty and well-being of the people. Always, of course, some champions of the people's liberties sought power for themselves or for less than benevolent causes. But both true and false people's heroes remained indebted to a revolution founded on the distrust of centralized power.[6]

In still another way the ferment of the Revolution helped to create a political culture with markedly populist features. Historians recently have called attention to a relatively widespread sense of efficacy among Britons on both sides of the Atlantic during the eighteenth century. Kevin Phillips notes the extraordinary political "assertiveness of ordinary Englishmen— and English*women*," which was "a staple of wry continental comment from the tracts of Montesquieu to the operas of Mozart."[7] Popular participation in Britain's polity was remarkable, compared with the European continent, but in British North America there flourished an "always potentially highly participatory politics." During the Revolution, ordinary men and women engaged in meetings, tavern gatherings, crowd and mob actions, parades and demonstrations, and military service in the Revolutionary War itself. Largely encouraged by native (and often wary) elites, the ranks of participating middling and ordinary Americans expanded, and, as important, so did their sense of efficacy.[8]

The Revolution's potential promise of independence for such dependent classes as women and African Americans would be unrealized. Although overturning the traditional patriarchal relation between king and subjects, republican ideology retained a great deal of paternalism and hierarchy, and citizenship was defined as white, male, and masculine in that manly republicanism was associated with "freedom from effeminacy." Yet the public sphere inexorably grew larger during the Revolution and had roots in the remarkable economic development of the colonies during the eighteenth century, which contributed to a "broad diffusion of an expansive sense of self-worth throughout the independent, mostly land-owning, adult male population." Although the colonies had experienced no common political life before 1765, two different ideas of empire formed on each side of the Atlantic, and the clash between them "turned into a revolution when the settlers firmed their common resistance to Britain by providing themselves with an historical-mythological identity, allowing them to declare them-selves a *people*."[9] But again, notions of who and what constituted "a people" or "the people" still varied, though the momentum to establish "a people" as the nation, as well as "the people" as possessors of sovereignty, was gathering force.

The populist phase of the Revolution, with publics operating "out-of-doors," often expressed anti-elite and anti-aristocratic sentiments. In 1789 David Ramsay observed that the conflict with England "gave a spring to the active powers of the inhabitants, and set them on thinking, speaking, and acting far beyond that to which they had been accustomed." This was liter-ally so in the case of public speaking, as "democratic idioms" and populist rhetoric began to gain a footing alongside the "classical rhetoric" of the elite. This shift appeared also in public prints, as the "printed text retained little of the written word's historical association with elite power, and the less privileged often found that textual appeals allowed them the social space to challenge authority."[10]

A spreading, expanded notion of "the people" also emerged in innovative state constitution making during the 1770s and 1780s. Aside from incorpo-rating the fear of executive power, several constitutions lowered property qualifications for voting, specified voting by ballot rather than viva voce, had the lower house chosen annually, limited terms of office, and dramati-cally increased the size of legislatures. Governors and upper houses lost some powers to lower houses, and the latter often delegated much to local governments. Georgia, Vermont, and Pennsylvania simply had no senate. The Pennsylvania constitution of 1776, with its weak executive, unicameral legislature, and embrace of popular ratification by all adult white males, has been taken to epitomize the era. Perhaps more tellingly, debates over the extent of the suffrage began to reveal a view of voting as a franchise, that any individuals who could not vote were therefore unrepresented.[11]

At the same time, "stake-in-society" thinking remained common among many gentlemen, who believed that government should mirror the social hierarchy. Thus, several new state constitutions contained property qualifications for officeholding and voting. The commitment to property-based citizen rights was so strong that in 1776 the New Jersey constitution enfranchised all adult inhabitants with £50 of property, even though its framers realized that this would allow unmarried women who qualified to vote. Some women did vote until 1807, when their suffrage became a casualty of partisan politics.[12] Clearly, antipopulist impulses were present in the populist phase of the Revolution, and they would become even stronger in the 1780s.

The anonymous *The People the Best Gove[r]nors* (1776) argued for keeping the freedom for which the people were contending "in their own hands" and against "reintroducing the worst parts of British rule," and it posed the question: "Are we fighting and lavishing our blood and treasure to establish the freest and best government on earth, or are we about to set up a formidable court interest? . . . The origin and essence of government is in the people." In contrast, conservatives warned that "the staff of power never was, nor never can be, in the nature of things, in the people's hands. As a people we have no power in our hands we can safely exercise, but of choosing our guardians once a year. . . . We are not fighting for this or that form of government, but to be free from *arbitrary power* and the *Iron Rod of Oppression* on one hand, and from *Popular Licentiousness and anarchy and confusion on the other.*"[13]

As the centrifugal forces released by the Revolution continued into the 1780s and bedeviled the confederation of states that had stumbled to victory over the British, both antipopulist and populist action and sentiment mounted. The Articles of Confederation (1781) laid out several important responsibilities for the Continental Congress: foreign affairs, conducting war, deciding disputes between the states, a postal service, coinage, and Indian and territorial affairs. But the new quasi state did not possess the power to enforce its decisions, to levy taxes, or to deal in a unified way with foreign powers. The situation worsened with an economic downturn in the two years following peace, 1783–85, as British goods flooded into the country and specie poured out. A chain reaction of debts and merchant failures and lost jobs ensued. American leaders had looked forward to free trade with the arrival of independence, but the British erected mercantilist barriers, closing the British West Indies to American shippers and placing high duties on the import of American staples to Britain. The states individually failed at retaliation, and the situation worsened as Spain closed the Mississippi to U.S. commerce.

Increasingly, the nationalists and proto-Federalists who wanted to reform the articles articulated a broad "pro-developmental vision" that encouraged native manufactures as well as "an expanding oceanic commerce."[14] For these things, they needed a government with "energy." Instead, the confederation government grew more insolvent, so that by 1786 seven states had issued some form of paper money, North Carolina and Rhode Island recklessly so. The latter became a byword among nationalists for democratic tyranny, but the state acted partly from an effort to ease the burden on taxpayers resulting from state and federal levies that had been designed primarily to pay off wealthy investors who had bought up wartime securities. Throughout New England, such taxes provoked resistance, especially in New Hampshire and Massachusetts, where angry farmers and their supporters resorted to crowd actions characteristic of the Revolution to get the attention of state authorities.[15]

During the later 1780s modes of popular protest that had often been encouraged by elites in the resistance to British authority became unwelcome when a conservative reaction set in after the war was won. Nationalists and conservatives throughout the country increasingly grew alarmed at unrest in the backcountry among farmers and other rural folk burdened by taxes, debt, and other grievances. Although most accounts of the 1780s have focused on the events in Massachusetts in 1786–87 known as "Shays's Rebellion," such a narrative marginalizes disturbances or threats of insurgency that rippled through New England, Pennsylvania, Maryland, Virginia, North Carolina, and South Carolina during those years. These populist protests and uprisings from the 1750s to the 1790s displayed common features, with a focus on immediate alleviation of distress by more direct democracy and a shortcutting through what they regarded as burdensome and unfair legality. Land rioters during the late eighteenth century embraced the notion that their labor entitled them to land, taking precedence over what they regarded as the often fraudulent claims of great landlords, while Revolutionary ideology taught them that republican citizenship must rest on property ownership.[16]

Pre-Revolutionary insurgencies stretched back most immediately to the 1750s, when settlers on the huge "manor" estates of the Livingston and Van Rensselaer families in the Hudson River valley engaged in sporadic violence over land claims. Another outbreak began in 1764, when heirs of the

Philips lands began to evict squatters, as well as tenants with leases. Yankee farmers, who had replaced the original and more "subordinate" Dutch settlers, claimed that local Indians, whom they deemed the original owners of the land, had conveyed title to them. Resistance escalated into a "no rent" movement by 1766, with vigilantism and rioting against law officers.[17] Soon after, Yankee settlers in what would become the state of Vermont, then New Hampshire, some of them refugees from the Hudson Valley, began to resist New York colonial authorities' claims to northern New England lands on behalf of large speculators. After initially submitting to a trial before the New York Supreme Court in June 1770, the Vermonters realized that the justice system was stacked against them (all the prosecutors, as well as one of the justices who ruled against their New Hampshire titles, held large tracts in the disputed area). Well-organized resistance, which would become the Green Mountain Boys, emerged on a communal basis, repelled surveyors and sheriffs sent from New York, and burned out and drove off settlers with Yorker land titles.[18] These insurgencies would be followed by others in New York, anticipating the far greater Anti-Rent upheaval in the same region during the 1840s.

In the 1760s two very different insurgencies swept the Carolinas, both adopting the term "Regulation," a concept that originated long before in colonial and British history. Both adhered to the meaning of Regulators as "persons" who regulate "great abuses," or "correct abuses," or "correct by control." The South Carolina episode involved planters and substantial yeomen in 1768–69 launching vigilante violence against rampaging outlaw gangs in the absence of colonial law enforcement. The North Carolina Regulation, however, was directed against corrupt officials and a legal system tilted in favor of oppressive landlords. Its North Carolina meaning would be adopted later by other rural protesters in Pennsylvania, Maine, Vermont, and notably, Massachusetts.[19]

Events leading to the American Revolution strongly influenced insurgency in North Carolina. Although unrest began building among the yeoman farmers of the Piedmont before 1765, the formation of the Sons of Liberty inspired the farmers first to pursue more militant petitioning and then to direct action. Although early protests were remarkable for their "generally humble tone," the blatant corruption of royal officials and the legal system soon provoked riots, court closings, and finally, an unwanted "battle," followed by severe repression.[20]

Large speculators through political connections acquired land claims with promises to settle colonists, then let settlers go onto the land and improve it, only to charge them high prices for the very improvements the settlers had made. As local officials and county courts repeatedly backed the speculators, while using the legal system to enrich themselves, disturbances mounted. The tax system similarly favored the wealthy and large speculators, and the sheriffs who collected the taxes "failed to pass on much of the money to the colonial treasury. [The sheriffs] were £64,013 in arrears between 1754 and 1770."[21]

The first systematic airing of grievances came, significantly, from radical Protestant farmers influenced by the Whig leaders' defiance of the Stamp Act and whose "backcountry Protestantism provided a climate conducive to the organization of a mass protest movement." Not all the Regulators, who came into existence in 1768, were radical Protestant sectarians, but many of those acting against "unjust Oppressions" were pious folk led by "the struggle to rid the colonies of imperial tyranny . . . to imagine more egalitarian and godly communities at home." More egalitarian, but still patriarchal. The Regulators feared that not only the security of their rights and property was at stake, "but also their capacity to function effectively as men," and they feared "being deprived of that capacity, of being reduced to impotence and the abject conditions of slavery."[22]

When Governor William Tryon assembled a militia of over 1,000 men in 1768, it was top-heavy with officers and "a gentlemen's affair." The governor reported to London that "not a person of the character of a gentleman appeared among the insurgents," which typified and mirrored elite arrogance toward middling rural folk elsewhere. But unlike later Regulators in Massachusetts, for example, the Piedmonters treated gentlemen roughly when they came to possess lands or collect taxes, and in Orange County in 1770 they pulled judges bodily off their benches, leaving a defiant statement of their actions in the court record. Besides the replacement of corrupt officials, Regulator demands included ballot voting (instead of viva voce), taxation in proportion to wealth, collection of taxes in commodities, and the printing of money with land as security.[23]

The denouement in North Carolina came when a well-armed force of almost 1,200 militiamen, laden with "gentlemen" and artillery, met a huge, unorganized mob of 2,000–3,000 at Alamance, where observers reported a "general reluctance of both sides to fight." After much gesticulating and fist-fighting, gunfire ensued, resulting in thirty deaths and two hundred casualties. The Regulators broke up and did not again gather to threaten armed resistance. Although Regulator leaders had been drawing on the same Anglo-American traditions of resistance to oppression invoked by

Whig leaders of the resistance to Britain, they "soon learned that North Carolina's revolutionary leaders conferred legitimacy only on popular resistance that bolstered their own position, characterizing as rank rebellion all popular actions that challenged their privileges." Elites in all colonies "agitating for 'American' liberties," according to Marjoleine Kars, "quickly understood the dangers of condoning popular protest and the importance of containing the political aspirations of those below."[24]

One consequence of the repression of the Regulators was resentment of the Whig leadership and hence Loyalist dissent from the revolutionary movement. In addition, after independence, during the period of state making, former Regulator areas became persistent advocates for more popular, representative government. Indeed, from the Carolinas to New England the resentments and residues of backcountry protest before and after the Revolution fed into opposition to the new federal constitution, notably so in Massachusetts.

During the 1780s "relief advocates, populists, Anti-Federalists, and resisters" complained of unresponsive state legislatures and too little democracy. Throughout the country, crowds attacked tax collectors and court officers and released debtors and taxpayers from prison. Courthouses were burned in Virginia and assaulted by crowds in South Carolina, Maryland, and Massachusetts. Although events in this last state constituted but one part of a much larger set of disturbances, it is instructive to examine the so-called Shays's Rebellion as a prime example of how elites suppressed and discredited the traditional modes of popular protest that had animated the American Revolution.[25] The Massachusetts insurgency also bears some remarkable resemblances to the Carolina Regulation, including a desire to avoid bloodshed by mobilizing large numbers, resistance to an elite perceived as corrupt (or, at best, selfish) and abusive of the law, and a legacy of popular distrust. Moreover, in several of the Regulations from the 1760s to the 1780s (Pennsylvania, Massachusetts, Maine, and Vermont), egalitarian religious leaders played important roles in rural protest.[26]

Before 1765 in Massachusetts popular mobilizations had been infrequent in a political culture generally marked by deference and low participation. The most notable had arisen in the 1740s, when a land bank proposal led to unusual levels of citizen activity in opposition, motivating many towns that had not previously done so to send representatives to the General Court. Rumors of a huge mob planning to march on Boston turned out to be unfounded, and one result was the British authorities' moving to curb increased representation in the legislature.[27] The 1780s insurgency known as "Shays's Rebellion," however, properly understood as the Regulation and recently labeled "the mother of all populist insurgencies against government run in the interest of financial elites," was far more consequential both on the state and national levels.[28]

For three years or so before 1786 towns and counties in central and western Massachusetts had been petitioning the General Court for tax relief and a change in the state's fiscal policy favoring wealthy investors, and for a leaner and less expensive court system and government. Some towns engaged in "passive resistance" by refusing to send delegates to the general assembly, believing the state legislature to be "deaf to their complaints." In the summer of 1786 several counties held extralegal conventions, to which the resisting towns proved willing to send representatives. The largest county convention, in Hampshire, detailed the protesters' demands and asked the legislature to reconvene immediately to address their grievances and proposals. Soon the impatient westerners took matters into their own hands, as hundreds of men, some armed with muskets, swords, clubs, or "sticks," and some not, marched to Northampton and prevented the opening, by forcing the adjournment, of the courts of common pleas and general sessions. Similar closings or adjournments followed in early September in Worcester, Concord (Middlesex County), Taunton (Bristol County), and Great Barrington (Berkshire County). These actions, as the clerk of the House of Representatives put it in a later book, constituted "a mode of awakening the attention of the legislature."[29]

In September Governor James Bowdoin reconvened the legislature, which passed some moderate measures to ease the tax burden but also a Riot Act and Militia Act, giving authorities new powers to crack down on protesters. In late November the governor sent 300 horsemen into Concord to arrest three insurgent leaders—but court stoppages continued into late December, in two of which Daniel Shays, a former Revolutionary captain, took part. Besides the reports of mob rule broadcast beyond the state, state officials and the merchant elite were embarrassed by the refusal of western militias to discipline the insurgents. In early January 1787 Bowdoin therefore issued a call for an army of 4,400 troops, most of whom would be drawn from Boston and environs. Knowing that communities and neighbors were divided by the Regulation, the governor wanted overwhelming numbers explicitly to avoid bloodshed: "A large force will never be opposed," he proclaimed.[30]

The Regulators petitioned the government not to send the army, but on

January 19 a force commanded by Benjamin Lincoln, a well-known Revolutionary general, set out in a winter storm. Shortly after, knowing the force was en route, an insurgent group outside Springfield, commanded by Shays and others, decided to try to seize the arsenal there, perhaps as a way of checkmating Lincoln's troops. Some 1,000 to 1,200 men defended the arsenal, commanded by William Shepard. Shays, with perhaps 700 to 800 men, sent an ultimatum to Shepard because he expected to be joined by another insurgent commander, Luke Day, with a contingent comparable in size to that of Shays. On January 25 Shays's group marched on the arsenal, but Day, supposed to advance from another side, stayed put. After warning the approaching insurgents with two cannon shots over their heads, Shepard ordered a volley into their ranks. Shays urged his men to keep marching, though not to return fire, but they turned and ran, leaving four dead on the field.

The combined remnants of Shays's and Day's men would be followed by Lincoln's army to Shays's hometown of Pelham and then to Petersham. Shays continued to try to negotiate favorable terms up to the morning of February 4, when Lincoln's troops, after marching all night through a near blizzard, surprised Shays's camp. Shays again refused to order his men to fight and instead allowed them to flee. Except for separate skirmishes to come in Berkshire and elsewhere in the spring, the Regulation had ended.[31]

The conventional interpretation of the Regulation, beginning with its name, and until recently largely unchallenged, is an object lesson in how the victors get to write history. The "Shays's Rebellion" construct not only has distorted a complex populist movement but has also obscured its central meaning. The populist rationale for the Regulation was articulated no more effectively than by a maverick member of the elite, Chief Justice William Whiting of the Berkshire County court. In writings privately circulated or used for public remarks, Whiting declared that the people suffered from real grievances and criticized the state's tax policies, the judicial system, sheriffs, and lawyers for "plundering" ordinary farmers and mechanics ("the Midling and Lower Orders of the people"). Although scolding ordinary citizens for their lack of attention to public affairs, which he said helped allow the control of government to pass to a greedy aristocracy, Whiting declared that whenever any encroachments were made on the liberties or properties of the people, if redress could not be had, "it is Virtue in them to disturb the government." He likewise condemned the beneficiaries of the status quo for stigmatizing insurgents driven to unwise measures as

"Profligate Licentious Banditti." But article five of the state constitution declared "that all Power is originally Vested in the People and is derived from them," and that all officials are their "Substitutes and agents . . . at all times accountable to them."[32]

A set of disturbances disconnected in both time and place has been given the name of a circumstantial and highly unwilling "captain" who in reality was very much an accidental leader. Daniel Shays was only one of many grassroots leaders of one phase of the Massachusetts protests that had epicenters in several counties. Shays's anointment as the principal leader, or "Generalissmo" in some hyperbolic conservative accounts, served a useful purpose for elites who would constitute the core of Federalism and for whom "Shays" and "Shaysism" became useful weapons in their campaign to influence public opinion.[33] If Daniel Shays had not existed, proto-Federalists would have invented him. In fact, they did create "Shays" and "Shaysism" through their newspapers and prints, making Shays into the supreme leader of a movement and advocate of doctrines, neither of which he was. The constructs of a "rebellion" and a would-be "monarch and tyrant of America," believed in to varying degrees by their disseminators, helped the nationalist elites working toward a stronger central government to foster a climate of crisis conducive to the creation and acceptance of a new constitution.

Aside from the political uses that could be made of "Shaysism," conservatives' hierarchical view of society also led them to attribute the insurgencies to one demagogue and would-be dictator. They preferred to believe that the disturbances were not a true popular uprising, and their worldview dictated that there be a single leader.[34] As late as July 1787 small bands of fugitive "regulators"—or desperate men who had turned to banditry—crossed the Vermont border for raids into Massachusetts. These incidents generated newspaper reportage of wild rumors and kept "the spectre of Shays" before the public.[35] That "spectre" included not just the threat of a dictator but also the late eighteenth century's version of socialism or communism. "Shaysites" were those who wanted "no law, and . . . a share of the property of others; these are called levellers, Shaysites." Henry Knox solemnly averred to George Washington in October 1787 that the "creed" of the insurgents was that the property of the country "Ought to be the common property of all."[36]

Contrary to their opponents', and to some historians', interpretations, the Regulators never contemplated radical changes in government, much less its overthrow, and they did not intend to engage in military combat and bloodshed. Even John Jay, an arch conservative, acknowledged the Regulators' restraint in a letter of December 1786: "These People," he wrote to Thomas Jefferson, "bear no resemblance to an English Mob. . . . They are more temperate, cool, and regular in their Conduct—they have hitherto abstained from Plunder; nor have they that I know of committed any outrages but such as the accomplishment of their Purpose made necessary." They wanted, as did Governor Bowdoin in response (but not Shepard at Springfield), to make a show of overwhelming military force and to appear willing to risk battle. Their actions fell in a gray area between fighting and ritual, between actual combat and symbolic show. The Regulators accepted that gentlemen would rule, but they insisted on their right to intervene with measured force when convinced that the rule of law was out of balance. They sought to regulate, not to change, the relationship between rulers and ruled; to stabilize government, not to overthrow it.[37]

The populism of the Regulators was further limited, even undercut, by their own continuing deference to social superiors. Their printed rhetoric "resounded with themes and images that had mobilized colonial resistance to the British," but in personal, public confrontations with authority their "inability to talk back to their social superiors revealed to them the insecurity of their position and contributed to their defeat." The scene of an often-described court closing in Worcester in early September 1786 illustrates this point. Captain Adam Wheeler and 100 men blocked the courthouse door, preventing Chief Justice Artemas Ward from entering. Following the sheriff through the crowd, Ward demanded to know who commanded "these people," only to get no answer; a second time "Wheeler answered, but did not own the command." Ward then asked to speak, and the protesters told him to put his comments in writing. He refused, and he got his wish to stand atop the courthouse steps to try to reason with them. Although some heckled Ward, when he insisted that he would not answer questions unless the questioner gave his name, he thus denied the protesters' anonymity and enforced "conditions of face-to-face address," "demonstrat[ing] his understanding of the power of an authoritative performance." Previously and subsequently, Regulator spokesmen were much more assertive with written and printed texts.[38]

But the character of the Regulation as a populist movement driven by communal loyalties cannot be qualified so readily. Not just poor and debt-ridden farmers joined the ranks of demonstrators and armed marchers.

Rather, debtors and creditors, joined by kinsmen and neighbors, made the Regulation. In the typical mode of the eighteenth-century backcountry, "the Regulation was a family affair." As a pro-government defender of a convicted rebel from Shays's hometown of Pelham wrote, "He told me he wished he was out of it, but he could not live in Pelham unless he joined them."[39]

"A family affair," meaning kinsmen. But what of wives, daughters, sisters, and other female family members? Of women's role in the Regulation very little has been written, and apparently very little is known. But men's gendered definition of citizenship clearly mattered as one dimension of insurgent perception. The Regulators' grievances often manifested a concern that their manhood was threatened. The tax and monetary policies of their rulers, they believed, prevented them from fulfilling their duties as patriarchs of their families. A petition from the Regulators who closed the Worcester court complained of "those sufferings which disenabled them to provide for their wives and children." A New Hampshire sympathizer in 1786 wrote that only in states that provided relief to debtors and taxpayers were men able to "meet their families with conjugal and parental affection." A protester in New Jersey said that debt and taxes meant that farmers could hardly remain "useful members of the community."[40]

The last phrase resonates with E. Anthony Rotundo's description of the ideology of "communal manhood" that developed in colonial New England and lingered on into the early decades of the nineteenth century. In the eighteenth century, says Rotundo, a man's identity was "inseparable from the duties he owed to his community," and masculine fulfillment came through "public usefulness" rather than "individual achievements."[41] If Regulators and insurgent farmers generally held to this ideal of manhood, they also frequently contrasted yeoman republican masculinity to the alleged effeminacy of elite opponents.

During New Hampshire (later Vermont) settlers' land disputes with New York officialdom in the 1770s, Green Mountain Boy leader Ethan Allen gradually articulated what Robert Shalhope has characterized as a "yeoman persuasion." Allen's construct emerged from a struggle he depicted as taking place between rich and powerful men and poor, ordinary people: "a small faction of aristocratic gentlemen and an entire community of hardworking farmers." Allen's "yeoman persuasion" validated ordinary citizens' place in society while revealing "the fraudulent practices and pretensions of all gentlemen." In contrasting manly yeomen and effete gentlemen, he described his New York adversaries as "Favourites and Gentlemen of Influence"; in court the "Plaintiffs appearing in great Fashion and State . . . made a brilliant appearance," while the defendants appeared "in but ordinary Fashion, having been greatly fatigued by hard Labour." The defendants had been forced to "put on Fortitude" or flee, and they chose to stand, while the gentlemen attorneys, "a cringing, fawning, deceitful Fraternity; not enured to the Horrors of War, or anything Heroic, durst not Fight for their own claims." Instead, they pursued their accustomed cheating strategy "under a pretence [sic] of law."[42]

In the 1780s in northern New England a "populist ethos" waxed strong. "Ethan," a correspondent to the *Vermont Gazette* in 1786, declared "common sense . . . and good natural powers" to be worth more than "the flowers of oratory, the rhetoric of schools, or the duplicity of courtiers." A "Land-Holder" asked who should be in Congress and the state legislature: "Who are the *great body* of the people? Are they lawyers, Physicians-Merchants-Tradesmen? No—they are a respectable *Yeomanry, Farmers.*"[43]

Americans generally in the era of Revolution and independence associated effete, deceitful gentlemen with British manners, as in the first American comedy produced commercially for the New York theater, *The Contrast*, by Royall Tyler. Tyler, a Boston lawyer, had served as an aide-de-camp to General Benjamin Lincoln during the Massachusetts Regulation. In its immediate aftermath Lincoln had sent Tyler on missions to Vermont, western Massachusetts, and then New York City in efforts to pursue insurgents who had fled the Bay State. Five weeks after arriving in New York, Tyler had written *The Contrast* and seen it performed on April 16, 1787. Echoes of recent events in Massachusetts found their way into the comedy, which poked fun at British degeneracy as well as more gently at republican virtue. The play's main contrast was "between the polished but hollow and insincere Dimple, with British affectations, and the forthright, honest Manly, who may have fewer social graces but is a loyal son of liberty."[44]

Manly expressed, at times somewhat pompously, the republican virtues of simplicity and love of country while complaining, as many of his countrymen from John Adams to Thomas Jefferson were, of Americans' becoming slaves of fashion and "pernicious foreign luxury." Dimple, a competitor with Manly for the affection of young women, represented the manipulative Europeanized dandy, hypocrisy, surface polish, and insincerity. But a second contrast, between the two men's servants, is of central interest here.[45]

Jessamy, Dimple's servant, resembled his foppish master, while Jonathan,

Manly's attendant, was a straightforward, guileless country bumpkin. As a comic figure touchy about his station in life, Jonathan had a flawed manhood. Objecting to being called a servant by Jessamy, Jonathan retorts, "Servant! Sir, do you take me for a neggar,—I am Colonel Manly's waiter." Jessamy answers, "A true Yankee distinction, egad, without a difference. Why, sir, do you not perform all the offices of a servant? Do you not even blacken his boots?" Jonathan replies, "I do grease them a bit sometimes; but I am a true blue son of liberty, for all that. Father said I should come as Colonel Manly's waiter, to see the world and all that; but no man shall master me. My father has as good a farm as the colonel."[46]

Jonathan further reacts to Jessamy's snobbery by swearing that "we don't make any great matter of distinction in our state between quality and other folk."

> JESSAMY: This is, indeed, a levelling principle.—I hope, Mr. Jonathan, you have not taken part with the insurgents.
> JONATHAN: Why, since General Shays has sneaked off and given us the bag to hold, I don't care to give my opinion; but you'll promise not to tell. . . . I vow I did think the sturgeons were right.

But Jonathan adds that he did not join them because Colonel Manly had said it was a "burning shame for all the true blue Bunker Hill sons of liberty . . . to have any hand in kicking up a cursed dust against a government we had, every mother's son of us, a hand in making."[47]

Tyler thus represented the Yankee Regulator as a figure preferable to the effete, and less masculine, Jessamy, but also as a country innocent, whose ignorance and simplicity had helped the likes of "General Shays" to lead his countrymen astray. By reducing the Massachusetts farmer (and insurgent) to caricature, Tyler also defused the purposeful populism that had animated the Regulation.[48]

Yet even if misled, Jonathan revealed the protesting farmers' desire to protect the core of their manhood. More than one historian has emphasized that a key feature of manhood in the late eighteenth and early nineteenth centuries was "less about the drive for domination and more about the fear of others dominating us."[49] The Regulators of the late eighteenth century believed, with considerable justification, that they were resisting domination and protecting their manhood. They soon would be followed by other populist protesters entertaining similar perceptions.

*The oftener power Returns into the hands of the people, the Better, and when*
*for the good of the whole the power is Delligated it ought to be done by the whole.*
—Resolution of Westminster, Massachusetts, inhabitants, 1778, quoted in
   Jackson Turner Main, The Antifederalists: Critics of the Constitution,
   1781–1788 (1961)

*These lawyers, men of learning, and moneyed men, that talk so finely, and gloss over*
*matters so smoothly, to make us poor illiterate people swallow down the pill, expect to*
*get into Congress themselves; they expect to be the managers of this Constitution, and get all*
*the power and all the money into their own hands, and then they will swallow up all us little*
*folks.*
—Amos Singletary, Massachusetts farmer, circa 1788, quoted in Edmund S. Morgan,
   The Birth of the Republic, 1763–1789 (1956)

The Anti-Federalist opponents of the Philadelphia constitution of 1787 gave quintessential expression to the central tenets of populist thinking in Anglo-American political culture—a mentality that preceded the American Revolution, was heightened by it and the period of constitution making, and continued on indefinitely in the politics of the United States. The Anti-Federalists, like the Levellers of the seventeenth century, called attention to the inherent tension already noted between democratic ideology ("the power of the people") and representative government by elites chosen by the people.[50] This distinction captures the essence of the basic division between the nationalist constitution-makers of 1786–89, the Federalists, and their opponents. The Federalists emphasized "ways that 'the people' could act *through* representative structures. . . . Thus it would not be necessary . . . to enumerate the rights or powers of the people *as distinct from* those of government." The Anti-Federalists, in making arguments against consolidated power and for state sovereignty and for a bill of rights, "repeatedly relied on distinctions between 'the people' and 'government.' Of particular importance, they argued that an enumeration of rights would affirm the right of citizens to act *independently* of government." In addition, the Anti-Federalists saw correctly that Federalists wanted to ensure gentry rule, by the "better sort," at the national level and to block the kinds of populist policies states had resorted to in the 1780s.[51]

Anti-Federalism surfaced in 1787–88 in reaction to an interstate group of leading nationalists initiating a movement to replace the Articles of Confederation with a stronger central government. Some of the reformers had grown genuinely alarmed at the economic and geopolitical insecurity of the newly independent states; some possessed a vision of national development and grandeur. However much they believed that "Shaysism" really existed as a threat to property and social order, their magnification of the threat served the highly useful purpose of promoting a new constitutional framework.[52]

In September 1786 national-minded delegates from several states met at Annapolis ostensibly to consider amendments to the articles. Instead, they issued a call for a convention that would consider the wholesale revamping of the government. In the next weeks and months, they and their allies superbly manipulated the specters of backcountry "agrarianism" and paper money. A sense of crisis percolated, in part real, in part manufactured. The following spring in Philadelphia, the reformers crafted a constitution that would enable the creation of a more effective central government. Based on an ideal of balanced government with separation of powers, the constitution sought to protect Liberty from Power.

The Constitution was made possible by two major compromises: one between large and small states, which resulted in bicameralism, and a second protecting slavery, which recognized it in all but name, particularly through the counting of three-fifths of all slaves for the purposes of representation. More important, the Constitution reserved to the states all powers not specifically enumerated for Congress, thus creating a hybrid government of dual sovereignty that amounted to a standing invitation to contest the federal government's power.[53] Neither the protections afforded liberty nor the ambiguity of dual sovereignty placated those who feared the concentration of power in the new constitution.

The Constitution's creators differed little in their expectation that gentlemen would continue to rule throughout the land, as they made clear through such mechanisms as the indirect election of senators and the president, as well as the restriction of one representative for every 30,000 persons. "The people" might be the ultimate sovereign but not the actual rulers. The lower orders would continue to show deference to "the elevated classes of the community." The new republic would be—and this was hardly a matter of self-conscious debate or reflection—a white men's republic.[54]

Women's inclusion was not considered, though the Founders' construction of women played an important role in their thinking about political life. Historians of gender have argued that the "Founding Fathers" (recently renamed "Founding Brothers") used a "grammar of manhood" that defined citizenship according to manly virtues in opposition to womanhood. "The construction of the autonomous, patriotic male citizen required" the founding generation to emphasize "the traditional identification of women with unreliability, unpredictability, and lust." This discourse excluded from the body politic not only women, African Americans, and Indians but also disorderly white men who were not fit for citizenship. Although American leaders had themselves engaged in a revolution against patriarchal authority, they saw themselves as a new kind of benevolent patriarchy— "enlightened paternalists"—who would care for the welfare of dependent groups excluded from their "fraternity of citizenship."[55]

To gain legitimacy for the Constitution, James Madison and his fellow Founders brought the people into the process by calling for ratification conventions in the states, thus making the states into battlegrounds over adoption of the document. In the fight over ratification (1787–88), the nationalists called themselves "Federalists," thereby stealing their opponents' names and adding to the advantages of wealth, status, resources, and influence they already enjoyed. "The better sort," said one Anti-Federalist, "have the means of convincing those who differ from them." Those means included organization and control of most newspapers. Urban and commercial farming areas tended to support the Constitution, as did most merchants, especially ship owners, professional men, most mechanics, and other small tradesmen. Anti-Federalism tended to flourish in the backcountry, but some prominent wealthy men and state officials who anticipated the loss of power in their own fiefdoms also opposed the Constitution, as did agrarian-minded gentlemen. Similarly, some farmers and rural areas favored it, while in Dutchess County, New York, "the binding element of Anti-Federalism . . . was hostility to the aristocratic landlord families."[56]

For a long time some historians maligned Anti-Federalists in terms commonly employed to discredit populist movements: Anti-Federalists were ignorant, narrow-minded, short-sighted, "men of little faith." In recent years, however, Anti-Federalists have gained respect from various historians not only for contributing to the shaping of the Constitution—not to mention pressing for a bill of rights—but also for expressing a "hostility to large concentrations of power that lay at the core of the left and right wing variants of Populism," anticipating, for example, "Goldwater Republicans and Students for a Democratic Society."[57]

An equally significant trend in contemporary literature regarding the Anti-Federalists is the recognition that they spoke in several voices, representing at least three distinct varieties of Anti-Federalism, identified by Saul

Cornell as elite, middling, and plebeian types, and that their arguments against the Constitution changed with shifting political dynamics. Some came to accept its inevitability, compromised, and thus sought to limit the damage it might do to "liberty."[58] Substantial agreement has existed, however, that the "Federalists viewed themselves as friends of the nation; Anti-Federalists depicted themselves as friends of the people."[59]

Elite, middling, and plebeian Anti-Federalists reflected the views of different social strata, addressed different audiences, and, like many in the late eighteenth century on both sides of the Atlantic, held different views of "the people." But all expressed a distrust of centralized authority and of power per se, and believed that "the people can never be too jealous of their liberties." Generally, Anti-Federalists argued that states posed less of a threat to liberty; the more local the government, the more the people had access to it.[60]

Under the Constitution, Anti-Federalists believed, not only would Power be centralized and thus inevitably consume Liberty as it grew, but also the mechanisms of representation would ensure that power would reside in the hands of the rich and influential, that it would create a political aristocracy. Middling and plebeian Anti-Federalists especially gave voice to this concern, the latter claiming a close connection to ordinary people "because they were themselves common folk." Therefore, they did not hesitate to rail against wealth and privilege. Plebeian Anti-Federalists and many middling Anti-Federalists believed that a relative equality of social condition should prevail and not be unbalanced by government action.[61]

While Madison wanted large representative districts for Congress to ensure the election of responsible gentlemen like himself, Anti-Federalists preferred that legislators "resemble those they represent. They should be a true picture of the people." Melancton Smith of New York, a prominent middling Anti-Federalist, did not object to representatives being persons of education and influence, but they "should also include ordinary people." In Massachusetts the fate of the Regulators created "a widespread fear of the governing elite," which fed Anti-Federalism: "Every critic, it seemed, envisioned the 'little people' being stomped on by 'the well-born,' 'the gentlemen,' and 'the aristocracy.'"[62]

For a variety of reasons, most Anti-Federalists championed the virtues of localism in politics as well as economic affairs.[63] Although not all Anti-Federalists were egalitarian democrats, they looked on "democracy" far more favorably than their opponents did. Federalists rarely referred to "democracy" approvingly. Some elite Anti-Federalists also shared with Federalists a more restricted view of public opinion and the public sphere and held reservations regarding the wisdom of ordinary folk. But Federalists, again, were more skeptical of the common man's judgment. They assumed that gentlemen would debate issues among themselves and guide the decisions of those below them. Middling and plebeian Anti-Federalists (and even some elite Anti-Federalists), however, possessed a much broader conception of the public sphere.[64]

"Popular" Anti-Federalists advocated a more inclusive public sphere "filled with debate in newspapers, pamphlets, broadsides and speeches . . . [and] imagined a form of robust politics defined by a free press and free speech that would extend across the whole of America. They were, as a result, quick to challenge efforts to mobilize traditional legal rules of libel, sedition, and prior restraint."[65] They also called attention frequently to the Federalists' ability to dominate public opinion through control of most newspapers. It has been estimated that Federalists controlled as many as seventy-five newspapers, while Anti-Federalists could rely on never more than twenty; moreover, the latter came under economic pressure from "the merchant-banker-lawyer community that was anxious for quick ratification," while "cancelled advertisements and discontinued subscriptions took their toll." Anti-Federalists complained also—not without cause—of the blocking of the circulation of Anti-Federalist newspapers along the seaboard by unfriendly postmasters. When news of New York's ratification reached Manhattan in July 1788, a mob celebrated by marching to the Anti-Federalist *New York Journal* and smashing furniture and typecases.[66]

Expressions of fear of domination, and the implied threat to manhood, as well as mockery of their elite opponents as less than masculine, pervaded Anti-Federalist rhetoric. The letters to the newspapers by the populist Anti-Federalist "Centinel" in Pennsylvania referred to opponents in terms that bring to mind the deceitful and manipulative Dimple and Jessamy of *The Contrast*. Gendered adjectives suggested the effete corruption of British and European manners (and the masculinity of the Anti-Federalists). The proponents of the new constitution were "harpies of power," "conspirators," masters of deception, fraud, and surprise, who used "base stratagems . . . to hoodwink" their countrymen. Centinel marveled at the "machiavellian talents of those who excel in ingenuity, artifice, sophistry and the refinements of falsehood, who can assume the pleasing appearance of truth and bewilder the people in the mazes of error." In Maryland an anonymous Anti-Federalist "effeminized the Constitution's 'featherist' supporters. . . . Contemporary magazines frequently attributed social degeneracy 'to unrestrained desires for feathers, gauzes, and ribbons, both the lack of restraint and the specific objects of desire being conventionally associated with foolish women' and decadent aristocrats."[67]

Centinel also believed that the wealthy and ambitious "in every community think they have a right to lord it over their fellow creatures." Free men even might be reduced to "slavery," a danger highlighted by other Anti-Federalists. "Cato," a New York Anti-Federalist, pointed to the tendency of rulers to enslave the ruled and argued that now that his fellow citizens had thrown off the British yoke, "new masters" loomed, whose principles of government would "fetter your tongues and minds, enchain your bodies, and ultimately extinguish all that is great and noble in man."[68]

But perhaps no Anti Federalist put the issue of manhood more pointedly than "Philadelphiensis," who declared the subject before the public (the new constitution) of such importance that there could not be a man in the United States, "except some base assassin or mean coward, who can be indifferent on this momentous occasion." Is there anyone who could be unconcerned or neutral? "If there be, I say he is not a *man*; no certainly he is unworthy of that character; such a wretch can have no claim to the title of free citizen of America, he is a pitiful sycophant, a cringing spaniel, a menial slave."[69]

Thus, Anti-Federalist rhetoric breathed a spirit of assertive masculinity while at the same time it defiantly declared its resistance to domination by, as Centinel put it, "aristocratic juntos of the *well-born few*." Historian Dana Nelson has argued insightfully that the federal constitution amounted to a "reformulated ideal of national manhood" that undercut "emergently radical democratic practices." The new constitution thus offered a "bribe of national manhood . . . that could be claimed through patriotic incorporation (or subordination . . .)" and that "effectively undercut the radicalizing energy of local democratic practices."[70]

But adoption of the Constitution hardly brought an end to radical democratic energy or to populist protest movements that were launched in the name of "the people" and claimed legitimacy on the grounds of a literal reading of popular sovereignty. The legacy of backcountry protest from the Revolution and Confederation era included both defeats and successes, and enough of the latter, along with ordinary citizens' deeply held belief in republican self-government, to sustain subsequent populist mobilizations against law and authority perceived to be exercised against the common good. The Massachusetts Regulation, despite the harsh repression that the Bowdoin administration levied in the immediate aftermath, led to a change in the state's fiscal policies. In the April 1787 election Bowdoin lost the governorship to the popular John Hancock by a three to one margin, and the legislature began restoring the suffrage to some 4,000 Regulators who had taken an oath of allegiance. The legislature reversed its policy that had resulted in big payoffs to speculators in state securities by enacting a moratorium on debts and drastically cutting direct taxes. Backcountry towns now enjoyed tax relief, and the average country family "still had a tax bill, but nothing like the earlier ones."[71]

Lingering resentment against the Boston elite and the Bowdoin government's repression of the Regulation made ratification of the federal constitution in Massachusetts a close call. But when Treasury Secretary Alexander Hamilton's program of assumption (of state debts) went through Congress in 1790, Massachusetts's debt burden was assumed by the federal government, benefiting, as Hamilton intended, wealthy and powerful elites. It also proved a boon to the farmers of central and western Massachusetts since the state's "immense debt" would no longer impact their lives.[72] The federal excise tax on whiskey, however, would lead to a different outcome in western Pennsylvania, Kentucky, North Carolina, and elsewhere.

Anti-Federalists, of course, lost the struggle over the Constitution, and they probably would have taken small comfort from Edmund Morgan's observation that "Antifederalists were right. Government and people could not be the same." But the Anti-Federalists contributed substantially to the final Constitution, and they gave voice to many Americans' preference for localized government, which would reflect in its representation the middling and ordinary citizens who stood on equal footing in face-to-face relationships in their civil units and neighborhoods. Further, the middling and plebeian Anti-Federalists' populist vision of an expanded public sphere would, especially during the elite political factionalism of the 1790s, increasingly become a hallmark of American political culture.[73]

Historians often quote the seemingly inflammatory remarks of Thomas Jefferson in response to news of the Massachusetts Regulation, to the effect that a "little rebellion" now and then was a good thing, and that the tree of liberty needed to be watered from time to time "by the blood of patriots and tyrants." Less acknowledged has been Jefferson's concern that

popular disturbances would generate a dangerous reaction. . . . Admitting that a certain "turbulence" was an endemic "evil" of a popular regime, he nevertheless insisted, first that these "irregularities" were "nothing" in comparison to the oppressions of a European regime—

"a government of wolves over sheep"—and second that the evil was itself productive of some good. "It prevents the degeneracy of government, and nourishes a general attention to public affairs." "An observation of this truth should render republican governors so mild in their punishment of rebellions as not to discourage them too much. It is a medicine necessary for the sound health of government."[74]

# Chapter 3

# The Taming of the American Revolution

It is Not ondly Implyed But fully Expressed in almost all the Constitutions on the
Continent—that all Men are born free & Equal & have an Equil Right to Defend their
Lives Libbertyes & propertyes—& that govrnment was Instituted to for the Common
Good—not for the profit honour or private Interest of any one Man—family or Clase of
Men—& that the Desires & Interests of the Majority of the Grate body of the people
ought to Controle in all Matters of government.
—William Manning, "A Response to Hamilton's Funding Plan" (1790)

The rhetorical ascent of "the people" was not only gradual, but from the
outset any lip service paid to the people's sovereignty also came with implicit assumptions as to just who—in the eyes of the gentry—the people
were. In theory, "the people were everything." Abstractly, the people ruled.
But as governments actually operated, "the sovereigns were asked to assume
their proper place. . . . In a well-ordered republic, the leaders instructed, the
people learned, leaders acted, the people responded." Indeed, the honor
code by which gentlemen conducted themselves dictated that they make
clear their avoidance of any activity designed to court popular favor—the
people's approbation.[1]

Yet, as already pointed out, assertions of the people's sovereignty over
time contained an unintended dynamic of raising popular expectations
for a greater degree of popular participation and that the people's will be
satisfied. The Revolution itself had generated considerable momentum for
the idea of popular sovereignty as an ideal, and it had infused backcountry
populist movements of "regulation" into the 1790s and beyond. Moreover,
elites could react sharply against popular attempts to extend traditions of
popular resistance that predated 1775 and that had flourished during the
Revolution. In the 1790s rural insurgents who followed in the footsteps of
earlier Regulators from New England to the Carolinas found the Federalists
who controlled the federal government ready to launch excessive legal and
military force against any defiance of the central government's authority.

Thus, after 1789 the Revolution continued to serve as a template for popular action. Yet during the decades after the Revolution, elite keepers of public memory and culture acted as if mobs, crowds, effigy burning, tarring and feathering, and property destruction had nothing to do with the Revolution. In Boston, for example, the popular side of the town's resistance went into eclipse. The organization of a Republican opposition to the Federalists in the 1790s made no difference in the taming of the memory of the fight for independence, as both Republicans and Federalists in Massachusetts buried the "plebeian heritage of the Revolution."[2] This process occurred in other states to a lesser or greater degree. Yet the momentum toward expanded involvement of ordinary citizens in the public sphere continued on into the 1790s and beyond, and backwoods populist insurgencies by no means ended with the Regulations of the 1780s.

Elite divisions in the 1790s over domestic and foreign issues that resulted in the formation of the Federalist (court) and Republican (country) parties helped to foster a populist spirit, particularly as competing elites appealed to hitherto only sporadically mobilized sectors of the population. The new nation's political class held different ideas of just what republicanism meant. So their disagreements regarding what the federal government could or could not do, and the United States's relations with England and France, turned into issues they saw as affecting the very survival of republican government. As the "ferocity and passion" of political conflict increased during the 1790s, the formerly cooperative Revolutionary generation moved to "complete distrust of the motives and integrity, the honesty and intentions" of their partisan opponents. This drove the political class to reach out increasingly for popular support to a citizenry of which only a fraction was paying attention. But citizen attentiveness expanded, and middling men urged to participate by Federalist and Republican gentry came to regard the public sphere as less an elite space and as more open to ordinary people like themselves. To be sure, Federalist and Republican gentlemen worked within structures of social hierarchy and organized politically through notables, but they began to do so "on an unprecedented scale," working from the concept of the people "as a well-ordered militia."[3] Eventually, a more active electorate was one unintended consequence of gentry exertions, as well as middling and ordinary people's acquiring an enhanced sense of their own virtue and thus their capacity as citizens.

Elite division also led to a break in the ruling class's monopoly of information. Here, too, the American Revolution had been liberating, breaking an information "bottleneck" and accelerating information diffusion. Republican ideology called for an informed citizenry, of course, but the partisan fusillade of Jeffersonian and Federalist gentlemen's writing in pamphlets and newspapers prompted a flood of information into the public sphere well beyond elite ranks, similarly flattering the political self-assurance of ordinary folk.[4]

A parallel sense of efficacy was spreading throughout churches everywhere. A "religious populism" also given momentum by the American Revolution impelled ordinary people in new and old religious groups to struggle to make their voices heard, according to historian Nathan O. Hatch, and democratic sentiments engulfed religious practices everywhere. "Democratic or populist leaders associated virtue with ordinary people" and advocated that sermons, hymns, and religious tracts be couched in vernacular, easily accessible to common people.[5] Religious leadership now often became people-oriented and sprang from the grass roots, and deference to traditional religious authorities declined.

The rise in religious populism occurred as conflicts percolated in various states over disestablishment and the role of the church in society. Eleven of the thirteen original colonies had possessed established churches that had been routinely involved in public affairs or social services and expected to remain so, with most of them supported by taxes on all citizens. While states such as New York and Virginia disestablished their churches during the Revolutionary era, the process took longer in New England, with state-sanctioned religious taxes ending in Vermont in 1807, in Connecticut in 1818, in New Hampshire in 1819, and in Maine in 1821 (as soon as it became a state). Although Massachusetts did not formally disestablish until 1833, Republican legislatures in 1811 and 1824 already had removed the most onerous features of tax and legal requirements. The contest over established churches spilled over readily into politics and elections, with dissenting religious groups usually taking an antiestablishment, populist posture. More important, the triumph of disestablishment represented a victory for voluntarism and individual choice, reinforcing the stimulus from other quarters, instilling in ordinary men and women faith in their own wisdom and judgment.[6]

Disestablishment hardly removed the role of churches and demands for moral conduct from the early republic's political life. The push for complete separation of church and state that republican liberals carried out of the Revolution, together with the growth of a market economy perceived as undermining traditional moral and community relationships, created great anxiety among conservative religious leaders. Therefore, they sought to counteract the steps taken to separate church and state by launching evangelical societies and missionary efforts to keep America a Protestant Christian polity, to retain a role for churches in public affairs, and to lobby legislatures for blue laws that regulated moral conduct, punished "the vices or immoralities of the times," and enforced keeping the Sabbath. Although Virginia enacted Jefferson's well-known Bill for Religious Freedom in 1786, religious issues and the role of churches continued to be contested in the legislature and the public sphere for decades afterward. As Virginia and other states confronted evangelical pressure to support religion or legislate morality, whether successful or not, many citizens, and not just among the dissenting sects or denominations, remained fearful of ecclesiastical elites who threatened the religious liberties won or promised by the Revolution.[7]

Dissenters in religion often supported or formed political alliances with the Jeffersonian Republican opposition as it developed in the 1790s, and in New England, particularly, the sermons of the orthodox Congregational clergy often resembled Federalist political campaigning, thus creating the impression that the Republicans were populists fighting a powerful politico-religious establishment.[8] The Jeffersonians' political rhetoric reinforced this perception, but although Republican leaders routinely contrasted their popular support with the elitism of the Federalists, "the Republican message did not announce a new venture in majoritarian politics." As much as the Federalists, the Republicans also regarded themselves as mentors of the people. Even Jefferson "heard little authority in the faint dissonant voice of the people." Indeed, like some ardent republicans of the 1790s, Jefferson was not comfortable with the word "democrat." Conservatives had done their best to put the word in "bad odor," but the term lacked definition, and many Republicans, like Jefferson, hesitated to embrace it.[9] Yet as organized opposition to the policies of the Washington administration over both domestic and foreign policy gradually emerged, members of the "republican interest," clustering around Jefferson and Madison and dismayed with the administration's policies, which they saw as threatening republican principles, would bring the term "democratic" into bolder relief.

The political culture of the early republic (1789–1828) was undergoing transition from eighteenth-century deferential politics to a deferential-participant and more egalitarian politics. It was a mixed period, deferential and democratic, elitist and participatory at the same time. In Massachusetts, for example, Republicans proved as capable as Federalists of fusing habits of deference to mass participation. Although the Federalists relied more on social position and influence, derived from property and status, to mobilize their followers, and Republicans invested more in organization, the latter by no means could be considered populist democrats.[10]

Yet populist democratic outbursts punctuated the politics of the 1790s and profoundly affected the formation of a Republican opposition to the dominant Federalists, who controlled the central government during the Washington (1789–97) and Adams (1797–1801) administrations.[11] Minor conflicts between tenant farmers and landlords, and between government officials and rural dissidents, continued after 1789 all through the back-country from Maine to Georgia. Land disputes in New York's lower Hudson River valley resulted in small-scale but sometimes violent resistance and riots against landlords, surveyors, and law officers.[12] Historians' narratives of unrest in this period, as in the case of the Regulations of the 1780s, have tended to focus on specific, delimited "rebellions," such as the "Whiskey" and "Fries" episodes, thus marginalizing if not obscuring more widespread and persistent resistance to central authority. Agrarian turmoil in Pennsylvania in the 1780s and 1790s illustrates the incongruity between ongoing populist insurgency and historians' interpretations that leapfrog from one "rebellion" to another.

## BACKCOUNTRY POPULISM AND THE "WHISKEY REBELLION"

Conventional understanding of the "Whiskey Rebellion" in western Pennsylvania emphasizes the immediate reaction to Treasury Secretary Hamilton's persuading Congress in 1791 to enact a federal excise tax on distilled spirits. Thereafter, resistance to tax collectors and violence against complying distillers mounted in several states, but especially in western Pennsylvania, culminating in 1794 with President Washington's leading an army of 13,000 across the mountains to quell unrest.

Since the end of the Revolution, rural Pennsylvanians all across the state, during postwar economic hard times, had been resisting foreclosures and tax collection. With money and credit scarce, state leaders had reduced the supply of both, and angry farmers and their neighbors and townsmen engaged in traditional crowd action to frustrate sheriffs and collectors. Before 1787, farmer networks could extend to "the bulk of a county, a region, or, in some locales, even a broad and ambiguous notion of 'the people.'" State leaders responded by enacting stiffer punishments for officials who did not enforce the law, and they joined creditors and Philadelphia money men in a campaign to replace the democratic 1776 Pennsylvania constitution and to revamp a "decentralized revenue system" reliant on local officials and independent constables and militia. The new 1790 constitution transferred authority from locally elected justices of the peace to new state-appointed judges.[13]

After 1790, however, popular resistance increased in the form of farmers' protecting themselves and their neighbors by closing roads with fences, ditches, and log piles and often preventing officials and jurors from attending court. Some vigilantes disguised themselves with blackened faces, Indian garb, and even women's clothing, a mode of resistance that would reappear in New England and New York into the 1840s. More such actions were recorded in the years after 1787 than before and took place not just in the backcountry but even in long-settled areas around Philadelphia. In western Pennsylvania many farmers saw the excise tax and Hamilton's financial program generally as an extension of policies they had opposed since the Revolution.[14]

More recent frustrations with the federal government added to the westerners' grievances. Instead of taxing whiskey, the westerners wanted the government to do something about the Indian threat in the nearby Ohio region, as well as the continuing British occupation of northwest posts and their incitement of Indians. The Mississippi River, they complained also, was still officially closed to American navigation by Spain, and trade through Pittsburgh on the Ohio was increasing. The tax itself was hardly inconsequential in a region that produced the highest per capita volume of spirits than any other. Moreover, the Scotch-Irish of the area had carried in their cultural baggage an inbred hatred of the excise collector. The state excise laws of the 1780s had gone unheeded; whiskey was central to the economic and social life of this developing region, one that now believed itself "being arbitrarily hemmed in, contained, and sat upon."[15]

Petitions and protests against the tax began in 1790 even before Congress enacted it into law, and the Pennsylvania legislature by a large majority passed a resolution condemning it. From 1791 on, both peaceful protest and intermittent small-scale vigilante action against tax collectors and farmers who complied with the tax continued, especially in western Pennsylvania and nearby backcountry areas. Prominent and wealthy men, distillers and landowners, took part in the mostly political phase of protest. "Nearly every member of the region's officeholding elite—representatives to the state assembly, local judges and justices of the peace, county commissioners, and even members of Congress, attended . . . meetings, signed petitions . . . and joined 'committees of correspondence,'" and they made sure proceedings of meetings were published in the local newspapers. Evasion and violence came to a head in the summer of 1794 when vigilantes, mostly of Scotch-Irish origin, roamed western Pennsylvania and Kentucky, terrorizing anyone who sought to comply with or enforce the tax, blowing up or shooting holes in stills, closing courts, robbing the mails, and assaulting collectors. In July several hundred men besieged the house of John Neville, a local notable and excise inspector for the four western counties, resulting in several casualties and the rebels' setting fire to the property. In August 5,000–7,000 insurgents assembled in military fashion for a march on Pittsburgh; this "rural mob" paraded through town, did a great deal of shouting and gesticulating, and was persuaded to march away, but only after burning a barn belonging to Neville's son. By now many prominent men associated with the earlier, peaceful protests urged moderation, but a few days later President Washington issued a proclamation calling for an end to defiance and calling out militiamen from several states. On September 24 he directed that the rebellion be suppressed.[16]

What the Federalists succeeded in labeling the "Whiskey Rebellion" bore striking parallels to the Massachusetts Regulation and other backcountry insurgencies, beginning with the repression selectively targeting resistance. In August and September 1794 violent resistance to the excise occurred in twenty-seven trans-Appalachian counties in four states and the Northwest Territory. Before that, petitions seeking repeal had come from across the frontier. As in Pennsylvania, three other state legislatures, Virginia, North Carolina, and Maryland, had passed resolutions condemning the whiskey tax. In Kentucky the law was "a dead letter." While it was enforced in coastal areas of Virginia and the Carolinas, in northwest Virginia and western parts of North and South Carolina the resistance was nearly as effective as in Kentucky. Revenues received in the Carolinas and Georgia were far below the costs of enforcement. Indeed, Hamilton at first had planned to single out North Carolina for punishment but switched to Pennsylvania for several reasons, including its proximity to "the immediate seat of government" and the presence of local Federalist allies. "In terms of both violence and refusal to pay the tax, nothing singled out western Pennsylvania as unique," one historian has argued. Federalist authorities also assumed, as in the case of Massachusetts, that popular protest in Pennsylvania was due to manipulation by elites. On the contrary, unrest "bubbled up from below," and more often, "elites were manipulated by the rage of small farmers and laborers."[17]

Although the federal administration's charges that scheming men in western Pennsylvania had fomented the insurrection were exaggerated, local political leaders had exacerbated opposition by their strident denunciations of the tax. One of them, up to his acceptance of office as an excise inspector in early 1792, was John Neville, who as state legislator, and to retain his popularity, had roundly condemned the tax and voted for the legislature's resolution declaring it unconstitutional. His neighbors thus saw the wealthy Neville as taking a bribe to betray them; the fact that he and his relatives' and connections' businesses stood to profit from government contracts for whiskey and other supplies provoked them further.[18]

The "Whiskey Boys"—whom Federalist critics accused of being "Shaysites"—had no radical designs against government in general, but a massive deployment against them nevertheless was justified on those grounds. Further, many vigilante farmers, as with the Massachusetts Regulators, did not believe an armed force would be sent against them, and if it were, they believed that the soldiers would join them or be overawed by the local population. Generals Henry Lee and Hamilton, however, who commanded an army larger than Washington had ever led in the Revolution, met no resistance and eventually marched back with twenty alleged conspirators who were mostly poor country folk, some unbalanced mentally. "It now seems astonishing," writes historian Mary Tachau, "that the Federalists—for this was a partisan issue—could manage the news (and therefore history) as successfully as they did. Thousands of people knew at the time that resistance to the tax was neither as isolated or contained as it was alleged to have been, nor did it end with the appearance of the troops." In unruly Kentucky, especially, with the connivance of Jeffersonian officials and members of local elites, "massive resistance" continued, but the Washington administration chose to ignore Kentucky (as well as North Carolina).[19]

Hamilton immediately sought to shape popular understanding of these events by writing a narrative portraying the military action as a successful exercise of force and moderation by the new government, thereby establishing its authority. It did not matter to him and the Federalists that widespread noncompliance continued after their symbolic victory against a phantom threat to the government. What Jefferson called a rebellion that "could never be found" had provided the occasion for an impressive show of military might that was more political than strategic. Indeed, the political utility of the "Whiskey Rebellion" extended well beyond the central government's theatrical demonstration of suppressing insurrection and punishing lawbreakers.[20] In addition to the continuing delegitimization of popular insurgency, begun in the 1780s, the Federalists used the "Whiskey Rebellion" to discredit an emerging opposition more broadly critical of the policies of the Washington administration.

## THE QUESTION OF OPPOSITION
## AND THE DEMOCRATIC SOCIETIES

Jefferson as secretary of state in Washington's cabinet and Madison in the House of Representatives early on had opposed the centralizing policies of Treasury Secretary Hamilton. They spoke for shifting coalitions in Congress that had objected to the funding and assumption of Revolutionary War debts, a national bank, a tariff to protect manufacturing and the excise tax to raise revenue, nationalization of the militia, and creation of an army of 5,000 men. The Virginians did not share Hamilton's vision of binding the wealthy and ambitious to the new government through his fiscal policies or of attaining national prosperity through a system modeled on Great Britain's, which they regarded as leading inevitably to excessive government centralization, undue influence flowing to "aristocrats," and corruption. Jefferson believed that the government was rushing headlong toward a European-style despotic regime.

Opposition to administration policies spread outside official circles as early as 1790, when the *New York Journal*, the *Boston Independent Chronicle*, and the *Pennsylvania Gazette* and *General Advertiser*, both of Philadelphia, criticized Hamilton's very first proposals. Then Madison took a more deliberate step toward establishing a partisan press, persuading a former Princeton College classmate, the poet Philip Freneau, to come to Philadelphia to edit a weekly paper and give a voice in the capital to the "republican interest." Jefferson offered Freneau a position as "translator" in the State Department at $250 a year, and in October 1791 the *National Gazette* began publication. In 1789 the administration had established, in the fashion of the British government, an official organ, the *Gazette of the United States*, to support its policies and print official communications, orders, and laws, which was financed in part by government printing and advertising. During 1792, as Jefferson's suspicions of the Federalists' aristocratic and monarchical designs grew, and as Hamilton became enraged at Freneau's stinging attacks, a newspaper and pamphlet war broke out from Boston to Virginia, making increasingly obvious the disunity within the government and initiating the spread outward to attentive citizenry what were still largely personal differences among extended but relatively small groups of gentlemen.[21]

Attitudes toward France and England among the political leadership, already part of the mix since the inception of the federal government and the French Revolution of 1789, increasingly injected more passion into political differences in the new nation. Most Americans had welcomed the French Revolution, and as European monarchies waged a reactionary war against the new republic, many Americans sympathized with embattled France. But when England became part of the alliance against France in 1792, and as the revolution became radical during 1793 with the beheading of Louis XVI, the Terror of 1793–94, and the attack on Christianity, sharp divisions followed in the United States, with the Washington administration seeming to tilt toward Great Britain and the "republican" opposition remaining pro-France.

With Britain and France at war, Washington proclaimed the United States's neutrality, but France expected special consideration as a former ally, and Britain imposed new restrictions on American shipping and seized U.S. ships in the West Indies. Despite Britain's continuing treatment of the new nation as an inferior, Washington and Hamilton preferred to work for an accommodation with the former mother country, which they regarded as the United States's natural trading partner. Meanwhile, the arrival of a new French minister, Edmond Genet, seemed to auger well for redressing the balance, as Jefferson and Madison wished, toward France. Genet met with enthusiastic crowds in the South and warm cooperation from Jefferson, but the overconfident Genet proceeded to defy the administration's neutrality by seeking to outfit French privateers in American ports and even to raise an army in Kentucky to liberate Louisiana from Spain. Soon Jefferson was forced to disown Genet, vote with the cabinet to request the French government to recall their minister, and try to contain the fallout that could only damage sympathy for France and the "republican interest." During 1794 Washington appointed the aristocratic arch-Federalist and Anglophile John Jay as special envoy to Britain, and the treaty that Jay brought back in 1795, more than any other policy difference, caused partisan polarization in Congress and led to the divided ruling gentry reaching out to a broader public and mobilizing popular demonstrations for and against the treaty. From this point on, citizen attentiveness began to rise, participation in the public sphere increased, and Jeffersonian Republican party organization began in earnest.[22]

The latter cannot be regarded as a populist movement, though it often used populist rhetoric. Its organization came from the top down: aside from communications in newspapers, its central core consisted of gentlemen writing letters and networking with other gentlemen. But in 1793–94 a new political entity appeared on the public stage that, while not a widespread popular movement, nevertheless expressed a thoroughly populist mentality and justified its actions as rooted in the sovereignty of the people.

These were the associations historians have labeled "Democratic-Republican societies," which proclaimed their purposes as promoting citizen awareness, public discussion of government policies, and political education. While the societies presented themselves as a voice of "the people," the defenders of the Washington administration, or "Court party," could be excused for thinking of the societies as factional allies of the growing "republican" opposition, given the issues that concerned the societies.[23]

Two of the first societies appeared in Philadelphia in the spring of 1793, the "German Republican Society of Philadelphia" and the "Democratic Society of Pennsylvania" (most had either "Republican" or "Democratic" in their titles). At least three dozen more followed in the next two years from the Carolinas to Kentucky to Vermont, with at least forty-two established by 1798, though few were organized after 1795. Although not widespread grassroots movements, the largest societies contained from two to three hundred members, and most rosters reflected a cross section of occupations and socioeconomic strata. Substantial men of "wealth and power" took the lead in forming the societies and serving as officers, some with ties to leading Jeffersonians. The most prominent opposition political leaders, however, and the likes of Jefferson, Madison, and Aaron Burr, kept their distance.[24]

Historians have differed as to whether the societies' inspiration came from homegrown predecessors such as the Sons of Liberty or from the Jacobin clubs of revolutionary France, but in any case most of them expressed concern for the beleaguered French republic. Republicanism, the fellow "citizens" of the societies made clear, was threatened on both sides of the Atlantic. Some expressed disapproval of Washington's neutrality proclamation; some protested Britain's high-handed treatment of American shipping and their incitement of Indians on the frontier. Western societies above all petitioned for action to open up the Mississippi River, while several eastern societies deplored the whiskey tax but also any unlawful resistance to it. Those still active in 1795 protested the Jay treaty, but soon the dominant theme sounded was that of the societies' very right to exist and to create a voice in the contest for public opinion separate from that of the government.[25]

And this was something of a new concept. The societies presented a novel populist challenge to the new government. Not only did they assert repeatedly that it was the duty of citizens to maintain constant "vigilance" over their representatives, but they also contended, as the German Republican Society declared, that in a republican government every citizen needed "to offer his assistance, either by taking a part in its immediate administration, or by his advice and watchfulness." Other societies echoed this assertion of a duty of virtual participation in the government. The Democratic Society of Norfolk's address of June 1794 called on citizens to assist the magistrate "in the administration of justice, and the legal execution of the duties of his office," because "all power originated from the people, and there can be no legal authority, but by their consent." Some societies, such as the Democratic Society of the City of New York, went beyond the simple assertion of sovereignty of "the People," adding, "who have at all times the natural and inherent RIGHT to amend, alter, or abolish the form of Government which they have instituted."26

"The People," the societies came close to suggesting, were sleeping, or at least were inattentive and unaware of the threat to republican government posed by the administration's centralizing and pro-British agenda. The People, having formed a government and delegated authority, said the Massachusetts Constitutional Society, must stay vigilant between elections or risk falling under despotism. As a Vermont Republican declared in 1799, "When the people have deputed they are not defunct; the [their] sovereignty is not annihilated; and however constitutions may point out no way for the sovereign to make its will known, yet the power exists."27

For the Washington administration's proto-Federalists, this constituted heresy, and they found the presence of two of the original and largest societies in Philadelphia, the capital city, and nine overall in Pennsylvania, particularly irritating. The Court party believed that no intermediaries between the government and the people were necessary. Once the people spoke at elections, that ended the matter. The Federalists wanted "a unitary public sphere," with no dissonant voices challenging government measures: to "have but one opinion formed of all," said one critic of the societies. Administration loyalists rejected the societies' assertion of independence from the state and saw them not as speaking for the people but as partisans undermining confidence in established authority. A 1794 letter in the *New York Daily Gazette* put the antisociety case succinctly: "Do the people require intermediary guides betwixt them and the constituted authorities? . . . Are they chosen by the people? If not, as I know no other authority, I shall henceforth regard them as self-creators, as a branch, perhaps of the Jacobin Society of Paris."[28]

"Jacobin" was one of the milder invectives hurled at the societies by their opponents. Although opposition newspapers were gradually increasing in number, most papers were "lock, stock, and barrel" controlled by administration supporters, and accusations that the societies were illegitimate, unpatriotic, corrupt, and treasonous proliferated in public print. But the Democratic-Republican societies were swimming against a larger current: a political culture steeped in antipartisanship and unaccustomed to the legitimacy of political opposition. Thus the societies were attempting to overcome ingrained assumptions about political life that they themselves shared to a degree. Since a formidable political opposition did take shape in later years of the decade, historians have given the societies credit for beginning the process. But clothing themselves in a populist idiom was not enough to overcome all at once the cultural resistance to legitimate opposition, much less the acceptance of parties.[29]

Even without the "Whiskey Rebellion," then, the societies contended with fierce opposition and, perhaps, self-doubts concerning their legitimacy. Even before the violence in western Pennsylvania, Federalists had accused the societies of fomenting rebellion. President Washington entertained no doubts of the danger posed by the societies, and early on he warned his advisors that, left unchecked, "they would shake the government to its foundations." In August he had opined privately that the insurrection was "the first *ripe fruit* of the Democratic Societies." Returning to Philadelphia after the expedition west, Washington wrote to John Jay that he found a "general opinion" that the insurrection "having happened at the time it did was fortunate." The Democratic societies, he continued, had "precipitated a crisis for which they were not prepared" and were now vulnerable to "annihilation." In his November report to Congress on the insurrection and its suppression, Washington caused a sensation throughout the country by publicly blaming certain "self-created societies" for the insurrection. Rebellion had arisen in a climate "fomented by combinations of men," who had carelessly disregarded "the unerring truth that those who rouse cannot always appease a civic convulsion, [and] have disseminated, from an ignorance or perversion of facts, suspicions, jealousies and accusations of the whole government."[30]

The precise role of the Democratic societies in the insurrection has been a matter of dispute among historians. While associations outside of western Pennsylvania had nothing to do with resistance in the backcountry (though some had objected to the excise tax), in the Pittsburgh region some of the leaders in the rioting were also leaders in the Mingo Creek Society, and many of its members, as well as those of the Washington Society, participated in the attack on Neville's house. A recent account, (correctly) asserting "plenty of connection" between the local societies and the violence, however, also concludes that "the insurrection was the product of the region rather than its societies. The ones outside the region invariably tried to discourage them; conversely, it is fairly certain that even if there had been no societies there would still have been an insurrection."[31]

Nevertheless, already under attack, it was now open season on the Democratic societies. The Federalist-dominated Senate and all the administration's print media, as well as the conservative New England clergy, took up the drumbeat of condemnation. The fact that some societies had participated in election contests that fall, and with some success, intensified the Federalist onslaught. Deciding on a response to the insurrection divided the prestigious Democratic Society of Philadelphia, while many societies condemned lawlessness, proclaimed their innocence, and added staunch defenses of freedom of speech and liberty of the press. Jefferson had set the tone for the Republican rebuttal in a December letter to Madison in which he called the denunciation of the societies "one of the extraordinary acts of boldness of which we have seen so many from the fraction of monocrats":

> It is wonderful, indeed, that the President should have permitted himself to be the organ of such an attack on freedom of discussion, the freedom of writing, printing & publishing. It must be a matter of rare curiosity to get at the modifications of these rights proposed by them, and to see what line their ingenuity would draw between democratical societies, whose avowed object is the nourishment of the republican principles of our constitution, and the society of Cincinnati, *a self-created* one, carving out for itself hereditary distinctions.[32]

Hamilton recognized the political advantages accruing from insurrection and wrote to one of his confidants that its suppression "will do us a great deal of good and add to the solidity of every thing in this country." One Federalist congressman called crushing the rebellion "the happiest event that ever happened" because it would "give the Government . . . a tone, an energy, and dignity, which will defy all efforts of Anarchy and Jacobinism." Madison, too, saw the political dangers that the insurrection and

Washington's verbal anathema posed to any political opposition, and he labored to prevent the House from censuring the societies, writing to Jefferson regarding those who sought "to draw a party advantage" out of Washington's popularity and censure of the societies: "The game was, to connect the democratic Societies with the odium of the insurrection—to connect the Republicans in Congs. with those Societies—to put the P. [president] Ostensibly at the head of the other party, in opposition to both." Madison prevented the House from leveling a direct censure against the societies, but soon the societies would become far less active and give way to other political strategies and, for the time being, less controversial forms of association among Republicans to create an infrastructure for successful electioneering. The societies, indeed, had "laid the groundwork for the Republican party."[33] But in an antiparty political culture, subsequently and for some time each contending party would regard their *opponents* as a party yet regard themselves as transcending faction and particular interests and serving as the true representatives of the people. To that extent, at least, the populist ethos invoked by the Democratic societies continued.

### THE CENTER MOVES RIGHT

Many former Anti-Federalists, especially elite and middling, who were now Jeffersonian Republicans, parted company with plebeian or radical populist Anti-Federalists over the "Whiskey Rebellion." Cowed to varying degrees by the Federalists' association of dissent with insurrection, most elite and middling opponents of too energetic a government disavowed the backcountry resistance, while populist Anti-Federalists, continuing to espouse a radical egalitarianism, found themselves relatively isolated in seeing the actions of the Whiskey rebels as "the will of the people." Pennsylvania Republican leaders also modified their stance, having organized Democratic-Republican societies as part of the first stages of building a party organization. They denounced equally any Federalist attempt to stifle legitimate protest but now insisted that such protest be legal: violence and extralegal crowd action were no longer acceptable. Like the Federalists they defined the Whiskey protesters as rebels. Increasingly, according to Cornell, the Anti-Federalist heritage would itself be tamed, identified more "with a dissenting constitutional discourse used by elite and middling democrats to defend a vision of localism compatible with state authority."[34]

The next major insurgency of the 1790s also arose in Pennsylvania. Although on a smaller scale, it was more authentically a populist action and also indicated that "the people" were learning their lessons, or at least growing in political sophistication, under the Federalist ascendancy.

Once again Federalist prosecutors succeeded in inaccurately labeling a "rebellion" what was more of a regulation and a brief quasi-military show of force that reflected widespread and long-standing discontent. The Federalists' Direct Tax of 1798 triggered what came to be known as "Fries's Rebellion," but the tax was simply the most offensive of several Federalist policies—including the Alien and Sedition Acts, military spending, and the creation of a peacetime army—objected to by the German Lutherans and German Reform folk of eastern Pennsylvania. The 1798 tax applied to houses, land, and slaves, and while it taxed wealthy homes more than average ones, it taxed improved farmlands more than the uncultivated holdings of large speculators. Extensive tracts of land held by wealthy men, moreover, additionally represented a federal land policy much resented by the Lutheran and Reform Germans—who called themselves *"Kirchenleute"* (Church People) to distinguish themselves from Moravians, Mennonites, and other sects.[35]

After several months of political protest against Federalist policies, Jacob Fries, a former captain in the Revolutionary War, led some 400 militia from Bucks and Northampton Counties to Bethlehem to demand the release of seventeen Northampton County men imprisoned for resisting the 1798 tax. Federalist papers quickly denounced the "Northampton insurrection" as carried out by "miserable Germans" and "traitors," but the aim of the farmer-militiamen was to bring back the prisoners for local trials. Moreover, their overall goals were political: to change laws regarded as "unconstitutional," as well as to replace tax assessors who were Moravians or Quakers and who were regarded as hostile outsiders receiving Federalist patronage.[36]

Their goals were limited, too, despite a Federalist judge's charge to a grand jury that the farmer-militiamen, "moved and seduced by the instigation of the devil," intended "to raise and levy war, insurrection and rebellion against the . . . United States." But one militia leader testified that their motive in going to Bethlehem to rescue prisoners resulted "from a general aversion to the law, [and] an intention to impede and prevent its execution," because the law was unequal and wrong and should be changed. He could not say who "projected" the idea of rescuing the prisoners: "The township seemed to be all of one mind."[37]

"The township" probably referred primarily to its adult male inhabitants, whose patriarchal sway over families and neighborhoods was also threatened by the tax on houses, the symbol of a head of household's manhood. The rhetoric of protest, as with the Anti-Federalists, mentioned the danger of being reduced to slaves or, a new twist, famished Irishmen. The farmer-militiamen, not necessarily domestic egalitarians, "conceived of citizens as mature, responsible, sober men who enforced the laws."[38]

"Fries's Rebellion" no more belonged to Jacob Fries than the Massachusetts Regulation originated with Daniel Shays. When the Northampton militiamen who marched to Bethlehem were asked who commanded them, some replied that "they were all commanders." Like Shays, Fries joined his comrades of March 7 shortly before then, and the resistance rather "belonged to the thousands of German-American men, women, and adolescent children of eastern Pennsylvania . . . as well as some western counties, who engaged in the varied acts of resistance." They also saw themselves as acting in the spirit of the American Revolution. A majority of those identified with the resistance had fought in that war or were related to veterans (over three-fourths were connected to the Revolutionary War in some manner). For them the Revolution pointed toward an expansion of "local and personal control over daily life as well as increased power over broader collective policies."[39]

A recent, detailed depiction of "Fries's Rebellion" supports the argument made in this study regarding the populist character of backcountry Regulations. The various political activities before and after the march on Bethlehem constituted a localist, ethnic resistance framed in the rhetoric and ideology of Revolutionary republicanism and was based on "popular constitutionalism." The *Kirchenleute* held a conception of popular sovereignty that was more democratic than that of the Jeffersonian Republican party that sought (and received) their votes. They believed that, "as the people, they had the right to obstruct unconstitutional laws while they were petitioning to overturn them" and that such action held a legitimacy "that would bring no criminal charges or military reprisal."[40] Federal officials, however, did attempt to impose harsh punishment on Fries and a few of his friends, but the three sentenced to hang were pardoned by President Adams.

The cumulative impact of the national Federalist administrations' pursuing statist policies and aggressive action against backcountry Regulators in the 1790s contributed greatly to the victory of Thomas Jefferson in the 1800 presidential election. So, too, did the reaction against the nativist and repressive Alien and Sedition Acts, which continued, in effect, the post–Whiskey Rebellion attempt by the Federalists (now without Washington's "aegis") to silence dissent and undermine or eliminate organized opposition to the administration's policies. The Jeffersonian Republicans' reply to the Alien and Sedition Acts came, of course, in the form of the Kentucky and Virginia Resolutions of 1798, adopted by the legislatures of those states and authored, secretly, by Jefferson and Madison. The resolutions endorsed a strict-constructionist view of the Constitution as a compact by the peoples of the states, rather than the American people, thus modifying Madison's original theoretical appeal to the people's sovereignty as the foundation of the Constitution. In later decades the resolutions would be embraced by states' rights militants and nullificationists, but at the time Jefferson and Madison intended their statements to serve as an anticentralizing, anticonsolidation platform to rally the Republican opposition as the 1800 elections approached.[41]

Having learned from the Whiskey repression the uses the Federalist administration could make of violence, Jefferson counseled that there must be nothing done in protest that was disorderly or illegal, and above all no resort to force: "This is not the kind of opposition the American people will permit. But keep away all show of force, and they will bear down the evil propensities of the government, by the constitutional means of election & petition." Madison echoed, too, the defense of the Democratic-Republican societies against Federalist attacks when he asserted that the Sedition Act should arouse "universal alarm" because "it is leveled against the right of freely examining public characters and measures, and of free communication among the people thereon, which has ever been justly deemed the only effectual guardian of every other right." Nevertheless, the Republicans' call to vigilance did not result in a Republican tide in the 1798 fall elections or in the spring elections in 1799. Jefferson for one, however, remained confident that popular sentiment would turn against the Federalists. While the Alien and Sedition Acts mattered to the political class, to cultural minorities that favored the Republicans, and to editors, the tax that had provoked the farmers of eastern Pennsylvania blanketed the country. Thus Jefferson believed that the Federalist ascendancy, "this disease of the imagination will pass over, because the patients are essentially republican. Indeed, the Doctor is now on his way to cure it, in the guise of a tax gatherer." And so in reaction to the centralizing statism of the Federalists, the individualist gentry of the slaveholding South joined with northern representatives of religious, status, and cultural minorities in the middle and eastern states to form a coalition that represented a successful "mobilization of the periphery."[42]

Although defeated in 1800, and rendered marginal thereafter as a national political force, the Federalists had succeeded in the 1790s in pushing the center of American political culture to the right. As the Jeffersonians and former Anti-Federalists had distanced themselves from the Whiskey Rebellion, and as the Federalists exploited the rebellion to discredit and undermine the Democratic societies, their continuing cultural offensive from 1793–94 through the Alien and Sedition Acts of 1798 forced the Jeffersonian Republican opposition to move away from the tactics of Revolutionary "radical Whiggery" and to retreat to safer forms of political opposition, leading, gradually, to the organization of a political party whose first order of business was to establish its legitimacy as the loyal opposition and the true representative—but now more cautious—of republicanism.[43]

The Revolution had been tamed in other ways, as revealed by a sporadic popular insurgency by settler vigilantes in Maine (then part of Massachusetts) that extended from the late eighteenth century well past 1800 and the Republicans' national electoral triumph. The conflict between "Great Proprietors" and "Liberty Men" originated in the 1760s, lapsed during the Revolution, then revived in the 1790s. Settlers in Maine often held uncertain title to their land because of uncertain and conflicting boundaries between the original large land grants to politically influential wealthy men, whose own claims rested on "vague and occasionally fraudulent seventeenth-century Indian deeds or on equally vague royal patents of similar date." During and after the Revolution, new settlers established farms in Maine believing they were occupying free land. But the new state government upheld the claims of proprietors who were now part of the post-Revolutionary elite (such as the secretary of war, General Henry Knox) and who began to launch lawsuits claiming from settlers payment that exceeded not only the value of the wilderness land when it was originally settled but even the value of the improvements the settlers themselves had created.[44]

Worried settlers first tried petitioning the legislature, but in the 1790s they turned to vigilantism as proprietors started legal proceedings. Dozens of "incidents of extralegal violence" followed, many of them involving small parties of Liberty Men who intimidated deputies, surveyors and land agents, or "Tory" neighbors who cooperated with the proprietors; the last might be beaten as well as humiliated. But many settler actions involved hundreds of men enjoying broad community support, attested to often by peaceful mass meetings, as well as the voluntary and enforced community solidarity to which settler women often lent their emotional support. In 1808 a deputy sheriff reported that "several thousands" of resistors were organized in one county. After 1800 settler activists adopted Indian disguises and called themselves "White Indians" to suggest to their adversaries a willingness to

engage in savage violence, as well as to imply that "they too [were] a persecuted people at odds with the most powerful whites." On occasion several hundred "Indians" gathered to confront deputies or the proprietors'
agents.[45]

After 1800 acts of obstruction and intimidation grew dramatically, with
mounting resistance in 1807–8 coinciding with increased legal pressure
and "an unprecedented surge in evangelical revivalism." The White Indian
leaders often fused traditional millennial religious expectations with populist, antiproprietor rhetoric in appealing for community solidarity and
resistance. But the increasingly violent assaults on deputies and others in
1807–8, and the deliberate killing of a surveyor in 1809, split the settlers
and ended widespread organized resistance. The Liberty Men and White
Indians had learned from the repression of the Regulators of the 1780s not
to engage in outright insurrection, but the effectiveness of their "perfor-
mances"—mobilizing in threatening numbers and savage demeanor—had
waned.[46]

During the years after 1800 also, the Jeffersonian Republicans increased
their political presence in Maine (and Massachusetts generally), and, as the
backcountry became less isolated and more politically involved, the Republicans basically co-opted settler resistance. By appointing Republican justices of the peace throughout the riotous region, the Jeffersonians created
partisan friends who would now favor order and legal redress; because the
Federalists opposed all land reform, "the Jeffersonians cheaply obtained
backcountry support with sympathetic rhetoric and mild reform measures." In the 1808 meeting of the General Court, the Republicans passed
a "Betterment Act," initially designed to allow local juries to determine the
original wild land value of the property. However, the Republicans allowed
Federalists to add amendments that heavily favored proprietors and set land
values at the price of wild lands at the time of the trial, thus giving "the
enhanced land value imparted by settler population growth entirely to the
proprietors."[47]

Nationally, the Jeffersonian Republicans profited politically by aligning
themselves with backcountry grievances and, in contrast to Federalists who
presented themselves as "Fathers of the People," became, in historian Alan
Taylor's felicitous phrase, "Friends of the People." While they delivered
land reform at both national and state levels, they also, ironically, rendered
"Regulations," or what Jefferson had called "interventions of the peoples"
based on "popular constitutionalism," far less likely. First, President Jefferson and the Republicans in Congress repealed the Federalist excise and land

taxes and also changed federal land policies, making it easier for settlers and small buyers to acquire western lands. With varying success Republicans also reversed (or tried to change) state policies favoring large speculators. In dealing with the debate at the heart of so many earlier land disputes as to whether labor or title was the touchstone of property, Jeffersonians tried to write legislation using both in determining the value of a farm. At the same time, they undercut the legitimacy of extralegal violence by tightening state laws against it. The Republicans "sent a clear message that redress could and must come through constitutional mechanisms." Now in control of the national and most state governments, "they saw no need for violent crowds of Regulators once 'the people's friends' were in power."[48]

Nor did the kind of folk on the periphery who formerly filled the ranks of insurgencies see the need to mobilize, since the centralizing, strong-state builders no longer occupied the seat of federal power. Although Jefferson did not completely undo the Federalists' infrastructure, and actually adapted to some features of the Hamiltonian system, he signaled to his followers a move away from statism in his program, his rhetoric, and his personal style. But after he left office, the War of 1812, during the administration of James Madison, pushed Jefferson's heirs to a centralizing agenda. In a well-known irony of history, the Republicans adopted key policies of their former opponents: a second national bank, tariffs, internal improvements, a stronger navy, and other Federalist measures.[49] Thus, renewed activism on the part of the central government in a rapidly changing society would create the impression that the Republican ascendancy had turned into a Republican establishment. The Panic of 1819, coming in the midst of a rising climate of egalitarianism, would set off entirely new populist insurgencies.

# Chapter 4

# The Rise of New Social Movements

*I hold it to be a popular government, erected by the people; those who administer it responsible to the people; and itself capable of being amended and modified, just as the people may choose it to be.*
—Daniel Webster, speech in the Senate, 1830

## "THE PEOPLE" RISING, OR, THE RHETORICAL ASCENDANCY OF THE PEOPLE

While notions of what "the people" meant continued to vary after 1789 and on into the new century, the idea of the people's sovereignty became entrenched, and the inclusiveness of the term inevitably expanded. A glance at the appearance of the word "people" or "the people" in presidential inaugural addresses during the early republic reveals that frequent references to "the people" were accompanied often by the implication of the people's sovereignty. Ironically, the Revolutionary generation of presidents (through James Monroe), though having a more constricted view of the entity, used the terms somewhat more often than their successors.

George Washington's several references (in both inaugurals) to "people" or "the people" pointed to the collective sense of the terms, while that alleged elitist John Adams used forms of the term "people" no fewer than eighteen times, often to mean the same entity as his references to "this nation" and "my fellow citizens" (once each). Adams viewed the influence of the people as exerted "by their representatives in Congress and the State legislatures, according to the Constitution." Thomas Jefferson's preference, as an admirer of the French Revolution, led to his using "my fellow citizens" no fewer than five times in his first inaugural and eight in the second. James Madison referred to "the people" and "my fellow citizens" sparingly. None of the first four presidents sounded what might be called a populist note in reference to "the people."[1]

In 1817 James Monroe was not only the last of the Revolutionary generation to become president, but he also dressed the part, going about in out-of-date clothing that evoked the republican simplicity of the Revolutionary era. But it was Monroe whose inaugural rhetoric moved cautiously toward the populist themes that, in the next decade, would engulf various regions of the country. Using the terms "people" and "the people" often, he drew a strong connection between the necessity of the people to be educated and "intelligent," that is, informed, and the proper exercise of popular sovereignty. "The Government has been in the hands of the people," he stated. To the people, therefore, went the credit for success in the late war. "It is only when the people become ignorant and corrupt," he continued, "when they degenerate into a populace, that they are incapable of exercising the sovereignty."[2]

Monroe sounded this note again in 1821 in his second inaugural address, contrasting the American republic with ancient republics that contained distinct orders of nobility and people: "In this great nation there is but one order, that of the people, whose power, by a peculiarly happy improvement of the representative principle, is transferred from them, without impairing in the slightest degree their sovereignty, to bodies of their own creation, and to persons elected by themselves." Thus, Monroe's more overt expression of popular sovereignty nevertheless followed in the footsteps of his predecessors by stressing the representative principle. Given how satisfactorily such representation was functioning, Monroe congratulated his fellow citizens on a government "possessing all the energies of any government ever known to the Old World, with an utter incapacity to oppress the people."[3] Ironically, he uttered these words at the outset of a decade in which many movements would arise claiming to speak in the name of "the people" and protesting oppression of the people by various usurpers of power, including officeholding cabals, banks, evangelical moralists, monopolies, the Masonic Order, and landlords.

Still deeper ironies emerged from John Quincy Adams's inaugural, given that four candidates had split the 1824 electoral vote and Adams had received a third fewer popular votes than Andrew Jackson (108,740 to 153,544), and then had been elected in the House of Representatives by a process subsequently denounced by his adversaries as thwarting the will of the people. Uncharacteristically seeking a popular touch, Adams expressed in no small measure the spirit growing in the political, social, and cultural arenas of the 1820s: "Our political creed is, without a dissenting voice that can be heard, that the will of the people is the source and the happiness of the people the end of all legitimate government upon earth . . . and best guaranty against the abuse of power consists in the freedom, the purity, and the frequency of popular elections." More remarkably still, Adams went further than any of his predecessors, including Jefferson, in describing the United States as a "representative democracy." A recent biographer has observed that "no President before him had ever used the word 'democracy' in a public address."[4]

A few months later, however, Adams undid whatever reassurance he had given to the democratic temper in his inaugural with a singularly unfortunate first annual message. In one "eloquent but fatal passage," he called for an activist central government to improve "agriculture, commerce, and manufactures" and observed that "liberty is power" and that the Creator intended that power should be exercised for "beneficence" and improvement: "While foreign nations less blessed with that freedom which is power than ourselves are advancing with gigantic strides in the career of public improvement, were we to slumber in indolence or fold up our arms and proclaim to the world that we are palsied by the will of our constituents, would it not be to cast away the bounties of Providence and doom ourselves to perpetual inferiority?" Adams's rivals pounced on this impolitic declaration, as well as other parts of his often visionary message, to ridicule the president as an elitist and impractical fool, contemptuous of his fellow citizens. It constituted the first step to his subsequent defeat in the election of 1828. Andrew Jackson's supporters not only revived the fear of consolidated, too powerful government that had buoyed Jeffersonian Republicanism and Anti-Federalism, but they also sounded populist themes arguing that only the defeat of Adams and the election of Jackson could restore the country to pure democratic principles.[5]

Surprisingly, neither Andrew Jackson nor Martin Van Buren in their inaugurals spoke of the virtues of popular sovereignty, emphasizing instead the importance of states' rights as against the encroachment of the "General Government." Jackson balanced such warnings with an emphasis on the "incalculable importance [of] the union of these States," while Van Buren, concerned for his political standing in the South, attempted to reassure slaveholders that the Constitution's enshrinement of states' rights afforded ample protection against any interference with "domestic slavery." But the Jacksonian inaugurals are misleading since other messages abound with, as historian Marvin Meyers has observed, "relentless and apparently irresistible invocation of 'the people' in Jacksonian rhetoric." In the classic style of populists, Jackson pitted "the whole people" against the aristocratic few.[6]

Clearly, "the people" had ascended to the status of sacred shibboleth when a conservative such as Daniel Webster trumpeted their undisputed and indivisible sovereignty. In 1830, during his famous debate with South Carolina's Robert Y. Hayne in the Senate over the nature of the Union, Webster challenged Hayne's argument that the government was "the creature of the State Legislatures" rather than "the creature of the people." If it was the creature of the legislatures, said Webster, then it was "the servant of four-and-twenty masters, of different wills and different purposes, and yet bound to obey all." Webster labeled that an "absurdity": "It is, sir, the People's Constitution, the People's Government, made for the People; made by the People; *and answerable to the People.* . . . The State Legislatures, as political bodies, however sovereign, are yet not sovereign over the People."[7]

## THE CHANGING SOCIOECONOMIC CONTEXT, 1800–1830

In the decades after 1800, economic, social, technological, and demographic changes created a new context for social movements, and within it populist social movements arose of a character different from the agrarian and backwoods rebellions discussed in previous chapters. As early as the 1780s a "market revolution" spread from seaports, commercial centers, and manufacturing villages throughout society. Although the United States was still overwhelmingly agricultural, rural areas began to experience a reduction of subsistence farming and of localized economic activity in which bartering of goods was extensive, as its producers shifted to raising or making goods for exchange in a wider marketplace. However, up to 1815, cities, towns, and small manufacturing villages were preindustrial, and "industrialization" is too sweeping a term to be applied even to the large factories that came into being in the thirty years before the Civil War. But the early stages of the industrial revolution nevertheless wrought far-reaching changes in society and public affairs.[8]

Historians have debated extensively various features of the market revolution, including its timing and extent; the receptivity to it of various groups in the population; its relationship to the rise of reform movements; its impact on the class structure and opportunity; the mind-sets or *mentalités* present in the population before, during, and after the rise of commercialization; and the political responses and eventual party affiliations of individuals and groups differentially impacted by the market revolution.[9] What matters here is the simple fact of social change and the interaction of the intensifying of capitalism with improvements in transportation and communication.

A "transportation revolution" proceeded together with commercialization. In 1800 travel was difficult, easier by sailing ship along the seaboard than almost anywhere inland on often rough or muddy roads. An early wave of canal and turnpike building in the 1790s put more men, horses, and stages on the roads, but it was not until the 1820s that dramatic improvements in transport took hold. After 1819 parts of New York's Erie Canal were put into operation, and soon DeWitt Clinton's "Big Ditch" proved an enormous economic boon, inspiring a wave of imitation in other states. Railroads would not be built in Massachusetts until the mid-1830s, but in 1826 travelers could travel from Boston to New York City in just over three and a half days, a trip that would have taken a week not long before. In 1829 a Boston minister contemplated "the immense facility given to intercourse by modern improvements, by increased commerce and traveling, by the post-office, by the steam-boat, and especially by the press, — by newspapers, periodicals, tracts, and other publications."[10]

Changes in the workplace had even more impact on independent farmers, artisans, and mechanics. Jefferson's embargo of trade in 1808 and then the War of 1812 spurred manufacturing in the United States, as a home market grew larger with population migration westward. Manufacturing villages had begun to dot the countryside from the 1790s, and by the 1820s and 1830s large textile factories appeared in New England. Yet the factory would not dominate industry until after the Civil War, and there "were two distinct paths to industrial development," according to Bruce Laurie: "One was followed by textiles and the other by handicrafts. The first resulted in capital-intensive methods centered in large factories; the second in labor-intensive techniques, or the sweating system, carried on in homes and small shops." Both paths led to similar results, however: the degradation of craft skills and an increase in wage laborers. While mechanization led to job simplification, so did the outwork system. Both undermined the "preindustrial world of the self-sufficient yeoman and independent mechanic."[11] The erosion of autonomy for many artisans and yeoman farmers also struck at their traditional conceptions of manhood. At the same time that masculinity was becoming more defined by work and success in the marketplace, competition and insecurity in that realm increased. Achieving economic independence was central to the full realization of manhood, and the apprentice and craft system allowed young men to aspire to "'earn a competence' by learning an entire craft. Masculinity was gradually acquired during the apprenticeship term as a boy learned the skills necessary to do manly work."[12]

In the early decades of the nineteenth century, printers began to complain of apprentices who worked for one-half or two-thirds of a journeyman's regular wages as "half-way" or "two-thirds" men, "underscoring the significance of both training and wages as the measure of the man." Thus, apprenticeship was about acquiring technical skills as well as acquiring manhood. But the decline of apprenticeship and the degradation of craft skills interfered with this process, creating fears of dependence, if not domination or humiliation. These fears led to a "compensatory" preoccupation with manhood.[13]

To oversimplify, "dependence" connoted women, children, nonwhites, and servility, while "independence" (often equated with "a competence") connoted masculine citizenship. Most artisans and average farmers did not expect to become gentlemen, whose patrician ideal of manhood consisted of property ownership, patriarchy, and (usually) the expectation of deference from the middle and lower classes. But most did look forward to attaining "a respectable 'competency,' becoming master of a trade, or owning their own freehold." Autonomy, mastery of their household, contributing to the well-being of family, and above all meaningful work "formed the very core of adult manhood." But as revealed in the well-documented experience of a Vermont farming family, a man need not move cleanly from childhood to adolescence to adulthood and independence but sometimes remained "suspended in a state between dependence and semidependence for most of his adult life."[14] In the period 1800 to 1840, with the socioeconomic and other changes affecting town and farm and blurring the lines between dependency and independence, many men entered into a state of anxiety regarding their attaining independent manhood. In the years immediately following the Panic of 1819, those anxieties intensified.

## THE DEPRESSION OF 1819–1822

After an economic boom following the War of 1812, the United States in 1818–19 experienced severe deflation, following a similar economic plunge in Europe, and endured an economic depression that covered most of the country through 1822 and, in some areas, longer. Prices for agricultural commodities fell disastrously, with cotton going from 21.5 cents a pound in New Orleans in 1818 to 14.3 cents a year later. Corn, tobacco, rice, and wheat prices also declined rapidly (wheat had been $1.45 a bushel in 1818, then dropped to 91 cents, then to 72 cents in 1820). All occupational groups suffered—farmers, merchants, small tradesmen, speculators, those with fixed debts, and bank stockholders who had borrowed on unpaid stock. Unemployment spread, and pauperism became more noticeable than ever before in the new nation's history. *Niles' Register* estimated that some 50,000 men were unemployed or irregularly employed in the three cities of New York, Philadelphia, and Baltimore; soup stations to feed the hungry appeared in all three. Real estate values in those and other eastern cities fell along with rents, while a frenzy of buying public land in the West came to an end. Although President Monroe mentioned economic troubles in his December 1819 message to Congress, a year later he evasively presented a more upbeat picture, marred only by "pressures on certain interests" that constituted "instructive admonitions . . . teaching us lessons of economy." Privately, he and his advisors worried about the "alarming situation," and John Quincy Adams conceded that distress was "universal in every part of the country." "Government can do nothing," he added, "at least nothing by any measure yet proposed, but transfer discontents, and propitiate one class . . . by disgusting another."[15]

Too many banks extending too much credit: that diagnosis of the depression found almost universal expression at the time, and while modern historians have told a more complicated story, the overexpansion of debt and credit remain the bottom line. From 1813 to 1819 the amount of bank capital increased from $65 million to over $125 million. The notes of the many new banks helped create prosperity, speculation in all forms of commerce and manufacturing, and heavy speculation in public lands, with $23 million owed to the government in 1819. The Second Bank of the United States (BUS) came into existence in 1818 in part to promote a sound and uniform currency. But the bank and the secretary of the treasury, rather than checking the extension of credit, acted together to give too much leeway to state banks to extend credit, creating a perilous chain of debt. In the summer of 1818 the BUS suddenly reversed course, stopped discounts, and ordered its branches to call on state banks to redeem their heavy balances and loans. There ensued a "wave of bankruptcies, particularly outside New England" (where banks had been more conservative). Everywhere popular indignation mounted against banks and bankers, but especially against the Second Bank. "The Bank was saved and the people were ruined" was among the mildest epithets circulated in the wake of economic distress. Just as well known became Missouri senator Thomas Hart Benton's characterization of the bank as a "monster": "All the flourishing cities of the West are mortgaged to this money power. . . . They are in the jaws of the monster!"[16]

A clamor arose in several states to tax the Second Bank out of existence, and several moved in that direction, but in March 1819 the Supreme Court in *McCulloch v. Maryland* denied Maryland or any state the right to tax the bank—a decision that hardly lessened the antibank furor and not incidentally fed states' rights sentiment. But antibank sentiment did not fasten on the BUS alone but ran rampant throughout the country against all manner of banks and lending institutions. Although strongest in the West, criticism of banks erupted also in Pennsylvania, a state awash in banks and seat of the Second Bank. One critic there characterized bank directors as "a set of speculating and monopolizing gentry," while a state senate committee rooted the cause of the depression "chiefly in the abuses of the banking system."[17] The antibank furor raised the temperature of class resentment and released a considerable amount of animosity toward the wealthy, especially speculators. Accordingly, after 1819 the release of class resentment in political and social movements became more common; it provided an enormous boost to the expression of populist anger against monied or other powerful elites. Populist rhetoric escalated into vivid hyperbole reminiscent of the eighteenth-century "Country" ideology steeped in antipower, anticorruption, and anticonspiratorial rhetoric that had shaped the mentality of American colonists before the American Revolution. The depression of 1819–22 unleashed populist anger across the country and energized political movements seeking "relief" from economic distress.

Examination of two very different episodes of populist outburst in the early 1820s, in very different settings, illustrates the impact of the depression and the escalation of populist rhetoric.[18] In one, language condemning "monied" power and wealthy aristocrats permeated a "war" over "relief" in a western and border state, with the "relief" party claiming to represent debtors and "the people" against the aristocracy. Although debtors were also creditors and the line between relief and antirelief was not at all a strict class division, the episode merits attention because of its impact on political rhetoric generally. In a second case, a newly strident class rhetoric emanated from urban artisans, small businessmen, and rising entrepreneurs in a populist movement in Boston in the early 1820s, dominated by middling men in a cross-class alliance claiming to represent "the people."

KENTUCKY'S "RELIEF WAR"

Congress convened earlier than usual in 1819 but did little to alleviate the economic crisis. By 1821 it had acted to reduce the cost of government, abolishing offices, lowering salaries, cutting military spending, and calling in from active duty half of the naval force. Buyers of public land in debt to the federal government received help: they could keep that portion of public land for which they had paid and relinquish the remainder, while being forgiven interest owed in arrears and given easier conditions to pay the full debt.[19]

But the states became the primary political arenas in which struggles over relief occurred, and not just in the West. Eastern states as well considered two principal ways of affording relief to debtors: with stop, stay (of execution), or replevin laws that extended the period for payment of debts by months or years; and with minimal appraisal laws, providing for either neutral parties to appraise property before it was sold at auction or setting a minimum price (such as two-thirds) of the value of a property in a forced sale. The legislatures of Delaware, New Jersey, New York, Massachusetts, and Virginia considered and rejected stay laws, while those of Pennsylvania, Maryland, Vermont (though after the crisis was over), Ohio, Indiana, Illinois, Missouri, Louisiana, Tennessee, and Kentucky adopted various kinds of replevin, often tied to requirements for debt payment that kept the notes of state banks or state loan offices in circulation and thus also expanded or did not contract further the money supply.[20]

Five states passed minimal appraisal laws: Pennsylvania, Ohio, Kentucky, Indiana, and Missouri. The divisions within states over relief legislation cut across urban-rural and sectional lines, as well as class and occupational groups. Opponents and supporters of relief accused each other of representing profiteers and speculators. In Missouri, scene of a protracted battle over stay and other laws, the antirelief *Missouri Republican* charged that the legislation was designed to keep "the wealthy debtor in his palace."[21]

Historians have traditionally emphasized the antibank fervor in Tennessee and Kentucky as the breeding ground for the hard-money passion and animus against the BUS that Andrew Jackson and several of his key advisors from those states would bring to Washington. While Jackson undoubtedly imbibed many westerners' hostility to banks, he was allied with Tennessee's powerful Blount-Overton faction, political-commercial entrepreneurs whose competition with a rival political faction of wealthy men helped shape the state's initial response to the economic crisis. Before the depression began, Tennessee's legislature passed a law taxing any bank not chartered by the state $50,000 annually. This resulted less from hostility to the Second Bank, which did have a branch in Tennessee, than from the rivalry of factions to prevent one another from gaining control of any additional BUS branch that might come into the state. The legislation also added ten new village banks that became branches of the state's two existing banks located in Nashville and Knoxville.[22]

When the depression struck, outrage against all banks engulfed the state, but new relief legislation put even more paper money in circulation and created a state office that would issue notes; unless creditors accepted those notes at par the debtor would receive a two-year stay of execution. This program did nothing to alleviate the anger against banks and speculators, and a grand jury in Sumner County (near Nashville) expressed its belief that "relief" was a cry got up by well-connected, greedy speculators who had accumulated property that "belonged to other people." In 1819 the voters of Middle Tennessee, a region hard hit by the depression, elected to Congress a candidate who regarded banking "[as] a frank fraud upon the laboring and industrious part of society . . . a schem[e], whereby, in a silent and secret manner, to make idleness productive and filch from industry, the hard produce of its earnings."[23]

The following year, however, relief forces managed to create a state-owned bank that would make loans, but dissatisfaction increased along with hard-money opinion. In the 1821 state campaign both gubernatorial candidates called for repeal of the relief program. The leading candidate, William Carroll, a popular ex-general and Nashville merchant ruined by the panic, said he wished he "had never seen one [a bank] in the state." Carroll was swept into office on a surge of populist antibank anger, receiving 41,244 votes to 11,171 for his opponent. Carroll then pushed the state toward a specie resumption, hard-money policy that led within five years to the demise of the state's major note-issuing banks.[24]

While Tennessee's "relief" program stirred up antibank populism, Kentucky's unleashed divisions that would dominate the state's politics through the mid-1820s. The debtor interest, no more located exclusively in the lower orders or poor than that of Tennessee, carried forward its program on a rising tide of radically populist rhetoric.

Unlike Tennessee, Kentucky contained an abundance of banks, including thirteen branches of the Bank of Kentucky, two recently opened (1818) branches of the Second Bank in Louisville and Lexington, and forty-six independent banks that had been chartered in 1817–18, a total of one bank for every 6,700 inhabitants. Other private lending institutions also issued notes, such as the Kentucky Insurance Company and several factories. Economic distress began in mid-1818, and by the spring of 1819 produce prices were 51 percent below their 1817 average. Prices for land and slaves dropped sharply, and unemployed laborers began to leave the state. The Second Bank's contraction of credit led to thousands of lawsuits in federal courts, resulting ultimately in a massive concentration of property, as the courts consistently favored banks and creditors. The Second Bank became the largest proprietor of real estate in the state capital, and over a two-year period the courts conveyed to banks, merchants, and other creditors one-third of Kentucky's property. This juggernaut of sheriffs' seizures and forced sales at a fraction of a property's worth clearly cut across classes and occupations. Earlier in its history the state had enacted both stay and minimum appraisal laws, and the electorate registered its overwhelming desire for "relief" in the 1820 gubernatorial election, casting a total of almost 70 percent of the votes for the three candidates identified with relief; an estimated 75 percent of the eligible electorate cast ballots.[25]

Before 1818 a mania for banks had prevailed, but now Kentuckians joined the national chorus blaming banks for the depression. Radical antibank populism had emerged early on in the legislature when state senator Jesse Bledsoe, a colorful Baptist preacher, called for the abolition of these "monied combinations" because their "silent, corrupt, and all pervasive influence" led to moral corruption and subjugation. Those who commanded the money power "will command the government." But the legislature ignored him and moved first to levy taxes or fines on non-state-chartered banks and lenders—including the Second Bank, not its primary target—that would drive nonchartered lenders out of business. When the Seventh Circuit Court disallowed the tax while courts delivered the property and debt judgments favoring creditors and banks, both judges and banks became symbols of antirepublican tyranny. Amos Kendall, editor of the *Frankfort Argus of Western America* and later a close advisor of President Jackson, complained that "to preserve the credit of the banks, the people are to be sacrificed." Now "relief" men revived Bledsoe's rhetoric and, invoking the "Spirit of '76," agreed that "laws were made for the benefit of the people"; contracts that did not promote the people's happiness could be abrogated if the "good of the people" really was "the supreme law."[26]

In December 1819 and February 1820 the legislature, dominated by "relief" men, passed stay or replevin laws aiding debtors. It also repealed the charters of independent banks (now known as the "Forty Thieves"), declaring in the preamble to that law that "all legislative power proceeds from the people" and that it was self-evident that "all laws which grant to a few, the power to oppress the many" were opposed to the "primitive rights of the people, and therefore repealable."[27]

Antirelief interests, which included Kentucky's most prominent man, Henry Clay, preferred to let matters "take their course" and condemned relief legislation as irresponsible and unconstitutional. But relief advocates responded that if the Constitution and laws became destructive, then law, not morality, should give way: "Constitutions and laws were made for men, not men for constitutions and laws." The Lexington Public Advertiser exclaimed, "Good God! Was our constitution framed only for creditors? Laws are made for the benefit of the people, and not the people for the benefit of the law."[28]

In November–December 1820 the relief forces in the legislature went further, passing another stay law and creating the Bank of the Commonwealth, a state-owned bank authorized to loan up to $1,000 to any Kentuckian to pay "his, her, or their just debts" or to purchase livestock or produce for export. Additional relief measures followed, including a three-quarter minimum valuation law, but opposition hardly quieted. During 1822, along with most of the country, Kentucky began to climb out of the depression, and by year's end most of the relief legislation had been repealed.[29]

Meanwhile, the struggle over relief evolved into an entirely different fight. After the Kentucky Court of Appeals declared unconstitutional the stay laws because they impaired the obligation of contracts, the conflict moved to the court itself. After winning the 1824 state election, a furious relief legislative majority set about removing the appeals court judges from office. (In Kentucky's populist political culture, the legislature "had a penchant for tampering with the courts.") An impeachment effort fell short of a needed two-thirds majority, so by year's end the relief/new court party repealed the law organizing the court and legislated a new court into existence. This passionate political war elicited even more extreme populist rhetoric from the relief/new court champions. The General Assembly began its assault on the old court by asserting that "the will of the people is the sovereign power of the state." The people acting collectively, it declared, intend "the promotion of the general welfare." The people's will was a "moral agent" and the sole "controlling and paramount power, competent to all the purposes of government," expressed exclusively through their legislature. The judges' attempt to control the legislature amounted to a transgression against the sovereign people, and if allowed, the people "cease to be sovereign." The assembly's "Preamble and Resolution" continued with a bow to the minority but gave it no standing with this astonishing claim: unanimity was not necessary because the rights of each depend on "the will of all, and that will must be displayed by the agency or expression of the majority."[30]

But within a year the relief/new court party lost both the house and senate in an "astonishing reversal," as the voters installed old court majorities in both, and in 1826 lost again, ending finally the fallout from the "Relief

War." Historians of this episode have concluded that despite the rhetoric, men with very similar economic interests participated on both sides, and that each party necessarily resorted to populist rhetoric, claiming to represent ordinary citizens and debtors.[31]

Ironically, men who later became influential members of the Jackson administration and its hard-money orientation enlisted in this struggle generally with the inflationary relief/new court party. Amos Kendall, who had some misgivings about stay laws that forgave debts, was in the process of migrating from an alliance with Henry Clay into the relief and, eventually, Jackson party. The legislature had appointed as chief justice of the new court William L. Barry, later Jackson's postmaster general, and as court clerk the young journalist Francis Preston Blair, later a "Kitchen Cabinet" advisor to the president.[32] But while leaving behind paper money, these future Jacksonians brought with them an understanding of antibank sentiment's popular appeal. They carried with them, too, the populist rhetoric in which they and their opponents had been immersed in the early and mid-1820s and that would come front and center on the national stage when Old Hickory waged his war against Henry Clay, Nicholas Biddle, and the Second Bank of the United States.

## THE MIDDLING INTEREST

A People opposed to a Party.
　　Measures and not men; the People and not a Cabal; the many and not the Few;—Public and not Party spirit are the leading maxims of the Middling Interest politics.
—Bostonian and Mechanics' Journal, April 2, 1823

Boston of the early republic, still a Federalist bastion of elitism and deference into the 1810s, was an unlikely locale for an eruption of urban populism. In the early 1820s, however, an independent, antipartisan movement calling itself "the Middling Interest" emerged to challenge Federalist gentlemen's tight control of public affairs in Boston. It sought to empower middle- and lower-middle-class ordinary men, as well as self-made entrepreneurs, whose ability to influence public policy matched neither their numbers nor their hard-won affluence. It was a restrained, middle-class kind of populism, driven in part by class-conscious rhetoric but not deeply radical in its demands.[33]

It arrived at a turning point in Boston's civil history, as the town moved formally to city government, and as local discontents became sharpened by the Panic of 1819 and the hard times that followed for many Bostonians. The panic added to economic damage to the city's merchants that had resulted from the 1816 tariff's failure to protect U.S. seaports against goods coming in illegally. British manufacturers also used a new auction system of sending ships laden with goods into Boston harbor and bypassing local merchants through an open auction. Economic depression came to Boston in 1819, and by January 1820 Governor James Brooks devoted the first half of his address to the General Court to problems of "depression and embarrassment." From 1820 to 1822 over 3,000 inhabitants were imprisoned for debt, and in 1822 during a three-month period, 100 businesses failed. In 1820 both the Society for the Relief of the Distressed and a newspaper, the *Boston Debtor's Journal*, appeared, "to subdue aristocracy and promote our freedom and happiness, as Americans"; the latter's focus on imprisonment for debt was soon included in the coverage of other newspapers in Boston and across the state. Many men who would join the Middling Interest also had agitated to abolish or alleviate imprisonment for debt.[34]

Several other issues bubbled up to create discontent with the Federalist oligarchy that had run Boston's local, state, and national politics for years. As early as the spring of 1820 the incumbent board of Federalist selectmen had been defeated by a Union List of candidates backed by nontraditional auctioneers and small tradesmen at odds with established merchants and importers allied with the defeated selectmen. In the fall intra-Federalist division continued when dissidents nominated a Republican merchant to run against the Federalist caucus's nominee. Although the latter prevailed, in March 1821 the Union List board of selectmen generally won reelection.[35]

The Federalist Central Committee, consisting of three wealthy men, Harrison Gray Otis, William Sullivan, and Thomas H. Perkins, gradually became a magnet for resentment among the Federalist rank and file as much as among Republicans. One running source of complaint was compulsory militia duty, a burden on the lower and middle classes but rife with exceptions and loopholes for the upper class. More urgent, exposure of abuses in the administration of justice and taxes helped create a widespread perception that public policy served the interest of a wealthy cabal. Taxes were levied through an archaic system administered by the county-based court of sessions, and a town committee reported that tax laws were enforced unequally and that certain "opulent citizens" did not pay their fair share. Efforts to reform the system moved forward slowly in 1821, but the court itself, the core of the problem, sidetracked proposed changes. An angry town meeting then passed a resolution complaining of "disrespect to the People . . . [and] utter disregard to [their] interests."[36]

Thus, the movement to city governance was reinforced by the desire to escape the "hated Court of Sessions." More generally, as a correspondent to the *New England Galaxy* put it, adopting the new form of government would result in "the whole authority ̄ . . . emanating from the people." Simultaneously, city proponents had determined that the new framework would be meaningless without ward voting for state and federal representatives (Boston had elected city officials by ward since 1799). The town traditionally voted at one place, Faneuil Hall, where, Republicans often complained, mechanics, artisans, journeymen, and laborers could be intimidated and influenced by watchful merchant princes, who often personally handed out ballots to voters. As Samuel Adams put it, echoing an Anti-Federalist argument for localism, with decentralized voting "there would be no coaxing of mechanics, threatening them with loss of work. . . . We know each other [in our wards]. . . . Here [in Faneuil Hall] we are strangers." Federalist William Tudor argued that ward divisions would "break up old associations, good feelings, etc. . . . We had been a great family. If we choose by wards, there is a danger of our splitting into twelve little towns." Privately, Federalist Harrison Gray Otis urged defeat of ward voting since the example and influence of "the most respectable persons" caused the numbers or "class which is *acted upon* by this example and influence [to] realize a pride and pleasure in showing their colors upon a general review, which they cannot feel when trained in a gun house. . . . It is easier to manage the town of B—— by a Lancastrian system of political discipline than to institute numerous schools."[37]

In the winter of 1821–22 the supporters of ward voting—mostly Republicans initially—began calling themselves the Middling Interest. In early January reform forces gained a huge victory when a new city charter and ward voting won approval in referenda in which over 4,800 votes were cast. In the legislature, Boston's representatives sought to kill ward voting, but in March the city again by popular vote strongly endorsed the charter and a ward system "that ensured more democracy to Boston's ordinary citizens."[38]

During the debates over the city charter and ward voting, another issue had arisen that proved decisive in launching the Middling Interest into electoral combat and drew many ordinary Federalist voters into the movement.

Middle-class contractors, carpenters, and artisans had petitioned for repeal of an 1803 law that prevented wooden buildings from being built over ten feet in height. Major fires in 1787 and 1794 and lesser blazes in 1801 and 1802 had prompted the law. Taller wooden buildings burned more readily and spread sparks rapidly, and they posed greater dangers for firemen. Repeal proponents argued, however, that affordable housing was scarce, and many master carpenters (or contractors) and journeymen wanted more work; some entrepreneurs wanted to develop row houses. They promised to include new safeguards and to limit the height of new structures. During 1821–22 the repeal had been frustrated in town meeting and the legislature by the Federalist Central Committee. By March, however, the measure garnered immense support and over 4,500 Bostonians' signatures on a petition. It passed in town meeting by a huge majority (2,837 to 547). Federalist newspapers such as the *Columbian Centinel*, speaking for the elite, unwisely had disparaged the issue and the "ten-footers," as mechanics supporting repeal were called.[39]

The pro-repeal *New England Galaxy* responded with populist outrage. It declared that "the mechanics of Boston are as intelligent, and as respectable in everything, except the *respectability of wealth*, as any body of men that ever gave strength, support and security to any city or nation on earth." Acting on the advice of Harrison Gray Otis, who held extensive real estate in the city but who now urged compromise, the Federalist command tried to co-opt the ten-footers. But the perception was now widespread that the Federalist elite for too long had managed public policy for its own benefit. Ignoring the traditional leadership, a March 11 meeting of "citizens from all wards" nominated for state senate an independent Middling Interest list of candidates consisting of Federalists and Republicans to oppose the Federalist list. Professions of conversion to ten-footer principles and lingering deference helped the Federalist senatorial list prevail, though the independent candidates won a respectable vote.[40]

Undeterred, Middling Interest leaders turned their attention to the city's first election by popular vote of a mayor. The Federal grandees assumed that Otis, then a U.S. senator, would win easily. The Middling Interest decided to back Josiah Quincy, a maverick Federalist well known for vigorously opposing all things Jeffersonian, but also for clashing with the Federalist Central Committee. Quincy at first opposed city government but then accepted it and helped to write the new charter, making him an almost ideal Middling Interest candidate. He had shown open-mindedness and sensitivity in dealing with poverty and other city problems, and most of all, he had demonstrated his independence of the Otises, Sullivans, Tudors, and Perkinses. A delegation of Middling Interest citizens, accordingly, headed by a master carpenter, came to Quincy's home and asked him "to stand" as their candidate for mayor.[41]

Heading into the April election, Middling Interest populism had been laid out in a pamphlet titled *An Exposition of the Principles and Views of the Middling Interest*. It rehearsed the manner in which the city's elected representatives had "utterly disregarded" the wishes of "the people" in issues such as ward voting and wooden buildings. Ward voting was necessary, it argued, because "the majority are, and of right ought to be, sovereign; and that there is not, nor can there be danger in trusting to the majority, when every voter in the Commonwealth is left free to form . . . and act upon his opinion of men and measures." The *Exposition* denounced "the secret influence of a FEW" whose acquisition of money made them believe they were superior to ordinary people. For several years now, it added, patriotic men of both the Federalist and Republican parties had grown dissatisfied with "the wanton violence of party spirit," thus echoing an earlier town meeting resolution denouncing party spirit as a device used by the overbearing few to control the many.[42]

Quincy entered the mayoral election with the unanimous nomination of the "Middling Interest Political Caucus," which touted him as the candidate not only of majority rule but also of reform of the judiciary, imprisonment for debt, the militia, and treatment of the poor. Though Quincy won a plurality of the vote, mostly with Republican support, a third candidate denied him a majority, producing a standoff. The Middling Interest then used its influence to bring about the nomination and election of a compromise candidate, Federalist John Phillips. A year later Quincy, as the candidate of a new coalition of Middling Interest men and non-Otis Federalists, won a narrow victory over a Republican candidate.[43] In the following years he would leave his mark as one of Boston's most activist and memorable mayors.

As with earlier agrarian populist movements, the Middling Interest possessed its own religious component. A young minister recently arrived at one of three Baptist churches in Boston, First Baptist in the lower-class North End neighborhood, Francis Wayland, became prominent as a Middling Interest advocate and Quincy ally. His ward housed many laborers, mechanics, artisans, and small shopkeepers, and Wayland himself had been raised in such a family. Although later in his life a conservative, at the time Wayland believed that "whatever we would do for our country, must be done for THE PEOPLE [for] the people are not only the real but also the acknowledged fountain of all authority." He also strongly expressed Middling Interest distrust of traditional political parties, which came to represent, he said, only the party officials.[44]

By 1823 Boston's Middling Interest had run its course. It had succeeded in making the city a more democratic polity and realized the wishes of the majority especially with regard to ward voting and wooden buildings. More important, it changed the climate of Boston in bringing into the public sphere the middling and artisan classes, as well as more affluent self-made men. Concern for the well-being of the poor increased, and imprisonment for debt became more scrutinized than ever. In July 1822 the *Bostonian and Mechanics' Journal* appeared to champion the rights of "mechanics" and even addressed itself to the condition of truckmen, laborers who carried heavy loads about the city on two-wheeled carts.

The Middling Interest populist insurgency was hardly radical, but it did release powerful social tensions, as well as give currency to strong populist and class-conscious rhetoric. The broad and somewhat fluid coalitions it brought together included, as its own leaders claimed, "men of property" and "business." Despite their rhetoric about conflict with "a MONIED ARISTOCRACY" and a "contest between the DRONES and the WORKING BEES of the community," some Middling Interest leaders were "no mean or middling sort of men." Yet the army of the movement had been composed of men who previously had been deferential to their acknowledged social betters. It signaled a political culture becoming more outwardly populist, even in Boston, and into which was seeping a consciousness of growing inequalities of wealth at odds with the republican heritage of the Revolution.[45]

WORKING MEN'S PARTIES

In England first and then in the United States commercialization and early industrialism led to labor radicalism that was distinctly populist in style, espousing less a Marxist class consciousness than a producer ethic that included virtuous masters, employers, and proprietors among the many—"the people"—contending against the exploitative few. In his discussion of the early resistance of the common people of Britain to the industrial revolution, Craig Calhoun regards these movements as "populist," arguing that attributing class consciousness to them is misleading; rather, they were "deeply rooted in many cases in traditional communities of both craft and locality." Hence, Calhoun labels these populists as "reactionary radicals."[46]

These artisans, craftsmen, and small tradespeople sought to defend their communities against oppression and poverty and demanded rights that were largely "collective rights." They tried to retain past practices even while calling for changes in present ones. "They were acting in response to changes going on about them that were largely beyond their control," but they were not simply conservative or even restorationist. They "aimed at the creation of a radically different social order from that in which they lived, one in which traditional values would be better realized."[47]

Like populists who came before and after them, these English populists reacted to threats that could be summarized by "corruption," prevailing among thieving officials and aristocrats. Classically, too, they spoke "primarily on behalf of 'the people' . . . against those who would abuse the people, but not necessarily in favor of any specific segment of the population." Their blend of radical-conservative vision was expressed succinctly by William Cobbett in his 1816 "Address to the Journeymen and Laborers of England, Wales, Scotland, and Ireland": "We want *great alteration*, but we want nothing *new*."[48]

A more ambiguous American version of this populism first emerged with some force in cities and even rural towns in the years 1829 to 1836, and went hand in hand with a nascent trade union movement focused on the ten-hour day. The Workingmen's parties of the 1830s command attention less because of their ability to mobilize workers or voters, modest by most measures, and more because of their populist ideology.[49]

Before the emergence of the Workingmen's parties, Middling Interest rhetoric already was moving from the margins of the polity and taking over the mainstream. Various social and political movements of the 1820s would help to induce that populist transformation of politics and, in particular, of the organized, mass political parties of Democrats and Whigs that emerged in the 1830s. The major grassroots eruption of antipartisan populism of the late 1820s and 1830s that most influenced the political culture was Anti-Masonry, the movement and then party, to be discussed in the next chapter. Although coming onto the political landscape just after the debut of Anti-Masonry, the Working Men's parties of 1829–35 merit notice here because they not only expressed a populist ideology more radical than any other of the period but also for a brief time tried to bring it, however unsuccessfully, into electoral politics.

Movements such as the Middling Interest and Working Men's parties owed much to the awakening of English artisans and their unionist and political responses to early industrialism. Although factory workers and their hardships increased in number after 1800, agitation for amelioration of conditions for English workers came from artisans in traditional crafts (for example, tailoring, shoemaking, hatting, handloom weaving, printing, cabinetmaking, building). Throughout the eighteenth century, trade societies or unions, often short-lived, had increased in number and action designed to improve workers' hours and pay. The period from 1800 to 1830 was turbulent, marked by worker petitioning, strikes, and local attempts at association but accruing little advantage for workers. In 1805 weavers, for example, formed an association to petition for a minimum wage law, but in 1808 the House of Commons defeated it overwhelmingly. The "Luddites," who broke machines in 1811–12 in the Midlands, Lancashire, and Yorkshire, met with harsh repression. In August 1819 a peaceful demonstration for parliamentary reform by tens of thousands of workers at St. Peter's Field was attacked by local cavalry, who killed eleven persons and wounded hundreds of others. Although the "Peterloo Massacre" provoked outrage in many quarters, the state continued its repression of workers' associations. In 1824–25 Parliament changed the laws regulating "combinations," and both strike and unionist activity increased dramatically, especially in the years 1829–34. Although most strikes were unsuccessful, and attempts to form general unions in 1830 and 1833–34, the latter mostly in London, did not last long, nevertheless the decade 1820–30 laid the foundation for working-class ideas and organization in Britain. Trade union activity in the United States also emerged in the same years and turned to the ballot box.[50]

English influence on labor radicals in the United States appeared in the Americans' self-conscious references to English counterparts, as well as the British origins of several American radical leaders.[51] The first Workingmen's party appeared in Philadelphia in 1828. In a pattern that would be common elsewhere, in 1827 Philadelphia journeymen had launched a strike that failed, then organized the Mechanics' Union of Trade Associations, and early the next year the union amended its bylaws to provide for the nomination of legislative candidates pledged to advance "the interests and enlightenment of the working classes." In Boston, similarly, failed strikes in 1825 and 1830 for a ten-hour day led to the formation of an independent party, which soon was imitated in towns and villages throughout New England. A ten-hour day strike preceded the formation of New York's Workingmen's party, perhaps the most radical, which made a strong showing in the 1829 local contest for state assembly, winning about a third of the vote.[52]

Appearing in "scores of cities and towns in sixteen states," these political expressions of a broad-based unionism called themselves many names, including Working Men's Party, Working Men's Republican Association, People's Party, Working Men's Society, Farmer's and Mechanic's Society, Mechanics and other Working Men, and simply Workingmen.[53] As quickly as they appeared, for the most part they faded quickly. Trade union associations that had preceded or paralleled the electoral efforts lasted somewhat longer, but both lapsed entirely with the depression that began in 1837.

Not all Working Men's parties, tickets, or candidates that mushroomed in the early 1830s really represented the interests of artisans, mechanics, ordinary farmers, and journeymen. Opportunistic traditional politicians and others in various places quickly borrowed some version of a Working Men's label or persona for themselves. Often, wealthy men appeared as candidates or leaders of a party claiming to represent the horny-handed masses, but this factor alone does not suffice to determine the authenticity of any particular coalition, which varied by place and over the duration of even their short lives. New York City's party, for example, embodied in its brief career the conflicting elements at work. After its strong showing in the 1829 assembly elections, the party split into three factions, radical, moderate, and conservative.[54]

The Workingmen's parties had issued, nevertheless, a broad, populist appeal. Who were workingmen? All who performed "honest toil." Their message, according to the author of the most sympathetic and thorough study of their ideas, Edward Pessen, was both "idealistic and radical." In the various demands of the Philadelphia Working Men's Party can be seen the "nucleus of the program everywhere," as well as a connection to the issues of the early 1820s agitated by Boston's Middling Interest and the reforming editors and artisans associated with it. These issues were abolition of imprisonment for debt, reform of inequities in militia duty (favoring the well-off), equal taxation of property, and a district system of election. In addition, the Philadelphia reformers desired a free, tax-supported school system, abolition of all licensed monopolies (a form of that issue rose to the surface in Boston in 1827), no legislation on religion, and a mechanics' lien law. The Middling Interest, partly out of self-interest certainly, had called attention to the lack of adequate housing in the city for the middling and lower classes. In Boston and other cities radical craftsmen or their allies also had focused on the lack of sanitation and the overcrowding in poor neighborhoods. At various times, the Philadelphia Working Men also criticized the sale of liquor, the practices of banks, the use of prison labor, and the costs and complexity of the legal system.[55]

Workingmen generally believed that greater democracy would improve society, as well as advance the "down to earth issues" of Working Men's parties: "higher wages, shorter hours, an improved standard of living . . . [and] job security." They were concerned, says Pessen, "with social justice, broadly conceived, rather than with the amelioration of labor's lot alone."[56]

The Working Men's populist appeal also resonated in their consistent antipartisanship. They condemned all political factions and traditional parties as routinely unrepresentative of their interests—and those of the broad producing classes. Their social critique intertwined with this political distrust since, as one spokesman put it, "so all-controlling are the social relations upon political affairs."[57] Viewing the rise of merchant capitalism and manufacturing, they prophesied a growing accumulation of wealth and economic power in the hands of a "few," while the living standards of the mass of working people would steadily deteriorate. Labor radicals denounced, as few Americans dared, a privileged class of "accumulators" reaping an ever larger share of everyone's labor, aided by legislation enacted by party politicians.[58]

In expressing traditional republican themes, it is not surprising that the Workingmen viewed citizenship in predominantly masculine (and white) terms. Their rhetoric, accordingly, was "saturated with equations of autonomy and manhood. Loss of autonomy was equated with emasculation; economic dependence on wages paid by an employer was equivalent to social and sexual dependency." A trades union newspaper, *The Man*, asserted it would be "unmanly" and undignified for craft workers not to organize, "an abdication" of their responsibilities as citizens. Workingmen's newspapers regularly made invidious comparisons between male workers and women, immigrants, and black slaves. Indeed, nineteenth-century labor rhetoric, while preoccupied with worker manhood and unity, at the same time "gendered and racialised labour solidarity by constructing manhood in opposition to femaleness and blackness."[59]

Historians of Working Men often have noted the existence in their ranks and among the working classes generally of racism and antiabolitionism. In the 1830s advocates for wage earners generally distanced themselves from the antislavery cause or demonstrated open hostility. In part they were reciprocating the dismissal with which William Lloyd Garrison greeted the newly created New England Association of Farmers, Mechanics, and Other Workingmen in the very first issue of *The Liberator*. But Workingmen's advocates simply placed far greater importance on improvement of the lot of white workers before attempting to deal with the more distant problem of southern slavery. During the 1830s and 1840s most Workingmen's newspapers and orators sounded the theme that northern mill workers and other laborers were worse off than southern slaves.[60]

Despite occasional recognition by labor reformers of both "wage slavery" and the evils of race slavery, many lower- and middle-class wage earners and independent artisans engaged in mob actions against abolitionists and African Americans. In New York City a "virulent" racism and antiabolitionism intensified in the mid-1830s and resulted in crowds breaking up abolition meetings, attacks on the property of abolitionist leaders, and the ransacking of black homes and churches. The New York daily newspapers' fare for their working audiences regularly included scorn for antislavery agitators and racist invective. In 1836 an antiabolitionist mob in Cincinnati assembled at a time convenient for "most of those who labor in the foundries and shipyards, and elsewhere."[61]

At times, however, antiabolition mobs consisted of "gentlemen of property and influence," such as the "broadcloth mob" that in 1835 dragged Garrison through the streets of Boston with a rope around his neck. As the radical reformer Wendell Phillips observed later, "well-dressed men hire hungry mechanics to mob free speech." But some labor spokesmen, although not admirers of Garrison, protested the attack on freedom of speech because they perceived that upper-class "aristocrats" wanted to silence labor dissent as well.[62]

Further, in New York, New England, and elsewhere, many factory workers, artisans, mechanics, and small shopkeepers joined antislavery societies or signed antislavery petitions, or, later on, voted for the Liberty and Free Soil Parties. In New York City the most consistent support for abolition came from "evangelical master artisans," and evangelical workers in Lynn, New Bedford, and Worcester County, Massachusetts, were drawn to antislavery societies and later to an antislavery politics that stood on a broader base than the earlier workers' politics.[63] Overall, divergent attitudes, including some racism, existed in the ranks of radical workingmen's leaders and among lower-class and middling workers of all kinds.

In Massachusetts the Working Men's party entered the election for governor only after the New England Association of Farmers, Mechanics, and Other Workingmen, organized in 1831–32, had conducted a months-long and widespread campaign for the ten-hour day through negotiations and strikes. After recognizing that the ten-hour effort had ground to a halt by September 1832, the labor reformers reluctantly moved to electoral activity the next year, even as they called for the organization of more workers' unions and organizations to push the association's agenda. One speaker at its September convention said that in relation to the association's goals, the difference between the presidential candidates that year, Andrew Jackson and Henry Clay, dwindled into "utter insignificance."[64]

In 1833 the Workingmen nominated Samuel C. Allen for governor, a former Orthodox Congregational minister and Federalist congressman who shared the "Workies'" view that society was increasingly divided into "producers" and "accumulators" and that government invariably represented the latter. Allen won less than 6 percent of the vote statewide (3,459 votes), and only 9 percent in Boston, though he did better in some maritime towns. His highest percentage came in a small town in the western hills, Monroe, peopled largely by a clan of Universalists. Although several towns with Universalist churches gave no votes to Allen, Universalists elsewhere in the state also seem to have voted for Allen, indicating once again a tie between egalitarian religion and radical populism.[65]

Working Men's skepticism toward the traditional parties did not deter the local Jackson Republicans from trying to bring them into their fold. But a local Workie organ, the Boston Artisan, pointed out that the Massachusetts Jacksonians were not opposed to state banks, and too many of them were "slaves of mammon." Increasingly after 1831, Jacksonian partisans, at the state, local, and national levels, and notably President Andrew Jackson himself, appropriated the populist cadences of the Working Men (and the contemporaneous Anti-Masons). As noted above, the Jacksonian invocation of "the real people" against the powerful few—especially the "money power"—was relentless. Jackson's supporters saw nothing inconsistent about a southern, slaveholding planter championing the "humble members" of society—"farmers, mechanics, and laborers"—over the "potent and powerful" who turned government to their selfish interests. But neither of the emergent mass parties, Democrats or Whigs, though speaking of the promise of free labor, embraced the class interests of journeymen, artisans, or unions.[66]

A few Working Men's leaders, and some of their rank and file, were absorbed by President Jackson's emerging Democratic Party, carried there especially by Jackson's "Bank War." But the more radical labor leaders and the various short-lived Working Men's movements regarded neither Jackson nor his party as vehicles for the attainment of their goals. In addition, their antiparty populism, though failing to mobilize a significant following, offered a dissident view of American society that challenged prevailing dogmas regarding the existence of a harmony of interests, equality of opportunity, and even political equality.

# Chapter 5

# Anti-Masonry: A New Kind of Populist Movement

*I believe this . . . the strongest Government on earth. I believe it is the only one where
every man, at the call of the law, would fly to the standard of the law, and would meet
invasions of the public order as his own personal concern.*
—Thomas Jefferson, first inaugural address, 1801

## CHRISTIAN REPUBLICANISM

The trade unionism and Workingmen's parties of the late 1820s and 1830s, while issuing a populist message but failing to mobilize a broad grassroots movement, ran parallel to a new kind of populist insurgency that mobilized tens of thousands of men and women throughout New England and the middle states. Anti-Masonry was in many ways, as a contemporary commented as early as 1832, "*sui generis.*"[1] Although historians often have misunderstood or slighted its importance, as a mass enthusiasm Anti-Masonry was unparalleled, and its political career served as a catalyst for the formation of the first true mass party organizations in the United States. In the burgeoning climate of egalitarianism and individualism of the 1820s, several socioeconomic and cultural changes came together to make this new departure possible, above all a communications revolution that sped up and widely diffused information throughout an enlarged public sphere.

The seemingly unimportant origins of Anti-Masonry no doubt contributed to many scholars' failing to take it seriously. When in 1826 a destitute stonemason, who otherwise would have been unknown to history, tried to make money by exposing the secrets of Freemasonry, overzealous members of lodges in the Batavia and Rochester, New York, area kidnapped and probably murdered their onetime brother. That was the beginning, but only a small part of the story. Dozens of Masons across a 100-mile area probably were involved, and when, for years afterward, they and their allies successfully thwarted investigation and meaningful punishment, they provoked an enormous reaction against a secret fraternity now deemed at odds with republican values and Christian religion.

Interpretations of Anti-Masonry have varied widely, but until the 1960s most accounts of the phenomenon echoed views originally expressed by its critics and adversaries: that misguided fanatics began a movement, soon adopted by political opportunists, that along the way trampled on the civil liberties of many innocent citizens. More often, scholars have associated Anti-Masonry with illiberal excess, if not right-wing extremism. In the 1950s it became fashionable to depict Anti-Masonry and other populist movements as irrational and paranoid. Less judgmental observers, while granting that the movement often wreaked havoc on social comity, took a more neutral view and emphasized its egalitarianism and defense of republican values, as well as its moralism.[2]

Many studies of Anti-Masonry have pointed to a religious dynamic that powered the movement. The "blessed spirit," as many of its adherents called it, paralleled the surge of revivalism in the 1820s and 1830s known as the Second Great Awakening. An extensive study of Anti-Masonry, focused on New England, also highlights religion and morality, but within a larger, economic framework. Paul Goodman's *Towards a Christian Republic* (1988) interprets both Masonry and Anti-Masonry as divergent responses to a "Great Transition" from an agrarian republic to a market-oriented, industrializing society. The new social order bred stratification and inequality, transiency, and the decay of preindustrial communitarian norms; it disrupted traditional crafts, eroded deference, and unleashed class resentments. Masonry adapted to and symbolized the transition. Anti-Masons, however, feared social change and thus "displaced anxieties about the commercialization of society onto an institution easily identified, pervasive, and vulnerable to attack."[3]

Goodman also labels Anti-Masonry as a "social paranoia," although with "roots in reality."[4] His emphasis on irrationality and displacement thus echoes not only earlier historians' negative views but also those of antebellum enemies and critics of Anti-Masons, who condemned their alleged "fanaticism," "ultraism," "delusion," and "frenzy." Masonic militants and their political allies repeatedly used these terms to counterattack Anti-Masonry—indeed, all critics—in both the movement's early and late stages. Thus, fitting the pattern of historical treatments of agrarian insurgencies, contemporary enemies of a populist movement helped to shape and to anticipate interpretations that would prove enduring. The extent to which Anti-Masonry's adversaries shaped most historians' views of the movement as irrational cannot be overemphasized.[5]

One can learn an enormous amount about Anti-Masonry, Masonry, culture, and society in the early republic from Goodman's often insightful analysis, but his theory encounters problems on both deductive and inductive grounds. Late in the book Goodman makes a passing remark about the absence of Anti-Masonry in the South. Masonry did not emerge there, he suggests, because a market system did not "penetrate extensive areas" in the slave states. But historian Darrett Rutman has subsequently found abundant records not only of Masonry's existence in Georgia and elsewhere but also of the fraternity's decline. How, he wonders, could the fraternity, "the product and symbol" of the "great transition," flourish without its motive cause? Rutman concedes that Goodman's comment was "simply an aside," but Goodman's theory was contradicted by "evidence of a middle-class Masonry and its pre-capitalist antithesis" where Goodman's theory said it should not be.[6]

It soon became apparent that Rutman had uncovered the tip of an iceberg. Two years after his critique two studies appeared that provided historians with a much-needed account of the important role that Masonry played among political elites during the period from the 1780s to the 1820s. Masonry indeed "flourished" in the South, from Virginia and Maryland to Mississippi and Louisiana. Moreover, its political influence in the early republican era in states such as North Carolina and Kentucky was enormous. And while no organized Anti-Masonic movement or party existed south of the Potomac, the southern fraternity was "seriously damaged" and died a slow death during the 1830s.[7]

Moreover, collective biographies comparing the careers and socioeconomic status of Anti-Masonic leaders and Masons in western New York and Massachusetts found extensive similarity between the two groups. Massachusetts Anti-Masonic leaders were "usually upwardly mobile, aspiring individualists, fully attuned to the spirit of 'improvement,' and, compared with Masons, more involved in nontraditional enterprises." Similarly, Anti-Masonic voters differed little from those of other parties.[8] The most convincing rebuttal of the "anxious Antimasons" thesis (several historians earlier had characterized them as "alienated") comes from Genesee County in western New York, where it all began. There, in the Anti-Masonic heartland, the party's vote was huge in "economically mature townships" and the "most highly developed and populous towns." These places also experienced increased participation in religious revivals and increased voter turnout. Moreover, Anti-Masonic leaders came from the county elite and were involved heavily in commerce, banking, and internal improvements. In nearby Monroe, Chautauqua, and Wayne Counties, Anti-Masonry flourished in the busy ports of the Erie Canal, manufacturing towns, and fertile agricultural areas with the highest tax assessments.[9] Although Goodman's overarching economic thesis cannot be sustained, his characterization of Anti-Masons as striving for a Christian republic captures the essence of the movement.

Actually, Christian republicanism captures the two conjoined impulses of the movement. The long-standing stereotype of Anti-Masons as consisting of "fanatics" and "opportunists" has had a counterpart view of Anti-Masons as divided into "ultras" and pragmatists. There is some truth to this characterization, but it creates too rigid a dichotomy that imports too much of the original invidious distinction. Rather, many Anti-Masons, especially those men and women who wanted to purge their churches and local governments of Masons, reacted to Masonry as a threat to religion, moral behavior, and families. The more "republican" wing of Anti-Masons, while sensitive to the concerns of the "Christian" wing, wanted primarily to purge local governments of Masonic influence and restore faith in a system of law and equal justice before the law. They also focused intently on driving from office the political faction that controlled New York's state government, which they regarded as the enabler of Masonic criminality.

Anti-Masons surely were not the first Americans to fuse Christianity and republicanism.[10] Many Anti-Masons were to some degree prompted by both Christian and republican impulses, and it is an artifice of later analysis to separate the two. Probably the Christian and moral syndrome was stronger, although not necessarily prevalent, among the rank and file, while Anti-Masonic leaders tended to be thoroughly imbued with republican ideology and more sensitive to pragmatic political considerations.

A distinction must be drawn also between social movement and political party. Everywhere there existed a movement before and during a political organization's electoral efforts. Certainly the party attracted more pragmatists, while the movement attracted more "ultras," those men and women less willing to compromise for political gain. But the oft-stated assertion that the "ultras" remained more faithful to Anti-Masonry's original goals is misleading. Tension did often exist within Anti-Masonry between movement "ultras" and republican pragmatists, and the former often unleashed exaggerated, vituperative rhetoric. But the "republican" wing was committed to Anti-Masonry *as* Anti-Masonry.

The movement also generated what sociologists term "rancorous conflict" in communities, churches, and even families. But heated Anti-Masonic rhetoric and excess must be measured in the context of Masonic hyperbole and excesses, especially in New York State, which reached well beyond the original vigilantism and provided ample evidence of obstruction of justice. Passionate brethren defended their fraternity by attacking Anti-Masons' character with as much intemperance and venom as was hurled against them. Anti-Masonic party rhetoric, moreover, differed little in hyperbolic degree from that employed by mainstream political factions, parties, and other social movements of the 1820s and 1830s.[11]

Anti-Masonic passion in most areas flowed from religious and egalitarian impulses, which mobilized against Freemasonry as a threat to Christianity and republicanism. Anti-Masons who feared Masonry primarily as a threat to religion or republicanism believed that the fraternity fostered aristocratic pretension, special privilege protected by secrecy and fearsome oaths, and false benevolence and that it militated against the egalitarian and democratic spirit of the age. Religious Anti-Masons, especially, regarded Masonry as a threat to the family and women.

As with the temperance movement that began before Anti-Masonry and gained traction also with the expansion of revivalism after the mid-1820s, the conflict with Masonry was also one about the nature of American manhood. Many Anti-Masons championed an ideal of Christian republican manhood at odds with the practices of an exclusive fraternity based on male bonding, secret rituals, male conviviality apart from the family, and anti-egalitarian hierarchy.

## ORIGINS: MASONRY AND ANTI-MASONRY

Some New England Baptists had grown uneasy over Freemasonry as a competitor for their members' loyalty and funds as early as the 1790s, but before 1826 Masonry had provoked only occasional criticism, primarily from clergymen. As an eighteenth-century English import, it attracted a cross-section of men in most communities, though weighted toward cosmopolitan men in the middle class and professions. Its rituals, regalia, secrets, code words, and signals, along with grandiose titles for officers and degrees of progress in "the Craft," appealed to the need for ceremony in a non-Catholic culture, but Masonry also generated an intellectual attraction by way of its deist-rationalist compromise with Christianity and its emphasis on brotherhood. Secular-minded men weary of sectarian disputes gravitated to Masonry, as, after 1800, would men seeking male conviviality away from wives and families. Young Masons who moved to new communities could find their entrance eased by the society connection.[12]

Whatever misgivings various clergy, wives, and mothers may have nourished regarding Masonry, in the 1820s it grew rapidly, if not spectacularly, in popularity. In 1800 it counted 11 Grand Lodges, 347 subordinate lodges, and 16,000 members nationwide. Two decades later, though Masonry never included a large proportion of the adult male population, New York State alone contained almost 300 lodges with an estimated 15,000 members. By 1825 another 150 lodges and 5,000 members had swelled Masonry's New York ranks. Before the Genesee kidnapping, even in western New York "Masonry was highly esteemed and rapidly growing." Everywhere Masonic orators pointed with pride to former and current members—George Washington, Benjamin Franklin, Andrew Jackson, Henry Clay—and in 1824–25 Masons conspicuously participated in the festivities attending Lafayette's nostalgic tour of the United States.[13]

In New England, and in the diaspora of migrated Yankees to western New York and other parts of the North, Freemasonry nevertheless constituted an exclusive, secretive, and cosmopolitan "counterculture," perceived to be privileged, heterodox, and at odds with traditional orthodox and communitarian norms. In Genesee County, Masons tended to be members of Episcopal churches and more latitudinarian, nondevotional, and nonevangelical than Baptists or Presbyterians. Masons who were not church-affiliated men, as well as some connected with Universalism ("particularly detested and feared by evangelicals"), furthered the contrast with less religiously liberal neighbors. In addition, Masonry's "pseudo-aristocratic style" jarred uncomfortably with the rising egalitarianism of the 1820s, while its emphasis on social pleasure contrasted with a culture that, although becoming more secular, "was, at the least, ambivalent regarding hedonistic joy." Moreover, as a provider of "sponsored mobility," entrance into the fraternity was "ostentatiously exclusive."[14]

Aware of the occasional criticism and sensing undercurrents of resentment, Masonic orators frequently called attention to their society's benevolence and social utility. They also campaigned with increasing success in the 1820s to recruit clergymen, who then joined the front ranks of Masonry's advocates with sermons designed to demonstrate the order's compatibility with Christianity. Masonic apologetics, however, sometimes ran to bombastic boasting, as in the notorious case—among Anti-Masons at least—of a Connecticut Mason who in 1825 declared Masonry "POWERFUL," comprising "men of rank, wealth, office and talent . . . in almost every place where power is important . . . so as to have the force of concert throughout the civilized world."[15]

The 1826 kidnapping and its aftermath led Anti-Masons to believe that

Freemasonry possessed inordinate power throughout civil society, bending political factions and local and state government to the will of secret cabals. In fact, while Masonic lodges normally eschewed partisan action, they "included substantial numbers of politically active and aware men." Although Masonry did not "anoint" individual candidates, as "an organization of national reach and high social standing . . . Masonry formed part of the post-Revolutionary infrastructure of power and authority, helping to constrain, channel, and facilitate political activities." In New York State elite men and high-ranking Masons frequently ran against one another for governor, with the result that every governor but one from 1804 to the 1820s was a Mason. In Genesee County "large numbers of the 'best' men" were Masons and held influential offices "out of proportion to their numbers." Masons dominated local political factions, militia commands, and township and county offices. Masons more often than their fellow citizens came from professions and possessed resources that gave them time both for participation in the fraternity and for political activity. The "Masonic party" of Anti-Masonic imagination did not exist, but Masonic influence surely did.[16]

Another combustible element contributing to the coming conflagration derived from changes in Freemasonry that had arisen since the late eighteenth century. From the 1790s on the fraternity moved partially away from its Enlightenment origins by developing higher degrees of initiation that emphasized mystery over reason and more sensational and emotional rituals, along with the terrible oaths and punishments that so horrified non-Masons and Anti-Masons. Aside from the public relations disaster these rituals constituted after 1826, they created before 1826 cadres of more zealous and strongly committed members, men who, with what they regarded as an intolerable provocation, would take the law into their own hands to enact vigilante justice.[17]

Most historians of Anti-Masonry have noted the evangelical fervor of the movement and party, but they have ignored the equally high-pitched zeal of a counterattacking, "sectarian" Masonry after 1826. Most accounts have dwelled usually on the closing or suspending of lodges, but such emphasis on Masonry's institutional decline after 1826 has obscured the continuing militancy of those who carried the fight to the enemy and who, in New York State, were well positioned in public offices and political leadership to exert their influence to protect guilty individuals and the institution generally. Influential diehards centered in Albany and New York City lodges waged intense political warfare aimed at defaming the character of individual Anti-

Masons, while even in the "infected" western counties stubborn remnants fought on for years.[18] Historians' ignoring recalcitrant Masons' stonewalling of justice and spirited counteroffensive has also resulted in their missing how those actions backfired.

The protest—before there was a movement—grew out of a kidnapping and likely murder in western New York in 1826. Early that summer, an itinerant stonemason, William Morgan, and David C. Miller, struggling publisher of the *Batavia Republican Advocate*, set about publishing an exposé of the secret fraternal order of Freemasonry. Both hoped to profit from the venture, and both may have sought revenge against certain Masons or lodges. Miller had been briefly a Mason, while Morgan had been affiliated with the Batavia lodge before falling out with it sometime before 1826.[19]

Although renegades had previously revealed Masonry's secrets for profit or notoriety, local Masons became obsessed with thwarting this particular project. A Masonic seceder who had witnessed a meeting of Batavia Masons later claimed he "never saw men so excited in my life. . . . Everything went forward in a kind of frenzy."[20] When threats failed to deter Morgan and Miller, Masons harassed them with prosecutions for petty debt and, with the cooperation of Genesee County's sheriff, a Mason, jailed Morgan and took away papers from his quarters. Suddenly strangers, thought to be Masons from other areas, came and went through the villages of western New York.

In early September Miller and friends twice repulsed gangs of Masons intent on burning his printing offices. Then, at dawn on September 11, several Masons "arrested" Morgan on a charge of petty theft and took him to Canandaigua where they imprisoned him a second time. The following night a number of Masons spirited Morgan away from the jail. Masons later claimed that all this formed part of a publicity stunt, but Morgan was never seen again. Miller almost met a similar fate, but friends rescued him from Masonic vigilantes.

Miller's press then broadcast news of Morgan's abduction, stimulating meetings of concerned citizens across the region. Adhoc committees of inquiry formed throughout the countryside and traced the carriage that had taken Morgan over 100 miles from Canandaigua west by Rochester to Lewiston and finally to Morgan's last known incarceration at Fort Niagara. Rumors, spread by Masons, began to fly about where Morgan was now living, but most non-Masons believed dark deeds of vengeance had sent him to his death in the Niagara River.

These events, and those that followed in the next months, are significant because they gave rise to the Anti-Masonic protest and movement. The complicity of many local law officers in the abduction added to the shock of these "outrages," as the affair and aftermath came to be known. (The kidnappers had stopped to change horses several times, finding friendly jailers and sheriffs along their way.) Moreover, in the months after the kidnapping, the conspirators and their champions acted to sustain and increase the growing hostility to Freemasonry.[21]

In the next phase courtroom proceedings provided new "outrages" for some four to five years, as numerous trials in five different counties returned to the events of 1826 and kept them before the public. Some fifteen to twenty grand jury investigations were held in at least five counties, and dozens of Masons were indicted; at least eighteen separate trials took place; scores appeared as witnesses, hundreds watched. In Genesee County alone twenty-six men were indicted. Only six came to trial, however, and only four were convicted and given light sentences. These four had pled guilty, and the belief quickly spread that they had done so to suppress testimony that might bear on future trials. Masons repeatedly sat on juries, and five of seven judges presiding over trials in Genesee were Masons. Many witnesses who were Masons refused to testify, or disappeared, and the trials spawned additional indictments of witnesses for perjury, all of which added to the rampant impression that Masons, to protect brothers on trial, were putting their fraternal oaths above law and religion.[22]

Reports also circulated, and further fanned the growing rage at Masonry, that the few conspirators who spent time in jail "were cheered by their friends . . . and lavishly supplied with the comforts and elegancies of life" by contributions from Masonic lodges. In fact, New York's Grand Chapter and various lodges raised hundreds of dollars for "charity" for "the western sufferers," to pay for their defense and, quite likely, for amenities while in prison.[23]

Historians who have ignored or dismissed the widespread obstruction of justice in western New York that occurred in the months and years *after* the events of September 1826 have also overlooked the official reports of three different special counsels who were appointed by the state legislature to assist the prosecutions and to satisfy mounting Anti-Masonic demands for action. All three counsels were mainstream political figures, Daniel Mosely (1828), John C. Spencer (1829–30), and Victory Birdseye (1830–31), and all began their investigations sympathetic to "persecuted" Masons and hostile to Anti-Masonry's political turn. Yet all three produced narratives of a conspiracy, kidnapping, and murder—carried out by Masons, said Spencer and

Birdseye explicitly—that concurred with the many published Anti-Masonic accounts. They also pointed to the obstruction of the legal system, as well as the obstacles they themselves had encountered in seeking information: *"Difficulties which never occurred in any other prosecution have been met at every step,"* protested Spencer. Moreover, the counsels entertained no doubt that some Masons had committed murder, still unpunished.[24]

In early 1827 the legislature reacted with minor steps to allay the outcry against Masonic jury tampering and the light sentences given to Masons found guilty of only minor offenses. On April 16, 1827, Governor DeWitt Clinton (a Mason) signed laws making kidnapping a felony and giving town supervisors (not sheriffs) the duty of preparing jury lists. But attempts to have the legislature empower Clinton to offer rewards and to appoint a joint investigative committee failed. During the period from September 1826 to March 1827, citizens' meetings protesting the outrages continually called attention to official inaction, the silence or ridicule of too many newspaper editors, and acts of defiance and deception committed by Masons individually or in their lodges.[25]

It could not have been apparent in the first weeks and months in western New York that the protests would become a movement and then a political party bent on eradicating Freemasonry. Although David Miller and his *Batavia Republican Advocate* had begun a crusade against Masonry as a dangerous institution as early as October 1826, and although some early citizens' meetings of protest also moved to condemn Masonry, many protests remained moderate. In November, for example, a meeting in Monroe County on the "outrages" noted that indignation should not fall "indiscriminately upon all the fraternity." As late as December a Rochester meeting of Monroe County citizens chose a committee of inquiry that was headed by a diverse group of influential citizens, including several Masons. While condemning the "violence" and "villainy" perpetrated against Morgan, they held no "sentiments of hostility to the fraternity of Masons as a body." Similarly, in the first weeks, as some protesters declared that they could not support candidates for public office who were Masons and had not renounced Masonry, they were not nominating their own candidates.[26]

As the perception of continuing official obstructionism spread, calls for action at the polls increased. In February and March some protesters met explicitly "to make nominations" for town offices. The movement may have intensified, spread, and turned political no matter what, but the emergence of full-fledged Anti-Masonry was accelerated by defiant Masons and their allies who did their best behind the scenes to protect the guilty and who in public harshly denounced all critics of Masonry. In Batavia on June 25, 1827, Masons celebrated St. John's Day, complete with a parade, colorful regalia, and a feast. Anti-Masons, after heckling the brethren and causing a near riot, then held a large meeting that labeled secret societies dangerous, complained of legislative inaction and the ridicule of most newspapers, and called for a convention of delegates from the western counties to plan political action. Soon "Republicans" and "Republican antimasons" were meeting to nominate candidates and choosing delegates to county and other conventions.[27]

By September 1827 full-blown "political Antimasonry" had emerged. Over forty years ago, historian Lee Benson accurately described the initial political insurgency of Anti-Masonry as a "spontaneous" and "populistic reaction" to the failure of established Republican factions (led by Clinton and Martin Van Buren) to respond adequately to the outrages, protests, cover-ups, and Masonic defiance. By the end of 1827, "to an unprecedented degree in the United States, popular conventions had nominated candidates and the Antimasons had elected town and county officers all over western New York," including fifteen assemblymen in the state elections. Not all these opposition groups went by the "Anti-Masonic" label: in Monroe County (Rochester) Anti-Masons put forth a "People's Ticket" for the state assembly; elsewhere, insurgents offered "Antimasonic Republican" tickets.[28]

Benson also argued that a New York political phenomenon of the mid-1820s, the People's Party, had prepared the way for the Anti-Masonic explosion. Understanding that movement must begin with the recognition of New York in that decade as an advanced laboratory of political sophistication, where the foundations were being laid for the emergence of the mass political parties of the nineteenth century. The state was a swirl of political factions claiming to be the true heirs of Jeffersonian Republicanism, but two cadres dominated: the Clintonians, led by DeWitt Clinton, and the Bucktail Republicans, led by Martin Van Buren. The latter and his allies were busy on the national scene forging an alliance with Virginia Republicans that would eventually play a leading role in bringing Andrew Jackson to the presidency in 1828. On the state level the Bucktails and their partisan organs, the *Albany Argus* and the formerly Federalist *New York Evening Post*, were pioneering techniques of party regularity that their Republican rivals resisted as fettering political independence. A new state constitution (1821) had broadened the electorate, introduced elective offices at the county level, and given the governor and legislature more control over patronage. After easily taking control of the state in the 1822 elections, the Bucktails rashly decided to oppose a rising sentiment for popular election of presidential electors. The Van Burenites also moved to consolidate their power by removing Clinton from the Canal Board, the administrative arm of the successful Erie Canal, with which Clinton's name was already linked. A Bucktail proposal to tax bank stock also backfired.[29]

In the context of a wider and increasingly attentive electorate, the Clintonians seized on the popular reaction and rallied a new coalition, the "People's Party," against the Bucktails, whom they branded as the "Albany Regency," and "whipped up popular frenzy against the 'Royal Cabinet,' 'the cabal,' and 'the junto,' which had conspired against the 'people's' rights." According to Benson, "Populistic democracy had arrived in New York."[30]

In reality, the rhetoric of populist democracy now prevailed and had arrived even earlier at the local level, in New York and other states. Populist, antiparty rhetoric accompanying a "Farmer's Ticket" (of Clintonians) had emerged as early as 1822 in western New York in Genesee County, and probably in other localities, before a "People's Party" ticket of Clintonian candidates was put forward in 1823 for assembly in New York City. In 1824 Anti-Bucktails across the state used the "People's" label inconsistently, along with variations on "Republican." At the local level, if Genesee County was at all representative, Bucktails too paid lip service to populist, anti-organization, and antiparty sentiments. Thus, the People's Party prepared the way for Anti-Masonry by permeating the public sphere with populist rhetoric as never before.[31]

In its initial grassroots phase Anti-Masonry gave expression far more authentically to populist rhetoric that had become common currency among all political factions. Many Anti-Masons, especially the religiously oriented and evangelical, exuded the antiparty animus of the People's coalition. The protest and social movement had been created in a paroxysm of rebellion against Masonic wrongdoing and obstruction of justice and was aided and abetted by the Anti-Masons' perception of a secret power that Masons wielded among political and officeholding elites.

Anti-Masonic populism also differed from the People's Party in deriving its grassroots energy early on from a powerful evangelical religious impulse. Before carrying the "blessed spirit" to ballot boxes across the western counties, Anti-Masonic protesters first tried to cleanse Masonry from the churches of what was already known as "the burned-over district" due to its penchant for religious enthusiasm and moral reform. Baptist and Presbyterian laymen and women, as well as clergy, were most susceptible to Anti-Masonry, though religious people of a pietist and fundamentalist mentality opposed to liberal denominations (such as Universalism) also joined the crusade to put down Masonry and its influence in public life.[32]

## MOVEMENT INTO PARTY AND REFORM

As Anti-Masonic protest turned political during 1827, Adams-Clay Republican political leaders who were not Masons followed their constituents into the movement, demanding action from an unresponsive state government controlled by the Bucktail–Van Buren Republicans. Although the Anti-Masonic religious enthusiasts based in the churches sought above all else the destruction of Masonry, the pragmatists with political experience desired as much the defeat of the Albany Regency. At the national level they wanted to reelect President John Quincy Adams, a non-Mason, and defeat the Regency's candidate, Andrew Jackson, a proud Freemason. The tension between the Christian and republican wings in movement and party would carry on through to the end of both in New York State and elsewhere.

Another problem for Anti-Masonry arose from the continuing hostility of many Adams-Clay Republican Masons in eastern New York. Both of these fault lines in Anti-Masonry helped determine the outcome of the 1828 state election. The Bucktails put forth their strongest candidate, Martin Van Buren, who was looking forward to a Jackson presidential victory and a place in a new administration, but the opposition split between two candidates. The Adams Republicans nominated Smith Thompson, a former Bucktail. Anti-Masonic pragmatists, such as Thurlow Weed, editor of the *Rochester Anti-Masonic Enquirer* and at the start of a brilliant career as a political manager, hoped to unite the Anti-Masons behind Thompson and Adams. But after a series of conventions dominated by the Christian "ultras," one held at a Utica Baptist church, the Anti-Masons put forward Solomon Southwick, editor of the Anti-Masonic *Albany National Observer*. Weed and his fellow pragmatists regarded Southwick as "visionary and unsound" and unable to make converts to Anti-Masonry because of his extreme views. Jackson narrowly carried New York's popular vote (51 percent), while Van Buren became governor with a plurality (49.5 percent), with Thompson and Southwick dividing the opposition vote.[33]

Although Southwick's nomination and defeat marked the "zenith of evangelical religious Antimasonry" in New York, the party continued to find it difficult to make significant gains beyond western New York. As practical politicians such as Weed, William Seward, and Millard Fillmore gradually had joined in the protests against the outrages and then in political organizing, these "cool and calculating men" increasingly tried to balance Anti-Masonic zeal with a successful formula for winning elections.[34] Although often depicted as cynically using Anti-Masonry—as "opportunists" whose real goal was gaining office—these republican Anti-Masons nevertheless shared with the outraged citizens of the western counties a desire to correct the abuses of the legal system and the courts and to prevent any repeat of the arrogant abuse of power manifested by reckless Freemasons in the Morgan affair and its long aftermath. The fact was that the best way to get the state government to take action against Masonry was to defeat the Regency and take control. That careful historian of western New York Anti-Masonry, Kathleen Smith Kutolowski, rejects the notion that pragmatists betrayed the goals of the purists: "Principle and pragmatic politics coexisted and reinforced one another throughout the crusade."[35]

In the crucible of Anti-Masonry, Weed and Seward, later governor, presidential candidate, and secretary of state, formed an anti-Regency alliance and friendship that would last for decades. Historians often have regarded their Anti-Masonic involvement as at best a way station and at worst cynical manipulation for other purposes. But their private correspondence, along with that of their political associates, testifies to an involvement with Anti-Masonry no less real—or sincere—than that of pragmatic politicians in other factions and parties. The republican pragmatists carried their Anti-Masonic goals forward well into 1830–31, when they were moving to add other issues besides the destruction of Masonry to the party's agenda. In 1831, while Anti-Masons still cherished hopes of defeating the Regency and Jacksonism *as Anti-Masons*, Frederick Whittlesey of Rochester wrote to Weed that "it will be a proud day when the despised, abused and misrepresented cause of Anti-Masonry shall not only be respected but bear sway in this Union. . . . Let her be imposing . . . in her victories, as she has been firm and unshaken in her despised state. I want to see Anti-Masonry predominate in this government . . . as to show that she is worthy of power."[36]

During 1829 the Anti-Masons ran well again in the fall state elections in the western counties, but not elsewhere. In 1830 Weed left Rochester to edit the *Albany Evening Journal*, and he and Seward began to steer Anti-Masonry toward coalition not only with anti-Jackson Republicans but also with the newly emergent Workingmen's party. After the Workingmen's surprise showing in New York City's 1829 assembly election, "Workie" parties quickly formed in Albany, Troy, Utica, and other cities and towns. Accordingly, after nominating Francis Granger for governor, the Anti-Masons turned for lieutenant governor to Samuel Stevens, a young attorney and

Manhattan alderman associated with the Clay faction of the Workingmen.[37] Granger-Stevens lost a close race to the Bucktail Jacksonian ticket headed by acting governor Enos T. Throop (who as a judge had sentenced some of the Morgan kidnappers), 120,667 (48.3 percent) to 128,947 (51.7 percent).[38]

Coalition politics, however, led to the high tide of Anti-Masonic progressivism in New York. While appealing to anti-Jackson Republicans favoring Henry Clay's "American System" of protective tariffs and federal internal improvements (soon to be known as National Republicans), the Anti-Masons in the legislature simultaneously took up most of the Workingmen's platform, including abolition of imprisonment for debt (opposed by the Regency), equal education for all, amelioration of the care of the insane, abolition of all licensed monopolies, reform of the militia system, institution of a less expensive legal system, and tax reform. Weed (elected twice to the assembly) supported bills for a mechanics' lien law and exempting mechanics' tools from taxation.[39]

In the state senate Seward staunchly defended the Second Bank of the United States (BUS) against the Jackson administration but also supported measures favored by the Workingmen. His progressivism extended to advocacy of penal reform, especially separate prisons for women and direct election of mayors, and he even expressed his belief that railroads, like canals, should be owned and operated by the state. The Anti-Masons generally also appealed to farmers by proposing to change the system whereby lands returned to the state because of failure to pay back taxes were sold at Albany. Pointing out that many farmers lost land this way, Weed's associate Philo Fuller introduced a bill requiring that "returned" lands be auctioned at the courthouse of the county in which they resided. The *Anti-Masonic Enquirer* made political capital by charging that "hungry" Regency speculators in league with Masons used the existing system to get rich. Whether the issue was bank taxes or canal tolls, Anti-Masons aggressively took a populist stand against powerful elites, especially "*Masonic* aristocrats," and for ordinary farmers, artisans, and small businessmen.[40]

Less authentically, Anti-Masons postured as champions of tenant farmers against the absentee landlords of the large land companies of western New York. The powerful Holland Land Company owned 3.2 million acres stretching west from the Genesee River to Lake Erie and north from the Pennsylvania border to Lake Ontario. After the Panic of 1819 Clintonian Republicans (some of whom would become Anti-Masons) cultivated an image as champions of the tenants and debtor farmers, while in the legislature

Van Buren's Bucktails protected the company's interests. Albert H. Tracy, a congressman from Buffalo who became a leading Anti-Mason, by 1827 had established himself as an advocate for small farmers and entrepreneurs at odds with the company.[41]

At the local level, however, Anti-Masons' relations with land companies were more ambiguous. In 1830 settler unrest had mounted on the foreign-owned (English and Dutch) Pulteney estates to the east of the Genesee River, and there, too, Anti-Masonic candidates denounced the landlords. But Anti-Masonic entrepreneurs also supported developmental, commercial interests, and in Genesee and other counties, as Kutolowski has pointed out, Anti-Masonic lawyers profited by prosecuting suits against insolvent settlers: "Antimasons, not Masons, figured most prominently as . . . creditors and land speculators by the 1830s." This hardly prevented Anti-Masonic leaders from demagogically exploiting anticompany sentiment and assailing "Monied Aristocracies of every description." In 1830 Anti-Masonic candidates for the assembly in Wayne County blasted the Pulteney landlords with the same complaints raised by Holland tenants for over a decade: excessive original prices, compound interest, all payments required in money and no part in "any country produce," and no return of settler payments in the form of improvements. Albert H. Tracy presided over the state Anti-Masonic convention held at Utica in June 1832 and wrote its "Address," which included condemnation of the Masonic "monster" as well as the "monied aristocracy" that governed the state and impeded construction of internal improvements to expand prosperity.[42] Anti-Masons' embrace of the cause of tenant farmers, like that of the Whigs and Democrats after them, mixed together concern for the underdog with political calculation and posturing by the lawyers and speculators who were themselves involved in the land business.[43]

Despite the opposition of key members of the Regency, the 1830 legislature did abolish imprisonment for debt, a law written by Weed's Anti-Masonic allies. The "main specific grievance" of the Workingmen, claims historian Arthur Schlesinger Jr., was imprisonment for debt. The Anti-Masonic legislators' 1831 "Address to the People" took credit for the reform and, like their address of 1830, did not neglect restating their opposition "to all privileged orders, aristocracies and secret societies," and lamented the expiration of legislation directed at the prosecution of Morgan's "murderers and kidnappers."[44]

But by 1831, to the continued complaints of the Christian wing, Anti-

Masonic republican pragmatists downplayed opposition to Freemasonry. Dieharders' protests increased the next year when, after an Anti-Masonic national convention nominated its own presidential candidate (William Wirt, U.S. attorney general, 1818–29), the New York party nominated an unpledged set of presidential electors evenly divided between Anti-Masons and National Republicans who would vote for Henry Clay or Wirt depending on who won the popular vote. Anti-Masons in other states, still caught up in the "blessed spirit," reacted with disappointment and outrage.[45]

The 1832 defeat, again, of Granger for governor, this time by Regency stalwart William M. Marcy, and the coalition loss to the Jackson–Van Buren presidential ticket by an even larger margin, were the final blows for the republican pragmatists. The question for them now became not whether but when to abandon Anti-Masonry. The following year the party held no state convention and elected a handful of assemblymen in the fall elections. The pragmatists, led by Weed, Seward, Granger, and others, had realized earlier that Anti-Masonry's political career was finished, but they had been working to broaden the party's appeal for the twin goals of defeating the dominant Jacksonian party and of advancing the Anti-Masonic agenda. And it was no trivial cause to them. In 1835, with New York Anti-Masonry gone, Weed, who had labored energetically to redirect the once "blessed spirit" into a broader coalition, reflected privately to his friend Seward on the passing of a noble cause: "Will we ever again have our better and higher sympathies so warmly excited and so nobly directed? I fear not."[46]

Political Anti-Masonry declined in large part because the social movement in New York (and elsewhere) had been so successful—at least in most of the state west of New York City and the Hudson River. By 1830 the 480 lodges of New York had fallen to under 100; by 1835 some 50 active lodges remained, mostly in the east. By early 1834 Anti-Masonry in the Empire State was ready to move into the new Whig Party.[47]

During the preceding seven and a half years, however, Anti-Masonic ultras and pragmatists alike had labored diligently to spread their message at home and abroad. At first news of the outrages had traveled as a matter of course into nearby regions of adjoining states because of routine kinship and commercial intercourse. Masons, as well as future Anti-Masons, had been involved in travel between western New York and contiguous states even before Morgan was kidnapped. They relied both on emissaries (Frederick Whittlesey was one such well-traveled missionary), friendly newspapers, the establishment of independent Anti-Masonic papers, and a barrage of printed material. It is not far-fetched to describe what Anti-Masonic proselytizers were doing as, what has been termed in a later context, creating a "movement culture."[48]

In doing so never was a movement more obsessed with spreading "facts" and information, through speeches and discussion but above all via the printed page, whether through newspapers, books, or pamphlets. Conditions specific to Anti-Masonry, as well as the developing information culture of printed material and extensive reading, created this fixation. Partly it arose from the movement's origins in a dramatic historical narrative of crime and punishment—or rather, the avoidance of punishment by subversive actions that threatened the foundations of republican society. In the early days in western New York, alarmed citizens had seen firsthand how the facts of the case could arouse citizens to band together and work to right the scales of justice. This motivated some of the pragmatic politicians such as Weed, whose connection with Anti-Masonry began in early 1827 when he served on the so-called Lewiston Committee and became convinced that Morgan had been murdered and that the Masonic order had been used to thwart justice and undermine republican civil society on an extensive scale. Shortly afterward, he established the *Anti-Masonic Enquirer*. Many religious Anti-Masons, in addition, were increasingly participants in an "evangelical print culture" that transcended church congregations and was becoming habituated to core narrative structures produced by publishers of religious tracts and the Bible.[49]

Anti-Masons' focus on "facts" stemmed, too, from the professional mentality of the many practicing lawyers in the Weed-Seward group. During his travels in the United States in 1831, Alexis de Tocqueville noted that American lawyers, in following English common law, focused on "not general theories, but particular facts." Tocqueville's observation resulted in part from his conversation with former special counsel John C. Spencer, who told Tocqueville that with Americans there are no arguments about the law, because "everything reduces itself in some sort to a question of fact."[50]

For Anti-Masons nothing could improve on circulating "*facts well proven relating to the Western outrages.*" A Weed associate wrote from Albany in 1829 that "there is nothing now so much needed as a general circulation of writings, such as Ward's review, Parkers sermon, Stearns book &c. &c. and the attention of the [coming Anti-Masonic] convention ought to be particularly directed to this subject as it is the most important one. The People will be anti Masons only give them the facts to read." Anti-Masons employed agents, usually committed Anti-Masons, to enlist subscribers for books and pamphlets and then to sell them at cost plus a small commission—in one case six cents per pamphlet. From Pennsylvania that summer another Anti-Mason wrote to Weed of the need for local distribution of publications to "put people on further inquiry."[51]

When the special counsel John C. Spencer published his report on the outrages and cover-up, Anti-Masons welcomed it with enthusiasm. Although noting that Spencer had criticized some of the Committees of Investigation for connecting the matter with politics, Whittlesey, who had seen only excerpts at that point, believed that "if he has given the facts truly, he has done enough for our purposes." Though faulty, wrote another Rochester Anti-Mason, Spencer's report would strengthen the Anti-Masonic case "and fully show the justice and rectitude of our cause." In preparing for the Anti-Masonic national convention, Whittlesey expressed his firm belief in the power of literature to make converts: he would gather all the old papers and additional facts regarding Morgan, the trials, and all the instances in which Masonry "had interfered with the *administration of justice* since the Morgan affair." Then, "the reports of the different committees in the national convention should abound in *facts* rather than declamation. These reports . . . will be widely read and it should be our aim to make them convincing from the facts embodied in them and conclusive reasoning from those facts."[52]

What a New York Anti-Mason referred to as "this simple uncontradicted story [that] has made many converts" proved a powerful engine for Anti-Masonic organizers in other states.[53] As 1829 turned into 1830 Anti-Masons in Massachusetts held their first state convention, where delegates from eight counties (of fourteen) met in Boston, not to nominate candidates, but to explore the nature of Masonry and the dangers it presented to the republic. It asserted the political influence of Masonry in New York, condemned its aiding of kidnappers and alleged murderers, and requested Massachusetts Masons to disfellowship those responsible or to renounce the order and its oaths. Henry Dana Ward's New York *Antimasonic Review* described in glowing terms the convention's "prudent, temperate, and firm" deliberations: "They gathered at Boston, not to excite, but to inquire; not to proscribe their fellow-citizens, but to elicit truth; not to break the constitution and laws, but to join their counsel in relation to the newly discovered character of Freemasonry."[54]

Testimony to the durability of the original Anti-Masonic historical narrative and its facts came as late as 1834 from the state of Maine, where Anti-Masonry had made little headway politically. But a state convention of Anti-Masons recited afresh and as if from only yesterday the outrages, trials, and obstructions of justice occurring five to eight years earlier in western New York. Since Masonry had shown itself to be anti-Christian and antirepublican, it was necessary to fight it politically. The distance of the recounted events in space and time hardly mattered because Masonry was the same everywhere, corrupting and subverting "Republicanism by introducing a privileged class among us."[55]

Like Anti-Masons elsewhere, the Maine diehards complained of the "silence" of the established newspapers after the Morgan affair and the necessity of establishing "an independent press." They also argued that establishing a press "necessarily" dragged Anti-Masonry into politics: "It was found impossible to support one without forming a distinct party."[56] The larger truth, however, was that the ability to extend Anti-Masonic political organization and electoral success *depended* on the existence of allied newspapers.

During Anti-Masonry's career, some 115 to 125 Anti-Masonic newspapers overall may have existed, either created by activists or converted to Anti-Masonic principles. Many, however, were short-lived. Weed's first issue of the *Albany Evening Journal*, March 22, 1830, claimed sixty-eight similar papers nationally: thirty-one in New York, eighteen in Pennsylvania, eight in Ohio, four in Vermont, two each in Connecticut and New Jersey, and one each in Rhode Island, Michigan, and Alabama. The high-water mark probably came in 1831–32, with over a hundred in existence (fifty-two in New York in 1831, but forty-two in 1832, and fifty-seven in Pennsylvania in 1831). Economic pressure brought to bear by Masons also limited the number and career of Anti-Masonic newspapers: cancelled subscriptions, printing work and advertisements withdrawn, had their effect.[57]

Anti-Masonic leaders knew that most of the established press—perhaps as many as seven-eighths of the nation's newspapers—were hostile or neutral toward Anti-Masonry. This meant that they ignored printing accounts of the "outrages," the original crimes and subsequent thwarting of justice, the narrative that constituted a principal means of converting men and women to Anti-Masonry. These papers also ignored Anti-Masonic conventions, their resolutions, and addresses recounting the founding narrative of the movement and party.[58] After the Anti-Masons' demoralizing defeat in the fall 1832 New York elections, William Seward wrote to Weed a postmortem analyzing "the causes of this unexpected check in the advance of the 'blessed spirit.'" Among them, he noted, was "masonic influence which shuts up the Press the channel through which that information must flow without which AntiMasonry [sic] can never gain the public favor and which once freely diffused would be the precursor of the universal assent of the whole People."[59]

The extraordinary emphasis that Anti-Masons gave to newspapers, printed material, and "facts" reflected a dramatically expanded print environment that had come into being since the 1790s. This resulted, as historians have long known, from the transportation revolution and, as has been emphasized more recently, from a much broader market and communications revolution that created a culture in which printed material was abundant and extensive reading was joining intensive reading. It was now a "society where printing and public speech were ubiquitous." As historian Richard D. Brown has pointed out, in the late eighteenth century the flow of information was relatively scarce and controlled by elites. By the 1820s, however, the "changeover from scarcity to abundance [was] well underway."[60]

Although the creation of an extensive railroad network was some years distant, Anti-Masonry and other egalitarian movements of the 1820s and 1830s profited from the expansion of the public sphere brought about by changes in the economy and communications. The remarkable spread of the federal postal system had an enormous impact. The number of post offices rose from 73 in 1790, to 903 in 1800, 2,300 in 1810, 4,500 in 1820, and 8,450 in 1830; the ratio of population per office fell from 4,876 in 1800 to 1,289 in 1830, giving the United States a better developed system than England or any European nation. As important, the Post Office Act of 1792, which admitted newspapers into the mail on favorable terms, hastened a similarly phenomenal growth of the press.[61]

The total number of newspapers grew from 96 in 1790, to 234 in 1800, to 366 in 1810, to 861 in 1828. Due to the exchange feature in the 1792 law, in 1800 the postal system transmitted 1.9 million newspapers; in 1830, 16 million. When Anti-Masonry burst on the scene, the world of newspaper publishing had expanded to include a much greater range of offerings and had become far more plural and competitive.[62]

Citizens read more in part simply because more printed material was available. One historian has seen an "Age of Reading" coming into being in this period. The great expansion of print culture took place mostly in New England and the middle states, but its effect was felt everywhere. The parallel religious revivalism of the 1820s, so prevalent in western New York ("the burned-over district"), spread through most of the country, from Maine to Kentucky. Religious enthusiasm, too, was not just created by the spoken word but also carried forward on a flood of print: populist religious leaders, according to Nathan Hatch, "were intoxicated with the potential of print." The same could be said for many Anti-Masons, the enthusiasts as well as the pragmatists.[63]

Economic expansion, a rapidly changing material environment, and a rising level of aspiration contributed substantially to the emergence of a populist movement that, as Benson once claimed, "extended egalitarian doctrines to embrace all aspects of American life, invested the egalitarian impulse with a religious intensity, drastically changed the style and substance of American politics, and thereby accelerated the dynamic pace of American economic growth." Benson stressed that economic change was raising "the level of aspiration to unprecedented heights," thus making "'equal opportunity for all' . . . the perfect battle cry."[64]

Anti-Masonry's populism in fact possessed several dimensions, present from the beginning, that changed in relative importance as the movement and political party evolved. Most obviously, the first protesters in western New York objected to Freemasons' committing kidnapping and murder because their secret society held itself and its members above the law. At an early meeting in the Monroe County town of Victor on October 7, 1826, protesters denounced a society that "grants exclusive privileges to its members and gives them the advantage of others in their general intercourse." Thus, complaints regarding the "prostitution of the laws" ran quickly to the matter of equal opportunity. The protesters were angered by being told "we can do nothing; the power & officers are all in their [Masons'] hands; this is the very thing which has aroused us. . . . We look in the public journals for the horrid news from Batavia and Canandaigua, but they are silent on the subject." The Victor meeting therefore pledged itself to a long effort to give each citizen "an equal advantage to others in our country."[65]

Anti-Masons also depicted themselves as being ordinary people, at least more so than the typical officeholders and political leaders. Established politicians, wrote one contemporary later on, were slow to take up the cause, fearing it to be ephemeral. But gradually men more experienced in public life took up the reins. William Seward claimed in his autobiography that he came to the forefront of the party in Cayuga County because the Anti-Masons "had no men in their ranks in the county who were accustomed to speak or write on public affairs." Seward then wrote the county convention's "Address to the Farmers and Mechanics," whom he trusted would recognize the Anti-Masonic delegates as "men whose hands minister to their own wants and those of our families—with few exceptions, farmers and mechanics like yourselves." In contrast, said Seward, "Priests,

Merchants, Lawyers and Doctors have found too much advantage in Free-masonry to give their exertions to our cause." Similarly, Weed described the Anti-Masons' first state convention of February 1830 as differing entirely "from the hackneyed caucuses of political ambition connected with party names, and devoted to party men." Rather, representatives of the yeomanry of forty-three counties had assembled and "were the *people doing their own business in their own way.*" Regarding the convention that would meet later that year in August, Whittlesey wrote to Weed that it "will not embody as much talent as the last convention, but you may rely upon a quantity of sturdy independence and honest zeal to compensate for it. It is the democracy of the country . . . who are with us." But despite this useful self-image, if Anti-Masonry's leaders initially consisted of ordinary folk from the grass roots, they soon came to resemble, as they did in Genesee County, the leadership of other political factions—more representative of local and regional economic and social elites. And like those leadership groups, Anti-Masonic leaders continued to see and depict themselves in a populist idiom.[66]

Another dimension of Anti-Masonic populism blended with both a positive regard for the lowly and a resentment of elites, whether of the rural gentry or the urban wealthy deemed to be corrupted by luxury. The former impulse found expression frequently in references to the "poverty, and low standing" of Morgan, frequently idealized in Anti-Masonic accounts as one of the virtuous and even heroic poor. This portrait of Morgan had as little to do with reality as the Masonic depictions of him as the worst of knaves and scoundrels. But it fit with Anti-Masons' self-portrayal as close to the common people, and it reflected a genuine and widespread conviction among them that true patriotism and republican principles were lodged most firmly in the honest yeomen of the countryside and the middling classes of the towns and cities. Myron Holley, an associate of Weed and Seward who was described as a man "always of the laboring class," believed that "the great improvements of our race [i.e., humanity] have always originated with the poor; and . . . we must always chiefly look to them for future improvements." Indeed, the poor, wrote Holley, took to heart more deeply the Christian command to love God and man; they lacked prejudices and did not favor "any little class." All social improvements that are permanent, he thought, benefited "not the few at the expense of the many, but the many together with the few." Holley's Anti-Masonry reflected both its religious and republican impulses.[67]

Allied to an affinity for ordinary people was the less noble impulse of resentment against those above in wealth and social status.[68] Charles Francis

Adams, involved briefly with Massachusetts Anti-Masonry, saw in the movement "a strong secret cause, a tendency to the errors of radicalism, to the dislike of the established order of Society, by which talent does not always maintain the ascendency over wealth." An evangelical Anti-Mason of rural Allegany County, New York, expressed well this view of society in an 1828 New Year's address: "Truly, the time is come, there is a continual overturn, and those that were held high in the estimation of the community at large, and [who] viewed with contempt and indignation, and very unfit for offices of trust, because they made their iniquity to be remembered . . . [and] their transgressions discovered, . . . therefore, their places of trust must be taken from them, and given to those whose right it is, until they shall, by true and unfeigned repentance, abolish their works of darkness, and throw off their yoke of bondage."[69]

Finally, Anti-Masonic populism anticipated what Alexis de Tocqueville would term a decade later "the tyranny of the majority." The Anti-Masons reasoned that in America popular sovereignty meant that the will of people was supreme. They gave the widest possible latitude to the claim that "public opinion . . . must properly govern everything which is subject of governmental power." The people had the responsibility to judge "the evils which should be driven from among them." Thus, as Benson observes, evil "was defined by the majority, and whatever it defined as evil must be eradicated." As a Young Men's Anti-Masonic state convention put it in 1830, "The people, the democracy of the country, have passed sentence of extermination against Free Masonry. From their judgement there is no appeal, and against their will it is folly to contend." Anti-Masons would bring about the desired result by bringing the people's rejection of Masonry to bear at the ballot box.[70]

Anti-Masons' exaltation of public opinion established their kinship with earlier populist movements, reaching back to the American Revolution. Moreover, their enemies also echoed earlier *antipopulist* mentalities by arguing that public officials needed to resist the will of erring common people. "New York state legislators," according to Bullock, "often followed this line of argument in discussions of the Morgan case." One legislator warned the House of the need "to free themselves from the contagion of this excitement—boldly to stem the current of popular feeling." In relentlessly depicting Anti-Masons as desperate fanatics seeking power and "office," Masons and their allies repeatedly in this scenario cast the people as "dupes." Anti-Masonic electoral success depended, they said, on "the weak-minded and the ignorant . . . the prejudiced and depraved." In contrast, an Anti-Masonic state legislator complained that, in resisting popular demands for state action regarding the "outrages," the government was "treating the people like children that do not know what is good for themselves."[71]

The theory of Anti-Masonic majoritarianism enjoyed very little opportunity to be put into practice since the party failed to gain the political power needed to implement it. Although the party became a force in several northern states, Anti-Masonic political leaders' success in getting state legislatures to enact their agenda regarding Freemasonry was quite limited. The movement, however, generally succeeded in having a devastating effect on Freemasonry, and the political party powerfully shaped the emerging political culture of the 1830s that would soon be dominated by organized, mass parties.

# Chapter 6

# Anti-Masonry: Progressive and Reactionary

*The men who erect the public press to bear upon the fortresses of Freemasonry,
are the sons of those, who opened the batteries of freedom upon the strong holds
of British tyranny; they do honor to their Fathers. Faneuil Hall rings again with
the voice of struggling independence.*
—Henry Dana Ward, Antimasonic Review (1828)

*Persevere, then, and achieve for your country a Second Independence.*
—Timothy Fuller, An Oration, Delivered at Faneuil Hall,
  Boston, July 11, 1831 (1831)

Anti-Masonry as populist movement and political party, as New York's example indicated, exhibited both progressive and reactionary tendencies.[1]
Some of the latter long preoccupied historians, with the result that recognition of Anti-Masonry's egalitarian attitudes tended to be brushed aside.
Anti-Masonry fits the profile of populist movements of mixed character discussed in the introduction. An unequivocal reading of the movement as predominantly progressive or predominantly reactionary is inappropriate, and
all the more inaccurate because of regional and state variations. In addition,
much more is known about Anti-Masonry in some places than others, and,
except for the kind of research Kathleen Smith Kutolowski has done, there
is insufficient information regarding Anti-Masonry as it operated in localities, churches, social networks, and families before any political organization. This absence of detail from the grass roots impinges particularly on
a dimension of the movement with progressive implications, namely, its
potential relationship to the rise of women's rights consciousness and activism.

The organizational spread of Anti-Masonry is recorded in its newspapers,
conventions of inquiry, nominations of candidates, publications of meetings and conventions, and other activities carried out by men. Ironically, a
major vehicle for the conversion of multitudes of families to Anti-Masonry
has proved resistant to any but the most rudimentary historical discovery:
women. Kutolowski refers to the wives of Anti-Masonic men as "a largely

untraceable but essential segment of the Antimasonic army," while in her study of Connecticut Masonry Dorothy Ann Lipson observes the "private, unorganized, and familial efforts of women [that] help to explain the inexpressive efficacy of Antimasonry as a social movement." Paul Goodman found "Antimasonic women in the forefront of a movement that persuaded thousands of men that for the sake of domestic order no less than civic virtue Masonry had to fall." Apart from their families, women exerted influence through their churches and social networks, and perhaps scrutiny of church records may reveal more concretely what historical analysis at this point reasonably infers.[2]

At least one instance of women's independent Anti-Masonry has survived: the address and resolutions of a protest meeting of Wheatland, Genesee County, "Ladies" in November 1826. Moderation was not for the ladies, for, having been made acquainted with Masonic oaths, they believed "the atrocities" against Morgan and Miller to have originated with Masons. If the perpetrators were not brought to justice, then they favored "total suppression" of the order. With a historical flair the Wheatland women compared the "outrages" to popish atrocities of the Spanish Inquisition (a common analogy then and later among protesters). Uniquely, they called attention to the family of Morgan, "a WIFE . . . left with her infant children, to all the horrors of suspense and heart rending anticipation." They declared that "our Husbands, Sons and Brothers will rise in the might of wise councils and benevolent feelings," resolved to bring about justice. The women touched on themes important to Anti-Masonic women and many Anti-Masonic men: "The time and money spent in Masonic orgies, is robbing their families and connexions of their natural and just claims, and is calculated to excite distrust and create discord in families"; "Resolved— That every Mother should duly remember the degrading disadvantages and unmerited contempt to which they consign their Daughters by their union with Free Masons."[3]

The revivals and temperance movements of the 1820s and 1830s, driven along by middle-class evangelical church men and especially women, shared with Anti-Masonry a vision of Christian manhood with which Freemasonry seemed fundamentally at odds. Recent studies of the cultural struggle over drink have observed that it was in essence "a battle over the nature of manhood." Temperance agitation and local regulation of alcohol (usually unsuccessful) in effect deprived men of the tavern and other masculine social spaces from which women were excluded. Well before 1826, critics of Masonry had voiced complaints that the exclusively male lodge gatherings promoted excessive drinking and worse.[4]

But Masonry also posed an ideological challenge to Christian manhood that went deeper than the perceived practical effects of alcohol and male bonding. Masonry conflicted with the new conception of republican motherhood extant in the early nineteenth century, which depicted women as uniquely virtuous and therefore bearing primary responsibility for instilling morality and virtue in children and the broader society. Masons agreed that women possessed special virtue but bypassed the family and "claimed that men could attain morality through participation in an all-male brotherhood. Its simultaneous exclusion of women and portrayal of men as morally self-sufficient could not help being called into question at a time when so many Americans, both men and women, believed that virtue could be secured only by the agency of women." Masonic ideology thus marginalized women and the family and claimed the power to inculcate morality "without female intervention."[5]

Anti-Masonry's war with Masonry thus constituted both an earlier and then parallel part of an antebellum struggle conducted in several arenas over the nature of manhood. Christian republican Anti-Masons saw their ideal of manhood and masculinity as threatened by both intemperance and Freemasonry. Indeed, the two frequently overlapped in Anti-Masonic perceptions as they associated lodge gatherings with a male conviviality that deliberately excluded women and promoted alcohol consumption and philandering. Masonry undermined the family by exposing husbands and fathers to multiple temptations. "By excluding women, tolerating licentiousness, practicing indecency [in oaths and rituals requiring states of undress], shielding intemperance, and sowing distrust between men and women," Goodman argues, "Freemasonry, critics charged, menaced domestic order."[6] Anti-Masonry thus could be regarded as an *escalation* of the culture war for Christian manhood.[7]

Masonry had long been criticized for its exclusion of and even its alleged hostility to women. In the years before 1826, Masonic literature and oratory sought to address this criticism, and the fraternity sometimes included women in public celebrations. Masonic rhetoric about women, however, was couched in the language of separate spheres, and it paid lip service to women's superior virtue while emphasizing female physical and moral weakness, reinforcing the sense of female inadequacy. Masonry, observes Kutolowski, "championed the moral primacy of men and encouraged them to socialize away from the family at a time when the emerging ideal of domesticity stressed family life and the moral authority of women." Other all-male recreations also segregated men from women and the family, such as militia musters, fire companies, and election day congregations, but they were not cloaked in mystery or secrecy.[8]

Although complaints regarding Masonry's exclusion of women had gathered force from the 1790s on as reformers began to advocate putting women on a more equal footing in education and marriage, Anti-Masons' warnings regarding Freemasonry's threat to the family and domestic economy were relatively new and clearly owed much to the rhetoric of both the temperance movement and the ideal of republican domesticity. For example, an Anti-Masonic Declaration of Independence, July 4, 1828, at LeRoy, Genesee County, charged Masonry with promoting "habits of idleness and intemperance, by its members neglecting their business to attend its meetings and drink its libations. It accumulates funds at the expense of indigent persons, to the distress of their families, too often to be dissipated in rioting and pleasure, and in its senseless ceremonies and exhibitions."[9] Massachusetts Anti-Masonic leader Timothy Fuller praised his state's "schools and seminaries" as "designed to give manliness of character and enlargement of mind—to make you into a man; while [Masonry] . . . *finds* its votaries *men*, but by its follies and emptiness degrades them to children." The 1833 address of the Middlesex County Anti-Masons similarly scorned Masonry as "the arch-seducer of your brothers, and your sons, and the corrupter of their morals." Massachusetts Anti-Masons often called attention to Masonic lodges' devotion to "refreshments" leading to intemperance and worse.[10]

The Anti-Masonic ideal of manhood presumed virtuous sobriety, renunciation of self-indulgence, protection of families, moderation in sociability, and avoidance of hedonism. Solomon Southwick referred to Anti-Masonry in 1829 as this "celestial flame" now animating the hearts of tens of thousands "of virtuous and independent freemen, of men uncontaminated by the luxury and vices of our cities," men who had the patriotism of "real Americans" and "unsophisticated republicans."[11] Such men could be counted on to respect their wives and daughters and to protect their families, but not necessarily in the manner of the traditional patriarch who wielded supreme authority in the family, still the dominant model of family structure even in this transitional period.

It is unlikely that the views held by William Wirt regarding women and family influenced Anti-Masonic leaders in nominating him for president in

1832, but Wirt's ideas resonated with those of other Anti-Masons. Wirt had gained modest prominence as a lawyer, as U.S. attorney general under James Monroe and John Quincy Adams (1818–29), and as an author of social commentary and a biography of Patrick Henry (the father of his first wife). Not associated with Anti-Masonry before 1832, Wirt was a hesitant candidate and a lukewarm Anti-Mason. His candidacy emerged almost accidentally after several better-known possible candidates were either unacceptable or unavailable. Serendipity—it was quite probable that if the Anti-Masonic convention had not been held in Baltimore, Wirt's home, he likely would not have attended and not have been nominated—and Wirt's reputation in evangelical and benevolent circles recommended him to Anti-Masons. For some time after his nomination, Wirt tried unsuccessfully to withdraw, but his dislike of President Jackson and his sense of duty kept him in, "possibly the most reluctant and most unwilling presidential candidate ever nominated by an American party." During the campaign Wirt issued no public criticisms of Masonry, while his private attacks on the fraternity were matched by his scorn for the Anti-Masons for refusing to support Clay.[12]

Ironically, Wirt's kinship with Anti-Masons rested, albeit silently, on more than revulsion against that proud Freemason, Andrew Jackson, whom he regarded as despotic and immoral. Wirt shared with other Anti-Masonic leaders a deep respect for women and embraced the progressive ideal that women's education should be on the same footing as men's, including classical education as well as the traditional domestic arts. That this impulse went beyond preparing women for the task of raising republican children is indicated by Wirt's approach to marriage (his second marriage to Elizabeth Gamble after his first wife's death). Though he and his wife found it difficult to implement, they sought to pursue "the emerging ideal of companionate marriage," in contrast to the patriarchal ideal based on the assumption of fundamental inequality between men and women. Companionate marriage, rather, promised "a loving partnership of equals." Although undercut by frequent separation and the cultural context in which they lived, this remained the Wirts' lifelong project.[13]

Wirt's advanced ideas regarding women's education were shared by Timothy Fuller, whose daughter, Margaret, would leave her own mark on American history. Fuller, a former Jeffersonian Republican and congressman (1817–25), was the Anti-Masonic candidate for lieutenant governor in 1832. In 1820, after reading the early feminist tract by Mary Wollstonecraft, Fuller wrote to his wife that he wished for his daughter an education comparable to the best available for men. Her curriculum included classical and modern languages, philosophy, literature, and history, and "he [Fuller] forcibly cut her off from the female subculture, a world governed by etiquette books and sentimental novels."[14] Margaret, of course, became far better known than her father as a champion of women, slaves, workers, Indians, and other oppressed groups.

Another leading Massachusetts Anti-Mason, Amasa Walker, was a successful, young wholesale shoe dealer, a pious Orthodox Congregationalist, and involved in the peace, temperance, and antislavery movements. In 1833, as president of the Boston Lyceum, he addressed 1,200 young men, warning them of the corrupting influences of the city, of "confidence men and painted women" ready to seduce and destroy them. Masonry, of course, stood among those seducers. But Walker believed that reading rooms, libraries, debating societies, and lyceum lectures could purify the city— only, however, by enlisting "the sympathies and assistance of the *female mind*." Therefore, Walker led the campaign to open those institutions to women. Not until women, with their special affinity for benevolence and an aversion to avarice, exercised a "commanding influence" would the city and the nation be brought to virtue.[15]

New York Anti-Masonic leader Myron Holley moved easily between the republican and Christian wings of Anti-Masonry. After giving up law practice because he could not defend guilty clients, he went into business as a bookseller, joined DeWitt Clinton in promoting the Erie Canal, and served as treasurer of the New York Canal Commission from 1816 to 1824. Freemasons' obstruction of justice in western New York convinced him that the courts "were completely in the hands of the masonic fraternity, and bound by extra-judicial oaths not to do justice."[16] Holley also saw Masonry as subversive of the republican family and disrespectful to women. For Holley the family "was the focus of human happiness, and justice the vital principle of human society," and therefore "any institution which segregated a body of men from the rest of the world, including the wives and daughters of their own families, under oaths of secrecy, backed by horrible penalties," must cease to exist. Masonry had been used, he decided, "not only against the family, but against free government."[17]

Like Amasa Walker, Holley too warned of the seductive power of Freemasonry through its "harlequin attractions" and saw the "charity" of the fraternity as "wholly counterfeit." (Harlequins, usually masked and dressed in diamond-pattern costumes, evoked the regalia of Masonic dress, as well as the hocus-pocus and tricksterism.) Walker had spoken of "confidence men"; Holley saw "mountebank retainers" dressed in "party colored garments" now revealed as "dripping with the blood of the innocent."[18]

Holley rose quickly in the Anti-Masonic ranks, drafting the address of the New York Anti-Masonic convention at Albany in 1829, and then the "Address to the People of the United States" from the national convention at Philadelphia in 1830. Deeply religious and laboring for "the redemption of our country," Holley was a radical egalitarian who never joined a church but preached regularly in public buildings, such as schoolhouses, to the lower classes of society, whom he regarded as the salt of the earth. Holley scorned both churches and Masonry for their relegation of women to inferior status. Churches and lodges, he believed, "much as they seem to differ, had one thing in common—the male element grasped all the power. The lodge would not trust a woman with a secret, the church would not allow her to open her lips as a religious teacher. It is hard to tell which held her . . . in the greatest contempt."[19]

Holley was one of many Anti-Masons who by the late 1830s had taken up the cause of antislavery and was working for the new Liberty Party when he died in 1841. The connection between Anti-Masonry and antislavery has been remarked on often by historians. Many Anti-Masons simultaneously participated in the temperance and antislavery movements. As Anti-Masonry waned after 1834, many of their leaders became involved with antislavery societies' lobbying efforts and then with the new (1840) Liberty Party. Some became associated with the antislavery, antisouthern wing of the Whig Party, while a few became radical Democrats who would later be drawn to Free Soil in the late 1840s. But what about the women who participated in the Anti-Masonic crusade, through their families, churches and communities?

Again, the lack of obvious records and research necessitates inference. It follows, however, that Anti-Masonic women also reinforced the ranks of the temperance and antislavery movements. In the 1820s and 1830s great numbers of middle-class white Protestant women, and some free African American women in the North, moved into benevolent and reform activities in the public sphere, while continuing also to be caught up in the revivals of the Second Great Awakening. Was it not possible that the Anti-Masonic experience, combined with that of parallel reform movements driven by evangelical impulses, also propelled women into an awakening that led to a conviction, if not activism, of the need for an expansion of women's rights?

Some historians have posited a strong historical connection between abolitionism and feminism. In the 1830s antislavery women entering the public sphere confronted criticism from conservative men and women, who challenged them on grounds of propriety and morality. In responding to their critics, abolitionist women laid the groundwork for the passage "from seeking equality for women in order to free them to work against slavery, to working for women's rights as an end in itself."[20] An extensive literature on women's reform activity, however, warns that participation in antislavery/abolition did not necessarily lead to proto-feminism or the embrace of woman suffrage or women's rights generally. Several historians have questioned the notion of "a neat sequence of stages" from reform, benevolence, and abolition to women's rights. It appears that only some, a minority, of women reformers advanced to a radical position for women and, further, that the issue of women's equality more often divided female activists, "isolating ultraists from their benevolent and perfectionist peers."[21]

Further, while antislavery women's entry into the predominantly male public arena implicitly challenged the ideology of a separate sphere of domesticity for women, most antislavery women gave "moral and pragmatic reasons," couched in traditional Christian evangelical rhetoric, to justify their activism.[22] These qualifications to the pattern of evangelical reform and antislavery leading to early feminism carry considerable weight and are based on careful scrutiny of the complexities of female activism. Yet some women reformers clearly did develop a feminist ideology *and* a women's agenda because of their antislavery and other activist experiences. Moreover, in recent years historians have also uncovered evidence of numerous individual "women politicos" who engaged in all kinds of political activities, including editing partisan newspapers, giving campaign speeches, lobbying legislatures, and pulling wires behind the scenes at political conventions. Even these women whose actions reached far beyond traditional gender roles often professed an adherence to the ideology of separate spheres and women's domestic role—except, somehow, for them. These admittedly exceptional women acting in men's roles for the most part paid lip service to the ideology of separate spheres, even as their actions totally ignored it.[23] Perhaps, then, many other activist women in abolition and temperance found it tactically useful not to raise "the woman question" even as their consciousness was indeed changing.

The question of Anti-Masonry's impact on women's consciousness is even more difficult than assessing the influence of reform and abolition in developing a women's rights mentality. Unfortunately, the otherwise informative histories of women's antebellum activism contain nothing regarding Anti-Masonry, nothing suggesting any link between that crusade and women's rights. Yet Anti-Masonry and incipient feminism were influenced by the same evangelical impulses inspiring temperance, antislavery, and other moral reforms. Such a connection was likely, however, especially given the abundant evidence—noted above—of men moving from Anti-Masonry to antislavery and other moral reforms. The point is that women's participation in Anti-Masonry may also have contributed, as abolition certainly did in however limited and qualified ways, to developing women's consciousness regarding their status in society.[24] Myron Holley's ironic observation that he could not decide whether the church or the lodge held women in greater contempt may have occurred to many Anti-Masonic women as well. In any case, it seems reasonable to suggest that the controversy over Masonry, which impacted families, churches, and communities, served as a prelude to women's much better documented participation in antislavery and temperance reform. Anti-Masonic women's activism, prompted by their preservationist and conservative perception of Freemasonry's threat to religion, the family, and the evangelical model of manhood, contained a progressive element that prepared the way for women's increasing presence in the public sphere.

## PROGRESSIVE AND REACTIONARY ANTI-MASONRY OUTSIDE NEW YORK

New York Anti-Masonry mixed populism with mostly progressive, as well as reactionary, tendencies. For several other states enough evidence exists to discern how the mixture varied across the North. In Vermont, for example, Anti-Masonry enjoyed perhaps its greatest political success and was pervasively populist, expressing resentments against a "back-country aristocracy" and exalting "the will of the people," expressed through the ballot box, as the ultimate source of authority. Its kinship with reform and evangelicalism was nowhere more pronounced than in the Green Mountain State; however, such connections did not always lead in a progressive direction.[25]

By 1831 Anti-Masons had gained a plurality of the state's gubernatorial vote in a three-way contest with the National Republicans and Jackson Republicans, and the next year Vermont became the only state to vote for William Wirt, who received approximately 13,000 votes to 11,000-plus for the Nationals and some 7,800 for Jackson.[26] In 1833 Anti-Masons won the governorship outright over a National-Jacksonian coalition (20,565 to 15,683), and they elected three of the state's five congressional representatives. Anti-Masonic ascendancy, however, brought no severe legislative action against Masonry. In 1830 the legislature had repealed the charter of the Grand Lodge, but by the time it outlawed the taking or administering of oaths "not authorized by law," Masonic activity had all but ended.[27]

As in western New York, Anti-Masonry in Vermont fed off the two impulses powering Christian republican antagonism to Freemasonry: the desire for a Christian commonwealth and an anti-aristocratic egalitarian drive for equality of opportunity. Anti-Masonry cut across all denominations but especially attracted evangelical Calvinists, and in 1830–31 revivals spread just as Anti-Masonry gained momentum and became a political force.[28]

Historians have noted often that Vermont Anti-Masonry became a magnet for resentments born of social change and rising inequality. The most recent account of Vermont's "blessed spirit" emphasizes the populist dimension of its leaders, who came from a secondary level of "substantial farmers, clergymen, and young professionals" involved in religion and reform but not associated with politics or enterprise. New to politics, they tended to desire the Christian republicans' communal ideal and to care "as much about order and community as about prosperity and power."[29]

A perception that Masons occupied public office out of all proportion to their numbers fed Anti-Masonry, as did militant counterattacks by prominent Masons in the early stages of the movement. Lists of lodge members "resembled a roll call of the Legislature and the bar," while the governor, a majority of the Supreme Court, and the House speaker were Royal Arch Masons, which seemingly validated charges "that Masonry composed an aristocratic body in a political democracy." In contrast, Anti-Masonic ascendancy led to "more open access to office, both elective and appointive."[30]

Women in Vermont participated in temperance and antislavery societies and were "drawn to Antimasonry as to no other movement, troubled by the threat that these men's clubs posed to their families." Here, too, a different ideal of Christian manhood animated Anti-Masonic women, who were alarmed by "the broader dangers that society risked when it allowed bands of indolent, cigar-smoking, supposedly mature louts to set a poor example for weaker spirits under the protection of lodges that were removed . . . from public scrutiny." Convinced that Masons practiced false benevolence and spread immorality, Anti-Masonic women worked through their families, churches, and communities to eliminate Masonic influence.[31]

Though strongly populist in character, Vermont Anti-Masonry proved to be less progressive than its New York counterpart. Anti-Masonic legislators were divided on the issue of the abolition of imprisonment for debt, and the measure did not pass. Throughout Vermont's history, as one analyst of a state known for its maverick streak has commented, its political culture has been "distinctive," its politics throughout a mixture of "radicalism, populism, and conservatism."[32]

South of Vermont, the Connecticut River valley cut through central Massachusetts, and there, too, an evangelical populist brand of Anti-Masonry flourished. In eastern Massachusetts the movement and party expressed primarily a middle-class moral populism that contained progressive and reactionary elements. A powerful religious impulse made Anti-Masonry more of a reform crusade than a secular political party. Christian republican men and women joined the movement for religious and moral reasons and because they believed Freemasonry's New York assault on law and justice undermined republican society. Even as a political party, Anti-Masonry in Massachusetts sought to promote Christian manhood and morality, as well as equality of opportunity and equality before the law.[33]

Frustrated with Masonic influence within the National Republican political establishment, in 1831 Anti-Masons nominated an independent candidate for governor, Samuel Lathrop, who, though not an Anti-Mason, was well known to "the religious community" as the last (1824) Federalist candidate for governor and as an outspoken Orthodox critic of the Unitarian religious establishment. Lathrop ran well behind the Nationals' incumbent, Levi Lincoln, but outpolled the nominee of the as-yet weak Jacksonian Republican party (Lincoln 28,804, Lathrop 13,357, Marcus Morton 10,975).[34]

Anti-Masonry's electoral strength peaked in 1833 when former president John Quincy Adams allowed his name to be put forward as its candidate for governor. Hardly a man given to enthusiasms, Adams's public and private writings revealed that he had become convinced that Masonry's structure and oaths had permitted the fraternity to commit crimes, subvert justice, and go unpunished. Moreover, as perhaps the most prominent antipartisan political leader of his era, Adams was an appropriate choice for the antipartisan crusaders. He also hoped to unite the anti-Jackson forces, but instead he garnered 30 percent of the vote (18,274), running second to National Republican John Davis. With the election now to be decided in the legislature,

Adams withdrew in favor of Davis, and then in early 1834 left Anti-Masonry, but did so by issuing a scathing critique of Freemasonry and its antirepublican influence in the state's dominant party.[35]

The Masons waged an antipopulist crusade against their critics, particularly in Boston, as intensely as anywhere else in the country. They disrupted Anti-Masonic meetings in Faneuil Hall and in other towns during 1829–30, began a Masonic newspaper in Boston as early as 1828, and launched sustained personal attacks on the reputations and "character" of Anti-Masons. "Antimasonry," charged Masons, "like the cholera . . . dwells among the lower classes." In December 1831, 1,200 Masons issued a "Declaration" defending their society and attacking its critics. Masonic influence prompted the legislature to choose Paul Dean, a Universalist minister and Mason, to deliver the 1832 annual election sermon. Dean decried "political fanaticism" as well as "agitators" and "workingmen" who were calling for reform of militia service and debt laws. Well might Workingmen, like Anti-Masons, conclude that Masons and a "monied aristocracy" ran the state. In 1834 the Suffolk County Anti-Masons denounced "unnecessary acts of incorporation and other exclusive measures," which were designed to create monopolies and "to make the *few* rich."[36]

As elsewhere, continued Masonic defiance fed Anti-Masonry, but in Massachusetts so, too, did a continuing cultural-religious war between Orthodox Trinitarian Congregationalists and the Unitarian elite. Although an 1811 law had eased dissatisfaction with the church establishment by allowing any denomination to pay taxes to their own society, assessments were still collected by towns or parishes, and the Orthodox chafed under Unitarian political control of the state government and its pretensions to cultural preeminence. The Orthodox fought back by launching revivals and reform crusades to preserve communal values and a Christian republic. Before Anti-Masonry grew in Massachusetts, a prominent Orthodox minister had delivered a sermon charging that a Unitarian conspiracy existed within the legislature and the courts. Soon, the Unitarian and Masonic conspiracies, in the minds of many Orthodox, would overlap.[37]

Anti-Masonry's moral populism attracted men and women from various denominations, but men prominent in Orthodox evangelical activity provided much of the movement's leadership. Their fight with Freemasonry paralleled campaigns against dissolution and for foreign missions, Bible education, conversion of the poor, temperance, and other benevolent enterprises.[38] Although Anti-Masonry's state leaders included several Unitarians, a Unitarian-Orthodox fault line tended to divide Anti-Masons and Masons.

Anti-Masons believed that, outside the Unitarian orbit, "thousands of Christians of every denomination, who now stand *neutral* as regards free-masonry," could be brought to Anti-Masonry if only they could be presented with the information showing "that Freemasonry is as dangerous to true Religion as it is subversive of the Rights and liberties of the people!" The evangelical impulse in the Bay State's Anti-Masonry made the moralist element dominant in its Christian republicanism. Established political leaders among their opponents believed the Anti-Masons to be wholly unprincipled because the Anti-Masons, their eyes fixed on transcendent goals, did not acknowledge the rituals and implicit rules operative among public men. John Quincy Adams grasped the Anti-Masonic core in his parting declaration: political Anti-Masonry "is founded upon a pure, precise, unequivocal principle of *morals.* . . . Moral principle is the vital breath of Antimasonry."[39]

Connecticut Anti-Masons also at first exhibited an antiparty aura, but after running an independent Anti-Masonic candidate for governor in 1831, the political leadership shuttled between coalition and independent politics, and their constituency quickly became disillusioned. Rank-and-file Anti-Masons seem to have regarded Freemasonry primarily as a threat to religion and may have included church members who wished to restore the tax support of the Congregational church that had ended in 1818. Anti-Masonic votes came heavily from two eastern counties that "formed part of an extended region of Antimasonic strength that stretched into northern, industrial Rhode Island through Pawtucket into southern Massachusetts." Throughout this region a developing industrial society coexisted with a persistent "conservative evangelical Calvinism." Although Anti-Masonic leaders included the populist Myron Holley, a religious and social egalitarian, more typical was the paternalist manufacturer Smith Wilkinson, who dominated the state's leading Anti-Masonic town, Pomfret, and kept his employees under an orthodox regimen of Sabbath-keeping, temperance, and avoidance of idle play.[40]

Political Anti-Masonry faltered quickly in Connecticut, but the social movement "crippled Masonry" largely because of "a silent and unorganized Antimasonry among women," who exerted influence through "apolitical and private networks of opinion."[41] A reactionary evangelical populism insistent on moral homogeneity characterized Connecticut Anti-Masonry.

Rhode Island Anti-Masonry's obsession to strike at the secret fraternity led it into alliance with an entrenched reactionary party. The "blessed spirit" quickly became tainted by the state's oligarchic polity and the leadership's opportunism. By the 1830s Rhode Island could qualify as a rotten borough of American republicanism, with its highly restricted suffrage based on land ownership and an increasing number of its growing manufacturing population unable to vote. Although calls for reform had been made and would grow stronger during the 1830s, and while individual Anti-Masons came to advocate constitutional reform, the party itself ignored the issue.[42]

The limited electorate, however, as well as only intermittent newspaper support, hampered Anti-Masonry's growth. Moreover, most Anti-Masons in Rhode Island held political views closer to the National Republicans, and in 1830 the party decided to back incumbent National Republican governor Lemuel Arnold, helping him to win reelection over the Jacksonian Republican James Fenner, 3,780 to 2,877 votes (independent Anti-Masonic candidates usually polled some 600 to 700 votes).[43] As a result, the Nationals appointed a legislative committee to hold hearings on Masonry, but this forum backfired, as the National Republican chair of the committee repeatedly insulted Anti-Masons ("The Masonic dunghill has produced a great many Antimasonic vermin") and issued a report in early 1832 that infuriated Anti-Masonic leaders.[44]

The Anti-Masons retaliated by fielding an independent candidate for governor in April 1832, Warwick manufacturer and entrepreneur William Sprague Jr., whose 592 votes were enough to cause a protracted deadlock between Arnold and Fenner. Sprague's father, William Sr., mirrored the paternalistic populism of Connecticut's Wilkinson, eating meals with his employees at a huge table, dressing plainly, performing physical labor, and insisting on regulating morality. Early the next year, however, the Anti-Masons went rapidly into alliance with the Jacksonians, who supported a national administration at odds with Anti-Masons' policy preferences. In return, the Anti-Masons received a law, regarded as unenforceable, punishing extrajudicial oaths by a fine of $100. After the Anti-Masons again helped elect a Jacksonian as governor, John Brown Francis, in January 1834 the legislature repealed Masonic charters and required the remaining Masonic corporations to give detailed annual reports disclosing their proceedings to the General Assembly.[45]

These measures, and perhaps more so the ongoing Anti-Masonic agitation throughout churches and communities, damaged but did not wipe out Masonry in Rhode Island. Although Masonic membership dropped from about 3,000 to about one-third that number, adhering Masons continued to defy various legislative measures that had been designed to discourage or regulate the fraternity. On June 24, 1835, after three years of avoiding public display, 200 Masons marched in Providence to celebrate St. John's Day. Although Anti-Masons hired two burly African Americans to don colorful Masonic uniforms and march mockingly at the rear of the procession, to the glee of onlookers, the Masons' flagrant defiance of the ostensible will of the General Assembly brought no reprisals, and, in fact, both the Jacksonians and the new Whig Party had been nominating or appointing Masons to office right along.[46]

Anti-Masonic opportunism thus resulted in apparently harsh but largely symbolic measures against Masonry. The Spragues clearly were driven by populist resentment, Christian moralism, and a regard for republican values. But Anti-Masonic leaders' opposition to aristocracy and privilege did not carry over to the growing problem of the state's anachronistic, antidemocratic polity. Agitation for reform increased during these years but made little headway. Meanwhile, Anti-Masons bore responsibility for handing the governor's office for several years to the Jacksonian Republicans, the party then most opposed to suffrage reform. According to the leading historian of Rhode Island in this period, "the party of Jackson . . . was rural-based, agrarian-oriented, and thoroughly reactionary on nearly all local questions relating to political and constitutional reform."[47]

Ironically, Anti-Masonry attracted support from the voting and nonvoting mechanics and factory workers in Providence, Pawtucket, and industrial villages where suffragism also flourished. In Providence more than half of the city's Anti-Masonic voters resided in Ward 6, home to many mechanics, shopkeepers, and artisans. Pawtucket, heavily industrial, was a "hotbed of Antimasonry" and suffragism, attracting both leading manufacturers and artisans and laborers. But while some Anti-Masons became reform supporters, the party took no position on the issue that in the early 1840s would bring the state to the brink of civil war.[48] In Rhode Island the Antimasons gained what were ultimately phantom blows against Freemasonry by supporting one of the most reactionary political establishments in the American republic.

Anti-Masonry in Pennsylvania combined both progressive and reactionary tendencies in an occasionally volatile mixture. Anti-Masonry also elected a governor and lasted longer in Pennsylvania, continuing on well after 1834, though it persisted later more as a political faction or pressure group than as a moral, populist crusade. Freemasonry, as in Vermont, was well established throughout the state, with some 113 lodges and a Grand Lodge in

Philadelphia known for having built itself "a magnificent new edifice" in the 1820s. The order also enjoyed considerable influence among the state's elite, with its members including "the most outstanding men of the community." More significant, clergymen and others had criticized Masonry before the 1830s. The pietist Germans, as well as Quakers and Presbyterians, disliked the fraternity's oath-swearing, secrecy, and what they saw as aristocratic pretensions. These groups proved receptive to the charge that Masonry subverted Christian religion.[49]

On July 4, 1827, Philadelphia's Third Presbyterian Church's congregation heard its pastor, Ezra Stiles Ely, give a sermon calling for the formation of a "Christian Party in Politics." Every man chosen for public office, declared Ely, "should be an avowed and sincere friend of Christianity. . . . Our civil rulers ought to act a religious part in all the relations which they sustain." Ironically, Ely's preference for president in 1828 was duelist and Mason Andrew Jackson and not the moralistic John Quincy Adams, because Jackson was a fellow Presbyterian. By 1830, however, Ely had converted to Anti-Masonry, and the first national Anti-Masonic convention in Philadelphia that year declared that "freemasonry exerts a dangerous influence upon the Christian religion, affecting thereby the dearest interests and hopes of man."[50]

Although they organized slowly, the Anti-Masons' 1829 candidate for governor, Joseph Ritner, made a surprising showing against George Wolf, a Mason and candidate of the dominant Jackson Republicans. Ritner, who polled 51,776 votes to Wolf's 78,138, projected a populist appeal as a hardworking farmer of humble origins. A self-made prosperous farmer raised in a poor German family, Ritner had married into a prominent Mennonite family, and, while not a zealous Anti-Mason, he was associated with temperance and antislavery. Although the party attracted several established, mainstream politicians, Anti-Masonic leaders tended to be less experienced in politics than their counterparts in other parties.[51]

As a champion of equal rights, Anti-Masonry exuded a "democratic and egalitarian appeal" and continuously attacked Masonic and elite domination of public offices. These themes resonated with some of the same German religious sects that had been involved in "Fries's Rebellion" and who distrusted centralized power. Anti-Masons accused Wolf of being the Masonic candidate and of favoring Masons with appointments. Wolf in fact defended Masons as diverse in religion and politics and "our dearest friends, best neighbors, and most estimable citizens." But in 1832 Ritner again lost to Wolf, though by a narrow margin in a large turnout (91,385 to 88,115).[52]

During 1833–34, Thaddeus Stevens, future Radical Republican and "Scourge of the South" during Reconstruction, brought a new, uncompromising zeal to the crusade against Masonry. Elected to the state legislature, Stevens, a complicated, always controversial figure, embodied both the progressive and reactionary impulses of Anti-Masonry.

Stevens introduced numerous resolutions and bills aimed at preventing Masons who were serving as jurors or sheriffs from abusing the legal system as they had in New York. He tried to get the legislature to suppress secret societies "bound together by secret and unlawful oaths" or to outlaw all "extrajudicial" oaths. Only one Anti-Masonic proposal passed—making membership in a secret society good cause to challenge a juror—and by one vote. Stevens bargained first with National Republicans, then with Whigs, to obtain from the legislature a committee to investigate Masonry. In December 1835 Stevens's committee began to call before it prominent Masons and Democrats. When several witnesses refused to appear before what opponents called the "Stevens Inquisition," and those who did invoked their constitutional right not to testify, the enterprise backfired. Despite a reaction to Stevens's high-handed tactics, his legislative party continued to play a role as late as 1838, though by then Anti-Masonry largely had disappeared from the grass roots.[53]

Some accounts of Stevens's Anti-Masonic career have stressed his opportunism, and at times Stevens put aside principle for the sake of political gain.[54] On the other hand, Stevens could match the vitriol and sensationalism of the most evangelical Anti-Masons. In one 1831 speech Stevens quoted Masonic ritual and read several of the bloodthirsty Masonic oaths. "The presiding officer . . . *personates the* ALMIGHTY GOD," he charged, and Masons drank wine out of skulls, binding themselves to keep each other's secrets, "murder and treason not excepted." Masonry "was a base-born issue of a foreign sire . . . a prostituted harlot" who had "entered the Courts of Justice and seduced the venerable Judges with her foul embraces."[55]

Born a cripple into the family of a poor shoemaker, Stevens possessed a difficult personality, stubborn and headstrong, as well as highly sensitive to any slight. His hatred of privilege and exclusivity sprang from personal experience. As a poor youth at Dartmouth College, he had been rejected by the fraternities, and Masons may have blackballed him at the outset of his legal career. Throughout his life Stevens gave generously to the unfortunate, and his lameness, while prompting aggression toward those he feared or envied, also gave him lifelong "identification with those handicapped by accident of birth. . . . Stevens [eventually] defended the Indians, Seventh Day

Adventists, Mormons, Jews, and Chinese, and he battled over thirty years to bring freedom and civil rights to the Negro."[56]

A thoroughgoing populist, Stevens could be progressively so, as demonstrated by the crusade for free public schools that he waged simultaneously with Anti-Masonry and at significant political risk to himself. He began campaigning for free, tax-supported schools in 1826, before the struggle against Masonry began, arguing that Pennsylvania should "learn to dread ignorance more than taxation." The German sects in his district ran their own schools, taught mostly in German, opposed taxation for public education, and saw the tax-supported schools as a threat to their cultural preservation. Stevens not only braved constituents' ire but battled for the school law with members of his own party, all the while cooperating with Democratic governor Wolf—Stevens's Masonic and Democratic enemy.[57]

The fight fit with the kinds of battles he fought his entire political career. Under the existing system parents paid a tuition or state tax to send their children to school, while parents who publicly admitted their poverty could receive free education for their children. Thousands of parents who could not pay the tax or would not admit to poverty kept their children home. This situation aroused all of Stevens's passionate animus against invidious distinctions. After the bill passed, petitions against it poured into the legislature, but Stevens managed to block its repeal by lashing out at the privileges of the rich and labeling the repeal an enactment of a pauper law. "Hereditary distinctions of rank are sufficiently odious," he declared, "but the distinction which is founded on poverty is infinitely more so. Such an act should be entitled 'An act for branding and marking the poor.'"[58]

But Stevens also expressed the reactionary side of Anti-Masonic populism. Even as Masonry declined, Stevens's "Inquisition" had put Anti-Masonry on the wrong side of civil liberties. The backlash against the "Stevens Inquisition" brought the committee's investigation to a quick end, tarnishing Anti-Masonry and stamping it with a reactionary authoritarianism. As a result, Pennsylvania Anti-Masonry lost much of the aura it had enjoyed for several years as being an alternative to politics as usual.[59]

The lack of local studies for several states makes it difficult to discern the progressive or reactionary features, or even the populist content, of Anti-Masonry elsewhere. In New Hampshire, Maine, and New Jersey Anti-Masonry made little headway as a political party, but Anti-Masonic sentiment caused significant cessation of Masonic lodge activity.[60]

Anti-Masonry as a vehicle for Christian republicanism, however, was more obvious in eastern Ohio (on the border of New York) and in the eastern counties of Michigan Territory, where transplanted Yankee Protestants caused Anti-Masonry to flourish both as a social movement and as a political force. Ohio's Western Reserve, ten counties and areas of two others, constituted part of the New England diaspora where revivals and evangelical reform and, after Anti-Masonry, political antislavery flourished.[61]

In Michigan Territory Anti-Masonry's populism expressed itself in the form of evangelicalism and an intense antipartyism. Anti-Masonic votes came heavily from townships in eastern counties marked by revivals, temperance, and antislavery. Before moving on as the evangelical wing of the new Whig Party after 1834, Michigan Anti-Masonry constituted a "Christian Party" focused on creating a morally homogeneous community. The moral authoritarianism of many Anti-Masons and evangelical Whigs went beyond involvement in evangelical Bible and missionary societies, and they pushed hard in the public sphere for temperance, tougher standards in libel cases, Sabbath-keeping, adultery laws, and the death penalty. In addition to condemning Masonry as subversive of or a substitute for religion, Michigan's Anti-Masonry was charged with a heavy dose of anti-Catholicism, comparing Masonry to popery and both to the emerging Democratic Party (which in Michigan was relying heavily on Catholic voters).[62]

REFORM AND REACTION IN CONTEXT

Anti-Masons and abolitionists would not have recognized the terms "progressive" or "reactionary," much less have understood the ideological dichotomy that contemporary liberals and conservatives extrapolate from them. They might have found meaning in "populist," often using the words "popular" or "democratic" to convey some of its connotations. Many Anti-Masonic activists became abolitionists and labored to end slavery in the American South; some became (or were already) Sabbatarians, seeking to stop the mails on Sunday and to impose more uniform and hedonism-free observances of the Lord's Day in their communities.[63] Some abolitionists detested Catholicism as much as they favored emancipating enslaved African Americans (some Masons were also anti-Catholic).[64] A minority of abolitionists confronted the daunting task of lifting discriminatory statutes and combating racial prejudice against free blacks in the North. Some even moved on to women's rights, while others parted company. Many Anti-Masons became ardent Whigs and favored activist governments that would promote economic enterprise and moral improvement. A few Anti-Masons even drifted into the Democracy of Andrew Jackson and Martin Van Buren, a party whose rhetoric championing the common man became, by inclination and political circumstance, increasingly tied to a virulent racism as the sectional crisis intensified before the Civil War.

Thus, to the varying combinations of progressive and reactionary tendencies in Anti-Masonry across several regions is added the complexities attendant on what seem to be from the present vantage point wildly inconsistent postures across the political, social, and cultural spectrum.[65] To fair-minded observers then and since, the demand of Anti-Masons outside of New York to ban Masons from jury duty seemed clear evidence of the crusade's intolerance. Given the well-documented obstruction of justice in western New York by Masonic sheriffs, the packing of juries with Masons, and the lack of meaningful punishment for the perpetrators of the "outrages," the actions taken there to prevent further abuses seemed understandable. But not so in other states where, lacking evidence of Masonic or official wrongdoing, Anti-Masons called for the same discriminatory laws.[66] This constituted a straightforward issue of civil rights, and the Anti-Masons fell on the wrong side.

Yet the matter of tests for jury duty entailed another dimension that illustrates the need for caution in attaching what may be anachronistic ideological labels to groups and individuals living in a society still evolving toward secularism. Indeed, in the antebellum decades many state courts and statutes prevented witnesses from testifying in court because of their religious beliefs. Religious tests for witnesses, in fact, constituted an ongoing and contested issue in the early decades of the nineteenth century. Although never becoming as salient an issue as imprisonment for debt or militia reform, for example, the issue gained greater prominence in the late 1820s and 1830s in part because of its role in one of the important trials of Masons for kidnapping William Morgan.

Eli Bruce had been sheriff of Niagara County and participated in Morgan's abduction. Thereafter, he frustrated attempts to prosecute Masons in Niagara by packing juries with Masons, one of which sent a memorial to Governor Clinton testifying to Bruce's good character. Bruce himself, however, and two other Masons went on trial in August 1828 and were convicted of the crime of kidnapping. Anti-Masons and other observers believed the trial could have shed light on Morgan's probable murder, if a turncoat Mason, Edward Giddings, had been allowed to testify regarding his knowledge of Morgan's final hours. The Masonic defense lawyers, however, objected to Giddings's being allowed to testify on the grounds that he was "an unbeliever in the Christian religion" and therefore an incompetent witness. They called several witnesses to testify to the effect that they had heard Giddings often declare there was no God or higher spiritual being, and that he had no belief in "futurity." The defense even produced an 1827 letter containing some of Giddings's heterodox views.[67]

The prosecution called several persons who testified to the contrary— that Giddings in fact did believe in God or an overruling Providence and that virtue was rewarded and vice punished. When the prosecution also attempted to produce evidence testifying to Giddings's "good character," the judge intervened, pronouncing that quality irrelevant since "moral character, however stainless, would not obviate the objection" that the law required "a higher sanction for the administration of an oath." After further arguments the judge declared Giddings an incompetent witness, convinced that Giddings did not "believe in a supreme being who holds men accountable for their conduct."[68]

Thus, the Masonic lawyers, despite their order's reputation for deism, latitudinarianism, and free-thinking in matters of religion (not to mention what their critics believed of them), ironically insisted on application of an illiberal test for court testimony more characteristic of their conservative religious opponents. New York law and an 1820 state supreme court decision (*Jackson v. Gridley*) declaring a witness incompetent on the grounds of disbelief in future reward and punishment had encouraged the Masonic defense to resort to this tactic. From Ohio to Massachusetts Masons held aloft the banner of "Toleration and Equal Rights" against the "persecuting, proscribing spirit of Antimasonry," but in this case the "proscription" of certain religious beliefs (or disbelief) suited their purpose.[69]

The irony grew as Anti-Masons in the state legislature quickly took up the Jeffersonian cause of complete freedom of religious opinion and requested that the law be changed so that "all objections now made to the competency of witnesses on account of their religious belief, or want of it, shall hereafter go to the credibility alone." Giddings had complained of his exclusion to state senator John C. Spencer, one of those appointed in 1827 to revise the statutes of New York and who served as a special prosecutor investigating the "outrages" (1829–30). The statutes regarding witness competency then had been slightly revised and Giddings was sworn as a witness at trials in early 1831, though only after his religious beliefs had been examined once again. Some Anti-Masonic leaders were not satisfied.[70]

Thus in 1831 a young Anti-Masonic state legislator, Millard Fillmore, continued the effort to eliminate religious tests for witnesses in courts of law. Fillmore had earlier drafted a successful bill to abolish imprisonment for debt, and in that instance, as with witness competency, he received help from veteran state senator John C. Spencer, a member of a committee to revise New York's statutes in 1827. Spencer had also served as one of the state's special prosecutors to investigate the Morgan kidnapping and the obstructions of justice that followed and in the process became converted to the Anti-Masons' view of Masonic wrongdoing and tampering with the legal system. The legislature, however, rejected a thoroughgoing elimination of any religious test for witness competency.[71]

The following year Fillmore published a pamphlet making an extended and learned argument for abolishing any religious test. He did so under the pseudonym "Juridicus," anonymously, perhaps because, as one of his biographers pointed out, removing the religious basis for the oath troubled his "more orthodox constituents" and the more evangelical Anti-Masons. Fillmore reviewed the history of English and New York State legislation and concluded that "every change has been in favor of admitting persons to testify who were before excluded" and that bigotry and prejudice were giving way to liberal views. Fillmore advocated no test whatsoever, whether for belief in a future or present state of punishment or in a Supreme Being. He would admit persons of any religion. The fear of punishment from human laws, dread of shame, pride of character, love of justice, sense of right and wrong affected equally "the believer and the unbeliever, pagan and Christian, Jew and Mohametan." Inducement to tell the truth existed independently of religious beliefs. Fear of future punishment was of little use in preventing perjury, and false-swearing witnesses could easily get around any tests. Beliefs were not palpable, conscience indeterminate.[72]

The New York legislature, however, rejected a thoroughgoing elimination of any religious test for witness competency and in doing so stayed in step with most legislatures and courts during this period. Events in two other states are worthy of note because they involved Masons or Anti-Masons. In an 1829 superior court usury case in Connecticut, *Atwood v. Weldon*, a majority of the judges ruled that any "person who disbelieves in any punishment in a future state, though he believes in the existence of a Supreme Being, and that men are punished in this life for their sins, is not a competent witness." In dissent, one justice argued that "the moral character of a witness is the only safe criterion" and that a man's reputation for truthfulness "by his conduct in society" was more important than "*mere opinion*." The irony here arises from the court, presided over by former Federalist leader and prominent Freemason David Daggett, reversing an earlier decision allowing Universalists to testify.[73]

Jackson Republicans both publicized the issue and fought in the legislature to make religious beliefs irrelevant as to the competence of a witness. A compromise emerged the next year when the legislature decided that anyone who believed in a Supreme Being, without a requirement for a belief in future accountability, could be a competent witness. The law thus barred atheists and agnostics from appearing as witnesses but no longer prohibited Universalists.[74]

The position of Connecticut Anti-Masons on the issue is unknown, but Goodman reports that the question of Universalists' testifying in Vermont split the Anti-Masons in the legislature. Vermont law barred Universalists from testifying in court if they did not believe in divine punishment after death. An 1833 bill to end disqualification on religious grounds failed in the legislature, with just over half of the Anti-Masons voting against it. This was surprising because Universalists strongly supported Anti-Masonry in Vermont, though members of that group elsewhere, despite being attracted to antislavery and temperance, tended to be "over-represented" among Freemasons and found the fraternity "immensely appealing," according to that denomination's recent historian.[75]

Sufficient evidence exists in these instances to speculate that religious tests for witnesses divided republican and Christian Anti-Masons, but they also divided Masons and other opponents of Anti-Masonry, with no clear separation of progressives and reactionaries. The New York case particularly, however, provides strong evidence of progressive impulses coexisting with reactionary impulses in Anti-Masonry.

# Chapter 7

# Anti-Masonry, the Parties, and the Changing Public Sphere

*A politics largely rooted in elite-dominated factions gave way, by the late 1830s, to a populist-oriented, institutionally organized political nation dominated by a system of two-party politics.*
—Joel H. Silbey, The American Political Nation, 1838–1893 (1991)

Anti-Masonry as movement and party substantially influenced the creation of a populist political culture and an expansion and invigoration of the public sphere. Contemporaries observed the rise of egalitarian attitudes among the American people in the 1820s and 1830s, and historians early on pointed to this central theme of the period by characterizing it variously as "the Age of the Common Man" or "the Age of Egalitarianism." Less commonly now do historians assign credit to Andrew Jackson as a democratizing influence—rather, they see Jackson's popularity and rise to the presidency in 1828 as a result, rather than as a cause, of populist currents engulfing politics after 1815.

Anti-Masons were hardly the only champions of the people's sovereignty. Even before Anti-Masonry appeared, an "aggressive egalitarianism" laced the political rhetoric of short-lived movements such as the New York's People's Party, as well as countless other state and local movements against established elites or for greater opportunity. Very often rival entrepreneurial interests, representing networks of business or kin associates, used populist rhetoric in competing for charters or legislative preference, arguing that their projects held superior benefits for the public good. A nearly universal suspicion of established elites joined a widespread enshrinement of the people's right to majority rule. As early as the run-up to the 1824 presidential election, the major Republican factions and their leaders—that is, many of the elites themselves—had adopted rhetoric exalting the will of the people.[1]

"If the preservation of republican liberty depended on resting ultimate political authority in the people at large," as many political leaders insisted, "then all people should have an equal voice in the polity—provided they were white, adult, and male." Several states revised their constitutions to

expand the suffrage by eliminating remaining taxpaying or property qualifications for voting or office, and otherwise moved to enhance majority
rule—for example, in attempting to make electoral districts more equal in
population. In 1826 New York eliminated its taxpaying qualification for voting, thereby expanding the electorate and helping to create the conditions
in which a hyperpopulist movement such as Anti-Masonry could arise.[2]

During the 1820s and 1830s, local and state controversies over internal
improvements, temperance, Sabbath-keeping, and other issues increasingly drew more citizens into the public sphere.[3] Presidential elections,
too, sparked greater participation, and in 1828 the turnout of eligible voters
doubled over that of 1824. Though turnout tended to plateau after that, the
numbers of those voting rose impressively. In the acrimonious 1828 contest
between John Quincy Adams and Andrew Jackson, the total vote grew from
356,038 (with 153,544 for Jackson) in 1824 to 1,156,328 in 1828. Less dramatic increases followed in 1832 and 1836 (to 1.25 and just under 1.5 million) until 1840, when the antebellum electorate surged to a turnout of 2.5
million voters.[4]

By 1840 Anti-Masonry was no longer a factor as movement or party, but
it had left its mark on political culture by ratcheting up the prevalence of
populist rhetoric, helping to moralize politics, and pushing citizens into
participating in politics well above previous levels. In a detailed study of
Genesee County, New York, Kathleen Smith Kutolowski found that in the
years before Anti-Masonry's advent, nearly 300 persons had participated in
town government and politics, not an inconsiderable number. But during
six years of Anti-Masonry, over 600 individuals had involved themselves.
An expanding local economy and the constitutional changes of 1826, of
course, stimulated this widening of popular interest; however, Genesee
Anti-Masons innovated by establishing the first young men's political organization, and, despite Anti-Masons' pronounced antipartisan rhetoric, they
were "no less voter-oriented and no less attuned to new party opportunities
than were [their] opponents."[5]

Evangelical reform movements of the 1820s and 1830s that sought to
Christianize and purify the public sphere, together with commercial expansion and communications improvements, also injected political affairs
with greater moral intensity, thus raising the stakes and the affective temperature attending issue conflict. Evangelical efforts to regulate individual
behavior with regard to alcohol or Sabbath-keeping, for example, which
ran parallel to the Anti-Masons' efforts to champion a traditional Christian
republican version of manhood and to suppress the Masonic alternative, at-

tracted the attention of many men and women, bringing them into the public sphere and increasing interest in voting among men and within families generally.[6]

During the 1830s, as Anti-Masonry faded and two major parties emerged (Democratic Republicans, or Democrats, versus Whigs), populist rhetoric came to dominate national politics.[7] No event did more to advance this process than the "war" waged by President Andrew Jackson on the Second Bank of the United States (BUS). Although the bank had been created by Jeffersonian Republicans, Jackson and his advisors, who claimed to uphold Republican traditions, harbored prejudices against bankers and speculation, and specifically against the Bank of the United States, and had learned the utility of antibank rhetoric during the 1820s. The Jacksonians' hostility toward the bank extended to its president, Nicholas Biddle, and his branch officers, who were political allies of Henry Clay and the National Republicans. During Jackson's first year in office, partisan allies in New England and New York began to lobby to have Biddle appoint good Jackson Republicans to bank offices. In New Hampshire and Massachusetts Jacksonian political-entrepreneurs began to attack the BUS and argue that their states would be served better by removing the government deposits from the bank and transferring them to state banks. Jackson's advisors, led by Martin Van Buren, prompted the president to continue expressing doubts about the bank, as he had in his first message to Congress.[8]

At this point Jackson's political opponents made a strategic error: Henry Clay, preparing to challenge Jackson in the 1832 election, urged his congressional allies to push through a recharter of the Second Bank, even though its charter would not expire until 1836. Clay, Biddle, and friends were practically daring Andrew Jackson to veto the bank recharter and make it an issue in the 1832 election. The National Republican leaders calculated that if Jackson vetoed the bill, he would alienate the commercial classes, who benefited from cheap credit and a uniform currency. They also believed that it would reduce Jackson's strength in Congress, drive a wedge between his supporters, and call attention to the executive usurpation of power. Never one to shirk a challenge, the feisty president did just that and turned the tables on his political opponents.[9]

He did so with a ringing veto message that was a "masterpiece of political propaganda," according to historian Michael F. Holt, and that embraced populist rhetoric as no president had ever done before. Jackson blasted the bank as an engine of the "rich and powerful, [who] too often bend the acts of government to their selfish purposes." Though inequalities in society were inevitable, "when the laws undertake to add to those natural and just advantages artificial distinctions . . . to make the rich richer and the potent more powerful, the humble members of society—the farmers, mechanics, and laborers—who have neither the time nor the means of securing like favors to themselves, have a right to complain of the injustice to their government." In addition to using a radical populist rhetoric of class that horrified social conservatives, and denouncing the bank as an unconstitutional "monopoly," the president also appealed to nationalism and nativism by pointing to the bank's many European stockholders: the Bank of the United States was not only unrepublican but un-American. His veto message also incorporated states' rights principles that Jackson already had enunciated as a hallmark of his administration. Thus, in denouncing a monster of concentrated power, Jackson portrayed himself as a people's tribune and "enhanced [his] credentials as a champion of republicanism and strict construction and as a foe of the corrupt and entrenched political establishment in Congress."[10]

The veto also helped relieve political pressure on Jacksonian politicians and entrepreneurs in states such as Pennsylvania and New York who were being attacked for supporting state monopolies. Indeed, the situation in New York illustrates how the Jacksonians co-opted the rhetoric that Workingmen and Anti-Masons had been using against them, first at the state and then at the national level. In 1829 Van Buren's Albany Regency—now the heart of Jacksonism in New York—had created a Safety Fund System to give state banks greater stability by creating a general reserve fund to which banks would contribute. The state administered the fund as insurance in case any bank failed. Earlier laws (1804, 1818) prevented banks from operating without legislative approval, and while the Safety Fund was an innovative and useful advance in banking, the system was essentially monopolistic, and bank charters went primarily to political leaders, their kin, or partisan allies. In 1830 the Anti-Masons had protested vigorously against the Safety Fund legislation, which also relieved certain banks from taxation and imposed a new direct general tax to help fund the system. Francis Granger, Anti-Masonic nominee for governor in 1830, saw the Safety Fund system as no less than the "enslavement" of the people. Soon Anti-Masonic journals were denouncing the "gigantic political Bank scheme, projected by Mr. Van Buren," as a "monster" institution. As applications for state bank charters poured into the legislature from the Regency's friends, the Anti-Masons stepped up their attacks on "licensed monopolies." Thus, the "egalitarian impulse initially directed against the 'privileged Masonic order' . . . found an outlet in the campaign against 'licensed monopolies.'"[11]

But even before the president's veto message, New York Jacksonians began diverting hostility "from the 'monied *monopolies*' in New York to the 'monied *monopoly*' in Philadelphia." When this process began, the *New York Working Man's Advocate* observed that while it took little interest in the question of the BUS charter, it was concerned that "our legislature madly persists in granting charter after charter to private companies" and expressed its distrust of "the tender mercies of the Local Bankers." Some Anti-Masonic leaders were as eager to acquire stock in the new banks as Jacksonian and other politician-entrepreneurs, but the party's denunciations of the "monied speculations of the political aristocracy that rules the state" had put Van Buren's Albany Regency on the defensive—until Jackson's veto message.[12]

Every political faction, major or minor, sought to associate itself with "democracy" and its opposition with "aristocracy." The Jackson administration and its state allies now deployed this rhetoric, hardly new to them or their rivals, but with a new "monster" representing "aristocracy," which had taken the place of Masonry. The Regency, in historian Lee Benson's words, "adopted classic jiujitsu principles in the 1832 campaign." So, too, did Jackson and his advisors appropriate the egalitarian rhetoric of the Anti-Masons and Workingmen. "Masonry had been portrayed as a secret, sinister monster with powerful tentacles that reached everywhere and threatened everybody," Benson concludes. "But by 1832 Masonry had been reduced to a pathetic shadow of a monster. In contrast, the Monster Bank was flourishing and, through its branches, *influencing* economic development all over the country."[13]

Not all historians have stressed the bank veto and subsequent "Bank War" as originating partly as "a brilliant political counter-attack," but many have attributed Jackson's solid reelection victory—55 percent of the popular vote and a 219 to 49 electoral college margin over Henry Clay—to the dramatic populist posture Jackson thus assumed as the people's champion. Although the bank veto cost Jackson votes in some places, notably in Pennsylvania, it also dovetailed with the states' rights stance adopted by the administration, which, along with Jackson's image as a slaveholder and defender of slavery, enhanced his appeal in the southern states.[14]

The Bank War helped hasten the demise of Anti-Masonry and pushed most of its remaining leaders, activists, and voters into the Whig Party, which emerged during 1834 as the major opposition to the Jackson–Van Buren Democratic Republicans. Reelection in hand, Jackson moved to destroy the bank before its charter expired, discharging his obstructive secretary of the treasury and appointing a replacement who would follow orders to withdraw government deposits from the bank. The administration then deposited the funds in state banks around the country—soon known as "pet banks"—selected on the basis of party loyalty or business or kinship ties. The Bank War gave the Jackson party an enemy, "aristocracy" or the "Money Power," and it also helped to form the character of the Whig Party as a defender of republican government against executive usurpation and "King Andrew."[15]

During 1833–34 National Republican leaders revived the issue of executive tyranny and made the contest with the Jackson party less about the bank. Jackson's opponents also charged that a recession that had begun in December 1833 resulted from Jackson's reckless financial policies. Henry Clay and state opposition leaders such as Thurlow Weed organized opposition to Jackson around the issues of removal of the deposits, economic distress, and above all, executive usurpation. Clay told Biddle in 1834, "The Bank ought to be kept in the rear; the usurpation in the front." "If we take up the Bank," he continued, "we play into the adversary's hands." Instead, Clay invoked "the campaign of 1777" against executive tyranny, and hence in 1834 the name "Whig" made its first widespread appearance in the spring elections to denominate a new party, echoing the patriots of the Revolution and their opposition to king and Tory. The name signified opposition to "King Andrew" and resonated with the "republican values Americans had cherished since the eighteenth century [and] it fused National Republicans, Antimasons, and states' rights Southerners."[16]

For many years historians described the Whigs as an ideologically bankrupt party without principles, held together only by ambition and opposition to the Jacksonian Democrats. In line with recent decades of scholarship, however, Holt disputes this view and asserts that the Whig Party was based on principle—opposition to states' rights—and "a passionate devotion to the Revolutionary experiment in republican government." The Whigs saw themselves as defending liberty against the power of a chief executive who was upsetting the balance among the branches of government and who was corrupting government officialdom with a "spoils system" of party patronage and the influence of his pet banks, "thereby to crush popular liberty." The Whig name, appealing to the patriot cause of the 1770s, helped erase "the stigma of antirepublican elitism" that had become associated with the Federalist party.[17]

In directing their opposition to the Jackson administration away from defense of the BUS and the haughty Biddle, and toward executive tyranny, usurpation, and spoils, the Whigs, whose elite supporters included many wealthy capitalists, adopted far more of a populist posture than their immediate National Republican predecessors. The Whig name and their new rhetoric struck themes that appealed to Anti-Masons and facilitated their merger with the Nationals in the North. Anti-Masons had condemned the power and privilege of Masons and their use of fraternal oaths and influence to break the law with impunity. Now the Whigs boldly challenged a usurping executive who they said placed himself above the law and whose bank and patronage policies created a privileged class of officeholders and speculators. "Salvation from Jackson's 'unlawful' actions rested 'IN THE HANDS OF THE PEOPLE,'" Whig papers proclaimed. The tyrant must be resisted "'THROUGH THE MEDIUM OF ELECTIONS.'"[18]

Anti-Masonry originated (and spread) in reaction to Masons' placing themselves above the law during the western New York "outrages" and the subsequent frustration of justice in numerous trials. Holt observes that Anti-Masons insisted "that America must have a government of laws and not of men, that no man or group of men, however powerful, was above the law. Thus the Whigs' insistence that their true issue with Jackson was not the Bank, but 'law or no law, constitution or no constitution,' resonated with Antimasonry's deepest values."[19]

While the Bank War shaped both the Whig and Democratic Parties as they emerged in the mid-1830s, it also drew attention away from the issues—though not the rhetoric—raised by Anti-Masons and Workingmen. In Massachusetts the National Republicans/Whigs launched a massive campaign protesting Jackson's abuse of executive power and calling for relief from economic "distress." As in New York and elsewhere, the Whigs during 1834 shifted attention from the bank to Jackson's despotic and unlawful acts and the resulting economic hardships. While Whig spokesmen denounced Jackson in the U.S. Senate, the Massachusetts legislature passed resolutions protesting Jackson's actions and hundreds of citizens attended meetings throughout the state. Several mammoth petitions eventually found their way to Congress. Many Anti-Masons and some Workingmen signed the petitions, though most Anti-Masons still hesitated to go over to the Whigs, who competed with the Democrats in courting Anti-Masons through 1834. In the Bay State "King Andrew" became the rallying cry for Whigs to unite the opposition to the Jackson Democratic Republicans.[20]

Whiggery's co-option of populist rhetoric in the former Federalist stronghold did not include approval of the Workingmen's movement. With the owners of the rising factory system high in Whig councils, Whig speakers and editors often denounced the Workingmen as Jacksonian demagogues or infidel radicals. But Whigs now claimed that they best represented the interests of ordinary workingmen, and they described their 1834 candidate for governor, John Davis, as a "Furrow Turner" with "huge Paws": thus the cosmopolitan lawyer (Davis) was just another hardworking farmer. Their candidate for lieutenant governor, the wealthy printer and book dealer Samuel T. Armstrong, they described as "a Mechanic and Workingman."[21]

The Massachusetts Whigs' selected their 1835 candidate, the scholar-politician Edward Everett, deliberately to appeal to Anti-Masonic and "Workie" voters. Everett had vaguely endorsed some Workie goals and called himself a "workingman" (though he opposed the ten-hour movement and had taken no position on an artisan's lien law). Everett, however, had lobbied tirelessly to arrange a rapprochement between National Republicans and Anti-Masons and in doing so had earned the enmity of militant Masons. In 1835 many Anti-Masons drifted to support Everett, while others made a point of rejecting the Whig candidate for lieutenant governor, a well-known Mason. Many Anti-Masonic voters and probably most former Workie voters (about 6,500 total) voted for the Democratic candidate for lieutenant governor, William Foster, who ran well ahead of his losing ticket and who possessed excellent credentials as a maverick friend of the Workingmen and an Anti-Masonic sympathizer. Foster ran best in former Anti-Masonic strongholds.[22]

Massachusetts Jacksonians similarly ratcheted up their already populist rhetoric in the 1830s, especially drawing on the class-based idiom of the Workingmen. As Whigs, out of power in the nation, ran against King Andrew's despotism, the Jacksonian Democrats, out of power in Massachusetts, ran against the Boston "aristocracy." In the mid-1830s the Democrats received a powerful infusion of the radical rhetoric of the Workies and even endorsed, for a time, some of the latter's major proposals. The Bank War also unified the Democrats as it had the Whigs, and it helped them recruit a few of the public men associated with "political Workyism." Although a few prominent men associated with the Workingmen (Foster) and some Anti-Masons (Amasa Walker) became Democrats, most of the radical labor leaders moved on to activism independent of the major parties, and most of the Anti-Masonic rank and file eventually became Whigs or, later, voted for the antislavery Liberty Party.[23]

The egalitarian impulse manifested so recently in the challenging groups of the early 1830s reached full expression in the Democrats' state address of 1835. Like the Workingmen, the Democrats now pointed in vivid language to the rise of dangerous inequalities of wealth and social condition that threatened republican government. Equal opportunity for all classes of citizens, they said, was declining, and they accused the Whigs of wanting the people to be "subjected to the controlling influence of self appointed guardians." Democratic Republicans recognized that to be capable of self-government the people "should be in an equality in their social and political condition." The Democracy stood against all special laws for combinations of wealth or influence and would discourage charters of incorporation as aristocratic instruments that disrupted "our equal social condition," which would lead to an imbalance of power in government. The Democrats' address, very likely authored by newly committed Democrat and future historian and secretary of the navy George Bancroft, asserted that "pure democracy inculcates equal rights—equal laws—equal means of education—and *equal means* of wealth also, as incidental to the other blessings."[24]

For purposes of this analysis, it matters little that the specific proposals of the Democrats did not match their populist rhetoric. Their platform echoed clearly those of the Jeffersonian Republicans, calling for minimal state spending and economy and relief from legislative malapportionment. It attacked the BUS but remained silent regarding state banks. Mechanics should be protected against "unequal competition," but no endorsement of a lien law issued forth. Similarly, it asserted that laborers had a "universal right to leisure," but it avoided mention of a ten-hour day.[25] Still, by 1835 Whigs and Democrats in Massachusetts and other states employed populist rhetoric that was heavily influenced by the Anti-Masons, Workingmen, various People's parties (especially that of New York), and other challenging groups who were seeking greater opportunity and expressing unrestrained egalitarianism.

## ANTI-MASONRY AND THE ANTI-DEMOCRATS

Of the populist movements of the 1820s and 1830s, Anti-Masonry had the most significant effect on a major party after this period of political upheaval and transition. Simply put, most Anti-Masons became Whigs; in so doing they shaped that party and imbued it with a moralist, evangelical wing, primarily in the North, that pulled the conservative elements of the party in more egalitarian directions and also created a greater potential for schismatic fracturing than existed in the Democratic Party.

Although a few Anti-Masons became abolitionists and some became Democrats, most northern Anti-Masons became Whigs. The process varied by region and state. Some Anti-Masons held aloof from both major parties and politics generally, though it is impossible to estimate how many and for how long.[26] The Anti-Masons of New England generally tended to resist giving up the cause, partly because of a residue of antagonism toward the National Republicans—now reemergent as Whigs—and partly because of what their former rivals and would-be allies saw as their "proscriptive and intolerant spirit." "Nothing would satisfy them," said one Massachusetts Whig in 1835, "but some legislative brand to be affixed on the forehead of every mason." In Rhode Island, Pennsylvania, and elsewhere, Anti-Masonry, either as a rump organization or as a diehard sentiment, lingered into the presidential election of 1836. These and other causes made for a disorganized opposition to the Democrats and their candidate, Martin Van Buren. According to the most thorough historian of the Whig Party, "To call all who opposed Jackson before 1836 'Whigs' or to speak of a 'Whig party' in the mid-1830s is more a literary convenience than an accurate description of fact. Although the opponents of Jackson could cooperate in Congress and although they cheered on each other's efforts in different states, they had developed no central organization."[27]

The "Whigs" could not agree on a single candidate or to arrange a national convention, so they put forward three different regional candidates, the most successful of whom was a former general, William Henry Harrison of Ohio, who received 73 of the 113 electoral votes that went to the opposition, compared with 170 for Van Buren (and a popular majority of less than 50,000 out of almost 1.5 million total). Significantly, two of the three "Whig" candidates in 1836, Harrison and Daniel Webster, were regarded as sympathetic to Anti-Masonry, and both made statements designed to attract Anti-Masonic support. Webster, however, could not command united Anti-Masonic support in New England, or even in his own state, in part because of calculations regarding his electability and in part because his "aristocratic tastes" and continuing ties with Biddle's bank repelled the egalitarian sensibilities of many Anti-Masons. Throughout the North a variety of rump factions of Anti-Masonic leaders maneuvered on behalf of Harrison or Webster, and some for Van Buren, but most remained hostile to presumptive favorite Henry Clay. The intensity of negotiations between

Whigs, Whig/Anti-Masons, and Anti-Masonic holdouts indicates that these political leaders regarded lingering Anti-Masonic sentiment as an electoral force that their favored candidates would do well to propitiate—without offending still resentful Freemasons, if possible. In the end, in December 1839, former and still adhering Anti-Masons played a significant role at the national Whig presidential convention in Harrisburg, Pennsylvania, which nominated Harrison instead of Henry Clay.[28]

After 1836 Anti-Masonry—except in Thaddeus Stevens's Pennsylvania legislature—ceased to be an organized political force. But the new Whig Party, especially in those states where former Anti-Masons helped organize it, had absorbed not only most former Anti-Masonic voters but also the evangelical and egalitarian strains so prominent in the "blessed spirit." Many Whigs were neither evangelical nor egalitarian, and even those who favored a cause such as temperance could be at odds with the "moral authoritarianism" of evangelicals who would coerce moral behavior through prohibition or Sabbatarian laws.[29] But northern Whigs tended to uphold "the familiar Antimasonic principle that government and legislation should be used to improve society, 'morally and economically.'" Western New York, where religious and moral crusades continued to flourish, became "an unassailable citadel of Whiggery because it had been the holy land of Antimasonry." Even before the Bank War or the formal birth of the Whig Party, Anti-Masonic voters there "had stabilized into a long-lived voting coalition schooled in egalitarian and evangelical ideology and in new political tactics." It was also a region where most Anti-Masons were "caught up in the expanding economy of mill site and commercial farm," not only in Genesee County but also in the counties of Monroe, Chautauqua, and Wayne, where Anti-Masonry tended to gain votes in busy ports, manufacturing towns, and fertile agricultural areas with high tax assessments.[30] Former Anti-Masonic leaders in New York such as Seward, Weed, Fillmore, and others remained influential at the highest level of the state Whig Party and, consequently, also in the councils of the national Whig Party.[31]

Anti-Masonic influence in Whiggery could lead in very different directions: toward moral authoritarianism, as in the case of Massachusetts's notorious Fifteen Gallon Law, which enacted temperance/prohibition for the working and middling class, or toward humane compassion for Native Americans, as with many Whigs' opposition to Indian removal. In political economy, Anti-Masons favored the Whig Party's impulse to use government to advance commerce and to promote internal improvements and economic progress generally, just as they had supported similar policies of the National Republicans earlier.

Anti-Masonic leaders, especially in New York and Pennsylvania, backed Harrison's presidential candidacy for 1840, arranging a convention at Philadelphia in 1838 purporting to be national but of limited scope, then maneuvered on Harrison's behalf at the 1839 Whig convention and against Clay's nomination. Harrison, as a popular general, or at least a military leader who could be touted as popular, was more "available" than Clay, in part because he had never been a Mason. In accepting the support of various "Anti-Masonic" groups in the late 1830s, Harrison used tactfully noncommittal language, just enough to satisfy Anti-Masons and to avoid offending Masons.[32]

During the late 1830s the Democratic and Whig Parties consolidated their organizations, platforms, and symbolism and geared up for a contest in 1840 that commanded the attention of voters as never before. Women, already drawn into the public sphere by temperance, antislavery, and other reform and moral causes, participated in unprecedented numbers and enthusiasm in rallies, picnics, parades, and the preparation of political paraphernalia for a campaign that became legendary for its enthusiasm, spectacle, and buncombe. Tens of thousands assembled across the country for hours of oratory in the manner of camp meetings earlier. The Whig "Log Cabin and Hard Cider" campaign for Harrison and vice presidential nominee John Tyler resembled a form of secular revivalism, and indeed, Whig rallies in many locales owed much to the religious revivals of the Second Great Awakening of the 1820s and 1830s—revivals that had often preceded or paralleled the flourishing of Anti-Masonry.[33]

The 1840 campaign also constituted a total triumph of a populist style, by blanketing the country with populist slogans, rhetoric, poems, songs, and speeches devoid of any challenging—let alone radical—content. Harrison, born on a Virginia plantation and grandson of a signer of the Declaration of Independence, was more gentry than plebeian, but the Whigs claimed for him a humble "log cabin" origin and presented him as a folksy man of the people, "the Farmer of North Bend" among other sobriquets. Of course, "Old Tippecanoe" was the favorite Whig nickname because it referred to Harrison's 1811 victory in the Indian wars and invoked the purported glory of his other military exploits. In contrast, the Whigs attacked Martin Van Buren as an effete aristocrat who dined in the White House with gold spoons and drank expensive French champagne. At the risk of offending temperance elements in their coalition, the Whigs also made 1840 the "hard cider" campaign, liberally opening the spigots at rallies and parades and adding extra energy to already spirited hoopla. Temperance Whigs (and Democratic opponents) in fact complained of their party's massive contribution to public rowdiness and drunkenness, but party chieftains saw the "hard cider" component of their campaign as another way to connect with common folk.[34]

Amid the demagogy, buncombe, hard cider, and hoopla, the Whig campaign particularly also possessed a religious element. Though historians have usually noted the Whig emphasis on democracy, patriotism, and Harrison's military exploits, they have made much less, as Richard Carwardine has observed, of the "explicitly religious appeal in the Whig party's campaign literature." The Whigs chose Harrison in part because he was a candidate they believed would run well in areas where the evangelically oriented Anti-Masonic party had prospered. Their stress on the elderly general's integrity was not a ploy; rather, the Whigs' emphasis on his morality was as fundamental as Whig economic policy. Carwardine also points to the Anti-Masonic/Whig evangelical outlook, which arose from "their conception of the organic unity of society," and their view that "economic progress, like moral improvement, was to be realized by the prudent intervention of government and by the sobriety, thrift, and sense of responsibility of the individual."[35] Thus, as much as the Whigs favored state action to promote commercial and economic development, they also constituted, succeeding the Anti-Masons as such, the "Christian Party in Politics" that the Reverend Ezra Stiles Ely had called for in 1828.

Of course, not all Whigs were evangelicals, but for former Anti-Masons and Whig evangelicals Harrison's strongest credential, according to Carwardine, lay in his antipartyism. In 1838 Harrison made a commitment to Anti-Masons that he would not use the presidency to advance party interests; in September 1840, to a convention at Dayton, Ohio, he issued an extensive criticism of party regularity. Harrison's candidacy "reinforced the image of the Whigs as the party of moral rectitude and Christian influence in politics."[36] In a huge turnout of voters, the largest ever in a presidential election, "Tippecanoe" and the Whigs won a convincing victory, getting 1,275,000-plus (52.8 percent) to Van Buren's 1,128,000-plus (46.8 percent), with an electoral college vote margin of 234 to 60. Harrison carried Pennsylvania by 351 votes, and Anti-Masonic support was crucial there. Of thirty Harrison electors, twenty-three were former Anti-Masons, including former Pennsylvania governor Joseph Ritner. Former Anti-Masons played a similar role in denying Van Buren a victory in his home state of New York.[37]

Anti-Masonry's influence hardly ended with the practical roles its former adherents played in the 1840 election. The evangelical political impulse so prominent in Anti-Masonry continued on, as noted above, in the moral wing of the Whig Party and in other crusades to Christianize America. Carwardine has characterized the impulse as a "form of postmillennial political evangelicalism, with its roots in Antimasonry and sabbatarianism [that] nourished the Whig, Free Soil, temperance and Know Nothing parties and reached its apotheosis in the Republicans."[38]

In many areas Anti-Masonry also served as a springboard for antislavery and abolitionist activity. The affinities between the two, though much greater numbers had been involved in Anti-Masonry, became evident as prominent Anti-Masons embraced abolitionism simultaneously or eventually moved on to antislavery societies or political organizing. As the Masonic threat receded with the disbanding of lodges and as Anti-Masonry passed its peak in the early 1830s, "abolitionism picked up momentum." Indeed, it has been suggested that the demand for the total destruction of Masonry provided the force of example for the emergence of "immediate abolition," in contrast to the antislavery gradualism that prevailed during the 1820s.[39]

Many individual Anti-Masonic leaders transferred their energy to the abolition crusade or antislavery political activity. Myron Holley's reforming zeal has already been noted. New Yorkers Gerrit Smith and Lewis Tappan, who would pour large amounts of money and energy into the Liberty Party (organized in 1840), had been Anti-Masons.[40] In Lynn, Massachusetts, one-third of identifiable Anti-Masonic leaders joined the town's abolition society. In Rochester, New York, the links between Anti-Masonry and antislavery appeared early on. In Vermont William Slade originally was elected to Congress in 1830 with Anti-Masonic support and soon "distinguished himself as an uncompromising opponent of slavery, and with John Quincy Adams fought tenaciously against the gag rules." Many Vermont abolitionists and their presses were Anti-Masons in new garb.[41]

William Lloyd Garrison, though initially skeptical of Anti-Masonry, after launching his abolitionist newspaper the *Liberator*, became involved enough to attend the 1832 and 1834 Massachusetts state Anti-Masonic conventions as a delegate from Suffolk County (Boston). In 1832 he published enthusiastic reports of the convention in Worcester where, he wrote, hundreds had descended on the city. He praised his fellow Anti-Masons as "substantial, sober . . . intelligent" citizens, who were "the last to be suspected of sinister motives, or seeking popular preferment—the last to abandon the ground of principle and equality." He felt "proud in being admitted to a seat with them." Garrison's attitude to Masonry was as uncompromising as his call for the immediate abolition of slavery, and he envisioned a total reformation of American society: "I go for the immediate, unconditional, and total abolition of Free Masonry. Pillar after pillar is falling—the mighty Babel begins to shake, and, ere long, it will be broken into fragments by the American people, and scattered to the winds of heaven."[42]

Garrison's *Liberator* defended Anti-Masons and attacked the *Boston Masonic Mirror* for trying to intimidate Anti-Masons. In 1834 he urged abolitionists to vote for Anti-Masonic legislative candidates, and in endorsing Amasa Walker for Congress against a Whig capitalist who was equivocal regarding slavery, Garrison argued that a vote for the Anti-Masons was a vote against slavery.[43]

Both abolitionists and Anti-Masons refused to compromise with institutions that they believed were corrupting the American republic. Both attacked churches that would not purge those they saw as wrongdoers, slaveowners and Freemasons, respectively, causing rifts in congregations throughout the North. The abolitionist critique of the powerful interests in the nation that supported and justified slavery paralleled the denunciation of Freemasonry as protected by powerful elites in both major political parties.[44]

Another parallel consisted of the obstruction and suppression that abolitionists encountered initially and on a continuing basis. Aside from the opposition that radical antislavery activity engendered on its own, party and community elites, still smarting from the Anti-Masonic/Masonic controversy, had learned from the episode that they did not want "another Antimasonry," and they reacted more harshly to the agitation against slavery. Abolition, like Anti-Masonry, stimulated the conservative elite's fears by using new methods of communication and provoked resentment because of the involvement of women. In addition, abolition, like Anti-Masonry, threatened entrenched economic and political interests. But abolition, unlike Anti-Masonry, also unleashed racial hatred and, its opponents insisted repeatedly, "if unchecked, would destroy the Union." Therefore, Whig and Democratic Party politicians and northern business elites desired "to do something, almost anything, to silence abolition." As a result, abolitionists met with far more systematic repression, including mob violence.[45]

Anti-Masons had complained incessantly and with reason that many newspapers across the country had refused to print news regarding the original western New York "outrages," and Anti-Masonic meetings in eastern cities and towns had been harassed and Anti-Masonic speakers threatened. So, too, in broader fashion and with a heavier hand did northern elites seek to quiet abolitionist activism, playing often on the explosive ingredient of racial prejudice to stir up antiabolition mobs. Southern defenders of slavery and their northern allies accused abolitionists of promoting "amalgamation," meaning racial intermarriage and the degradation of the white race. Churches discharged antislavery ministers, while businessmen and bankers brought economic pressure against abolitionists (as many had against Anti-Masons). Cities and towns regularly denied abolitionists the use of public halls for meetings. In 1835 Garrison was pushed through the streets of Boston with a noose around his neck by a "broadcloth mob" that included many "gentlemen of property and influence." With the encouragement and sometimes participation of influential men, Irish Catholic laborers often provided foot soldiers for antiabolition vigilantes. Such mobs often were motivated in part by racial prejudice and sometimes by their antipathy toward Protestant evangelicals, some of whom were known also for their anti-Catholicism.[46]

The English writer Harriet Martineau shrewdly observed that local notables in Boston signaled that abolitionist agitation would be met with violence. Her comments followed an 1835 meeting of leading citizens at Faneuil Hall whose purpose was to warn abolitionists that any meetings they held might cause trouble, thus implicitly manipulating the threat of violence to suppress the agitation against slavery. "It is an invariable fact, and recognized as such," wrote Martineau, "that meetings held to supply the deficiency of gag laws are the prelude to the violence which supplies the deficiency of executioners under such laws. Every meeting held to denounce opinion is followed by a mob. This was so well understood in the present case that the abolitionists were warned that if they met again publicly, they would be answerable for the disorders that might ensue."[47]

When the American Antislavery Society attempted to circulate antislavery literature in the South directly to slaveholders, President Jackson and his postmaster general Amos Kendall instructed southern postmasters to prevent such "inflammatory" mail from being delivered. Kendall interpreted the Post Office Act of 1836 to mean that southern postmasters who did not immediately burn the "incendiary materials" could be fined. In New York the Jacksonian postmaster decided on his own to sort out and withhold abolitionist literature from distribution. Although the abolitionists aimed their first wave of printed material at "touching the moral conscience of slaveholders," their opponents promulgated the sensational accusation that they intended to incite the slaves to bloody rebellion.[48] With this stigmatization of antislavery activists from federal officials and from those who shaped public opinion, little wonder that abolitionists encountered stiff opposition.

Throughout the North antislavery men and women met with harassment "ranging from insulting and rude remarks to physical assault." From 1834 to 1837 three major abolitionist newspapers noticed 157 antiabolition mobs in the North. Mobs, as in the Boston case noted above, included influential men and drew from all ranks of society, "manufacturers and merchants, and working-class artisans, farmers, and unskilled laborers." Violence culminated in 1838 when 300 women gathered at the Second Antislavery Convention of American Women in Philadelphia in the newly built Pennsylvania Hall, which housed an abolitionist newspaper and a free produce store. A mob reported to be 10,000 strong first harassed the meeting and the next day burned down the building.[49] Antiabolitionism could be regarded as an episodic form of reactionary populism, one that was particularly uncivil, illiberal, and subversive of democratic values.

Antislavery activity in the North did not abate, however, and in 1840 the fledgling Liberty Party, whose promoters had broken with the more radical elements of the antislavery cohort but whose platform called for an end to slavery, entered the presidential election with a former Kentucky slaveowner, James G. Birney, as its candidate. After an insignificant showing in 1840, the Liberty Party managed to attract more votes in several states, especially as the question of slavery in the South became entangled with questions regarding white rights in the North. Although the Liberty Party remained a distinctly minor party, never achieving the levels of electoral success enjoyed by the Anti-Masons, it did manage to control the balance of power between the two major parties in some parts of the North. Its presence also pressured Whigs, as well as Democrats, in various northern congressional districts into stronger antislavery (extension) or at least more antisouthern positions.[50]

Although some writers have seen the antislavery movement as a populist political movement, neither the antislavery societies nor the Liberty Party, despite abolitionism's ideological and other similarities to Anti-Masonry, including a great deal of grassroots leadership, possessed the attributes of the "blessed spirit's" mass populism. The Free Soil Party, which succeeded the Liberty Party, was in contrast to the latter an anti–slavery extension rather than antislavery or abolition party, and while it swept together in a broad coalition reformist, populist, and even radical elements, it was primarily a third-party effort quickly taken over and managed by party politicians.[51] Though antislavery-abolition similarly owed much to the religious revivalism of the 1820s and 1830s, it hardly gained the traction in the evangelical churches that Anti-Masonry had enjoyed, despite the involvement of hundreds and thousands of churchgoing women.[52]

Much more is known regarding the antislavery activities of women, compared with the sketchy certainty of their involvement in Anti-Masonry. Abolitionism, too, concerned itself with promoting an ideal of Christian republican manhood, one that contrasted sharply with that of the southern slave-whipping arrogant master prominent in abolitionist literature. To be sure, the southern master's well-documented access to slave women imperiled his wife and family. Yet the threat of Freemasonry in the North to the ideal of Christian republican manhood was perhaps far more immediate and closer to home—literally—than the threat to family posed by the southern slave master.

Anti-Masonry's Christian republican spirit continued on in the moral wing of the Whig Party, as well as in abolition, in temperance, and in evangelical politics during the 1850s. Whig moralists, often frustrated by the conservative, property-oriented wing of their party, often broke off into third-party or other factional activity. Anti-Masonry's major legacy to the political culture generally, along with other populist movements of the 1820s and 1830s, was its impact on shifting the rhetoric of most spokesmen for the major political parties, and particularly the Whigs, to full-blown egalitarianism—at least in style. That rhetoric would play a prominent role in two localized "wars" of the 1840s, as well as provide inspiration for challenging movements that rejected the status quo of the political economy buttressed by the two-party system.

# Chapter 8

# Two "Wars" of the 1840s

*All political power and sovereignty are originally vested in, and of right belong to,*
*the people. . . . The people therefore have an indefeasible and inalienable right, in their*
*original, sovereign, and unlimited capacity, to ordain and institute government, and in*
*the same capacity to alter, reform, or totally change the same, whenever their safety*
*or happiness requires.*
— *"The People's Constitution" of Rhode Island, article 1, section 3 (1842)*

## THE PEOPLE'S SOVEREIGNTY

The demise of Anti-Masonry and the difficulties encountered by radical labor reformers did not diminish the continuing centrality of the idea of the people's sovereignty in American political culture. As universal white male suffrage became a reality in the 1820s and 1830s, movements to remove any restrictions came with "a new explicitness about popular sovereignty, a new assertion of the people's right actually to rule." As property qualifications were reduced or abolished, demands arose that "the people shall choose their judges, their governors, [and, as seen in New York] their presidential electors."[1]

By the 1840s, both major political parties had incorporated the principle that the people's right to rule was paramount, and each proclaimed that they, rather than their rivals, offered the best vehicle for representing the popular will. Both Democrats and Whigs made populist and egalitarian appeals to voters, and both sent out into the electorate many politicians who mingled "willingly along the class margins," dressing and speaking in the manner of ordinary folk, posturing as one of "the People" when electioneering.[2] Thus, a populist style of campaigning joined the enshrinement of the people's sovereignty at the forefront of popular party politics. It powerfully shaped, too, the rhetoric of third-party and antiparty challengers to the major parties.[3]

In his magisterial synthesis of the period "from the adoption of the Constitution to the eve of disunion," Robert Wiebe describes, as have other historians, a powerful democratizing process, especially during the 1820s to the 1840s, that dissolved the hierarchical society bequeathed by the Revolutionary gentry. He calls this the "opening" of American society, and other historians have identified the politics of the era as "open and malleable," especially when compared with "the stagnant and discouragingly predictable partisan politics in the twentieth century." By the 1830s and 1840s the United States possessed "a citizenry that boasted of its unique democracy to any European who would listen."[4]

Yet Wiebe and others have qualified the picture of an expansive democracy with the observation of a "society in halves" and a deepening "class line that separated those who were qualified to participate in a democracy of free choices from those who were not." Indeed, in what Lee Benson once called "the Age of Egalitarianism," the mantra of "equality" became a fundamental part of the American creed "at a time when economic inequalities were becoming highly conspicuous."[5] Some Americans felt palpably the incongruity between the image of an egalitarian society projected by both parties and the experience of their daily lives. This chapter illustrates that assertion by examining two episodes of populist discontent, one involving tenant farmers in New York engaging in civil disobedience, violence, and vigilantism, and a second involving voteless white males in Rhode Island and gentry reformers whose struggle with an entrenched, unresponsive elite embroiled that state in civil discord.

Insurgency sprang from sources other than advancing economic inequality, including the powerful conviction of the people's sovereignty in the popular imagination. As Baltimore's *Niles' Register* put it during the 1844 election, "*Every voter in the broad expanse of the Union knows and feels that the* PEOPLE *are this day* SOVEREIGNS; *one of whom he is. . . . All acquiescing in the decision bow to the majority of the people.*"[6] Another was the frequency with which the people, or voters, heard from party political leaders that the people ruled, and that their will prevailed, so they said, in the councils of party and government.

## THE "DORR WAR/REBELLION" AND THE PEOPLE'S CONSTITUTION

In the early 1840s a populist movement years in the making crested in Rhode Island and campaigned through political and then ineffectual quasi-military means to bring about a new constitution for the state.[7] The state's fundamental law still derived from a 1663 colonial charter that possessed no amending mechanism and that limited the franchise to "freeholders" owning land (originally £40 worth, revised in 1798 to $134). Population growth steadily disenfranchised more adult males and created inequities in representation. Every small agricultural town, ranging in size from 182 to 461 persons, sent two representatives to the General Court, while Providence and industrial Smithfield sent one representative for every 5,793 and 4,767 persons, respectively. Non-freeholders also suffered deprivations of civil rights in matters of jury service, debt collection, and assault.[8]

The reform movement appealed to the theory of the people's sovereignty inherited from the Revolution and the belief still current among many Americans that the people's sovereignty meant that the people possessed an inherent right to revise their constitutions whenever they chose, and not necessarily through established procedures. Revolutionary-era constitutional ideals, according to Christian G. Fritz, persisted long after adoption of the federal constitution: "Americans transformed the language of the revolutionaries' right to 'alter or abolish' government into an ongoing, inherent right of the people, as sovereign, to revise their constitutions." "Alter or abolish" provisions found their way into many constitutions well into the nineteenth century.[9]

Many Americans construed the theory of the people's sovereignty to mean that sovereignty remained in the people and was not transferred to governments created by written constitutions or to elected representatives. Therefore, the people as sovereign could act whenever they chose. But other Americans adhered to a different understanding of the people's sovereignty, one that came into conflict with the populist view in Rhode Island in the 1840s. The conservative position "asserted that this collective sovereign expressed its will only through the use of procedural mechanisms. After creating governments based on their power as sovereign, the people would henceforth be bound by the constitution." But many Americans, including the Rhode Island reformers, held a quite different view, "that 'the people' could express their will directly—just as they did during the Revolution—without using formal procedures before every move. . . . Government was subordinate to 'the people,' who, although normally quiet and acquiescent, could, when they desired, act as the ultimate sovereign."[10] These conflicting understandings of sovereignty characterized the opposing forces in Rhode Island's political and constitutional crisis of the early 1840s.

Ironically, Rhode Island's historic religious liberalism probably contributed to the persistence of a relatively undemocratic political culture. In next-door Massachusetts and Connecticut conflict over established churches had led to constitutional reform.[11] As factories and economic diversification increased in Rhode Island, making it the most industrialized state in the

Union, the legislature remained egregiously malapportioned, and a large part of the adult male population became disenfranchised. In 1840 probably around 10,000 or more white men qualified as voters (including elder sons of freemen); reformers claimed that a liberal suffrage would create a potential electorate of 22,000 or more, while conservatives, using Massachusetts as their standard, estimated an increase to 18,200. Nurtured by an increasingly participatory national polity and rising egalitarian rhetoric, pressure for reform increased, and during 1842 the existence of two rival state governments, both claiming legitimacy, brought Rhode Island to the brink of what the first scholarly study of the events, written a little over fifty years afterward, called a "civil war."[12]

The industrial revolution arrived early in Rhode Island, where Samuel Slater built the first textile mill on the Blackstone River, a stream north of Narragansett Bay. But the state's political culture still seemed mired in the eighteenth century. Those historians who have written glowingly of triumphant democracy during "Jacksonian America" could not have looked too long or closely at Rhode Island, where, up to 1840, the "thoroughly reactionary" Democratic Party, according to the leading historian of constitutional issues in this period, defended the privileged position of landholders and obstructed reform.[13] After 1840, however, party leaderships and constituencies realigned, and the Whig Party, augmented by previously Democratic agricultural and landowning interests, became the major obstacle to reform.

By 1840 just over half of the state's labor force was engaged in manufacturing. Although mills, foundries, machine shops, jewelry shops, and hundreds of small enterprises existed across the state, they were concentrated in the north, where landless artisans and operatives also filled the factory villages. This same development fed the long-standing fear of conservative elites that crowds of dependent workers posed a danger to representative government. Many Rhode Island mills remained small and dependent on local family labor, but some bustling factory villages contained mill-owned schools, churches, and stores, where mill owners and agents exercised a tight paternalism over their workers' lives.[14]

More so than elsewhere in New England and the United States, "influence"—that is, the power of wealth and status—acted on elections in Rhode Island through virtually open voting. The secret ballot was nonexistent. Influentials easily could know how debtors, tenants, employees, and other dependents voted since party ballots (or "proxes," as they were called in Rhode Island) were of distinctive colors.[15] In addition, before 1843 the freehold qualification allowed wealthy men to sway elections by creating "freemen" by temporary conveyances of small tracts of land. For security the landholder retained the grantee's note for a sum above the actual worth of the land, while the freeman-for-a-day "would vote as the grantor desired." In 1841 a prominent Democrat and defender of the freehold suffrage conceded privately to a suffrage Democrat that "there is fraud enough in our present system."[16]

Ironically, both reformers and conservatives pointed to the abuses of "manufacturing villages" to justify their positions. Reformers believed that the "work men employed in and about the Mills," if given the vote, "would not be controuled [sic] by the Agents and owners." Defenders of the "landed interest" instead claimed that "free suffrage" would "place the political power of this state in the hands of the aristocracy of wealth; [and] give a single manufacturer, or agent of a manufacturer, the power of putting into the ballot-boxes from 20 to 300 votes besides his own." Lumped into the "landed interest" were also several of the smaller southern towns benefiting from malapportionment that contained ports with thriving commerce, and they too resisted change.[17]

In the 1820s reformers had petitioned the legislature and held conventions but were ignored by the political establishment. At first disaffected members of the gentry took the lead, but by the 1830s mechanics, artisans, and shopkeepers joined in calling for reform, including the radical trades union advocate Seth Luther. Artisan radicals gradually gained allies among young lawyers and professionals who, without success, proposed constitutional reform in the legislature.[18]

By the late 1830s one such ally was Thomas Wilson Dorr, a scion of the Providence establishment. Born in 1805, Dorr attended Harvard College and then studied law in New York City with the eminent chancellor James Kent. He returned to Providence to clerk with other conservative luminaries, but by the time he entered the state legislature in the mid-1830s, and despite his elite background and affiliation with the National Republican/Whig parties, he was championing reform. Dorr's causes included abolition of imprisonment for debt, better prisons, softening of the state's harsh penal code, civil service reform, educational innovation, a more independent judiciary, and defense of the rights of antislavery petitioners and religious radicals. His Bank Act of 1836 checked usury by creating a 6 percent ceiling on interest and a permanent banking commission. Dorr's independence led him to break with the Whigs and to cooperate with radical Democrats, unlike those that dominated Rhode Island's Jacksonian party.[19]

During 1840–41 a militant suffrage movement emerged and gained adherents outside the ranks of radical artisans, mechanics, and shopkeepers. Non-freeholders often complained that while they could not vote, they constituted the majority of men required to do militia duty. Early in 1840 the General Assembly made this situation worse by levying criminal penalties on any man who refused to serve. About the same time, radical New York Democrats began disseminating literature in Rhode Island advocating that a constitutional convention be called, with or without legislative sanction. Moreover, the enthusiasm of the "Log Cabin and Hard Cider" campaign engulfed even politically backward Rhode Island. Hundreds, "even thousands," of men and women, according to one observer, "swelled the meetings and participated in the excitement . . . who had no vote." "People who could not vote," recalled another, "more than ever envied those who could."[20] The Rhode Island Suffrage Association grew out of meetings of mechanics in Providence and gradually acquired respectability, as well as the support of many freeholders. Soon a suffragist weekly was appearing, the *New Age and Constitutional Advocate*, supported by professionals and small businessmen.[21]

By 1841 suffrage association chapters had spread and inundated the legislature with petitions. Now, established politicians endorsed the movement, especially Democrats. Agrarian Democratic leaders had resisted constitutional change as much as commercial-manufacturing Whig chieftains, but nevertheless some Democrats joined the reform chorus. Whig partisans attributed the Democrats' conversion to frustration at their defeat in the 1840 election, and some opportunism was evident. Democrats countered that the Whigs' "grand hard cider POWOW of 1840" had sowed the wind by appealing "to the passions and senses" and now reaped the whirlwind of suffragism. The conservative Democrat Elisha Potter observed that the suffrage association imitated the Whig campaign with the "same machinery of music and processions."[22]

The new assembly continued to provoke the disenfranchised and reformers by ignoring a suffrage petition with 581 signatures and then responding to one from several African Americans also asking for the vote, denying that request but then exempting men of color from town and state taxes on real and personal property, which further inflamed white non-freeholders and increased hostility against blacks in the suffrage ranks. In February 1841 the legislature agreed to call a convention but refused to liberalize voting and apportionment rules, and it continued through May to turn aside efforts to do so. The suffrage association, enjoying widespread support, responded by affirming the right of citizens, inherent in the people's sovereignty, to call a constitutional convention on their own—to bypass the assembly, elect delegates, draft a constitution, and ratify it in the manner of states during the Revolutionary period. During the spring and summer suffrage reformers held massive parades, rallies, and barbecues and mobilized support among both the disenfranchised and freeholders, holding aloft the banner of the people's sovereignty.[23]

After an August election, the "People's Convention," whose delegates included well-known freeholders and lawyers, met in October and drafted a "People's Constitution," which extended the vote to adult white male Americans who had lived in the state for one year. It increased representation ratios for Providence and the larger towns, but not on an equal basis. The constitution also provided for a secret ballot, voter registration before elections, and an independent judiciary, but the delegates rejected Dorr's proposals to enfranchise African Americans and to abolish imprisonment for debt. Portions dealing with state debt, corporations, and banks reflected radical Democratic thinking about political economy. The document also required voters on fiscal affairs in towns to be taxpayers or owners of $150 worth of property, a restriction common in nineteenth-century America. The document would be submitted to a popular vote, to be held December 27 through December 29, 1841. Through Dorr's insistence, a clause provided for a timely referendum on striking "white" from the suffrage qualification, but prominent abolitionists, including Frederick Douglass and William Lloyd Garrison, nevertheless came into the state to campaign against the entire document. Some suffragists returned the favor by labeling the state antislavery society "a 'nigger party,' 'checkerboard party,' and 'amalgamationist' . . . raising the specter of race mixing."[24]

Abolitionist opposition proved ineffective, with almost 14,000 voters approving the People's Constitution, including nearly 5,000 freeholders. Some conservatives grumbled about fraud, but it was a model election, conducted with written or printed ballots identifying each voter and his status as an American citizen, state resident, and freeholder or non-freeholder. Supporters of the existing government boycotted the election, and only fifty-nine votes were cast in the negative. The coalition endorsing the People's Constitution cut across classes but was clearly anchored in the middling classes. A sharp sectional contrast appeared in the voting: in northern towns gaining in population, 63 percent of freeholders favored the constitution, in static towns 44 percent, and in declining (mostly southern) towns a mere 29 percent supported the new constitution.[25]

Seemingly triumphant, the reformers undercut their own momentum. The People's Constitution decreed that the charter government should exercise power until May 1842, when their successors under the new constitution would be elected. Thus, as Patrick Conley has observed, the reformers "gave the Charterites nearly four months to devise an official counteroffensive to prevent the People's Constitution from taking effect. Seldom have revolutionaries been so obliging."[26] The Charterites pursued a strategy of concession, intimidation, and repression, chipping away at the moderate middle of the reform coalition.

In February 1842 the freeholders reconvened and offered a revised constitution with a compromise on the suffrage, opening it to native-born citizens while keeping the property test for naturalized citizens and lengthening the state residency requirement. The concession to native citizens opened the door for the Charterites to launch an extreme nativist, anti-Catholic campaign against the People's Constitution. Other changes were modest, and overall the document offended reformers. Joined by many Democrats, reformers campaigned vigorously to defeat the "Freeholders' Constitution," while the Charterites launched a ferocious counterattack.[27] Now the ideological warfare over the meaning of the American Revolution and the people's sovereignty intensified.

Charterites, including prominent former Democrats, rejected the suffragists' "radical" theory of popular sovereignty, as well as provisions in the People's Constitution reflecting "locofoco"—that is, radical Democratic, anticorporation populism. Their concern for maintaining the predominance of agricultural-landowning influence was evident, as was their abhorrence of Irish Catholic voters coming into the polity. But amid the escalating war of words the issue at bottom remained "the never-articulated urge for political self-preservation."[28]

One of the starkest contrasts between the rival constitutions arose from the people's document embracing fully the people's sovereignty and "their inalienable right . . . to ordain and institute government, and . . . to alter, reform, or totally change the same, whenever their safety or happiness requires." The freemen's constitution spoke only of the citizens' right, "in a peaceable manner, to assemble for their common good, and to apply to those invested with the powers of government for redress of grievances, or other purposes, by petition, address, or remonstrance."[29]

Earlier, in January, federal district judge John Pitman had sent an address to the legislature urging that the extralegal "revolutionary movement" of the suffragists be suppressed. In March the three judges of the state supreme court issued a public letter declaring the People's Constitution illegal; attempts to carry it into effect, they warned, would be treason against the state and the United States. Lawyers for the People's Constitution answered with a pamphlet asserting the sovereign right of the people to form a constitution, but the threat of prosecution for treason, repeated in other forums by Chief Justice Job Durfee, would take its toll.[30]

So, too, would the Charterites' mobilization of antiforeign and anti-Catholic sentiment, led by Henry Bowen Anthony, editor of the Whig *Providence Journal*. Broadsides, pamphlets, and speeches pounded away at the threat of ignorant Irish Catholic voters under the sinister sway of priests and bishops. "Men were called upon not to vote for a Constitution but to vote against Irishmen. To support the laws, prevent a civil war, and vote down the Irishmen was the war cry of our opponents," said a Tiverton suffragist. In Providence Judge Durfee, in a speech at the town hall, ranted against "the Irish, the Irish, is to him and his party the raw-head and bloody bones *after all*. They won't vote the right way, to suit their Wig [*sic*] or Federal view, hence down with the Irish."[31]

Despite such Charterite tactics, the Freeholders' Constitution lost by a vote of 8,689 to 8,013. Yet the freeholders' compromises had attracted many moderates who would settle for partial reform and an end to controversy, indicating the fluidity of opinion among many hundreds of voters occupying the moderate center. Thomas Dorr recognized this in May in his "inaugural" speech, when he said that many who voted for the People's Constitution just shortly before in December had voted for the Freeholders' Constitution in March as a way of getting part of their rights "and of terminating all controversies."[32]

But the defeat of the Freeholders' Constitution spurred the state government to repression of suffragists. In April the assembly decreed harsh penalties for those voting in elections to implement the People's Constitution and declared anyone who assumed office under it as guilty of treason against the state and subject to life imprisonment. Reformers labeled this act the "Algerine Law" (and the Charterites henceforth as "Algerines"), after the despotic Dey of Algiers. The Charterites also went forward with the regularly scheduled April election.

The Algerine Law had a chilling effect on the suffragists' ability to recruit candidates for state office. So, too, did President John Tyler's assurance to the Charterites that the federal government would assist the existing state government against any future insurrection and would recognize no constitutional change except that effected "by legal and peaceable proceedings" pursued by state authorities. After several potential gubernatorial nominees withdrew, Dorr, assigned the task of enlisting candidates, offered himself as the People's candidate shortly before the People's election. On April 18, during a fierce storm, Dorr (unopposed) received about 6,400 votes for governor, and two days later the incumbent Whig governor, Samuel Ward King, received 4,864 votes to 2,211 for Democrat Thomas F. Carpenter, a moderate suffragist.[33] Soon after, the state government took additional steps to thwart the People's movement, stiffening the riot act, authorizing special police companies, and creating a "war council" to advise the governor on emergency measures. President Tyler added to the intimidation by reinforcing the federal garrison at Newport. In the wake of conflicting elections and declining support for radical measures, several suffragists defected.

Still supported by many moderates, suffrage militants pressed on. On May 3 Dorr's government assembled for an inauguration in Providence, with a parade led by a brass band, armed military companies, and troops of artisans and tradesmen. Unfortunately, the People's legislators marched past the locked statehouse and assembled instead in an unfinished foundry building. Under a symbolically leaky roof, the "Foundry Legislature," sixty-six of eighty representatives and nine of twelve senators, repealed the Algerine Law and created new election and militia laws. Dorr failed to convince them to take possession of the empty statehouse—the Charter legislature was about to meet at Newport on May 4—and this timidity led to what his friend Dan King later called "a fatal mistake, which no subsequent measures could remedy." A pro-Dorr historian commented acidly: "Men who dared to face a life sentence in the State prison dared not . . . force a lock or break a pane of window glass in the State House."[34] This lack of resolve marked the beginning of the end of the People's Constitution movement as a broad-based popular enterprise.

People's legislators included not only professionals and artisans from Providence but also farmers, lawyers, and entrepreneurs across the state, some of whom were pillars of their communities. Some remained obscure, but local leadership rested squarely in the middle ranks of society.[35] That suffragist middle steadily dwindled after the People's legislature's brief existence for two days in the leaky foundry, eroded by repression and apprehension.

The Charterite legislature declared that an insurrection existed and selectively began arresting members of the People's government, serving warrants for treason on prominent Dorrites and then releasing them on $5,000 bail. Dorr reluctantly joined a delegation to Washington to lobby President

Tyler, while sympathizers in the U.S. Senate tried unsuccessfully to pass a resolution admonishing Tyler not to intervene on the side of the Charterites. Returning by way of New York, Dorr paused to be lionized by Tammany Democrats who urged him to persist and promised military aid if needed. The Tammany exhortations and bravado may have persuaded Dorr to embark on a much more dangerous course of action on his return to Rhode Island, but the Democrats' posturing turned into "empty promises." On May 16, 1,200 admirers welcomed Dorr back to Providence. Tired and dusty, he gave a stirring speech professing his willingness to die defending the People's government, though he spoke of using military action primarily in defensive terms.[36]

A day later sixty armed Dorrites raided a Providence armory and seized two Revolutionary War–era cannon. Over the objections of moderate allies, Dorr decided to try to seize the state's arsenal. After midnight on May 17, he and a force of 234 men stood in an open field in fog and darkness before the arsenal. A well-protected and heavily armed contingent of 200 (including Dorr's father and younger brother) waited inside. By the time Dorr's antiquated cannon failed to fire (fortunately for his company), most of his men had vanished. Dorr fled the city and eventually the state. Meanwhile, the entire Providence delegation to the People's legislature had resigned and called Dorr's action "deplorable." This fiasco Conley has called "the death knell of the Dorrite cause."[37]

The "fear of prisons" waxed strong in Providence and the southern towns, yet northern suffragists continued to rally and to claim that new militia companies were being organized to support the People's governor. Dorr then announced his intention to return and reconvene the People's legislature in the northwestern town of Chepachet on July 4.[38] Dorr, who was receiving conflicting advice from his friends, repeated his intention to defend the legislature by force if necessary, but the erosion of moderate support had rendered the cause hopeless.

During June the Charterite or "Law and Order" legislature made some timely concessions by calling for a new constitutional convention in September, allowing all male citizens of three years' residence to vote for delegates, and making a slight improvement in apportionment ratios. This appeased the growing bloc of moderate and "no force" suffragists who now wanted an end to civil disorder. Conservative Elisha Potter wrote to President Tyler that the suffrage party "have come to their senses & with few exceptions are quite moderate." Meanwhile, Charterite propagandists spread rumors that the Dorrites intended to sack Providence, an excuse for Governor Samuel King to assemble a large force of militia from the trusty southern and western counties.[39]

Against the advice of moderates, on June 25 Dorr came to Chepachet at 2:00 A.M., having been told that large numbers of suffragists were gathering there to uphold a meeting of the People's legislature. But of the several hundred persons milling around Chepachet that weekend, most were sightseers and the curious from the countryside. By Monday, June 27, Dorr realized that no more than 225 stalwarts, mostly artisans and farmers, were on hand to defend their camp on Acote's Hill, and none of the members of the People's legislature. He ordered supporters to disband and sought refuge in New Hampshire. Charterite commanders, learning of Dorr's departure en route, still advanced a force of some 3,500 to Chepachet and "stormed" an undefended hill. Then, they terrorized and looted neighboring villages, indiscriminately rounding up and brutally mistreating suspected Dorrites.[40]

Many Charterites now saw little need to compromise on constitutional issues. Even before "having twice put Dorr down," reactionaries in the Charterite camp had never reconciled themselves to "any considerable change" in the suffrage. Law and Order authorities and militia continued to persecute suffragists into the fall. Repression—the "reign of terror," suffragists called it—had been ongoing since at least May, when Algerine employers dismissed workers and landlords turned out tenants suspected of supporting the People's movement. Even moderate Democrat Thomas Carpenter, who would be the opposition candidate for governor the next year, was arrested and briefly imprisoned. Punishment fell even on women who had written, spoken, or participated in lawful political activity. Arrests and forfeiture of bail bonds continued, while some Dorrites attributed new taxes on their property to political reprisals.[41]

The state government held a ratification election in November on the new Law and Order constitution, and widespread disgust with the repression led to a thorough boycott by opponents and approval by a vote of 7,024 to 51. The state government rewarded African Americans for service as firemen and guards of prisoners while loyal militia were away during the spring by allowing them to vote in this election, but the constitution itself mandated a special referendum at the next election on removing "white" as a suffrage qualification, as had the People's Constitution that had provoked the opposition of abolitionists. (In 1843 blacks gained the vote permanently by a margin of 4,031 to 1,798.) Most suffragists refused to dignify what many called "this bastard constitution" even with a vote against it. The new document combined a tone insulting to suffragists, a one-year residency requirement for freeholders, a two-year residency requirement for the native-born without real estate but owning $134 worth of personal property, and a temptation for tampering with elections by creation of a class known as "registry voters," native-born residents without property who could vote in general elections by paying a $1 poll tax (or by one day's militia service per year). Naturalized citizens still needed to clear the hurdle of the real estate qualification of $134. The legislative apportionment ratio gave growing towns increased representation in the House but capped large towns' representation there and cost Providence two seats, and in the state senate each small town was given one seat, ensuring rural Rhode Island a veto.[42]

The suffragist movement now merged into the Democratic opposition, carrying former Whig equal rights advocates and workingmen with it and focused on contesting the next state election under the new rules in April 1843. Thomas Carpenter ran as the "Democratic–Equal Rights" candidate for governor, while former Jacksonian governor James Fenner headed the "Law and Order–Whig Prox," a five-man slate for state officers consisting of three Whigs and two Democrats. After a heated campaign, Fenner won by a vote of 9,107 to 7,392. Reflecting the changes engendered by the conflict, northern industrial towns once strongly Whig now voted Democratic–Equal Rights, while Fenner easily carried previously Democratic towns in the less-populated south. Both of the new parties and their voting rank and file consisted of cross-class coalitions. Though most farmers and landlords were probably Charterites, many freeholders had supported the early People's movement. Five thousand had voted for the People's Constitution, and, said Dorr, those "sons of the soil . . . the mechanics and workingmen" who rallied to him at Chepachet included a majority who "were already partakers of the landed suffrage."[43]

Men of property and status led both major parties throughout this period, and leaders of the People's Constitution movement included young professionals and, like Dorr, descendants of "families of the first settlers." Although even some factory owners were Dorrites, the wealthy elite tilted heavily to Law and Order. Many large manufacturers opposed the People's Constitution, including former Anti-Masons such as the Spragues of Cranston and Warwick and the industrialist Wilkinsons of Pawtucket. "Dorrism" had replaced Masonry as a threat to the morals of their workforce.[44] Former Anti-Masons, however, also could be found in the reform movement, and artisans and working men in Providence's Sixth Ward and Pawtucket village supported both Anti-Masonry and suffragism. A conservative Democratic critic of "Dorrism" asserted a connection between it, Anti-Masonry, temperance, and abolition.[45] "Class warfare" existed during Rhode Island's constitutional crisis primarily in the degree of unity manifested by the upper classes.

Aside from the advantages of wealth and influence that the Law and Order–Whig party brought to the election of 1843, it had written rules of the game into the new constitution favoring its electoral success. By enfranchising African Americans, a population of 3,240 statewide with perhaps 200 potential voters in Providence, the Law and Order party added a reliable voting bloc to its constituency. Abolitionist William Goodell scorned the hypocrisy of Law and Order men who earlier had "hooted at" the reformers for wanting "the low Irish and niggers" to vote, but now "the city aristocracy were willing to have the help of the colored people, the most of whom were their dependents, their laborers, their coachmen and their domestics." Charterite Elisha Potter agreed that the blacks posed no threat as they were "conservative and go with the wealthy part of the community." Whig politicians thereafter attended to getting blacks to the polls, providing dollars as needed for the poll tax for any "registry voters."[46]

The new constitution also reshaped the militia to provide a Law and Order political base by abolishing compulsory militia duty (a reform!) and shifting state support to independent, chartered companies that had been mostly loyalist. Although Dorr believed the state-sponsored militia to be "charter men," and loyalist militia during the crisis had made a show of force in several factory villages to discourage "Dorr demonstrations," some companies in Providence and elsewhere were viewed by conservatives as "half and half" and unreliable. With state support, loyalty to Law and Order could be enhanced. African Americans also received support for a militia company, further provoking antiblack sentiment that already existed among some reformers. The partisan and negative reference group dynamics of Rhode Island now more closely resembled those found in other states. The Law and Order–Whig coalition extended paternalist benevolence to African Americans while appealing to nativist animosity against "foreign voters" and Irish Catholics; the Democrats tended to attract the support of working-class and immigrant whites who were profoundly resentful of blacks and their wealthy patrons.[47]

The greatest advantages that the Law and Order–Whig party enjoyed, however, derived from money and influence. Both Whigs and Democrats routinely had used money and coercion of dependents, but intimidation and bribery crested in 1843. Law and Order leaders Elisha R. Potter and John B. Francis (both former Democrats) knew that spending money was a necessary ingredient of campaign "exertions": for treating voters, paying campaign workers, and bribery. In 1837 a friend urged Potter to spend liberally in his own town because Whigs were boasting that there were "about 60 Surinames [sic] who can be bought with money and they will buy them. The term surinames is well understood among nautical men and it means those who will be bought and sold for a price." In 1842 Potter was cautious about spending, but wrote to Francis that "you know the people in the back parts of the country cannot be got to town meeting without exertion and expense." The following year a Potter agent in Westerly requested "a little of the ready [which] would be useful if properly applied. . . . A small sum would be better than a large . . . as there [are] but a few men who can be affected within the bounds of reason. . . . I could give a good account of $25 to $30."[48]

In 1843 the new category of "registry voters" made money even more important. Law and Order–Whigs charged that the Reform-Democratic coalition also used bribery and coercion.[49] But Law and Order landowners and manufacturers possessed more influence over workingmen and tenants, as well as more of "the ready." People's men reported extensive dismissals of workers to undercut their residential qualification for voting, and in January 1843 Providence Democrats charged that while individual manufacturers in the past often controlled the voting of their workmen, "never until now, has there been a general plan concerted and adopted to control an election." Law and Order merchants and lawyers for two weeks before the election systematically brought pressure to bear on debtors and small businessmen who were potential Equal Rights voters and on election day intimidated many artisans and workers. A Law and Order Providence businessman, Hiram Hill, recorded his approval of these tactics in his diary: "Those persons who employ many hands are determined to discharge such as will not agree to support the laws and constitution as now adopted; proscription will be the cry but let it come."[50]

Thus, Rhode Island's political establishment—despite some minor defections of elite and upper middling men and women—turned aside the People's movement for reform, though it grudgingly made concessions by some broadening of the suffrage and lessening of second-class status for native non-freeholders. The long-term result would be the perpetuation of a limited, oligarchic republicanism lasting well into the twentieth century.[51]

The short-term legacy of the defeat of populist constitutionalism carried more mixed results. In October 1843 Dorr returned to Rhode Island to allow himself to be arrested and was tried for treason in April 1844 before Chief

Justice Job Durfee, a vengeful opponent. Durfee ruled all of Dorr's defenses unacceptable and refused to consider the meaning of popular sovereignty. But his harsh sentencing of Dorr to life imprisonment in separate confinement backfired and even alienated some Whigs. In 1845 a "liberation campaign" calling for Dorr's pardon won a narrow victory in the state election, and Dorr was freed in June. In 1851 a Democratic–Free Soil coalition handed the Whigs another defeat, and the new legislature restored Dorr to full citizenship; in 1854 the legislature annulled the court's judgment in Dorr's treason trial. He died later that year at age forty-nine, his health long since broken by the twenty months he had spent in prison.[52]

While Dorr won eventual and complete personal vindication, in the immediate aftermath of the People's movement a climate hostile to all reform held sway. As with very different insurgencies reaching back to the Regulators of the 1780s, reactionaries exaggerated the threat. An extraconstitutional movement designed to expand democracy became an attempt to "destroy our lives and establish an agrarian despotism." The carryover of a repressive climate became evident in 1844, when conservatives charged that the ten-hour movement, agitation for a shorter work day, was "treasonable." A lecturer for the ten-hour day who visited several towns was warned in Providence that "the movement would be considered by some a 'second edition of Dorrism.' Can't help it said I; let them consider it what they will, we consider it a *moral* movement." The following day, however, he decided to postpone his "address" because the "movement of the *working men*, has been called . . . *an insurrection, Treason* and the like—which startling discovery has produced not a little excitement in this waspish city."[53]

The constitutional crisis, along with other circumstances, undermined as well the state's emerging antislavery movement. Although not a popular movement, the Rhode Island Antislavery Society had been thriving in the mid-1830s, establishing local societies and adding converts, especially in mill villages. The economic downturn of the late 1830s dried up antislavery's financial support, and the controversy regarding women's public activism in the cause hit hard in Rhode Island as it coincided with a sex scandal involving an antislavery preacher. This episode, together with the People's movement of 1841–42, resulted in the disappearance of male leadership from the cause. Thereafter, antislavery efforts were kept alive by women who became virtual caretakers of a network much reduced in significance.[54]

Even more women, however, intensely involved themselves in the conflict between suffragists and Charterites. Few Rhode Islanders seemed to be neutral in the state's most compelling and divisive episode since the American Revolution. Towns, churches, neighborhoods, and families took different sides and also divided internally over the competing constitutions.[55] Passions ran high on both sides, engulfing women, children, servants, and other dependents, but suffragist women followed in the footsteps of radical abolitionist women not only by engaging in traditional forms of benevolence to aid the suffrage cause but also by taking direct political action—short of voting. Invoking, as did suffrage men, the patriotic fervor of the American Revolution, suffrage women brought passionate support of Thomas Dorr and a radical militancy to "the People's" cause.[56]

Charterite women expressed themselves within the private sphere, or in the traditional modes of cheering and waving handkerchiefs and throwing flowers from windows as returning loyalist militia marched through the streets. But soon after the "Algerine" government began arresting reformers, suffragist women began organizing societies, raising money for legal fees, and bringing provisions to those in prison. In joining the ranks of Dorrite men by acting as couriers, transporting letters to Dorr and other exiled leaders, they did not regard themselves, as one Charterite woman regarded herself, as "poor helpless women . . . penned up at home." Most conspicuously, suffrage women took the lead in organizing several clambakes through the summer and fall of 1842, to raise reformers' spirits as well as funds. The largest of these, on September 28, drew an estimated five to eight thousand Dorrites from Rhode Island and Massachusetts to Acote's Hill. As suffragists threw their energies into preparations for the 1843 spring election, these women activists also raised money to pay the "registry fee" for landless native voters. In Pawtucket in March the Friends of Free Suffrage called a meeting for "both male and female" supporters.[57]

Dorrite women also stepped forward to speak at suffragist gatherings, at first it seems on an impromptu basis. Ann Parlin, the wife of a Providence doctor who had been imprisoned in June, told Dorr that "on impulse" she "gave a brief speech at the mass clambake" in August. Catherine R. Williams, a well-published writer and confidante of Dorr's, was "literally forced to the stump" at an October bake because she had recently visited "our exiled Governor; you might have heard a leaf move in the forest, so profound was the attention given."[58]

With attention shifted to electoral politics, women's activity receded. The Law and Order–Whig party also began to attack activist women and refer to them as Dorr's "masculine followers." Worse, according to Catherine Williams, the "Algerines have torn Mrs. Parlin's character in fragments, and several others so they boast." Parlin had gone to New York City to drum up support for her Rhode Island comrades, continuing to speak in public (no longer "on impulse") and fraternizing with male politicians, so much so that even suffrage men worried about her becoming "notorious."[59] Thus, conservatives accused suffragist women of sexual impropriety, as antiabolitionists had attacked abolitionist women in the same vein, and sought to repress women who asserted their rights as citizens by entering the public sphere and seeking to influence public opinion.[60]

But suffragist women's political activity continued at least into the 1845 "liberation" campaign that secured the state government and Dorr's release from prison. Further, Parlin may have unsettled even suffrage men because of her fiery advocacy of a military fight against the Charterites; it was a fight, however, that the suffrage male followers of Dorr had been unable to consummate. Parlin spoke of women taking steps that would "necessarily move the men to action," and she spoke directly of "one half of our valiant [suffrage] men, in peace are cowards in war, had they shown as much courage last spring and summer as they did at the roasting of the ox, they would not have been imprisoned." Dorr himself, who knew well the failure of nerve at the statehouse, at the arsenal, and at Chepachet, never put it quite so bluntly. Suffrage men, further, had endured Charterite taunts directed against their manhood, so hearing it from a woman in their own ranks must have been doubly uncomfortable.[61]

The goals for which suffrage men and women struggled extended well beyond obtaining the vote for disenfranchised adult males. While votes for women had nothing to do with the movement, perhaps the months and years of constitutional debate over the meaning of the people's sovereignty as well as "the people" helped to get women thinking about acquiring the vote for themselves.[62]

## NEW YORK'S ANTI-RENT WARS

The rhetoric of democracy employed by major and minor parties, as well as reform movements, helped inspire the People's Constitution movement in Rhode Island. That rhetoric played as large a role in stimulating the hopes of thousands of tenant farmers in eastern New York caught up in the Anti-Rent movement in the 1840s. Whereas an excess of power exercised by the Charter legislature shaped events in Rhode Island, the civil unrest in New York was influenced by an ongoing shrinkage of legislative capacity. This indirect source of discontent arose from a developing incongruity in the political culture.

From the 1820s on, as participation and democratization expanded, the responsibilities of governments at the federal and state levels diminished. Governments experienced "slipping authority," according to Wiebe. The federal government became highly decentralized, reflecting in part the decentralization of party organizations. More pertinent, state legislative authority was contracted, especially as Jacksonian Democrats insisted on limiting state power to regulate economic or social activity. President Jackson's destruction of the Second Bank of the United States symbolized the party's determination to minimize any centralizing authority. Though the Whigs and later Republicans wished to use the state to promote economic and moral development, government power, especially over political economy, began to recede. Although governments continued to promote the general welfare, "increasingly less and less direct supervisory activity was deemed appropriate."[63] Legislators in states across the country, as well as state supreme court judges, removed a wide range of substantive matters of political economy from the political agenda and from contestation in the electoral and representative arenas, the major result of which was to protect vested property rights and to privilege individual or private use over public or communal use. This circumstance profoundly affected the context of the episode known as the Anti-Rent Wars of New York in the 1840s.

So, too, did the republican ideal of the independent, yeoman freeholder, whose capacity as a citizen rested on the foundation of landownership. But in the Mohawk-Hudson region of eastern New York, what John M. Murrin and Rowland Berthoff have termed the "feudal revival" in the eighteenth century had created huge manorial estates where thousands of tenant farmers paid rents, services, and goods to landlords for several "lives" or in perpetuity. Moreover, "the [feudal] revival ripped relationships out of their original social context and seized what surviving obligations could be enforced for the income they might produce. And in fact, exploitation of legal privilege became the greatest source of personal wealth in the colonies in the generation before Independence."[64]

The original Dutch settlers on the manor estates had acquiesced in the leasehold system, but the migrant Yankees who came later into the region grew increasingly restive. A situation long fraught with contradictions and tension erupted in 1839 when tenants on the huge 726,000-acre Manor of Rensselaerwyck began a rent strike that spread to eleven counties over the next six years, engulfing 1.8 million acres and involving a farming population of perhaps 260,000 in the "most spectacular tenant rebellion in United States history." By 1844–45 as many as 50,000–60,000 tenants supported the Anti-Rent cause, some 25,000 had signed Anti-Rent petitions, and in the later stages of the movement thousands voted for Anti-Rent Party candidates. As a populist insurgency, Anti-Rent climaxed in 1844–46, but legal battles, pockets of resistance, and sporadic defiance of the law would continue until after the Civil War. Of primary interest here, however, is Anti-Rent's populist career in the 1840s and its inability to realize its goals, despite enjoying on balance favorable standing in public opinion as well as the rhetorical embrace of Whig and Democratic politicians.[65]

During the colonial era, landlords used political connections to acquire huge tracts of land, some of which they enlarged illegally by redrawing the boundaries. They originally encouraged settlement by offering tenants liberal terms and by building mills, schools, taverns, and other infrastructure. Most tenants held perpetual leases; a smaller number held leases in "lives," or occupancy for as long as one, two, or three persons named in the lease survived. Water, mill sites, and other resources were "reserved" for the landlord, who could lay out roads, build mills, and flood crop land on a tenant's premises without compensation. On the Rensselaer "Manor" freeholders paid the landlord a yearly rent of ten to fourteen bushels of wheat per hundred acres, plus "feudal dues" of "four fat fowl" and a day's work with horses or oxen. Most manors' leases also provided that if tenants sold their interest, landlords must be paid from one-tenth to one-third of the sale price—often the cut was one-fourth, as on Rensselaerwyck, and known as "quarter-sales." These conditions discouraged many tenants from making improvements, especially in hill towns with poorer soils. If tenants failed to meet their obligations, landlords had the right to "reenter" and take not only the land but also any improvements—houses, barns, fences, or crops—on the land. Charles McCurdy describes the system as "a *rentier* dream. The tenants absorbed all maintenance costs and paid any taxes; the quarter-sale . . . tended to forestall turnover and provided landlords with a bounty when conveyances did occur." The landlords needed to do nothing more than to receive from their lawyers "a fat check every year."[66]

During the 1820s and 1830s as the agricultural economy changed, the debts of both tenants and landlords mounted, and relations between them deteriorated. Conflicts over common lands, reserved rights, rent payments, and quarter-sales increased, with individual tenants becoming less cooperative and landlords less benevolent. At the same time, with a broadened suffrage and a burgeoning egalitarian political climate, the contrast deepened between the tenants' growing sense of economic insecurity and their enhanced feelings of political efficacy. Although the landlords' direct role in local and state political affairs declined, they retained political power behind the scenes, notably with the dominant Van Buren–Jacksonian party, though prominent Whigs also were lawyers and allies of landlords.[67]

The opening chapter of Anti-Rentism began in early 1839 on the death of Stephen Van Rensselaer III, "the last of the patroons," whose leniency with his tenants had resulted in a debt estimated at $400,000. His heirs, Stephen IV and William P. Van Rensselaer, turned the debts into mortgages, and Stephen IV, who now owned the manor land west of the Hudson, began to press his tenants for payments of back rents. Resentful and excited tenants held meetings and appointed committees, especially in the western townships of the Helderberg hills (in Albany County). In May a committee of twenty-five men from the hill towns, all "prosperous, influential working farmers," called on Van Rensselaer at the manor office. What followed illustrated both the economic and social dominance of the landlords and the bridling of the tenants at the traditional relationship.[68]

On arriving at the office, Van Rensselaer refused to speak with the tenant committee, walking stonily through where they stood waiting into an inner office without greeting them. His agent emerged to tell the committee that he would not meet with them and that he required them to submit their grievances in writing. Retiring to a nearby tavern, the committee prepared a written petition asking for new leases that included the landlord's converting feudal dues such as "four fat fowl" into cash, giving up "reservations" and quarter-sale rights, and allowing tenants to buy out their farms by effectively converting their value into mortgages (as the Van Rensselaers had done with their debts). A week later the landlord rejected all their demands and refused any negotiation until all back rents were paid. While he did agree to grant new leases that put all obligations on a cash basis, he insisted on higher rates than the tenants had proposed.[69]

The lord of the manor still would not greet or meet his subordinates, but whereas previously landlords had always dealt with tenants individually, now a nascent tenant organization was attempting to negotiate terms for all tenants. The following July 4 Helderberg-area tenants held a mass rally at the town of Berne and not only rejected the landlord's terms as an "outrage upon the laws of humanity" but also challenged his title and called him the "pretended proprietor." Further stalemate brought landlord suits for back rents and writs of ejectment. However, during the next months when sheriffs attempted to serve papers, they were met in the hill towns by hundreds of angry farmers who blocked roads and threatened the lawmen. In December an assemblage of over 1,500 farmers forced officers to leave the hills. Tenant networks posted sentries, who mobilized crowds on foot and horseback by blowing horns. The protesters issued threats, but "the tenants' entire strategy," reminiscent of long-standing Regulator traditions, "depended on their ability to intimidate their enemies without a fight."[70]

Governor William H. Seward, a Whig sympathetic to the tenants' situation, reluctantly responded to local officials' requests for help and called out militia to disperse the crowds and enable papers to be served. For the moment Van Rensselaer had won the "war," but it was really the first battle in what would be a protracted conflict. In September an Albany County tenant had written to the sheriff that Van Rensselaer's tenants had previously prayed "to their landlord like children to a parent," but no more; "the tenants have organized themselves into a body, and resolved not to pay any more rents until they can be redressed of their grievances." During early 1840 tenants petitioned the legislature and governor, and Anti-Rent sentiment began spreading from Rensselaerwyck into other manors and counties. Moreover, at Seward's urging, the Whig legislative majority began to look into "the manor difficulties," over vigorous protest from Democratic legislators, whose leaders retained strong political and business ties to most of the landlords.[71]

Whig legislators echoed Seward's criticism of the leasehold system, seeing it as an impediment to commercial progress by blocking the improvement and buying and selling of land. A Whig committee actually invoked the state's power of eminent domain as a theoretical solution, but while showing little respect for the paternalist relation of landlord and tenant, it also insisted that property rights (that is, the landlords') were inviolable. Whigs delivered, in short, radical rhetoric and no help for tenants. This pattern, a "politics of evasion," would prevail for several years.[72]

In the Helderbergs Van Rensselaer and his tenants remained at odds, and in April 1841 a mass meeting of tenants at Berne resolved on a "ten year contest with the Patroon of the colony of Rensselaerwyck, or until a redress of grievances is obtained." By now bands of tenant young men had donned disguises, wearing masks of calico or painted sheepskin, or posing as Indians, to intimidate law officers and landlord agents. Some painted their faces black or red, and many wore "loose pantaloons and tunics of brilliant calico, decked with fur, feathers, and tin ornaments." The "Indians" carried weapons as varied as their costumes, including muskets, pistols, spears, hatchets, axes, knives, scythes, and dirks, and some "chiefs" wore long dresses like a woman's nightgown. These bands worked closely with Anti-Rent associations and would rally when lookouts blew rams-horns to warn of approaching adversaries. Their mission, in the words of Anti-Rent leader and "Chief Big Thunder" Dr. Smith Boughton, was to provide beleaguered tenant farmers "the same kind of protection resorted to by the people of Boston" when the tea was thrown into the water of the bay.[73]

These "Indians" especially focused on disrupting distress (or repossession) sales, at which tenants could lose most of their personal property, but in 1842 the legislature passed a law, signed by Whig governor and former Anti-Mason William Seward, that extended property exemptions and ended most such sales. During the rest of the year and into 1843, landlords and sheriffs relaxed the pressure on tenants, and Indian activity quieted. Meanwhile, Anti-Rent sentiment and organization were spreading throughout eastern New York, from the west side to the east side of the Hudson River, along with a new strategy for undermining the leasehold system.[74]

Thus far, common law had prevented any challenges to landlord titles, but enterprising Anti-Rent lawyers discovered evidence that in their view proved Van Rensselaer's titles to be faulty, a conclusion that had immediately appealed to long-standing popular beliefs (grounded in considerable truth). The Anti-Rent movement now began an unfortunate focus on legislation that would require landlords to prove the validity of their claims (and in case they did, the law further provided a process to turn the lease into the equivalent of a mortgage). This shift was unfortunate because during 1843 decisions by the U.S. Supreme Court and the New York Supreme Court, in cases having nothing to do with the leaseholds, would undermine the already shaky basis of the proposed legislation.[75]

Specifically, the national court ruled that the state legislature could not in effect retroactively impair an original contract, saying this violated the contracts clause of the U.S. Constitution, and the state supreme court undercut the principle of eminent domain by ruling that the legislature could not take one person's property and give it to another. These decisions, however, did not diminish Anti-Renters' focus on state legislation aimed at overturning titles. Nor did they halt the momentum of Anti-Rentism or the efforts of Whig legislators to use Anti-Rent discontent to their party's advantage.[76]

During 1844 Anti-Rent took off as a populist movement, ultimately engaging tens of thousands of tenant farming families, including men, women, and children. As it spread throughout the Hudson-Mohawk hills and valleys, its adherents identified themselves as Anti-Renters or as "Down

Rent." Anti-Rent petitions with 25,000 signatures greeted the legislature, but lawmakers fanned the flames of tenant unrest with two reports containing opposing rhetoric. One spoke harshly of the leasehold system but offered no remedy, while a second criticized Governor Seward and asserted that "the degradations and hardships" complained of by tenants "exist but in the imagination." One affirmed the justice of the tenants' cause; the other (drawn up in a landlord's office, charged the Down Renters) goaded the tenant movement to further exertions. Anti-Rent associations also reacted to the Freeholders Committee of Safety, a landlord lobbying organization that financed the printing of 1,000 copies of the hostile report, and to landlords' renewing attempts to collect rent. The New York Supreme Court again gored the tenants by holding that the Exemption Act of 1842 could not apply to contracts made before its passage.[77]

In May Anti-Renters sent agents to other manors to form associations in Delaware, Columbia, Schoharie, and other counties, eleven in all. As the movement began to imitate the organizational methods of political parties, tenant farmers joined Anti-Rentism by the "tens of thousands"; by summer bands of Indians roamed the countryside, while Down Rent orators stumped through eastern New York. Democratic and Whig politicians and editors began competing for tenant votes, and "Anti-Rent was suddenly a big regional movement." Rent boycotts were resumed, and independent conventions nominated Anti-Rent or Whig/Anti-Rent candidates for state assembly. Though garnering mixed results, political action would grow, and some observers now referred to the Mohawk-Hudson region as "the infected district."[78]

Coercive resistance to rents and paper-serving by lawmen continued into December. Besides Indian activity and the tar and feathering of deputies, the disturbances led to one accidental death and the deliberate shooting of a tenant who was doing business with a landlord. Opponents seized on the deaths to generate negative publicity and more purposeful official activity to suppress the Indians. More important, among Anti-Renters divisions arose over the Indians' hard-line tactics, with moderate Anti-Renters joining critics in calling for an end to violence. Yet in January 1845 eleven counties sent delegates to the Anti-Rent convention in Berne, the original center of Anti-Rent in the Helderbergs.[79]

By the spring of 1845 Anti-Rent was a "commanding force on New York's manors and patents," with associations organized throughout the eleven counties, Indian auxiliaries active in several of those, and increasing political influence wielded through Anti-Rent/Equal Rights or Whig/Anti-Rent candidates or elected officials. In April the *Albany Freeholder* began publication, and during the next fourteen months three other newspapers joined it in spreading the Anti-Rent message throughout the leasehold district. In July, as in previous years since 1840, enormous Independence Day parades and rallies assembled as many as 5,000 persons.[80]

Yet despite the continuing enthusiasm of the Anti-Rent faithful, schisms deepened in the ranks. Indian activity already created a latent division between moderates and militants, and from 1844 radical reformers from outside the district associated with the National Reform Association had embraced the tenants' cause. National Reform was an outgrowth of New York City's radical artisan republicanism and was promoted by George Henry Evans, who published the *New York Working Man's Advocate*. During 1845 both the *Freeholder* and *Young America*, National Reform's journal, called for government regulation of "land monopoly," proposals that would soon energize the Free Soil Party and prefigure the National Homestead Act. Although the radicals' proposals of limited acquisition and free homesteads applied to unsettled public lands in the West, Anti-Rent factions now found themselves debating and rebutting charges of "agrarianism." Further, Evans and his allies in the leasehold district attacked the title test bill, the talisman of Whig/Anti-Rent politicians, as unconstitutional.[81]

The August 7 deliberate shooting of a deputy sheriff in Delaware County brought a wave of unfavorable public opinion and further turmoil among Anti-Renters. State oppression of the Indians now "outstripped anything that had preceded it." Governor Silas Wright, a Democrat, declared Delaware and two other counties to be in a state of rebellion, and posses rampaged through the district, destroying crops and property. In Delaware County almost 250 persons were indicted for murder, robbery, or other crimes, breaking the Indians as a major force of Anti-Rent resistance.[82]

Nevertheless, the legislature that convened in January 1846 held great promise for passage of Anti-Rent remedies. Seven movement men had been elected to the assembly and senate, while "numerous" fellow travelers won election as Whigs or Democrats. Governor Wright, who recently had cracked down on the Indians, had seen his party in the previous autumn's elections battered in the leasehold district and concluded that his own reelection hinged on propitiating Anti-Renters. He called for abolition of landlords' right of distress and the taxation of rent, but his key proposal would allow tenants to buy the landlord's interest in their farms after the current proprietors died (known as "devise and descent"). While the distress and tax bills passed, the important devise and descent bill died what

McCurdy has called a "strange" death, with both conservative Whigs and Democrats pleased that it failed. The tax and distress bills were the least important part of the Anti-Rent agenda, and much of the Anti-Rent movement remained committed to attaining a title test law.[83]

That fixation, along with changing political circumstances, also led to missed opportunity in New York's 1846 constitutional convention. The convention grew out of a movement, based largely in the Democratic Party, to impose restrictions on the state's power to borrow and spend money and to give special privileges to favored corporations. Under the banner of making the state government more democratic and the legislature more responsive to "the People," the state's power to regulate diminished relative to the power of the market. Worse, the new constitution's articles dealing with leaseholds and describing them as unrepublican, echoed the empty platitudes expressed by Democrats and especially Whigs in the last few years, and changed nothing.[84]

During 1846, political party divisions in both national and state arenas resulted in a loss of leverage for the Anti-Rent pressure bloc. The Democratic Party's division over the extension of slavery at the outset of the Mexican War struck particularly hard in New York, and was compounded by clashes over economic policy and patronage between Van Buren strict constructionist Democrats (Barnburners) and conservative Democrats (Hunkers), who were willing in Whig fashion to use the state to promote economic enterprise and to incur public debt. The Democratic split, which would soon lead to defection to Free Soil on the part of a Barnburner minority, ended the competition between Whigs and Democrats for the Anti-Rent vote.[85]

Anti-Renters influenced, however, the Whigs' nomination for governor in 1846 of John Young, a seasoned entrepreneur of Anti-Rent politics; and while Whig conservatives were outraged, they had little to fear from Young. In any case, Anti-Rentism had expired as a broad-based populist movement and political force, though its afterlife extended for several more years, primarily through the work of lawyers and the dwindling number of legislators committed to the tenants' interests.

Young's victory in the gubernatorial election resulted from a heavy vote for him in the Anti-Rent counties and factional division among the Democrats.[86] Down Rent voters received their reward from Governor Young when in 1847 he issued an address pardoning Anti-Rent militants who had been jailed for their actions in disturbances in 1844 and 1845. Following the rhetorical footsteps of many Whig politicians before him, Young described the tenant movement sympathetically and called for an end to the leasehold system. By arrangement, Whig/Anti-Rent legislators then postponed consideration of landlord-tenant relations to the next year. The Whig remedy presented in 1848, and supported in the tenant districts, was a legislative resolution—not a statute—that instructed the state attorney general to inquire into the validity of lands held "under manorial titles"—the title test scheme in new and just as ineffective a form. Lone voices of dissent met with savage criticism even from the *Freeholder*. The futility of the new approach would be apparent years down the road, but in the meanwhile it moved the leasehold controversy from the legislature to the courts. Young and the Whigs, facing a divided Democracy and, for the moment, sure of Anti-Rent votes, declared the manor troubles to be at an end.[87]

Meanwhile, another state supreme court decision in 1848 reaffirmed an earlier decision limiting the legislature's eminent domain power, undercutting the Anti-Rent fallback position should tests confirm the landlord's title. But in 1847 Anti-Rent organization at the local level had already collapsed. In 1846 a minority of Anti-Rent National Reform militants had broken off to join in the new Free Soil venture, getting a minuscule vote in the state election. Further, during 1847 Governor Young encouraged landlords, eager to avoid rent taxation, to sell their interest for an amount that, invested at 5 percent, would yield the annual rent. Over two dozen landlords on the Livingston and other patents (but not Rensselaer) spurred a "land rush" that in a short time resulted in as many tenants in those areas paying mortgages as were paying rent. Buyouts and migration and diminution of the Anti-Rent constituency contributed to the movement's decline along with its co-option by the Whig Party, collapse at the grass roots, and lessening political leverage.[88]

The story of how Whig and Democratic allies of the Anti-Renters began developing a proposal to distribute public lands in the West to actual settlers, at reasonable prices, in limited quantities, has been well told by others and need not be discussed here.[89] Nor is it necessary to recount post-1848 attempts in the courts and legislature to remedy the tenants' plight. Legal battles went on through the 1850s. But by 1850 the Anti-Rent *movement* was dead. In June 1851 the *Albany Freeholder* ceased publication.[90]

## ANTI-RENT AS A POPULIST MOVEMENT

During its time of growth and wide community support in the mid-1840s, Anti-Rent exhibited several familiar features of a populist movement. From the beginning in the Helderberg hills, Down Renters saw themselves not as a minority but as "the People." They saw their oppressors, as did Regulators, Anti-Masons, and other insurgents before them, as possessing unnatural power because of "special privileges" bestowed by the government that undermined republicanism and threatened their well-being.[91]

The Indian disguise that referenced the Boston Tea Party was just one of the ways that Anti-Renters continuously invoked the American Revolution. They compared themselves early and often to the patriots of the Revolution who had fought against aristocratic tyranny. They held their largest, most festive, and most defiant celebrations on July 4. While serving a jail sentence resulting from his activities as an Indian chief, Smith Boughton appealed to his friends to help his family in the spirit of the "true-souled republicanism . . . that tore the Stamp Act to pieces, and threw the fragments into the face of the blockhead George the Third," and "that dished up the salt-water tea long ago."[92]

The climate of the Age of Egalitarianism and the pragmatic political culture of the parties operated in general and specific ways to enhance Anti-Renter populist expectations. Horace Greeley, a leading voice of Whiggery through his *New York Tribune*, offered advice on a regular basis to his party and the Anti-Renters regarding the manor troubles. Although he rejected extralegal action and favored conservative remedies, Greeley understood "that much of the Political theorizing of our day—our Fourth-of-July gatherings, Orations, etc., have contributed essentially to fan into flames the long inflammable material at the bottom of the Anti-Rent excitement." Beyond "theorizing," Whig and Democratic political leaders alike, competing for Anti-Rent votes, continually condemned the leasehold system as an unwholesome economic anachronism, out of place in a republican society. Both political parties bore a major part of the responsibility for failure to enact a compromise remedy, primarily because neither wished to allow its opponent to claim credit. At the same time, both parties fed the populist expectations of the tenants that "the People's will" would ultimately prevail over property rights.[93]

Horace Greeley imagined the language of human rights and the Declaration of Independence as inspiring some "unknown Gracchi of a rural neighborhood" to break the law, but local Anti-Rent leaders tended to be among the most substantial citizens in their towns. The twenty-five men who called on Stephen Van Rensselaer in 1839 were "prosperous, influential working farmers who had already demonstrated their capacity to lead their neighbors." In Albany and Delaware Counties generally, Anti-Rent activists tended to be well-respected community leaders. The Indians, in contrast, generally were young men, landless, and relatively poor. Thus, the Anti-Rent movement cut across classes in eastern New York with networks based in neighborhoods and towns.[94]

It also engaged women, who took over male tasks while relatives were away and served the movement as sentinels and horn blowers and assisted in hiding fugitives from the law. In 1845 their involvement expanded to holding their own meetings, passing resolutions, sending off petitions, and writing letters to newspapers. But Reeve Huston insists that within the patriarchal order of tenant farm families "citizens" meant men (white men, of course; men of color also were noncitizens). Anti-Renters depicted women as dependent or auxiliary, even when they were not.[95]

Although Huston's depiction of women's subordination may be over-drawn, it is consonant with the economic anxiety and threatened manhood that formed part of the bedrock of tenant farmers' resistance to the semifeudal leasehold system.[96] The youthful Indians, who usually lacked property or authority or the vote, could through their displays of horseman-ship and bravado lay claim to masculine virtues. In disguise they could even garner respect from their elders. They knew, too, of other white men who, since the American Revolution, had pretended to be Indians to engage in civil disorder and unlawful actions in defense of their communities.[97]

Their elders also experienced, though they might not acknowledge it, the damage inflicted on masculine self-esteem by the lease in fee. Greeley, in a controversial essay in 1845 called "The Pro and Con of Anti-Rent," imag-ined well the dynamics at work. After recounting the circumstances of how tenants easily could fall behind in rent payment, Greeley described the "day of reckoning" when feelings of dependence took hold: "At home, he [the tenant farmer] is the equal of the best around him; when he approaches the landlord or agent for forbearance, he feels himself an inferior being. He is a slave addressing a master, who has power to work him deadly injury."[98] Thus, the more the credo of the white male citizens' republic equated manly citizenship and popular rule with yeoman independence, the more the obli-gations and long habits of deference of tenants to landlords not only con-flicted with the economic interests of the tenants but also cast a shadow on their claim to manhood. Why not, then, disguise oneself as a lowly Indian or in long, womanly skirts?

Many familiar criticisms of populist movements suggest themselves in assessing the Anti-Rent movement. That the Indians and their neighbors often put themselves above the law, and thereby damaged their standing in public opinion—which they counted on to ease their burdens—is the most obvious, and perhaps one of the least relevant to their ongoing frustration. More important was the practically suicidal adherence to the title test strategy, the end result of which offered overturning of the landlords' ownership and, in a sense, getting "something for nothing." This could be viewed in an antipopulist perspective as typical of populist movements' often "simplistic" approaches to complex, legal problems. Of course, in the eyes of tenant Down Renters "nothing" was far from the case; rather, decades, generations, or "lives" of rent payments had been rendered.

Anti-Renters repeatedly spoke and wrote about not wanting to pay more for something whose value had been paid many times over. They wanted landlords or the state government to show them proof of title, not papers of eviction or repossession. After the shooting of the deputy sheriff in Delaware County in 1845, the New York Herald, vehemently hostile to the tenants' cause, sent a reporter to the town of Delhi where he interviewed old men who told him that they believed that until a good title, "honestly, fairly and constitutionally acquired is shown by the landlords, they are usurpers." Paraphrasing the Down Renters, the reporter wrote sympathetically that they believed "there was a time when these lands belonged to the State, and so they do unless it had in exchange good and lawful consideration. Show us what that was!" The reporter also saw the depressing effects of the leasehold system in discouraging improvements and wondered who would "cherish and enrich land and accumulate property or improvements on it, while he knew that he could not dispose of it at his decease, nor sell, nor convey by deed or mortgage, nor in any way alienate it. He who suffers from these oppressive conditions is bound hand and foot, and he would be more than a man if he did not feel his energies prostrated and courage daunted by their pressure."[99]

In justifying the resort to Indian disguise and extralegal coercion that sometimes resulted in violence, Boughton explained that "our all was at stake. The law was on their [landlords'] side and we were at their mercy." But violence and their opponents' magnification of it damaged the Anti-Rent cause in the court of public opinion, prompting harsh criticism from no less than that "chanter" of "democracy," Walt Whitman. Of course, in the 1840s Whitman was editor of the Democratic Brooklyn Eagle, patronized by Democrat-landlord interests, and strongly supportive of Governor Silas Wright's reelection, and he condemned the Anti-Renters as "the most violent faction which has disgraced the State since laws were heard of in this hemisphere." True patriots must vote for Silas Wright: "Let the people of the State themselves judge whether the Indians shall again raise their fiendish cries, their fires blaze forth anew, and the blood of legal functionaries again be shed."[100]

But public opinion was as hostile to the leasehold system itself as to sporadic Indian violence. Ultimately, the Anti-Renters failed because of decisions made by partisan legislators and judges ever more protective of property rights, and of those holding the most property.

The Anti-Renters certainly, as McCurdy observes, "overestimated the promise of democracy. . . . At no point could the people of New York State speak directly with one voice capable of trumping all other voices"; rather, "agents of the people, not the people themselves" would decide the issue.[101] Since before the American Revolution, as noted at the beginning of this history, that disjunction laying at the heart of "the people's sovereignty" between the people and their elected representatives had propelled many other popular insurgencies and would continue to do so through the rest of the century.

# Chapter 9

# The Know-Nothings

## POPULISMS, PARTIES, AND GOVERNANCE

During the era of the American Revolution, many ordinary white Americans, men and women, believed that the people's sovereignty enabled them—or perceived majorities representing "the people"—to "regulate" wayward authority. Throughout different regions of the country, many Americans saw ultimate authority as invested not in particular governments but in the people. By the end of the eighteenth century "Americans had come to the view that ultimately 'sovereignty . . . remains in the people,' that all government is but 'the *trustee* . . . of the people and *accountable* to them.'"[1] These beliefs underpinned not only various efforts to change fundamental law in the states but also popular insurgencies that sought to counter the effects of bad laws or to bring those who administered the laws into conformity with the (perceived) will of the majority.

By the 1830s and 1840s, as Christian Fritz has shown, many Americans still believed that constitutions sorted out powers to government and reserved certain powers and ultimate authority to the people. But so, too, did many hold the opposing view that constitutional change, and the power to "alter or abolish," could come about only by following established procedures or the lead of sitting governments. As seen in the last chapter, by the 1840s the former view, of majoritarian nonprocedural sovereignty and change, was losing ground. Although during the 1844 presidential election the Democratic Party used Rhode Island's "Algerine" repression of constitutional reform as a campaign weapon (ignoring the "substantial Democratic contribution to the cause of law and order"), in reality the episode split the Democrats both in Rhode Island and nationally and "caused the Democracy to back away from an unconstrained popular sovereignty."[2]

If the People's movement in Rhode Island had succeeded in establishing its constitution, it might have enhanced the lingering recognition of the nonprocedural view of the people's sovereignty and right to alter or abolish. But having failed, the episode has been labeled, in the fashion of other populist insurgencies, the "Dorr Rebellion" or the "Dorr War," even though the movement for the People's Constitution was peaceful up until Dorr's misguided decisions of May 1842, at which point he lost much of his support. Subsequently, legal scholars and historians have tended to view the suffragists' position as illegitimate, which even a historian sympathetic to the Dorrites called an "archaic and potentially dangerous relic of our Revolutionary era." But at the time, as Fritz has observed, Dorr and his supporters saw their opponents as violating the Revolutionary principle that the people could alter or abolish a government that no longer represented them. "What is most notable," says Fritz, "is how Dorr's many followers were surprised about what happened." Suffragists "spoke of their 'astonishment' at having 'to vindicate . . . the great principle' on which the American Revolution 'turned.'"[3]

To bypass established procedures would have been constitutional "circumvention," a mode that Fritz describes as not unusual. For example, Pennsylvania's radical 1776 constitution offended a large segment of the state's professional and upper class, with one house, a weak executive with no veto power, a broad franchise, and term limits on judges. The document allowed for its amendment by convention every seven years if called by a Council of Censors. When the council did not act in the first appointed year, 1783, elite opponents of the constitution began campaigning for change and pushed a resolution through the legislature by appealing to the constitution's "alter or abolish" provision and the people's sovereignty. Thus, a new constitution replaced the old in 1790 and contained no mechanism for amendment except in its retention of the alter or abolish provision.[4]

A very different scenario played out in Maryland in 1836, where Democrats began a process to democratize a polity perhaps as out of balance with popular rule as that in Rhode Island. Maryland's lower house was elected by popular vote without property qualifications (which had been abolished in 1802) but was grossly malapportioned. Each of eighteen counties had four delegates, while the growing population centers of Baltimore and Annapolis had two. Further, if a party could win in the eleven most sparsely populated counties, it could control all the seats in the senate through an anachronistic mechanism in the state's 1776 constitution. Senators were selected by an electoral college composed of two electors from each county and one each from the two cities. Thus, eleven counties could choose the entire senate, of their party, and then by joint ballot the legislature elected the governor and executive council. In 1836 a majority of electors had been elected from counties with a total population of 85,179 white men, while the minority represented counties and towns with a population of 205,922 white men. Democratic-Republican agitation for reform grew in the populous areas of the north and west.[5]

In the smaller rural counties, dominated by long-entrenched oligarchies, opponents of reform echoed the "agrarian interest" in Rhode Island and its fears of being "ruled by a [city] mob" and specifically of foreigners. Newly arrived German and Irish immigrants in Baltimore and other growing urban places and ports represented a threat of illegal voting—and future legal voting—already being exploited by Jacksonian politicians.[6]

A crisis began in September 1836 when Democrats won a majority of 3,000 (of 44,000 total) in the vote for electors, but Whigs stood poised to control the senate with twenty-one of forty seats in the electoral college. Frustrated by the legislature's repeated rebuffs of proposals for electoral reform, and partly from political calculation, the nineteen Democrats decided to block the Whigs by absenting themselves from the college. This action denied the Whigs the required quorum of twenty-four votes. The Democrats agreed to attend only if the Whigs guaranteed selection of at least eight reform Democrats for the fifteen-seat senate. The state government now ground to a halt; there would be no senate and no General Assembly to choose the governor and council. Then, the Democrats scheduled a constitutional convention to be held in Baltimore, appealing to the Maryland Bill of Rights and the people's power to remake their government.[7]

Democrats called meetings in various counties to support the nineteen absentee electors as well as the process for carrying out "the will of the people." A Frederick town meeting declared the electoral college majority "deaf to the voice of the people," and Baltimore reformers claimed the right of the people at any time and manner they deemed effectual to change their government. But the Democrats' gambit faltered. Both Jacksonians and Anti-Jacksonians in the populous counties of Frederick and Baltimore had called for reform, and a bipartisan backlash developed against Democratic political leaders for turning reform into their partisan issue. The Democrats' complaints that the government as constituted was based on "antirepublican" principles was trumped by the Whigs and moderate Democrats, who stood against "revolution" and "anarchy" and for "constitutional reform." In the October elections for the House of Delegates and in the November balloting for president, the Whigs won decisive majorities. Maryland's Whig governor called for a special session of the legislature (with the senate elected previously in 1831) and issued a proclamation calling for military preparedness. The Democrats backed down, and several appeared at the electoral college to make a quorum. At the next session of the General Assembly, the Whig majority accepted in modified form the reform proposals desired by the Democrats. Though the Democrats and some Whigs from populous areas voted against the changes, legislative apportionment was improved, and the governor and senate would now be elected by popular vote.[8]

The Whig leadership probably persuaded a majority to vote for reform by adding a new voter registration law applicable to Baltimore County and designed to control illegal voting by Irish and German immigrants. The nativist intent of the bill resembled similar Whig efforts in other parts of the country. However, the registration law proved ineffective as Democrats managed to find ways around it, thus gaining most of what they aimed for when they began their boycott. Although the strategy of nonprocedural constitutional change had been derailed, by the 1840s Maryland possessed a lively political culture characterized by high voter turnout and competitive party politics.[9] The movement for reform was not a populist insurgency, but the outcome indicated the rising ascendency of procedural constitutional change and the increasingly constrained environment such movements would encounter.

A similar signal came, though somewhat ambiguously, from the 1849 U.S. Supreme Court decision in a case arising from Rhode Island's troubles, Luther v. Borden. Although evading a clear statement on the merits of procedural versus circumventional constitution making, the Court dealt the latter another setback. In assessing the actions of the "political department" of government, Chief Justice Roger Taney argued that the legislative and executive departments in Providence and Washington consistently had legitimized the Charter government. Congress had throughout the crisis accepted the state's representatives, the People's government had not sent its own representatives, and the president had recognized Governor King by promising military aid if needed.[10] Taney's claim that the Court declined passing judgment "upon political rights and political questions" was somewhat misleading, however, since the Court's opinion implicitly validated procedural people's sovereignty.

Ironically, also implicit in Taney's opinion and explicit in Justice Levi Woodbury's dissent (Woodbury was a New Hampshire Democrat sympathetic to Dorr) was reasoning that, if carried to its logical conclusion, meant that the suffragists and People's government had not gone far enough to establish their power and authority. Woodbury implied that the Whigs of 1776 had succeeded and won independence because they had resorted to the uninhibited use of force, and the People's movement failed because it had not.[11]

Of course, Rhode Island's reformers, though not gaining as much as those in Maryland, did gain some concessions from the Freeholders, notably in the enfranchisement of natives of two years' residency owning $134 of real property and of the "registry voters," though the latter, with no secret ballot provided for in the constitution, led to abuses that lasted until 1888. Despite other liberalization measures, including allowing nonvoters to be members of a school committee, opening the door to women serving, the final landholders' constitution perpetuated a severely restricted form of republicanism in Rhode Island.

The real estate qualification for naturalized citizens made the state's suffrage "the most nativistic in the nation from the moment of its inception." The targets of the restriction were the largely Irish Catholic immigrants flooding into Providence and factory villages. Property also "ruled" in other ways, as registry voters could not cast ballots in Providence city council elections and could not vote on financial questions in any municipality. While the Freeholders broadened legislative representation for the house (expanding towns received 52 percent of the representatives, thirty-six of sixty-nine, a better ratio than allowed by the People's Constitution), an upper limit of twelve immediately cost Providence two seats and prevented its representation from growing. Worse, in the senate each municipality of whatever size had one vote, making that body an oligarchic seat of power for rural towns. In 1925 rural towns with 8 percent of the population held twenty-two of thirty-nine senate seats. From 1901 to 1935 under a new law the "rotten-borough senate" also acquired control over state apportionments and the state budget. Finally, the constitution contained no provision for future conventions and made amendments extremely difficult: two successive legislatures needed to pass any amendment with a general election in between, then gain approval by three-fifths of the voters.[12]

The contrasting outcomes of somewhat similar movements for constitutional reform in Rhode Island and Maryland suggest how diverse political cultures could be in the antebellum states and the very different receptions that could be accorded to populist insurgencies of various kinds. Some time ago historians buried the notion that Andrew Jackson personally was responsible for the advance of political democracy in the 1820s and 1830s, but they have tended to persist in holding that a democratic political culture was fully developed by 1828. In reality, in that year fourteen states still had some sort of property or taxpayer qualification for voting. Not until the 1840s did

Connecticut, New Jersey, and Louisiana drop their taxpayer qualification; Virginia waited until 1851; South Carolina held on until Reconstruction. Moreover, suffrage expansion was not always accompanied by other democratic reforms, though it was followed often by a stiffening of registry laws. New Jersey's governor was not elective until 1844; Illinois retained open or viva voce voting to 1848, Kentucky to the 1890s; North Carolina held on to a property qualification to vote for state senate until 1857. Throughout the South, "progress toward representation based upon population and the acceptance of political individualism was hindered by the existence of slavery. During these years, some combination of 'people and property' survived as the basis of representation in most states." Throughout the North, Rhode Island municipalities were hardly alone in requiring taxpaying or property qualifications to vote on matters of public finance.[13]

This is not to suggest that the vibrant, highly participatory politics (for adult white males) of the nineteenth century "party period," described by so many historians, did not exist. Despite the qualifications presented here and by others recently regarding the "limits of political engagement" in what has been seen as "the golden age of participatory democracy," when the historian looks away from Rhode Island (and South Carolina) the picture, especially compared with trends that set in at the turn of the century, is one of extraordinary citizen attentiveness and high voter and activist mobilization.[14] More important, a broad sense of efficacy prevailed among many citizens, including many nonvoting women who entered the public sphere on missions of benevolence and reform, who believed that their participation could make a difference in their local community, in the shape of their society, or in public policy.[15]

But events in Rhode Island, New York, and elsewhere indicate that the Revolutionary-era climate of ideas concerning the people's sovereignty and "regulation" had weakened. Although many Americans still retained a belief in the principle that sovereignty and authority resided ultimately in the people and not in a particular, delegated government, a changing political context was steadily diminishing the capacity and willingness to act on that belief. For a long time after the Revolution, many Americans assumed the right of the people (or a perceived local majority) to "regulate" their rulers—to watch, monitor, petition, remonstrate, and then to take action, including extralegal action, to restore the balance between them and their representatives. After the 1840s, populist movements would tend to take different forms and employ different strategies.

The forerunners of New York's Anti-Renters had been "White Indians" and Regulators from the Carolinas to Boston and northern New England, as well as western and eastern Pennsylvania farmers and rural opponents of taxes and officials whose legitimacy or authority they did not recognize. The Anti-Renters would hardly be the last of their kind in American history. They would have descendants who would resort not only to collective action but also to vigilantism and violence.[16] But during the last half of the nineteenth century, the major populist movements would attempt to work through the political system and the ballot box, though not necessarily through either of the two political parties.

Anti-Rentism had combined collective action, vigilantism, and electoral activity (nominating independent or coalition candidates for office) in its attempt to overthrow the manorial leases. Its frustrations signaled the increased significance of political parties in the formation of public policy and, at the same time, the decline of legislative/representative authority wielded by those very party organizations. The enduring tension between the people's sovereignty and representative government highlighted at the beginning of this narrative increasingly became, by the 1840s, a disjuncture between the people's sovereignty and majority will as against *party governance* within representative institutions, with increasing limits set by the courts on legislative authority.

Ironically, during the 1840s the judiciary began to become more democratic, as most old states and, from 1846 to 1912, every new state entering the Union provided for the popular election of state supreme court judges. But, as noted above, these same courts were swinging the balance of authority over property and economic regulation away from legislatures. In New York, for example, after 1840 there occurred a "dramatic upsurge" in judicial review. The courts' invalidating legislative statutes in record numbers stemmed from several causes, not least of which was concern over the potential power of the state to use eminent domain to redistribute wealth. Anti-Rent lawyers and legislators had brought eminent domain power into the discussion at the start of the "manor troubles," and it was the landlord-tenant conflict that prompted a divided court to rule that the judiciary, rather than the legislature, would decide what takings of private property were of a public nature (and that a court would know it when it saw it). As the New York judiciary shut the door on resorting to eminent domain, during the 1840s and 1850s "courts everywhere" turned away from the view that a public purpose inhered in state-sponsored activity that promoted economic growth.[17]

The courts' role in both Anti-Rentism's short-term demise as a populist movement in the late 1840s and in its long-term inability to overcome property law should not be exaggerated. The unwillingness of the Whig and Democratic Parties to allow the other to gain credit for enacting a reasonable solution loomed even larger while Anti-Rentism was an electoral force. As Anti-Rent factionalism increased, and as Anti-Rent voting leverage decreased, the Whigs and Democrats, with the latter divided over state patronage and national issues in the late 1840s, lost interest in tenant problems, but not in partisan advantage.

This narrative is not intended to be one of declension, though if it ended with the two "wars" of the 1840s it could be. Certainly, those events suggest that both the public space and contested legitimacy once claimed by populist insurgencies and movements in the early decades of the nineteenth century seemingly had grown more restricted. Moreover, they pose ironic sidebars on grand narratives chronicling the "rise of democracy." But the course of American political culture as representative republican government cannot be summarized in linear fashion. Republican institutions differed by region, by state, by locality, and over time.

With the courts increasingly setting limits on legislative governance, and with the Democratic and Whig Parties increasingly encased in the kind of political calculation that placed partisan advantage over the public good, populist movements that were energized to bring government closer to the will of the people in the late 1840s and early 1850s tended to use antipartyism and antipolitics as central organizing themes. Political insurgency flowed into nonpartisan, independent forms of political action focused on elections. The next great populist mobilization would differ strikingly from the Regulations of the early republic and would build on several streams of popular aspiration and discontent gathering force in the 1840s and early 1850s.

THE KNOW-NOTHINGS/AMERICAN REPUBLICAN PARTY

The Know-Nothing movement of the period 1853–56, primarily nativist and anti-Catholic, was one of the largest populist mobilizations of U.S. history, gathering into its fold a host of reforming and reactionary impulses, including, throughout the North, anti–slavery extension and anti-southernism (*after* Congress in 1854 passed the Kansas-Nebraska Act repealing the Missouri Compromise). It resembled less the Regulations of the earlier period and more the Anti-Masonic movement and party; however, Know-Nothingism, although short-lived, proved more powerful and more national in scope than Anti-Masonry and created an enormous upheaval in politics.

Know-Nothingism long has posed a problem for historians, partly because of its seemingly contradictory elements and partly because of an impulse to dismiss or minimize the intensity of anti-Catholic and nativist sentiment in nineteenth-century American society. The movement's populism has been acknowledged for some time. Historians have been slower to grasp, however, that Know-Nothingism was populist *and* progressive *and* reactionary. It was not progressive because it was populist, or reactionary because it was populist. Rather, all three of these currents came together, making it a classic case of the combination of progressive and reactionary elements in a populist movement described in the first chapter.

Before the multifaceted nativist movement emerged as a political force in the northern states, it was preceded by a powerful prohibition movement calling for state legislation to eradicate the evils caused by demon rum. Although the ravages of alcohol were often homegrown, native Protestants associated them with German and Irish immigrants. Temperance societies had existed since the 1810s, followed in the 1820s and 1830s by local and state efforts at limiting grog shops and alcohol consumption, but what emerged by 1850 resembled a populist movement in its own right. Thousands of men and women became engaged in this much expanded evangelical crusade, petitioning and lobbying as a pressure group. After Maine enacted strict regulation of alcohol in 1851, prohibition played a major role in state elections in 1853 and soon became merged in the Know-Nothing and other antipartisan, independent political reform movements arising across the nation.[18] Conflict over temperance, as noted earlier, was very much a struggle to assert the predominance of Christian (Protestant) manhood, and it inevitably overlapped with culture wars between Protestants and Catholics, as well as old native groups and new and old ethnic groups.

Know-Nothingism began as a small secret fraternity, the Order of the Star Spangled Banner, founded about 1850, which gradually merged with other similar patriotic groups. Native American parties had appeared briefly in several cities and had contested elections in the mid-1830s and mid-1840s. Like Freemasonry and other fraternities, the Order of the Star Spangled Banner intrigued recruits with a modest degree of hierarchy and ritual, including secret oaths and passwords. Part of the fraternity's ritual involved answering certain questions with "I know nothing." The movement devoted itself to reducing the corrupting influence on public life and elections of "foreigners," especially Catholics. Its "lodge" members, therefore, would vote only for native-born Protestants and advocated extension of the naturalization period for citizenship to twenty-one years. This approach reflected in part the deep-seated hostility long held by many native, evangelical Protestants toward popery, joined in the late 1840s to a perception that foreign Catholic influence was growing and, if not checked, would undermine republican government. In many cities, too, the fraternal lodges attracted native-born mechanics, artisans, and workers who were adversely affected by immigration and also fighting for better wages or shorter hours.

Know-Nothings, and many native Protestants throughout the country who did not join the order, reacted with equal hostility to the party politicians, Democratic and Whig, whom they held responsible for enabling the foreign and popish degradation of government and public life. Everywhere that Know-Nothingism or its political successor, the American Republican Party, arose, whatever the mix of opportunists or sincere defenders of republicanism in their ranks—and many were committed—the movements presented themselves as "reformers" who would clean up elections and "political corruption" and restore the sanctity of the ballot box.

In addition to nativism, Know-Nothingism gathered up temperance, antislavery, and evangelical moralism—though some Know-Nothings were not particularly moralistic, antislavery, or ardent for temperance. Besides a bundle of dissident and imperious cultural elements collected into one great antipartisan and antipolitical mobilization, its lodges offered many men a chance to show their patriotism and enhance their status by the fact of native birth, and they also provided a fraternal bond allowing members to express their manhood.

The reaction against foreign Catholics and partisan politics began in 1852–53 in city and local elections across the country, often prompted by Catholic-Protestant conflict over issues relating to the public schools. This culture war was not a simple case of bigoted natives victimizing Catholics. Catholic bishops, priests, laymen, and their representatives had entered into state and local politics aggressively after 1850, demanding, for example, a share of public school money to support independent Catholic schools, and that the Protestant Bible not be read in public schools attended by Catholic students. These issues merged with Protestant-Catholic disagreements over taxation and ownership of church property, the latter leading to the excommunication of Catholic laymen infected with "Protestant ideas" proposing lay rather than clerical control of property. The Vatican then inflamed American Protestants by sending a papal nuncio to settle the trusteeship disputes, whose tour of the country provoked hostile and violent demonstrations, especially after knowledge of his role in the harsh suppression of republican revolutionaries in Italy became known.[19] During the 1853 state and local elections Know-Nothings or their antecedents caused conventional partisan contests to be overwhelmed by the victories of numerous antipartisan and independent "People's" and "Fusion" candidates and tickets.

National politics also fed the mounting anti-Catholic fever, with Whig politicos offending Protestant militants by an uncharacteristic and egregious courting of Catholic voters during the 1852 campaign. Their presidential candidate Winfield Scott's clumsy efforts to flatter Catholics ("I love to hear the Irish brogue") backfired, and resentment among native Protestants intensified when newly elected president Franklin Pierce nominated Catholics to office, most provocatively James Campbell as postmaster general. The prospect of a Philadelphia Catholic controlling thousands of patronage appointments infuriated nativist Protestants of all political stripes, including Democrats, while nativist Whigs blamed their presidential defeat in part on the Democrats' bringing swarms of illegal voters to the polls.[20]

In addition to culture wars and social upheaval, in 1854 northern politics would be thrown into turmoil by renewed controversy over slavery extension. The passage of the Kansas-Nebraska bill (repealing the Missouri Compromise) in May "infuriated the northern public and spawned the creation of the exclusively northern and overtly anti-Southern, antislavery Republican Party." It also helped wreck the Democratic Party in the North. But as Michael Holt contends, "antiforeign and anti-Catholic sentiment was just as important in causing Democratic defeat in 1854 and 1855 [as Kansas-Nebraska], just as it was indisputably more important than antislavery or free-soil sentiment in killing off the Whig Party in the North."[21]

The Know-Nothing movement in 1854 and its political party (American Republican) in 1855 constituted the most powerful force in northern politics during those two years and had considerable impact in southern cities and states. Initially operating wholly in secret and backing either regular Whig or independent Fusion nominees, the Know-Nothings dominated or played major roles in People's, Fusion, or Independent anti-Democratic coalitions in Maine, New Hampshire, Ohio, Illinois, Michigan, and Indiana, buried the opposition in Pennsylvania and Massachusetts, and mounted a strong, competitive independent race in New York.[22]

In 1855 the American Republicans or Know-Nothing-dominated Fusionists carried every New England state except Maine and Vermont, ran ahead of the Republican or anti-Nebraska tickets in the middle states and California, formed a powerful element in anti-Democratic coalitions in the Midwest, and won in Maryland, Kentucky, and Texas. In the South generally the Know-Nothings had replaced the Whigs as the major opponent of the Democrats. Throughout the slave states Know-Nothings attacked "political corruption" and in southern cities organized and rioted during elections to prevent voting fraud by immigrants.[23]

It was hardly coincidental that the peak of Know-Nothing/American success came in the very years that unprecedented numbers of immigrants arrived in America—over 400,000 in 1854. The influx of close to 3 million new immigrants from 1844 to 1854 amounted to 14.5 percent of the nation's 1845 population. The culture shock registered in countless ways, most notably in the political tsunami of nativism and anti-Catholicism. Nativists complained that poor immigrants, particularly the Irish, overran poorhouses and, along with Germans, contributed to intemperance and alcohol-related problems, including crime, indigence, and violence at polling places.[24]

Besides culture shock, historians have also emphasized that economic dislocations created rising insecurity among common laborers, workers, and artisans. Immigration was seen as "the root cause" of a deep "hidden" depression that struck native mechanics and tradesmen from 1848 to 1855, leading to a wave of strikes in many cities, with about 400 occurring in 1853–54. Employers responded with aggressive countermeasures, such as bringing in troops and police to crush strikers and replacing discontented native workers with cheap and malleable immigrant labor. Economic hardship and turmoil in the workplace fed the "political revolt of northern workers."[25] While rapid shifts in the economic and demographic landscape helped to create the conditions for a populist upheaval, the crisis of the 1850s was profoundly, as Michael Holt has emphasized, a political crisis.[26]

Know-Nothings regarded themselves as defenders of republican purity against the corrupting influences of party politicians and immigrant interlopers who owed allegiance not to the United States but to a foreign "potentate," namely the Roman pope. They saw themselves as reformers out to reclaim politics from cynical wire-pullers and unprincipled representatives who disregarded the public interest for patronage and profit. Although the movement was soon infiltrated by seasoned and opportunistic politicians, initially it proclaimed its lack of connection to the spoils system and the routine machinations of Democratic and Whig officeholders. At first they targeted Democrats for defeat more than Whigs because the former were notorious for enabling illegal voters. Everywhere, Know-Nothingism was, if nothing else, "a revolt against the Politician, above all in his role as manipulator of the voters."[27]

That manipulation depended in most regions of the country on the absence of the secret ballot, rituals of mostly open voting, with brightly colored ballots supplied by parties and their presses, and widespread voter acquiescence in local rituals of "showing one's colors." These practices led as well to close scrutiny of ballot casting by sharp-eyed partisan lawyers representing creditors, employers or their agents, and party poll watchers, checking on the allegiance of those beholden or otherwise intimidated or compromised in some way. Most interference and violence associated with elections took place in cities or larger towns, and soon nativist rowdies themselves perpetrated a good deal of such abuses in the mid-1850s. Many elections throughout the country in the nineteenth century functioned properly and testified to the strength of widespread norms of civility. But while most adult white males (and in some places some nonwhites) usually participated in fair elections, by the late 1840s complaints about tampering had risen dramatically.[28]

The Know-Nothings' secret maneuvering testified implicitly to the conditions under which elections were conducted and to the ways open voting permitted intimidation and management. Their defiant rejection of partisan norms and the secrecy they employed in 1853–54 to wield their votes in elections speak volumes about their determination to escape the monitoring of party and other agents. Indeed, before election day the traditional parties routinely sent spies to their opponents' caucuses and conventions to contrive ways to undermine them, but the Know-Nothings' stealth organization walled them off. Their tactics expressed the ordinary citizens' populist rejection of party managers' and elites' manipulation. Although many former Anti-Masons found the Know-Nothings' secrecy difficult to accept, where the Masons' secrecy had reinforced the fraternity's sense of exclusivity and their opponents' perception of antirepublican elitism, the Know-Nothings' secretiveness at once protected them from elite retribution and gave them a sense of proud defiance. It sprang, too, from the strategies of workers' fraternal orders for organizing strikes and other workplace actions to circumvent anticonspiracy statutes that made it a crime for workers to combine to leverage employers to raise wages or improve working conditions.[29]

In Massachusetts, where in 1854 Know-Nothings working in the shadows surprised the regular parties by sweeping the state and electing almost every one of the 400-plus legislators, support for a secret ballot was tied closely to the push for labor reformers' movement for a ten-hour workday. Again, the implication of a drive for unfettered, unmonitored suffrage resonates in the coupling of these two measures, as does resistance to the political and economic pressure against a ten-hour law brought by mill owners agents' to bear on factory operatives.[30]

Massachusetts could serve as the poster child of Know-Nothingism as a vehicle for populist progressive reform *and* reactionary populism. Nowhere else were anti-Catholicism and nativism as intense, and nowhere else did the movement and party enact such a broad array of reforms affecting both social welfare and political democratization. During the 1840s conservative Whigs' dominance of Massachusetts and their habitual blocking of reform had led to a logjam that was partially broken when a "Coalition" of Free Soilers and Democrats controlled the state government in 1851 and 1852. The Coalition anticipated the Know-Nothings by passing several long-overdue reforms and by combining populism, antipartyism, and nativism, as well as hostility to slavery extension and to southern power in the national government. Its most notable success was passage of a secret ballot law, adamantly opposed by the Whigs, and one of its most controversial measures was a prohibition law modeled on the "Maine Law." With labor reformers a key element of the Coalition, it tried mightily to pass a ten-hour workday law but fell short in what was the most significant challenge to the state's manufacturing-capitalist elite in the antebellum era.[31]

The Coalition had nevertheless struck at several pillars of the state's Whig-Unitarian economic establishment, and it extended that populist assault by calling for a constitutional convention and writing a new constitution. The document contained progressive political, social, and economic reform measures but also imposed an undemocratic measure to enhance the power of western rural towns at the expense of eastern population centers.[32] In a referendum the constitution met defeat by a narrow margin (51.9 percent), and the Coalition disintegrated as the Whigs returned to power in 1853.

But in their frantic campaign against the constitution's approval, the Whigs promised their support for several major reforms and also appealed to eastern Massachusetts's growing Irish Catholic population to defeat the document. Although referendum voting followed partisan and regional lines (eastern voters mostly against), frustrated Coalitionists, especially Free Soilers, singled out the Irish Catholics for defeating "reform," adding to the mounting nativist and anti-Catholic sentiment spreading across the entire nation. Moreover, the Whigs, back in power, immediately repealed the secret ballot law and then largely reneged on their recent promises of reform, fueling the mounting populist antipartyism and frustration with politics as usual.

Thus, Know-Nothingism arrived in Massachusetts in a polity seething with the very elements that propelled it forward everywhere. The result was an unprecedented outpouring of reform and reaction.

First, reaction. The nativist and Free Soil legislators fired foreigners in the police force and state agencies, took away from state courts the power to grant naturalization, disbanded Irish militia companies (that had provided escort for the rendition of fugitive slave Anthony Burns, for example), required the daily reading of the Protestant Bible in public schools, summarily enforced the pauper law and deported hundreds, called for the federal government to extend residency for naturalization to twenty-one years, proposed a state constitutional amendment to that effect, and even purged Latin words and other "foreign" symbols from public proceedings and buildings. Equally excessive, and ultimately damaging, was the appointment of a committee to inquire into Catholic convents and schools regarding "acts of villainy, injustice, and wrong" perpetrated within their walls. When the "Hiss Nunnery Committee" became notorious for the scandalous behavior of its own members, it contributed to the decline of Know-Nothing influence.[33]

Before then, however, "the Know-Nothings outdid the Free Soilers on anti-Southernism and antislavery," passing resolutions calling for restoration of the Missouri Compromise and repeal of the 1850 Fugitive Slave Law, while also passing a Personal Liberty Law to protect fugitives. Remarkably, in 1855 the nativist legislature passed a law desegregating by race the Boston public schools, a measure that was related to the assault on Catholics (an earlier law banned the use of public money for sectarian schools) and expressed "the nativism that had long commingled with antislavery." The legislature also voted to send avid Free Soiler (and nativist, for the moment) Henry Wilson to the U.S. Senate and called on President Pierce to protect free-state settlers in Kansas against violent proslavery mobs from Missouri.[34]

Nativist moralism and evangelical willingness to control private behavior found expression above all in a new prohibition law, with penalties so extreme that jury conviction was doubtful, and also in stronger penalties for keepers of dens of gambling and vice, in fines on bowling alleys and billiard rooms that admitted juveniles or operated on Sundays, and, in line with its concern for education and rehabilitation, in the state's first reform school for girls.[35]

With regard to matters of domestic economy and governance, the Know-Nothings, according to the most detailed recent account, "brought a radically different attitude toward the proper uses of government." Addressing the backlog of socioeconomic and welfare issues avoided by the Whig ascendancy, the nativists increased state spending by 45 percent in a single year and spent 40 percent more on welfare than the previous legislature. They lavished funds on public education; made vaccination compulsory; increased funds for school libraries, for the mentally handicapped, and for the recently established school for the blind; authorized cities and towns to provide free textbooks and paper; and required factory children under age fifteen to attend school at least eleven weeks a year.[36] Although the nativist legislators made concessions to commercial enterprise, they subjected railroads, banking, and insurance companies to more regulation, transparency, and accountability than had been the case in past decades. They required railroads to adopt new, uniform safety measures and created a Board of Pilots to supervise shipping traffic. Labor reformers welcomed abolition of imprisonment for debt and extension of the existing homestead exemption and lien law for mechanics, increasing the value of property protected. Although the legislature revived the measures most dear to labor advocates, namely, the ten-hour law and secret ballot, both went down to defeat in what many nativists regarded as their most frustrating failures.

After 1855 Rhode Island defenders of that state's limited republicanism could no longer point to unrepresentative features of the polity in the nearby Bay State. The Know-Nothings expanded political democracy while reducing partisan patronage by abolishing property qualifications for the legislature and executive council; allowing the governor and all state offices to be elected by a plurality, ending a system that had led to abuses; basing representation on population for both houses; reducing the executive council and making it, as well as secretary of state, treasurer, auditor, and attorney general, elective; providing for election of sheriffs, probate registers, clerks of the court, and district attorneys; and establishing that state and national elections would be held on the same day, thereby increasing turnout for the former. Finally, in a nod to "alter and abolish," the nativists incorporated machinery into the constitution for amending it.[37]

Outside of Massachusetts, detecting the amount of reform blended with reaction in the nativist, populist outburst becomes more difficult, though the combination waxed strongest in the other New England states. How much reform or reaction ensued depended obviously on how much electoral success the Know-Nothings enjoyed or, subsequently in the North, how much leverage they could bring to bear on the Republicans. In all states, with the exception of Massachusetts, Know-Nothing *reaction* has been most assiduously documented, revealing the widespread efforts to restrict foreign or Catholic influence by disbanding foreign militia companies; reducing the number of paupers of foreign origin; making naturalization take longer and voting more difficult; preventing Catholics from holding any government office; requiring the Protestant Bible to be read in public schools; and broadcasting in newspapers and in an outpouring of pamphlets and books the conspiracy of Roman popery to acquire dominion over the American republic.[38]

The great fear of the popish plot has been rightly compared to red scares and other hysterical reactions to exaggerated threats of internal subversion. But also feeding anti-Catholicism were rational fears arising from cultural conflicts based on what Protestants saw as Catholic encroachments on American republican values, as in the case of church property laws passed by Know-Nothing, Fusion, and Republican legislatures. That issue arose first as a division within the Catholic Church, when in the 1840s the hierarchy launched a crackdown on lay trustees who they believed had become infected with "Protestant" and "American" ideas, instead insisting that church property should be owned and controlled exclusively by clergy. In the 1850s, partly as a visceral reaction to Roman imperiousness and partly to support dissident American Catholics, nine states (Massachusetts, Connecticut, New Jersey, New York, Pennsylvania, Maryland, Indiana, Michigan, and Arkansas) enacted laws protecting lay trustee ownership and in some cases making clerical ownership illegal.[39]

A similar fusion of reform and reaction, impossible to disentangle, permeated Know-Nothings' obsession with their generous support of public schools and their desire to eliminate Catholic influence and keep Protestant values ascendant. The 1855 Ohio American Republican platform, for example, declared its strong support for funding a public school system, denounced attempts to exclude the Bible from schools, and hence believed it was endorsing "unlimited *Freedom of Religion* disconnected with politics."[40]

Although nativists, like Whigs before them, were divided on antiliquor legislation, "Know-Nothings enacted temperance legislation in every northern state in which they gained significant political power." Prohibition agitation and legislation, already bursting into politics before the advent of the

Know-Nothings, mingled with the nativist campaign, not just to enforce morality and reduce crime and pauperism, but also to further the effort to clean up illegal voting and violence during elections and to reduce foreigners' political influence. Laws limiting the sale and consumption of liquor were tied to the purging of foreigners or Catholics from fire and especially police departments and were often accompanied by city administrations' expanding and making those services more efficient. "Efficiency" for nativist reformers meant enforcement of prohibition laws, on Sundays, for example, and on election days.[41]

Temperance reformers sought to drive up the cost and difficulty of selling spirituous liquors, but the early Maine Laws often had received no enforcement because of the overrepresentation of immigrants on many police forces. Thus, the Know-Nothings increased penalties and replaced foreign-born policemen with native-born officers. In 1854 Philadelphia's Know-Nothing mayor fired all the foreign-born policemen precisely for that reason. The nativists' special targets were the immigrant-run "groceries" and saloons, which they regarded not only as hatcheries of crime and pauperism but also as intimately associated with immigrants' influence on elections. On election day immigrant squads of voters and "poll watchers" often mobilized at saloons; in New York City's immigrant neighborhoods, saloons housed 89 percent of polling places.[42] Thus, temperance "reform" and political "reform" overlapped in the Americanist movement.

The outcome of elections in many city wards often depended on who controlled the public space outside the room or "voting window" where tickets were taken. After gathering at saloons, immigrant rowdies and gangs (foreign-born and native) went forth to intimidate and drive away opponents. Toughs known as "shoulder strikers" bumped into would-be voters for the rival party, knowing them by their clothing, the ballots they carried, or their ethnicity. The Know-Nothings countered by organizing secretly in several cities to ensure orderly voting at the polls, and after taking control of city governments, they put their new police forces into play. Whoever controlled the police often controlled polling places, and police frequently acted as agents of the incumbent party's electioneering force. If rival partisan gangs clashed, the police could tip the balance to those aligned with their party. Hence, the importance Know-Nothing mayors attached to making a clean sweep of Irish and other foreign-born from the police force.[43]

Nativist control did not always result in a decrease in election day violence. For example, Baltimore's elections had earned a reputation as the most violent in the country before the advent of the Know-Nothings. Quasi-political clubs and gangs ruled several city wards with shoulders, fists, weapons, and bloodshed. Opposing partisans might even be locked up, or "cooped," for a day or so. The Know-Nothings imitated their opponents, fighting fire with fire to prevail, and after taking office continued to use organized violence, justifying themselves as truer practitioners of republicanism. Their gangs viewed violence "as normal practice" and raised it to unprecedented levels of illegality and mayhem. While Baltimore was exceptional, in other cities, too, Know-Nothings ended up using tactics that "reform" had arisen to purify.[44]

In New Orleans Know-Nothing intervention resulted primarily in more orderly elections. Fraud and violence associated with Democratic Irish and Creoles marred the city election in March 1854 when the nativists first entered the lists to challenge illegal voters, and as the fall elections approached, the city became a scene of continuous riots and brawls. But during a November election for state legislators, the nativists sent out a poll-watching army of well-organized, well-armed "reformers," who ensured an uneventful election, as well as a heavy Know-Nothing victory. The nativists' aimed above all, however, to capture the city government, which, under a Democratic administration, had spent a $500,000 surplus and run up a corresponding debt, raised taxes, and seemingly run the city for the benefit of a Creole-immigrant coalition. The March 1855 contest for city council brought a sweeping Know-Nothing victory, with bands of "American" brothers constantly guarding the polls and virtually eliminating all rowdyism and possibility of fraud. In subsequent elections, however, the Democratic opposition fought back in kind, and, as the nativists kept the pressure on to challenge cases of fraudulent naturalization, some wards became battlegrounds, with Know-Nothing police siding with the nativist election fighters. By 1856 the anti-Catholic Americans dominated New Orleans using the same ruthless methods as their predecessors and, remarkably, retained control of the city government until the Civil War.[45]

In San Francisco Know-Nothings brought order to elections at least temporarily. They first mobilized for the 1854 fall city election behind a "Citizen's Reform" ticket. The Democratic mayor appointed extra police to maintain order, but the Know-Nothings countered with their own squads of poll watchers. In the First Ward a crowd of thugs and "shoulder strikers" went for the ballot box, and the Know-Nothings fought them off with thirteen shots fired, three wounded, and one killed before order was restored. Trouble broke out in other wards, usually after noon as rowdies gathered and liquor took effect. When a gang of "Irishmen" threatened in the Fifth, the Know-Nothings looked "so spunky" that their opponents backed off. Amazingly, given the mayhem wrought by both sides, most newspapers agreed that the election was more orderly than previous city contests. By September 1856, however, the Know-Nothings, Democrats, and Whigs had disintegrated before a new "People's Party" that put "an exaggerated local focus on the reformist, antiparty ideology that had provided the initial strength of the Know-Nothings."[46]

As in northern cities, Know-Nothing success in western and southern cities did not spring solely from nativism and coercion. Across the urban South, native Protestant workers, especially skilled workers, shifted their allegiance to the American Party as it emerged as a prolabor party supporting striking workers and bringing labor leaders into its leadership. Attacked by Democrats as antislavery, the Know-Nothings responded by claiming to be the better protectors of slavery. Indeed, Baltimore Know-Nothings upheld white supremacy as a way of advantaging native white workers in potential competition with black or immigrant labor.[47]

Getting to the polls and approaching the ballot box, where intimidation, rowdyism, and worse prevailed, clearly often required a stout heart and could be a test of manhood. In fact, when the Massachusetts Whigs attacked the secret ballot in 1852–53, they declared that secrecy was unmanly and that truly independent men did not fear open voting. In contrast, the Know-Nothings, using secrecy and stealth, provided a brotherhood of confidence, support, and strength to allow the expression of both patriotism and manhood. It took numbers, organization, and unity, and frequent calls on one's cohorts, to display "manhood and strength."[48]

The gangs of Baltimore and New York expressed in a more primitive form the lure of fraternal bonding that had drawn thousands of men into the patriotic secret societies and the Know-Nothing lodges. As a "refuge of brotherhood and security" steeped in ritual, mysticism, and a communication system of grips, passwords, and signs, Know-Nothingism provided self-esteem and a sense of patriotic masculinity. Its fraternalism also constituted a source of "oppositional political identity," shaped by antipartyism, and thus "literally was an alternative to the politics of party." Thus, the antiparty Know-Nothings ironically emulated in accentuated form the male culture of the major political parties and their exclusion of women that became more ingrained in the latter half of the nineteenth century.[49]

Yet despite the aggressive masculinity of nativist politics, women participated in the Americanism campaign to an extraordinary degree. And the

Know-Nothing, anti-Democratic, and Republican legislatures of the 1850s rewarded women to an extraordinary degree.

Women already had been drawn into increasing activity in the public sphere by temperance lobbying and contributed to sixteen states' passing either Maine Laws (thirteen) or laws restricting alcohol use (three). The threat that the abuse of alcohol posed to the family, women, and children was, of course, a staple of evangelical temperance advocacy. Nativism and anti-Catholicism similarly engaged women in conspicuous activity, including establishing female auxiliaries to the men's lodges, writing pamphlets, giving speeches, and, in the case of one Mississippi widow, editing her late husband's newspaper and becoming a "woman politico" in her own right. Precisely because it was a "complex blend of conservatism [or reaction] and liberal reformism," nativism/antipopery attracted women.[50]

The dictates of "republican motherhood" predisposed many women to resist the threat posed by Roman authoritarianism as they, too, perceived that their version of Christian manhood was under attack by foreign influence. In Massachusetts the Know-Nothings' advocacy of a ten-hour law impacted women because of their growing presence in the industrial workforce. There and in Connecticut and Pennsylvania middle-class women approved of the nativists' efforts to enact laws limiting child labor.[51] For a variety of reasons, native Protestant women embraced Know-Nothing and then Republican initiatives to change government policy and to impose Protestant moral values on public life.

Know-Nothings, the various anti-Democratic coalitions of the mid-1850s, and the Republicans succeeded the Federalists and Whigs as being welcoming to women in the public sphere and friendlier to women's rights than the Democrats. Accordingly, sixteen states passed laws recognizing married women's property rights and giving married women independent financial rights separate from their husbands. Massachusetts even made divorce and remarriage easier and sought to protect the rights and sustenance of divorced women with children. In Oregon nativist activity prompted protofeminist criticism of women's status solely as childbearers and domestic workers, but this rising women's self-consciousness was limited to a minority. Indeed, the most politically active women often cloaked their obvious transgression of women's place by paying lip service to the idea of "separate spheres."[52] But the nativist upheaval of the 1850s, a populist movement mixing extremes of progressive and reactionary tendencies, with respect to women on balance tipped in a liberalizing direction.

The more progressive attitude to women, as just suggested, existed in the emergent Republican Party, which contended with the Know-Nothings to replace the Whigs as the alternative to the Democrats. In its early stages the newly formed Republican coalition, succeeding the Know-Nothings, as well as host of usually Know-Nothing-dominated People's, Independent, and Fusion tickets, itself constituted a populist insurgency. Its regard for women's rights counted as just one of several ways it absorbed the various impulses—temperance, prohibition, hostility to slavery and southern domination—that had also suffused the northern nativist movement. Women's political activism, too, continued and increased in behalf of Republicanism. Although moving to moderate the extreme nativism and anti-Catholicism of the American Party, the Republicans absorbed former Know-Nothing voters and leaders while echoing and appropriating features of the nativist populist insurgency—notably, in its early days, antipartyism.[53]

Historians have debated at length to what extent Republicans incorporated Know-Nothings and their focus on anti-Catholicism and political corruption as the American Party declined during 1856 and after. One group of scholars has maintained that the nascent Republican Party was thoroughly antislavery and did little to accommodate or negotiate for nativist support.[54] Other historians have emphasized that the acquisition of nativist support along with various gestures to former Know-Nothings—proposal of laws tightening voting requirements, nominations of former Americans for office—was essential to Republican success in coalition building. Some have also insisted that distinctions must be drawn between antislavery as a moral posture, and anti–slavery extension and antisouthernism. In any case, most recent scholarship has confirmed the case for continuity, while logically conceding that as the sectional crisis deepened, antislavery, anti–slavery extension, and antisouthernism became dominant but without, even in 1858–59, totally jettisoning nativism.[55]

## CONCLUSION

For a long time the historical fate of the Know-Nothings and the American Republican Party resembled that of earlier, albeit quite different, populist movements stretching back to the Revolution. Memory and then historians sought repeatedly to marginalize the Know-Nothings, and nativism and anti-Catholicism, as peripheral to American political culture, when in actuality those impulses were as mainstream as tolerance and pluralism—coexisting and contesting, side by side.[56] But the tendency, hardly extinct, has often prevailed to diminish Know-Nothingism and its cultural and popular sources as a "flash in the pan," an aberration or abnormality due to short-run circumstances. It is true enough, however, that specific conditions in the early and mid-1850s (and at other times) intensified the expression of nativism and anti-Catholicism (think of the 1928 presidential campaign with the Catholic Al Smith as the Democrats' nominee), but those cultural conflicts continued on in American politics as part and parcel of the substance of political management, conflict, and partisan identities. But many historians and selective memory pushed the complex blend of reaction and progressivism and of its economic *and* cultural sources that was Know-Nothingism into an ideological straitjacket, in part, too, because of the desire to categorize social movements as *either/or*, a tendency that has been difficult to overcome. However, populist movements have been and remain not either/or, but are often combinations of contradictory political, social, and cultural elements.

The ideological encrustation of Know-Nothingism had another source as well, what Robert Penn Warren once called the North's "Treasury of Virtue" regarding the Civil War. Northern memory avoided the truth that while thousands of white northern men and women joined antislavery societies, many thousands more were indifferent to the horrors of southern slavery. Like most of the nation's founders, for many northerners slavery constituted a "distraction," not a moral issue to be confronted. As the sectional crisis built in the 1850s, the northern white majority became less tolerant of slaveholders' political aggressions and reacted less to the immorality of slavery as an institution and more to the Slave Power's threat to white rights and northern white "free labor" and its perceived (and real) domination of the national government. After the war, memory and celebration increased the numbers of northern abolitionists well beyond what they had been. In this context, the enthusiasm for nativism and anti-Catholicism that exploded across the country before *and* after the passage of the Kansas-Nebraska Act became, especially among the memory-keepers, something of an embarrassment.

Finally, historians have been reluctant to recognize that the alliance of anti-Catholicism and reform, including democratization, was typical of Anglo-American and Protestant culture. While the Catholic Church in the 1840s and 1850s did not uniformly oppose European nationalist and liberal movements and revolutions, men and women in Great Britain and the United States who regarded themselves as liberal believed that popery usually aligned itself with reaction and the suppression of progressive change.

Of more significance for this analysis, however, is recognition of the populist antipartyism that everywhere structured nativism and Know-Nothingism. Everywhere the nativist movement had taken on the mantle of reform against political corruption; everywhere it had denounced party managers as deceivers and manipulators with no regard for the public welfare or republican values, who trampled on public welfare for partisan and private ends, including lining the pockets of the party faithful. The sincerity or opportunism behind these declamations, depending on who issued them and where, may be questioned, but not their ubiquity.

The Anti-Rent experience in eastern New York in the 1840s possessed no known connection to, say, the Know-Nothing upheaval in Massachusetts, or Pennsylvania, or Michigan. Perhaps it did in New York State, but whether it did or not the absolute bedrock of nativist reform in the 1850s represented a rejection of the Whigs' and Democrats' partisan politics that had held out rhetorical mirages of hope and relief from tenant distress while hamstringing the Anti-Renters and determining what would be proposed within the limits of partisan calculation.

A common pattern has emerged from this analysis of populisms from the Revolutionary era to the 1840s and 1850s. Previous interpretations of the insurgencies and movements covered in this narrative often have incorporated ingredients of the self-serving constructions that their contemporary opponents imposed on them.[57] Those imposed frameworks of understanding benefited the populists' adversaries and gave them political and social advantage, as well as the ideological upper hand in the short and the long run.

From the late eighteenth century to the 1840s, populist insurgencies contended with inflammatory charges of "agrarianism," with accusations that they intended to overthrow or redistribute property and entertained no respect for debts, laws, or social order, often when nothing could have been further from the truth. Until recently, for example, otherwise dispassionate scholars could assert that the Massachusetts Regulators of the 1780s intended to overthrow the state government, echoing the "Friends of Order" and their rationale for harsh suppression of the insurgency.

The "Regulator" insurgencies of the Revolutionary and early republican era justified and tied their actions much more closely to the ideology and traditional last-resort tactics of the late eighteenth century. They assembled numbers of people—their kin, neighbors, and strangers sharing their grievances—in quasi-military fashion to overawe officials and overturn bad laws by creating a physical presence of "the people's sovereignty."

Across space and time, the various Regulators shared common views of the people's sovereignty and of republican government and society. To isolate one as "Shays's Rebellion," or another as "Fries's Rebellion," not only continues the distortions pointed to in earlier chapters whereby a widespread community effort was shrunken and attributed to a leader who never was, but also obliterates the cultural capital and memories of the populist participants themselves.

# Notes

CHAPTER ONE

1  Ghita Ionescu and Ernest Gellner, eds., *Populism: Its Meaning and National Characteristics* (London: Macmillan, 1969).

2  Two provocative studies that analyze conflicts arising from clashes between global capitalism (and democracy) and the resurgence of religious and ethnic fundamentalism are Benjamin R. Barber, *Jihad vs. McWorld: How Globalism and Tribalism Are Reshaping the World* (New York: Ballantine Books, 1995); and Amy Chua, *World on Fire: How Exporting Free Market Democracy Breeds Ethnic Hatred and Global Instability* (New York: Doubleday, 2003).

3  See, for example, Susan J. Tolchin, *The Angry American: How Voter Rage Is Changing the Nation* (2d ed.; Boulder, Colo.: Westview Press, 1999); and Gideon Doron and Michael Harris, *Term Limits* (Lanham, Md.: Lexington Books, 2001), xiv–xv, 74–85.

4  Paul Krugman, "For the People," *New York Times*, October 29, 2002, A31. Krugman's reflections came on the untimely death of Senator Paul Wellstone (D.-Minn.), whom he regarded as a genuine populist. George McKenna calls populism "the perennial American 'ism'" (*American Populism*, ed. George McKenna [New York: G. P. Putnam's Sons, 1974], xii).

5  Michael Kazin, *The Populist Persuasion: An American History* (rev. ed.; Ithaca, N.Y.: Cornell University Press, 1998), 1–7 ("I do not contend that my subjects *were* populists. . . . [Rather] all these people employed populism as a flexible mode of persuasion" [3]). See also, regarding the post–World War II changes, Thomas Byrne Edsall with Mary D. Edsall, *Chain Reaction: The Impact of Race, Rights, and Taxes in American Politics* (New York: W. W. Norton, 1991); Dan T. Carter, *From George Wallace to Newt Gingrich: Race in the Conservative Counterrevolution, 1963–1994* (Baton Rouge: Louisiana State University Press, 1996); J. David Hoeveler, "Populism, Politics, and Public Policy: 1970s Conservatism," *Journal of Policy History* 10, no. 1 (1998): 75–98; and Thomas Frank, *What's the Matter With Kansas?: How Conservatives Won the Heart of America* (New York: Henry Holt and Co., 2004).

6  Alan Ware, "The United States: Populism as a Political Strategy," in *Democracies and the Populist Challenge*, ed. Yves Mény and Yves Surel (Houndmills, U.K.: Palgrave, 2002), 101; Marco Tarchi, "Populism Italian Style," in ibid., 120–38; regarding England, see Peter Mair, "Populist Democracy vs. Party Democracy," in ibid., 81–98.

7  A useful introduction is Margaret Canovan, *Populism* (New York: Harcourt Brace Jovanovich, 1981); see also Paul Taggart, *Populism* (Buckingham, U.K.: Open University Press, 2000); and Margaret Canovan, "Two Strategies for the Study of Populism," *Political Studies* 30 (December 1982): 544–52.

8  The antipopulist tilt has been noted by others, including Carole Pateman, *Participation and Democratic Theory* (London: Cambridge University Press, 1970), 1, 104; and Allen D. Hertzke, *Echoes of Discontent: Jesse Jackson, Pat Robertson, and the Resurgence of*

*Populism* (Washington, D.C.: Congressional Quarterly Press, 1993), xiii, who sees populists often depicted "as demagogues or backwater nativists." For a discussion of studies that "the understanding of the ordinary citizen might be different from that of the elite, but was not thereby necessarily less coherent or democratic," see Vivien Hart, *Distrust and Democracy: Political Distrust in Britain and America* (Cambridge, U.K.: Cambridge University Press, 1978), 7. See also Ron Formisano, "Interpreting Right-Wing or Reactionary Neo-Populism: A Critique," *Journal of Policy History* 17, no. 2 (2005): 241–55.

9 First quotation, Josiah Ober, *Political Dissent in Democratic Athens: Intellectual Critics of Popular Rule* (Princeton, N.J.: Princeton University Press, 1998), 6–7; second quotation, Peter Bachrach, *The Theory of Democratic Elitism: A Critique* (Boston: Little, Brown and Co., 1967), 2. For a radical contrast with democratic elitism, see James Surowiecki, *The Wisdom of Crowds: Why the Many Are Smarter Than the Few and How Collective Wisdom Shapes Business, Economies, Societies, and Nations* (New York: Random House, 2004).

10 William H. Riker, *Liberalism against Populism: A Confrontation between the Theory of Democracy and the Theory of Social Choice* (San Francisco: W. H. Freeman and Co., 1982), esp. 238, 241–42.

11 Richard D. Parker, *"Here the People Rule": A Constitutional Populist Manifesto* (Cambridge, Mass.: Harvard University Press, 1994), 54–60. For treatment of populists as uninformed, unrealistic, impatient, and possessed of a "theocratic temptation" to purify, see Rainer Knopff, "Populism and the Politics of Rights: The Dual Attack on Representative Democracy," *Canadian Journal of Political Science* 31 (December 1998): 704–5.

12 Such "disdain" may also "embolden elites to claim transcendence, securing an elevated position from which to try to contain, control, or manipulate ordinary political energy" (Parker, *"Here the People Rule,"* 62, 64–65). See also Bachrach, *Theory of Democratic Elitism,* 4. This study attempts to emulate efforts by such scholars as Christopher Lasch, Alan Brinkley, and others to avoid what Richard Hofstadter complained of as American liberalism's "self-indulgent" tendency in its history writing "too much altogether to ignore . . . blemishes in its own past. And in 'the people.' And in the 'grass roots'" (Hofstadter quotation, Robert M. Collins, "The Originality Trap: Richard Hofstadter on Populism," *Journal of American History* 76 [June 1989]: 161).

13 For examples of the tendency to portray "populists" as right-wing or extreme radicals, see Catherine McNicol Stock, *Rural Radicals: Righteous Rage in the American Grain* (Ithaca, N.Y.: Cornell University Press, 1996), 2; Michael P. Federici, *The Challenge of Populism: The Rise of Right-Wing Democratism in Postwar America* (New York: Praeger, 1991); and Chip Berlet and Matthew N. Lyons, *Right-Wing Populism in America: Too Close for Comfort* (New York: Guilford Press, 2000). Ironically, Berlet and Lyons begin with an analytical framework that recognizes populism's variety and complexity but then relentlessly associate populism with the "mentally unbalanced, politically dysfunctional, or 'fringe'" (*Right-Wing Populism,* 14). A more theoretical hostility to populism can be found in John Lukacs, *Democracy and Populism: Fear and Hatred* (New Haven, Conn.: Yale University Press, 2005).

14  Norman Pollack, *The Humane Economy: Populism, Capitalism, and Democracy* (New Brunswick, N.J.: Rutgers University Press, 1990); Gene Clanton, *Populism: The Humane Preference in America, 1890–1900* (Boston: Twayne, 1991); Robert C. McMath, *American Populism: A Social History, 1877–1898* (New York: Hill and Wang, 1993); Elizabeth Sanders, *Roots of Reform: Farmers, Workers, and the American State, 1877–1917* (Chicago: University of Chicago Press, 1999). The modern literature on Populism began to turn in the 1960s and especially with the publication of Lawrence Goodwyn, *Democratic Promise: The Populist Movement in America* (New York: Oxford University Press, 1976).

15  Saul Cornell, "The Changing Historical Fortunes of the Anti-Federalists," *Northwestern University Law Review* 84 (Fall 1989): 39–73; E. J. Hobsbawm, *Primitive Rebels: Studies in Archaic Forms of Social Movement in the 19th and 20th Centuries* (New York: Frederick A. Praeger, 1959). The various popular insurgencies referred to here will be discussed in chapters 2 and 3.

16  In recent years historians have shown less interest in using the concept of "modernization" to describe the large socioeconomic and cultural changes that ensued in the decades after the nation's founding and have emphasized more the impact of a "market revolution" or, to a lesser extent, a "communications revolution." None of this is particularly new, given its foreshadowing in 1951 by George Rogers Taylor's *The Transportation Revolution: 1815–1860* (New York: Rinehart, 1951).

17  Eric Hobsbawm and George Rudé, *Captain Swing* (London: Phoenix Press, 1969), 249; George Rudé, *Ideology and Popular Protest* (New York: Pantheon, 1980), 31, 35. See also George Rudé, *Paris and London in the Eighteenth Century: Studies in Popular Protest* (New York: Viking Press, 1971), 22–23.

18  Alan Brinkley, *Voices of Protest: Huey Long, Father Coughlin, and the Great Depression* (New York: Alfred A. Knopf, 1982), 133–48, quotation, 144.

19  Bernard Bailyn, *The Ideological Origins of the American Revolution* (Cambridge, Mass.: Harvard University Press, 1967).

20  Christopher Lasch, *The True and Only Heaven: Progress and Its Critics* (New York: W. W. Norton, 1991), 172–80, quotation, 180; Lasch, "Communitarianism or Populism?," in *Rights and the Common Good: The Communitarian Perspective*, ed. Amitai Etzioni (New York: St. Martin's Press, 1995), 59, 60, 65; Lasch, "Liberalism and Civic Virtue," *Telos* 88 (Summer 1991): 67–68. For a critique of Lasch as a confused antiliberal, see Stephen Holmes, *The Anatomy of Antiliberalism* (Cambridge, Mass.: Harvard University Press, 1993), 124–40; but see also Holmes's requirements for constitutional restraints on majority rule in Stephen Holmes, *Passions and Constraints: On the Theory of Liberal Democracy* (Chicago: University of Chicago Press, 1995), xi–xiii, 8–10.

21  Lasch, *True and Only Heaven*, 387, 530–32, quotation, 378 (a phrase that originated with Reinhold Niebuhr). Regarding Lenin, see J. F. Conway, "Populism in the United States, Russia, and Canada: Explaining the Roots of Canada's Third Parties," *Canadian Journal of Political Science* 11 (March 1978): 110–18. Lenin's emphasis on Russian populism's combination of economic grievance and unrealistic nostalgia was echoed in Richard Hofstadter's seminal critique of the "agrarian myth," *The Age of Reform: From Bryan to F.D.R.* (New York: Vintage, 1955).

22  For discussion of the "redneck myth" that disproportionately assigns racial preju-

dice to the lower classes, see Ronald P. Formisano, *Boston against Busing: Race, Class, and Ethnicity in the 1960s and 1970s* (2d ed.; Chapel Hill: University of North Carolina Press, 2004), 233–34.

23 Hertzke, *Echoes of Discontent*, xii, 5, 241. Of course, real differences existed between Democrats and Republicans and between the knowledge elite and the business elite, but for Hertzke's analysis, "both the knowledge elite and the business elite are children of liberal individualism," and neither articulates a "communalist vision" (ibid., 242). Sanders, *Roots of Reform*, has a similar view of Bryan.

24 Hertzke, *Echoes of Discontent*, 33–39, quotation, 37; for a similar view, see Barry Alan Shain, *The Myth of American Individualism: The Protestant Origins of American Political Thought* (Princeton, N.J.: Princeton University Press, 1994). For an emphasis on religious faith in 1890s North Carolina populism, see Joe Creech, *Righteous Indignation: Religion and the Populist Revolution* (Urbana: University of Illinois Press, 2006). Hertzke also echoes Lasch in rejecting psychological explanations that tend "to minimize the genuine grievances of protesters" (*Echoes of Discontent*, xiii–xiv). Hertzke's approach to Pat Robertson also fits with a developing trend among U.S. historians to take seriously "the grassroots right" and conservatism generally. Although these studies registered an immediate impact on the understanding of the 1960s, the Goldwater campaign of 1964, and the rise to power in the Republican Party of right-wing conservatives, especially the religious right, for the most part they do not focus on populist movements. See the bibliography in Lisa McGirr, *Suburban Warriors: The Origins of the New American Right* (Princeton, N.J.: Princeton University Press, 2001); see also Michael Kazin, "The Grass-Roots Right: New Histories of U.S. Conservatism in the Twentieth Century," *American Historical Review* 97 (February 1992): 136–55; and Alan Brinkley, "The Problem of American Conservatism," *American Historical Review* 99 (April 1994): 409–29.

25 Formisano, "Interpreting Right-Wing or Reactionary Neo-Populism."

26 Quotation, Carlos De La Torre, "The Ambiguous Meanings of Latin American Populisms," *Social Research* 59 (Summer 1992): 413. As the title indicates, De La Torre is hardly uncritical of authoritarian leaders and other features of Latin American populist movements. For evaluations stressing inclusiveness and expansiveness, see Torcuato S. Di Tella, "Populism and Reform in Latin America," in *Obstacles to Change in Latin America*, ed. Claudio Veliz (London: Oxford University Press, 1965), 74; Michael Conniff, "Introduction: Toward a Comparative Definition of Populism," in *Latin American Populism in Comparative Perspective*, ed. Michael Conniff (Albuquerque: University of New Mexico Press, 1982), 5, 6–7, 12–13, 22; Torcuato S. Di Tella, "Populism into the Twenty-First Century," *Government and Opposition* 32 (Spring 1997): 188; and Michael Conniff, "Introduction," in *Populism in Latin America*, ed. Michael Conniff (Tuscaloosa: University of Alabama Press, 1999), 6–7, 21.

27 Alan Knight, "Populism and Neo-Populism in Latin America, especially Mexico," *Journal of Latin American Studies* 30 (May 1998): 223–24, 229.

28 Regarding a conservative-populist ascendancy in the United States since the 1970s that is probusiness and antigovernment, see Hoeveler, "Populism, Politics, and Public Policy." In Argentina left- and right-wing traditions joined together to form

Peronism; see Alberto Spektorowski, "The Ideological Origins of Right and Left Nationalism in Argentina, 1930–43," *Journal of Contemporary History* 29 (January 1994): 155–84.

29  William B. Hixson, *Search for the American Right Wing: An Analysis of the Social Science Record, 1955–1987* (Princeton, N.J.: Princeton University Press, 1992), 43 (quoting Brinkley, *Voices of Protest*, 283).

30  Hertzke, *Echoes of Discontent*, 71, 73, 75, 76–77, 80.

31  Margaret Canovan, "Taking Politics to the People: Populism as the Ideology of Democracy," in *Democracies and the Populist Challenge*, ed. Mény and Surel, 27. See also Canovan, *Populism*, 3; and Canovan, "Trust the People! Populism and the Two Faces of Democracy," *Political Studies* 47 (March 1999): 2–16. Canovan's 1981 book was the first to give the concept of populism sustained analysis.

32  For an exemplary treatment of women in a progressive movement, see Michael Lewis Goldberg, *An Army of Women: Gender and Politics in Gilded Age Kansas* (Baltimore: Johns Hopkins University Press, 1997).

33  Mark Wahlgren Summers, *Rum, Romanism, and Rebellion: The Making of a President, 1884* (Chapel Hill: University of North Carolina Press, 2000), 314.

34  The Know-Nothings will be discussed in chapter 9; Kathleen M. Blee, *Women of the Klan: Racism and Gender in the 1920s* (Berkeley: University of California Press, 1991). For women active in Boston's "antibusing" movement in the 1970s, see Formisano, *Boston against Busing*, 146–50.

35  Tiziano Bonazzi, "Civic Nation and Ethnic Nation," in *Communities and Identities*, ed. Anna Krusteva (Sofia: Petekston, 1998), 64–85.

36  John R. Howe Jr., "Republican Thought and the Political Violence of the 1790s," *American Quarterly* 19 (Summer 1967): 147–65; John L. Brooke, "Ancient Lodges and Self-Created Societies: Voluntary Association and the Public Sphere in the Early Republic," in *Launching the "Extended Republic": The Federalist Era*, ed. Ronald Hoffman and Peter J. Albert (Charlottesville: University Press of Virginia, 1996), 319–21; quotation, Donald H. Stewart, *The Opposition Press of the Federalist Period* (Albany: State University of New York Press, 1969), 487.

37  Bailyn, *Ideological Origins of the American Revolution*, 144, 95, 150–51.

38  Gordon S. Wood, "Conspiracy and the Paranoid Style: Causality and Deceit in the Eighteenth Century," *William and Mary Quarterly*, 3d ser., 39 (July 1982): 406, 407, 408, 411.

39  The foundational works here are David B. Davis, "Some Themes of Counter-Subversion: An Analysis of Anti-Masonic, Anti-Catholic, and Anti-Mormon Literature," *Mississippi Valley Historical Review* 47 (September 1960): 205–24; Richard Hofstadter, *The Paranoid Style in American Politics and Other Essays* (New York: Knopf, 1965); and David B. Davis, *The Slave Power Conspiracy and the Paranoid Style* (Baton Rouge: Louisiana State University Press, 1972). In an essay similar to Wood's that engages in historical contextualizing of attitudes and mentality, James H. Hutson has explicitly argued that the "paranoia" ascribed to Revolutionary leaders is better understood by the eighteenth-century concept of "jealousy," a term connoting vigilance, suspicion, and distrust. Further, the fears of Revolutionary leaders, Anti-Federalists,

Federalists, and Republicans of "a persecutory conspiracy of power holders are altogether credible." Up to 1830 the term "*paranoid*, with its connotation of pathology, is not a suitable term to apply to the beliefs in persecuting power which surfaced so frequently in American politics." But after 1830 fears of conspiracies hatched by Freemasons, the Catholic Church, or "the so-called Slave Power" tended to be held by those on the margins, and "at this point . . . it becomes possible to speak of those fears veering off toward pathology." See James Hutson, "The Origins of 'the Paranoid Style in American Politics': Public Jealousy from the Age of Walpole to the Age of Jackson," in *Saints and Revolutionaries: Essays on Early American History*, ed. David D. Hall, John M. Murrin, and Thad W. Tate (New York: W. W. Norton, 1984), 341, 347–49, 367, quotations, 371–72. For a positive view of distrust, see Hart, *Distrust and Democracy*.

40  Richard Rorty, *Achieving Our Country: Leftist Thought in Twentieth-Century America* (Cambridge, Mass.: Harvard University Press, 1998), 52–53.

41  In a similar vein R. R. Palmer noted that the difficulty with the theory of popular sovereignty "was that the conditions under which it could work were seldom present. No people really starts *de novo*; some political institutions always already exist; there is never a *tabula rasa*, or state of nature" (R. R. Palmer, *The Age of the Democratic Revolution: A Political History of Europe and America, 1760–1800*, 2 vols. [Princeton, N.J.: Princeton University Press, 1959], 1:215–16).

42  Edmund S. Morgan, *Inventing the People: The Rise of Popular Sovereignty in England and America* (New York: W. W. Norton, 1988), 49, 50, 53. "We assume too easily that popular sovereignty was the product of popular demand, arising from the many against the few. It was not. It was a question of the few enlisting the many against the rest of the few" (ibid., 169).

43  Ibid., 66, 68–69; "The Case of the Army Truly Stated (15 October 1647)," reprinted in Howard Shaw, *The Levellers* (New York: Harper and Row, 1968), 111. Another way of formulating Morgan's observation of bringing the "fact" into line with the "fiction" would be to consider "the rise of democracy" in the United States, as with Sean Wilentz, *The Rise of American Democracy: Jefferson to Lincoln* (New York: W. W. Norton, 2005). Anyone familiar with Wilentz's book will recognize that this narrative takes a very different approach to many topics considered by Wilentz; for example, "populism" is not to be found in his index.

44  Morgan, *Inventing the People*, 73.

45  Regarding the inherent instability of the people's sovereignty, see Seymour Martin Lipset, *The First New Nation: The United States in Historical and Comparative Perspective* (New York: Basic Books, 1963), 12. Bruce Ackerman has observed that a government makes decisions on a daily basis: "Decisions by the people occur rarely [Morgan argued never] and under special constitutional circumstances" (Ackerman, *We the People: Foundations* [Cambridge, Mass.: Harvard University Press, 1991], 6–7). Books dealing with other dimensions of what can be called the democratic disconnect include Samuel P. Huntington, *American Politics: The Promise of Disharmony* (Cambridge, Mass.: Belknap Press, 1981); and James A. Morone, *The Democratic Wish: Popular Participation and the Limits of American Government* (New Haven, Conn.: Yale University Press, 1998).

1    Pauline Maier, *From Resistance to Revolution: Colonial Radicals and the Development of American Opposition to Britain, 1765–1776* (New York: Alfred A. Knopf, 1972), 3–9; Gordon S. Wood, "A Note on Mobs in the American Revolution," *William and Mary Quarterly*, 3d ser., 23 (October 1966): 635–42; Edward Countryman, "The Problem of the Early American Crowd," *Journal of American Studies* 7 (April 1973): 88–89; quotation, Barbara Clark Smith, "The Adequate Revolution," *William and Mary Quarterly*, 3d ser., 51 (October 1994): 691 (emphasis in original). For discussion of the "radical and conservative" character of the American Revolution, see Alfred F. Young, "American Historians Confront 'the Transforming Hand of Revolution,'" in *The Transforming Hand of Revolution: Reconsidering the American Revolution as a Social Movement*, ed. Ronald Hoffman and Peter J. Albert (Charlottesville: University Press of Virginia, 1996), 469–92. Young (406–7) calls attention to R. R. Palmer's anticipation of this view in *The Age of Democratic Revolution: A Political History of Europe and America, 1760–1800*, 2 vols. (Princeton, N.J.: Princeton University Press, 1959), 1:235.

2    Gordon Wood, *The Radicalism of the American Revolution* (New York: Alfred A. Knopf, 1992), 8. The qualification of Wood's thesis reflects the critiques made by, among others, Alan Taylor, "Common Revolutionaries," *Historical Journal* 35 (December 1992): 943–44; Smith, "Adequate Revolution," 687; Edward Countryman, "Revolution, Radicalism, and the American Way," *Reviews in American History* 20 (December 1992): 480–85; and Michael Zuckerman, "Rhetoric, Reality, and the Revolution: The Genteel Radicalism of Gordon Wood," *William and Mary Quarterly*, 3d ser., 51 (October 1994): 695–97.

3    Liah Greenfeld, *Nationalism: Five Roads to Modernity* (Cambridge, Mass.: Harvard University Press, 1992), 6; Jon Cowans, *To Speak for the People: Public Opinion and the Problem of Legitimacy in the French Revolution* (New York: Routledge, 2001), 2–25, quotation, 22. Before the change "people" usually referred to the population of a region and most frequently was used in a derogatory fashion to refer to "rabble" or "plebs." "National identity in its distinctive modern sense is, therefore, an identity which derives from membership in a 'people,' the fundamental characteristic of which is that it is defined as a 'nation'" (Greenfeld, *Nationalism*, 6–7).

4    This paragraph has drawn on the Declaration itself; Greenfeld, *Nationalism*, 426; and Elise Marienstras and Naomi Wulf, "French Translations and Reception of the Declaration of Independence," *Journal of American History* 85 (March 1999): 1311, 1324. See also John M. Murrin, "A Roof without Walls: The Dilemma of American National Identity," in *Beyond Confederation: Origins of the Constitution and American National Identity*, ed. Richard Beeman, Stephen Botein, and Edward C. Carter II (Chapel Hill: University of North Carolina Press, 1987), 333–48.

5    Regarding Jefferson, see Michael Kazin, *The Populist Persuasion: An American History* (rev. ed.; Ithaca, N.Y.: Cornell University Press, 1998), 16–17; Seymour Martin Lipset, *The First New Nation: The United States in Historical and Comparative Perspective* (New York: Basic Books, 1963), 77; and Andrew W. Robertson, *The Language of Democracy: Political Rhetoric in the United States and Britain, 1790–1900* (Ithaca, N.Y.: Cornell University Press, 1995), 3; but regarding nationalist movements and "the political baptism

of the lower classes," see Tom Nairn, *The Break-up of Britain: Crisis and Neo-Nationalism* (London: New Left Books, 1977), 41; and Benedict Anderson, *Imagined Communities: Reflections on the Origin and Spread of Nationalism* (London: Verso, 1983).

6 Bernard Bailyn, *The Ideological Origins of the American Revolution* (Cambridge, Mass.: Harvard University Press, 1967); Paul K. Conkin, *Self-Evident Truths: Being a Discourse on the Origins and Development of the First Principles of American Government—Popular Sovereignty, Natural Rights, and Balance and Separation of Powers* (Bloomington: Indiana University Press, 1974), 27–43; M. J. Heale, *The Making of American Politics, 1750–1850* (London: Longman, 1977), 32–35; Daniel T. Rodgers, *Contested Truths: Keywords in American Politics since Independence* (New York: Basic Books, 1987), 84–85. For skepticism regarding the idea that antistatism is "a timeless national essence," see Jill Quadagno and Debra Street, "Ideology and Public Policy: Antistatism in American Welfare State Transformation," *Journal of Policy History* 17, no. 1 (2005): 52–71, quotation, 67.

7 Kevin P. Phillips, *The Cousins' Wars: Religion, Politics, and the Triumph of Anglo-America* (New York: Basic Books, 1999), 516, 517; Heale, *Making of American Politics*, 31–33; Linda Colley, *Britons: Forging the Nation, 1707–1837* (New Haven, Conn.: Yale University Press, 1992); David Hackett Fischer, *Albion's Seed: Four British Folkways in America* (New York: Oxford University Press, 1989). This and the next three paragraphs draw on previously published material in Ronald P. Formisano, "State Development in the Early Republic: Substance and Structure, 1780–1840," in *Contesting Democracy: Substance and Structure in American Political History, 1775–2000*, ed. Byron E. Shafer and Anthony J. Badger (Lawrence: University Press of Kansas, 2001), 8–10.

8 Jack P. Greene, *Pursuits of Happiness: The Social Development of Early Modern British Colonies and the Formation of American Culture* (Chapel Hill: University of North Carolina Press, 1988), 200. For a stirring narrative of the first phases of the Revolution in Massachusetts as a populist, collective enterprise, see David Hackett Fischer, *Paul Revere's Ride* (New York: Oxford University Press, 1994); see also David W. Conroy, *In Public Houses: Drink and the Revolution of Authority in Colonial Massachusetts* (Chapel Hill: University of North Carolina Press, 1995); and Paul A. Gilje, *Rioting in America* (Bloomington: Indiana University Press, 1996), 35–59. Regarding women's expanded sphere of thought and action, see Mary Beth Norton, *Liberty's Daughters: The Revolutionary Experience of American Women, 1750–1800* (Boston: Little, Brown, 1980), 195–227. For the impact of the Revolution on religion, see Nathan O. Hatch, *The Democratization of American Christianity* (New Haven, Conn.: Yale University Press, 1989), 6.

9 First quotation, Linda K. Kerber, "The Paradox of Women's Citizenship in the Early Republic: The Case of Martin vs. Massachusetts, 1805," *American Historical Review* 97 (April 1992): 351; Greene, *Pursuits of Happiness*, 195, 200; last quotation, Tiziano Bonazzi, "'Men Like Flowers or Roots, Being Transplanted Take After the Soil Wherein They Grow': Reflections on Alterity and Politics Regarding the Origins of the United States of America," in *Multiculturalism and the History of International Relations from the 18th Century to the Present*, ed. Pierre Savard and Brunello Vigezzi (Milano, Italy: Unicopoli, 1999), 26. In creating a new national identity, the "new *homo America-*

*nus*," Carroll Smith-Rosenberg has asserted, "was male, white, and, increasingly, middle-class" ("Dis-Covering the Subject of the 'Great Constitutional Discussion,' 1786–1789," *Journal of American History* 79 [December 1992]: 844).

10  Gordon S. Wood, *The Creation of the American Republic, 1776–1787* (Chapel Hill: University of North Carolina Press, 1969); Ramsay quotation, Joseph J. Ellis, *After the Revolution: Profiles of Early American Culture* (New York: W. W. Norton, 1979), x; second quotation, Sandra M. Gustafson, *Eloquence Is Power: Oratory and Performance in Early America* (Chapel Hill: University of North Carolina Press, 2000), xxi–xxii. A neoprogressive view of popular politicization that summarizes much recent literature is Michael A. McDonnell, "Popular Mobilization and Political Culture in Revolutionary Virginia: The Failure of the Minutemen and the Revolution from Below," *Journal of American History* 85 (December 1998): 946–98.

11  Jackson Turner Main, *The Anti-Federalists: Critics of the Constitution, 1781–1788* (Chapel Hill: University of North Carolina Press, 1961), 17, 19; John M. Murrin, "The Great Inversion, or Court Versus Country: A Comparison of the Revolution Settlements in England (1688–1721) and America (1776–1816)," in *Three British Revolutions: 1641, 1688, 1776*, ed. J. G. A. Pocock (Princeton, N.J.: Princeton University Press, 1980), 400; Calvin Jillson, "Patterns and Periodicity in American National Politics," in *The Dynamics of American Politics: Approaches and Interpretations*, ed. Lawrence C. Dodd and Calvin Jillson (Boulder, Colo.: Westview Press, 1994), 32; Marc W. Kruman, *Between Authority and Liberty: State Constitution Making in Revolutionary America* (Chapel Hill: University of North Carolina Press, 1997), 156, 159–60. On the mixed results of the Revolution with regard to the franchise, with an emphasis on the "modest" gains in formal democratization, see Alexander Keyssar, *The Right to Vote: The Contested History of Democracy in America* (New York: Basic Books, 2000), 15–25.

12  Jillson, "Patterns and Periodicity," 32; Heale, *Making of American Politics*, 37–40; Judith Apter Klinghoffer and Lois Elkis, "'The Petticoat Electors': Women's Suffrage in New Jersey, 1776–1807," *Journal of the Early Republic* 12 (Summer 1992): 159–93. North Carolina, for example, required assemblymen to own 100 acres and senators, 300 acres; New York allowed only £1,000 freeholders to vote for senators and governor, about one-third of adult white males.

13  *The People the Best Gove[r]nors: Or, a Plan of Government Founded on the Just Principles of Natural Freedom*, quoted in Elisha P. Douglass, *Rebels and Democrats: The Struggle for Equal Political Rights and Majority Rule during the American Revolution* (Chapel Hill: University of North Carolina Press, 1955), 172 (pamphlet itself quoted in *Boston Independent Chronicle*, July 10, 1777). Douglass says that the anonymous tract probably was printed in Boston, Worcester, or Hartford, and it was reprinted in an appendix in Frederick Chase, *History of Dartmouth College* (Cambridge, Mass., 1891). Antipopulism expressed by "Faithful Friend," *Independent Chronicle*, August 7, 1777, quoted in Douglass, *Rebels and Democrats*, 172. Bailyn, *Ideological Origins of the American Revolution*, 293–94 (n. 61), discusses *The People the Best Gove[r]nors* and gives the place of publication as "Hartford?" (294). The "staff of power" surely was a gendered image.

14  Lance Banning, "Political Economy and the Creation of the Federal Republic," in

Devising Liberty: Preserving and Creating Freedom in the New American Republic, ed. David Thomas Konig (Stanford, Calif.: Stanford University Press, 1995), 24–26, 30; Heale, Making of American Politics, 50–51. This paragraph is also drawn from Formisano, "State Development in the Early Republic," 10.

15  Woody Holton, "'From the Labours of Others': The War Bonds Controversy and the Origins of the Constitution in New England," William and Mary Quarterly, 3d ser., 61 (April 2004): 271–316.

16  Thomas J. Humphrey, Land and Liberty: Hudson Valley Riots in the Age of Revolution (DeKalb: Northern Illinois University Press, 2004), 9. Regarding the character of backcountry rebel leaders (which could be characterized as populist), see Richard Maxwell Brown, "Back Country Rebellions and the Homestead Ethic in America, 1740–1799," in Tradition, Conflict, and Modernization: Perspectives on the American Revolution, ed. Richard Maxwell Brown and Don E. Fehrenbacher (New York: Academic Press, 1977), 87. For early insurgencies see also Edward Countryman, "'Out of the Bounds of the Law': Northern Land Rioters in the Eighteenth Century," in The American Revolution: Explorations in the History of American Radicalism, ed. Alfred F. Young (DeKalb: Northern Illinois University Press, 1976), 37–69; and Pauline Maier, "Popular Uprisings and Civil Authority in Eighteenth-Century America," William and Mary Quarterly, 3d ser., 27 (January 1970): 3–35.

17  Humphrey, Land and Liberty, 5–9. Sung Bok Kim argued earlier that the conflicts in the 1750s and 1760s arose less over tenant grievances with the leasehold system and more from conflicting land claims and title disputes, and also from Massachusetts's "expansionism," in Landlord and Tenant in Colonial New York: Manorial Society, 1664–1775 (Chapel Hill: University of North Carolina Press, 1978), 281–415, esp. 412–13, 415. Staughton Lynd viewed the uprising as one of class conflict and prefiguring Anti-Federalist sentiment in Anti-Federalism in Dutchess County, New York: A Study of Democracy and Class Conflict in the Revolutionary Era (Chicago: Loyola University Press, 1962), 37–54.

18  Robert E. Shalhope, Bennington and the Green Mountain Boys: The Emergence of Liberal Democracy in Vermont, 1760–1850 (Baltimore: Johns Hopkins University Press, 1996), 70–97.

19  Richard Maxwell Brown, The South Carolina Regulators (Cambridge, Mass.: Harvard University Press, 1963). Brown points out similar Regulator movements that followed South Carolina's and that the term "vigilante" eventually replaced "Regulator" (ibid., 141). For an emphasis on governmental corruption in creating discontent in the North Carolina backcountry, see A. Roger Ekirch, "Poor Carolina": Politics and Society in Colonial North Carolina, 1729–1776 (Chapel Hill: University of North Carolina Press, 1981), 161, 168–74. On the role of the Scotch-Irish in the Carolina Regulations, see James G. Leyburn, The Scotch-Irish: A Social History (Chapel Hill: University of North Carolina Press, 1962), 301–4.

20  Douglass, Rebels and Democrats, 85.

21  For a superb treatment of economic and religious conditions in the Piedmont leading to the Regulation, see Marjoleine Kars, Breaking Loose Together: The Regulator Rebellion in Pre-Revolutionary North Carolina (Chapel Hill: University of North Carolina Press, 2002), 27–67, quotation, 67. Kars stresses, as have historians of the Massa-

chusetts Regulation, the commitment to a "moral economy" on the part of the Piedmont farmers, but she insists they were not averse to participating in the market. Indeed, she asserts, they understood the market very well and knew they could not pursue their "economic well-being and independence" for themselves "without participating in the market both as producers and consumers. However, they quickly discovered that the playing field was not level. The rules of the market advantaged elites eager to turn the Piedmont into a world dominated by large plantations and the exploitation of enslaved workers" (ibid., 215–16). See also Ekirch, "Poor Carolina," 168–69.

22 Kars, *Breaking Loose Together*, 77, 110–11, 113; last quotation, James P. Whittenburg, "Planters, Merchants, and Lawyers: Social Change and the Origins of the North Carolina Regulation," *William and Mary Quarterly*, 3d ser., 34 (April 1977): 215 (n. 2). See also Marvin L. Michael Kay, "The North Carolina Regulation, 1766–1776: A Class Conflict," in *American Revolution*, ed. Young, 71–123.

23 Douglass, *Rebels and Democrats*, 88, 89, 90. Ekirch describes the Regulators as consisting mostly of small to middling planters and including a few wealthy men, and quotes a contemporary description of a force of 700 Regulators in 1770 as "regulating gentry" (Ekirch, "Poor Carolina," 166).

24 Regarding Alamance, see Douglass, *Rebels and Democrats*, 93–99, first quotation, 98; and Kars, *Breaking Loose Together*, 134. The numbers present and casualties are from Ekirch, "Poor Carolina," 165. In 1777 Whig leaders in New York helped landlords suppress a tenant rebellion as the British had in 1766. Alfred F. Young, *The Democratic Republicans of New York: The Origins, 1763–1797* (Chapel Hill: University of North Carolina Press, 1967), 26. Ekirch argues that the Regulators shared the "Country ideology" invoked against Britain but also acknowledged the disaffection of many from the Whig cause (Ekirch, "Poor Carolina," 183–92, 208–11).

25 John P. Kaminski, Gaspare J. Saladino, et al., eds., *The Documentary History of the Ratification of the Constitution*, 21 vols. to date (Madison: State Historical Society of Wisconsin, 1976–), 9:xxxxv; Woody Holton, "An 'Excess of Democracy'—Or a Shortage? The Federalists' Earliest Adversaries," *Journal of the Early Republic* 25 (Fall 2005): 368, quotation, 381; Jean Butenhoff Lee, "Maryland's 'Dangerous Insurrection' of 1786," *Maryland History Magazine* 85 (Winter 1990): 329–44. In September 1786 New Hampshire farmers surrounded the state legislature demanding the abolition of debts and taxes. Kaminski and Saladino, *Documentary History of the Ratification of the Constitution*, 13:35. In Vermont during the same year farmers petitioned authorities to expel lawyers, cancel or delay debts, or give relief from taxes; angry crowds gathered at courthouses; and in October a mob was talked out of closing the Windsor court. In November some 100 "Regulators," many of them veterans, held the court building a few hours, then left before a large force of militia arrived. In Pennsylvania's Wyoming Valley, settlers won a dispute with land speculators after Vermont's Ethan Allen visited the region, mobilized them to resist, and negotiated a compromise with the state government allowing them to keep their titles. Michael A. Bellesiles, *Revolutionary Outlaws: Ethan Allen and the Struggle for Independence on the Early American Frontier* (Charlottesville: University Press of Virginia, 1993), 246–51; Shalhope, *Bennington and the Green Mountain Boys*, 188–91.

26  Hatch, *Democratization of American Christianity*, 32; Shalhope, *Bennington and the Green Mountain Boys*, 3–13, 35–43, 55–56.

27  George Athan Billias, *The Massachusetts Land Bankers of 1740* (Orono: University of Maine, 1959), 32–35, 40–41; Ronald P. Formisano, *The Transformation of Political Culture: Massachusetts Politics, 1790s–1840s* (New York: Oxford University Press, 1983), 25–26.

28  Robert A. Gross, review of *Shays's Rebellion: The American Revolution's Final Battle*, by Leonard L. Richards (Philadelphia: University of Pennsylvania Press, 2002), *New England Quarterly* 76 (March 2003): quotation, 126. The *Oxford English Dictionary*'s first definition of "regulator" is "one who regulates." A 1655 usage: "Such judges as may be appointed Regulators of the great abuses done thereunto." The second and third definitions of the infinitive similarly suggest persons, indeed officials, with special authority to correct abuses, as do the usages given ("b. To bring or reduce [a person or body of persons] to order. . . . 1687. . . . There are 6 commissioners appointed, who are to inspect all the corporations of England, and regulate them, by turning out such as are against taking away the penall laws and test" and "c. To correct by control").

29  Quotations, Holton, " 'Excess of Democracy,' " 372; Ronald P. Formisano, "Teaching Shays/The Regulation," *Uncommon Sense: A Newsletter of the Omohundro Institute for Early American History and Culture* 106 (Winter 1998): 27–28; Leonard L. Richards, *Shays's Rebellion: The American Revolution's Final Battle* (Philadelphia: University of Pennsylvania Press, 2002), 6–12. Regarding western Massachusetts's use of tactics against the British in the 1760s and 1770s that would be used in the 1780s, see Ray Raphael, *The First American Revolution: Before Lexington and Concord* (New York: New Press, 2002). Richards emphasizes state fiscal policy and taxation and points out that "debtors" lined up for and against the Regulation (Richards, *Shays's Rebellion*, 50–62). Regarding Worcester County, John L. Brooke agrees that debt alone did not separate political actors in 1786 but rather kinds of debt: Regulators tended to be indebted to merchants and gentry in the county's leading towns. See John L. Brooke, *The Heart of the Commonwealth: Society and Political Culture in Worcester County, Massachusetts, 1713–1861* (New York: Cambridge University Press, 1989), 210–13.

30  Bowdoin quotation, Robert A. Feer, *Shays's Rebellion* (New York: Garland, 1988; a reprint of Feer's 1958 doctoral dissertation from Harvard University), 339; Richards, *Shays's Rebellion*, 16–21.

31  Formisano, "Teaching Shays/The Regulation," 29–31. Richards, *Shays's Rebellion*, 16–22, gives a different account of Petersham.

32  Whiting documents reprinted in Stephen T. Riley, "Dr. William Whiting and Shays' Rebellion," *Proceedings of the American Antiquarian Society* 66 (1957): 131–66, quotations, 132, 140, 146. For his opinions, Whiting was convicted of seditious libel and fined (ibid., 130–31). Understanding of the insurgency began to change substantially with the publication of Robert A. Gross, ed., *In Debt to Shays: The Bicentennial of an Agrarian Rebellion* (Charlottesville: University Press of Virginia, 1993); for an excellent introduction to the literature, see Gross, "White Hats and Hemlocks: Daniel Shays and the Legacy of the Revolution," in *Transforming Hand of the Revolution*, ed. Hoffman and Albert, 286–345.

33 An extended version of the argument in this and the succeeding paragraphs can be found in Formisano, "Teaching Shays/The Regulation," 26–35. Significantly, in the private correspondence of the "Friends of Government" *during* the Regulation, they referred uniformly not to "Shaysites" but to the "Insurgents": for example, Artemas Ward, Shrewsbury, to Governor Bowdoin, January 12, 1787; "A Sincere Friend" to Isaiah Thomas, Worcester, December 8, 1786; Sam. King, Worcester, [to Governor Bowdoin], (1786 or 1787?); all in Shays' Rebellion Collection, Miscellaneous Documents, 1786–87, folder 43, American Antiquarian Society, Worcester, Mass. So, too, the first history of the Regulation, a progovernment account, written by the clerk of the Massachusetts legislature: George Richard Minot, *The History of the Insurrection in Massachusetts* (1788; Worcester, Mass.: Isaiah Thomas, 1838), 43, 47, 53, 112, 113.

34 For the operation of a similar mentality during Bacon's Rebellion, see Bertram Wyatt-Brown, *Southern Honor: Ethics and Behavior in the Old South* (New York: Oxford University Press, 1983), 85.

35 Kaminski and Saladino, *Documentary History of the Ratification of the Constitution*, 13:92, 94–96.

36 "Federal Farmers: Letters to the Republican," November 8, 1787, in Kaminski and Saladino, *Documentary History of the Ratification of the Constitution*, 14:50; Knox to Washington, October 23, 1787, in ibid., 13:93. See also Samuel Phillips Savage to George Thacher, March 7, 1788, in ibid., 16:334; and "Publius: The Federalist 74," *New York Packet*, March 25, 1788, in ibid., 16:480. For similar expressions, see Formisano, "Teaching Shays/The Regulation," 32 (n. 37), 33 (n. 42).

37 Jay quotation, Maier, "Popular Uprisings and Civil Authority," 17; Formisano, "Teaching Shays/The Regulation," 26; Alan Taylor, "Regulators and White Indians: The Agrarian Resistance in Post-Revolutionary New England," in *In Debt to Shays*, ed. Gross, 146; the last sentence is a paraphrase from John L. Brooke, "A Deacon's Orthodoxy: Religion, Class, and the Moral Economy of Shays's Rebellion," in *In Debt to Shays*, ed. Gross, 207, 208. Holton refers to the insurgents' mode as traditional "intimidation tactics" in "'Excess of Democracy,'" 371. William Lincoln also stressed "the Regulators'" unwillingness to inflict harm, as well as Shays's reluctance to be a leader, in *History of Worcester, Massachusetts, From Its Earliest Settlement to 1836* (1837; Worcester: Charles Hersey, 1862), 124–26, 128–29.

38 Sandra M. Gustafson, *Eloquence Is Power: Oratory and Performance in Early America* (Chapel Hill: University of North Carolina Press, 2000), 205–6. Several sources cited herein describe this incident. For the protesters' early populist rhetoric, see, for example, "Grievances mentioned in the Various Petitions," Shays' Rebellion Collection.

39 Jonathan M. Chu, "Debt Litigation and Shays's Rebellion," in *In Debt to Shays*, ed. Gross, 81–99; Richards, *Shays's Rebellion*, 89–116, first quotation, 89; second quotation, William Pencak, "'The Fine Theoretic Government of Massachusetts Is Prostrated to the Earth': The Response to Shays's Rebellion Reconsidered," in *In Debt to Shays*, ed. Gross, 131. Richards points out that Daniel Shays was actually atypical of the Pelham folk (Richards, *Shays's Rebellion*, 89–90). Brooke's analysis of the Regulation's "center of gravity" in Worcester County residing in towns with a strong sense of mutual obligation, moral economy, and orthodox religious unity thus par-

allels Richards's emphasis on community (Brooke, *Heart of the Commonwealth*, 213–15, quotation, 214). This dimension of the Regulation is relevant to Edward Countryman's critique of Wood's *Radicalism of the American Revolution* for ignoring popular traditions of resistance and "the intertwined beliefs that small communities should form moral and economic wholes, that these could close out the external world in a time of crisis, and that popular action was justified if gentlemen failed in their duty" (Countryman, "Revolution, Radicalism, and the American Way," 483–84).

40  Quotations, Holton, "'Excess of Democracy,'" 354, 358. Holton points out that sometimes when a man served time in debtors' prison, the designation of head of the household passed from husband to wife (ibid., 354–55).

41  E. Anthony Rotundo, *American Manhood: Transformations in Masculinity from the Revolution to the Modern Era* (New York: Basic Books, 1993), 2.

42  Shalhope, *Bennington and the Green Mountain Boys*, 94, 95.

43  Ibid., 200.

44  G. Thomas Tanselle, *Royall Tyler* (Cambridge, Mass.: Harvard University Press, 1967), 19–20, 22–23, quotation, 60.

45  Royall Tyler, *The Contrast: A Comedy in Five Acts* (Boston: Houghton Mifflin Co., 1920), 79.

46  Ibid., 54.

47  Ibid., 55, 56.

48  Tyler, as Robert A. Gross has put it, drained off the "social tension in the real Jonathans of New England." But on stage thereafter, Gross added, Jonathan "upstaged everyone else" and "eventually became a heroic figure in his own right" (Robert A. Gross, "The Confidence Man and the Preacher: The Cultural Politics of Shays's Rebellion," in *In Debt to Shays*, ed. Gross, 319).

49  Michael Kimmel, *Manhood in America: A Cultural History* (New York: Free Press, 1996), 7; see also David Leverenz, *Manhood and the American Renaissance* (Ithaca, N.Y.: Cornell University Press, 1989), 72–73.

50  Yves Mény and Yves Surel, "The Constitutive Ambiguity of Populism," in *Democracies and the Populist Challenge*, ed. Yves Mény and Yves Surel (Houndmills, U.K.: Palgrave, 2002), 8.

51  Wayne D. Moore, *Constitutional Rights and Powers of the People* (Princeton, N.J.: Princeton University Press, 1996), 67, 68. Edmund S. Morgan has similarly observed that the Federalists' insistence on the "new fiction" of "we the people" over "we the states" led the Anti-Federalists "to a healthy insistence on the ultimate fictitiousness of popular sovereignty itself. . . . In the interests of sanity and self-preservation the people who submitted to a government of their own supposed creation had to remember that government is always something other than the actual people who are governed by it, that governors and governed cannot be in fact identical" (Morgan, *Inventing the People: The Rise of Popular Sovereignty in England and America* [New York: W. W. Norton, 1988], 282). Gordon S. Wood has asserted that the Constitution "was intrinsically an aristocratic document designed to check the democratic tendencies of the period, and as such it dictated the character of the Antifederalist response. . . . Aristocratic principles were in fact 'interwoven' in the very fabric of the pro-

posed government" (Wood, *Creation of the American Republic*, 506–15, quotations, 513, 514–15).

52 Formisano, "Teaching Shays/The Regulation," 32–34; Richards, *Shays's Rebellion*, 139–40. Peter S. Onuf has described the way in which "Shays's Rebellion" became a synecdoche for the crisis of the American republic, though he notes that terms like "civil war" and "anarchy" "did not necessarily falsify 'reality'" (Onuf, *The Origins of the Federal Republic: Jurisdictional Controversies in the United States, 1775–1787* [Philadelphia: University of Pennsylvania Press, 1983], 174–85, quotation, 184).

53 Banning, "Political Economy and the Creation of the Federal Republic," 29–30; Heale, *Making of American Politics*, 51–52; Forrest McDonald, *Novus Ordo Seclorum: The Intellectual Origins of the Constitution* (Lawrence: University Press of Kansas, 1985), 276–78. This paragraph and the preceding and following paragraphs are based in part on material in Formisano, "State Development in the Early Republic," 10–11.

54 Heale, *Making of American Politics*, 60; Rodgers, *Contested Truths*, 86. By 1840 the "white men's republic" would become a "tyrannically uniform 'white man's democracy'" (James Brewer Stewart, "Response," in "SHA Roundtable: The Emergence of Racial Modernity and the Rise of the White North, 1790–1840," *Journal of the Early Republic* 18 [Summer 1998]: 234).

55 Mark E. Kann, *A Republic of Men: The American Founders, Gendered Language, and Patriarchal Politics* (New York: New York University Press, 1998), 1, 3; Kerber, "Paradox of Women's Citizenship," 351; Jay Fliegelman, *Prodigals and Pilgrims: The American Revolution against Patriarchal Authority, 1750–1800* (Cambridge, Mass.: Harvard University Press, 1982); Jan Lewis, "'Of Every Age, Sex & Condition': The Representation of Women in the Constitution," *Journal of the Early Republic* 15 (Fall 1995): 359–87; Joseph J. Ellis, *Founding Brothers: The Revolutionary Generation* (New York: Vintage, 2000). For analysis of the Constitution as a "patriarchal legal text," see Joan Hoff, *Law, Gender, and Injustice: A Legal History of U.S. Women* (New York: New York University Press, 1991), 22–23; regarding paternalists, see also Wood, *Radicalism of the American Revolution*, 145–68. Rosemarie Zagarri has argued that although male elites managed to circumvent the extension of natural rights principles to women at the time of the Revolution, natural rights ideology worked (and was invoked) to subvert women's exclusion. Zagarri, "The Rights of Man and Woman in Post-Revolutionary America," *William and Mary Quarterly*, 3d ser., 55 (April 1998): 203–30.

56 "Madison was inventing a sovereign American people to overcome the sovereign states" (Morgan, *Inventing the People*, 267). Jack N. Rakove, *Original Meanings: Politics and Ideas in the Making of the Constitution* (New York: Random House, 1996), 128–30, 190; Heale, *Making of American Politics*, 44–47, first quotation, 63; Banning, "Political Economy and the Creation of the Federal Republic," 27; Simon P. Newman, "Principles or Men?: George Washington and the Political Culture of National Leadership, 1776–1801," *Journal of the Early Republic* 12 (Winter 1992): 477–507; Paul A. Gilje, *Road to Mobocracy* (Chapel Hill: University of North Carolina Press, 1987), 97–99; second quotation, Lynd, *Anti-Federalism in Dutchess County*, 85. The phrase "agrarian-minded," in contrast to "commercial-minded," is from Lee Benson, *Turner and Beard: American Historical Writing Reconsidered* (Glencoe, Ill.: Free Press, 1960), 216–18. See

also Forrest McDonald, *E Pluribus Unum: The Formation of the American Republic, 1776–1790* (Boston: Houghton Mifflin Co., 1965), 189–208.

57  Saul A. Cornell, "The Changing Historical Fortunes of the Anti-Federalists," *Northwestern University Law Review* 84 (Fall 1989): 64.

58  Ibid., 43–46, 52; Paul Finkelman, "Antifederalists: The Loyal Opposition and the American Constitution," *Cornell Law Review* 70 (November 1984): 182–207; John P. Kaminski, "Antifederalism and the Perils of Homogenized History: A Review Essay," *Rhode Island History* 42 (February 1983): 29–37. Young described New York's Anti-Federalist leaders as typically respectable and middling or newly risen to property, most of them lacking the status and polish of the richest Federalists (Young, *Democratic Republicans of New York*, 42–54).

59  Forrest McDonald, "The Anti-Federalists, 1781–1789," *Wisconsin Magazine of History* 46 (Spring 1963): 214.

60  Saul A. Cornell, *The Other Founders: Anti-Federalism and the Dissenting Tradition in America, 1788–1828* (Chapel Hill: University of North Carolina Press, 1999), 1–15, 38–41; quotation, Main, *Anti-Federalists*, 9. According to Cornell, Anti-Federalists addressed nine issues repeatedly: consolidation; aristocracy; inadequate representation of the people; separation of powers; judicial tyranny; the absence of a bill of rights; taxes; the standing army (not prohibited); and executive power (Cornell, *Other Founders*, 30–31).

61  Cornell, *Other Founders*, 38–40, 41, 83; Main, *Anti-Federalists*, 10, 30, 108.

62  Morgan, *Inventing the People*, 277, 278; Saul Cornell, "Reflections on 'the Late Remarkable Revolution in Government': Aedanus Burke and Samuel Bryan's Unpublished History of the Ratification of the Federal Constitution," *Pennsylvania Magazine of History and Biography* 112 (January 1988): 105–27; Richards, *Shays's Rebellion*, 148. For another source advocating the election of middling men as representatives, see "Observations Leading to a Fair Examination of the System of Government Proposed by the Late Convention, Letters from the Federal Farmer (1787 and 1788)," in Herbert J. Storing, ed., *The Complete Anti-Federalist*, 7 vols. (Chicago: University of Chicago Press, 1981), 2:275–76. According to Richard L. Bushman, "In the minds of people a sharp line divided plain and genteel culture, just as they distinguished in their minds a class of people called 'gentlemen.' 'Polite,' 'fashionable,' 'gentlemen' were the categories of a widespread vernacular culture" (Richard L. Bushman, "American High-Style and Vernacular Cultures," in *Colonial British America: Essays in the New History of the Early Modern Era*, ed. Jack P. Greene and J. R. Pole [Baltimore: Johns Hopkins University Press, 1984], 374). For a critique of the Storing collection, see Finkelman, "Antifederalists."

63  Main, *Anti-Federalists*, 127–29; Cornell, *Other Founders*, 109; Cathy D. Matson and Peter S. Onuf, *A Union of Interests: Political and Economic Thought in Revolutionary America* (Lawrence: University Press of Kansas, 1990), 154.

64  Main, *Anti-Federalists*, 104, 169, 171–73; Saul Cornell, "Politics of the Middling Sort: The Bourgeois Radicalism of Abraham Yates, Melancton Smith, and the New York Antifederalists," in *New York in the Age of the Constitution, 1775–1800*, ed. Paul A. Gilje and William Pencak (Rutherford, N.J.: Fairleigh Dickinson University Press, 1992),

157; Michael Schudson, *The Good Citizen: A History of American Civic Life* (Cambridge, Mass.: Harvard University Press, 1998), 55.

65  Hendrik Hartog, review of *The Other Founders: Anti-Federalism and the Dissenting Tradition in America, 1788–1828,* by Saul Cornell (Chapel Hill: University of North Carolina Press, 1999), in *Journal of Southern History* 67 (November 2001): 837–38.

66  Robert Allen Rutland, "The First Great Newspaper Debate: The Constitutional Crisis of 1787–1788," *Proceedings of the American Antiquarian Society* 97, pt. 1 (1987): 50, 54–55, 57. In addition to other advantages enjoyed by the Federalists, David Waldstreicher has argued, they more successfully used patriotic displays celebrating the Constitution to suppress opposition to it and drew on Revolutionary traditions the better to contain them (David Waldstreicher, *In the Midst of Perpetual Fetes: The Making of American Nationalism, 1776–1820* [Chapel Hill: University of North Carolina Press, 1997], 12, 85–107).

67  Storing, *Complete Anti-Federalist,* quotations, 2:171, 175, 182, 183, also 193, 196; Eric Robert Papenfuse, "Unleashing the 'Wildness': The Mobilization of Grassroots Antifederalism in Maryland," *Journal of the Early Republic* 16 (Spring 1996): 98. Federalists also ridiculed the New England Regulators as effeminate and having a taste for feathers and other luxuries. See Smith-Rosenberg, "Dis-Covering the Subject of the 'Great Constitutional Discussion,'" 854–55.

68  Storing, *Complete Anti-Federalist,* 2:137 (Centinel) and 107, 113, 125 (Cato); for Centinel's references to the danger of slavery, see ibid., 2:171–73, 177, 182; and to rich and powerful seeking more power and "submission" from the "less able," see ibid., 2:172. Cornell has observed that among Anti-Federalist essayists "none employed a more assertive and class-conscious rhetoric" than Centinel (Cornell, *Other Founders,* 100). Bailyn has pointed out that references to "slavery" for the Revolutionary generation referred to "a specific political condition, a characteristic of the lives of contemporary Frenchmen, Danes, and Swedes as well as Turks, Russians, and Poles." While it applied also to the obviously worse-off black plantation slaves, it generally meant subjects of governments "under the absolute and arbitrary direction of one man" (Bailyn, *Ideological Origins of the American Revolution,* 233–34).

69  Philadelphiensis, in Storing, *Complete Anti-Federalist,* 2:109; see also "Address of John Humble," *Philadelphia Independent Gazeteer,* October 29, 1787, in ibid., 89–90. The latter was a mock "address of the low born . . . to their fellow slaves, accepting the dominion of the wellborn over ordinary citizens," agreeing to "leave all *power, authority,* and *dominion* over our *persons* and *property* in the hands of the *well born,*" and contending that "we shall in future be perfectly contented if our *tongues* be left us to lick the feet of our well born masters."

70  First quotation, Cornell, *Other Founders,* 100; Dana D. Nelson, *National Manhood: Capitalist Citizenship and the Imagined Fraternity of White Men* (Durham, N.C.: Duke University Press, 1998), 33, 34.

71  Richards, *Shays's Rebellion,* 32–42, 119. Regarding different opinions in the country regarding tax and relief policies of the state legislatures, see Woody Holton, "Did Democracy Cause the Recession that Led to the Constitution?" *Journal of American History* 92 (September 2005): 442–69.

72  Richards, *Shays's Rebellion*, 143–50, 153–58.

73  Morgan, *Inventing the People*, 284. McDonald, too, holds the Anti-Federalists "right" in the sense that the new government established by the Constitution was not "republican" according to contemporary meanings (McDonald, *Novus Ordo Seclorum*, 285). See also Hartog, review of *Other Founders*, 838.

74  Lance Banning, *Jefferson and Madison: Three Conversations from the Founding* (Lanham, Md.: Madison House, 1995), 60.

CHAPTER THREE

1  Robert H. Wiebe, *The Opening of American Society: From the Adoption of the Constitution to the Eve of Disunion* (New York: Knopf, 1984), 38, 39. See also Joanne Freeman, *Affairs of Honor: National Politics in the Early Republic* (New Haven, Conn.: Yale University Press, 2001).

2  Alfred F. Young, *The Shoemaker and the Tea Party: Memory and the American Revolution* (Boston: Beacon Press, 1999), 92–98, 110, quotation, 113. For a more sweeping thesis that the Revolutionary heritage of "liberty" and "freedom" was crushed during the 1790s, see Larry E. Tise, *The American Counterrevolution: A Retreat from Liberty, 1783–1800* (Mechanicsburg, Pa.: Stackpole Books, 1998). See also related discussions in Kimberly K. Smith, *The Dominion of Voice: Riot, Reason, and Romance in Antebellum Politics* (Lawrence: University Press of Kansas, 1999), 11–83; and Donald S. Lutz, *Popular Consent and Popular Control: Whig Political Theory in the Early State Constitutions* (Baton Rouge: Louisiana State University Press, 1980).

3  First quotation, John R. Howe, "Republican Thought and Political Violence of the 1790s," *American Quarterly* 19 (Summer 1967): 148–49; Paul Goodman, "The First American Party System," in *The American Party Systems: Stages of Development*, ed. William Nisbet Chambers and Walter Dean Burnham (New York: Oxford University Press, 1967), 59; Ronald P. Formisano, "State Development in the Early Republic, 1780–1840," in *Contesting Democracy: Substance and Structure in American Political History, 1775–2000*, ed. Byron E. Shafer and Anthony J. Badger (Lawrence: University Press of Kansas, 2001), 13–15; second quotation, Wiebe, *Opening of American Society*, 81.

4  Richard D. Brown, *Knowledge Is Power: The Diffusion of Information in Early America, 1700–1865* (New York: Oxford University Press, 1989), 270–71, 290–91, quotation, 290.

5  Nathan O. Hatch, *The Democratization of American Christianity* (New Haven, Conn.: Yale University Press, 1989), 5–7, 67–68, quotation, 5. Hatch adds that some of the dissenting religious groups eventually became themselves hierarchical and authoritarian. "Yet despite these authoritarian structures," he concludes, "the fundamental impetus of these movements was to make Christianity a liberating force" (ibid., 11).

6  Mark Douglas McGarvie, *One Nation under Law: America's Early National Struggles to Separate Church and State* (DeKalb: Northern Illinois University Press, 2004), 4, 10–11; Ronald P. Formisano, *The Transformation of Political Culture: Massachusetts Parties, 1780s–1840s* (New York: Oxford University Press, 1983), 154–59, 170, 217–19. In his exhaustive study of disestablishment in New England, William G. McLoughlin

emphasizes that the state laws ending compulsory religious taxation represented a "victory of the common man," while Federalist politicians and Congregational clergy defending the Standing Order viewed its repeal as the "'leveling spirit of democracy'" (William G. McLoughlin, *New England Dissent, 1630–1883: The Baptists and the Separation of Church and State*, 2 vols. [Cambridge, Mass.: Harvard University Press, 1971], 2:1065, quotation, 811).

7 McGarvie, *One Nation under Law*, 13, 17; Mary Kupiec Cayton, "Who Were the Evangelicals? Conservative and Liberal Identity in the Unitarian Controversy in Boston, 1804–1833," *Journal of Social History* 31, no. 1 (1997): 86–92; Thomas E. Buckley, "After Disestablishment: Thomas Jefferson's Wall of Separation in Antebellum Virginia," *Journal of Southern History* 61 (August 1995): 445–80. Fear of conspiracy by an ecclesiastical elite had constituted part of the threat posed by English power against American liberty perceived by the emergent colonial revolutionaries (Bernard Bailyn, *The Ideological Origins of the American Revolution* [Cambridge, Mass.: Harvard University Press, 1967], 97–98, 246–71).

8 Hatch, *Democratization of American Christianity*, 45–46, 59. While dissenting sects regarded the Democratic Republicans as their allies, and the Republicans usually received their votes, the relationship was often complex because of Republican concern for other groups in their coalition, including some Congregationalists (McLoughlin, *New England Dissent*, 2:808–9, 877–93, 1006–1024, 1065–1185).

9 Wiebe, *Opening of American Society*, 81–83, quotations, 85, 40; R. R. Palmer, "Notes on the Use of the Word 'Democracy,' 1789–1799," *Political Science Quarterly* 68 (June 1953): 207, 208, 224.

10 Formisano, *Transformation of Political Culture*, 130, 135, 137. Neither were Virginia Republicans populist reformers; see William G. Shade, *Democratizing the Old Dominion: Virginia and the Second Party System, 1824–1861* (Charlottesville: University Press of Virginia, 1996), 57–59.

11 Although the term "Federalist" as party label did not come into common usage until later in the decade, it will often be used here, in addition to the more accurate label of proto-Federalists, to characterize the Washington administration and its supporters.

12 Thomas J. Humphrey, *Land and Liberty: Hudson Valley Riots in the Age of Revolution* (DeKalb: Northern Illinois University Press, 2004), 112–38, 142; Alan Taylor, *Liberty Men and Great Proprietors: The Revolutionary Settlement on the Maine Frontier, 1760–1820* (Chapel Hill: University of North Carolina Press, 1990), 229.

13 Terry Bouton, "A Road Closed: Rural Insurgency in Post-Independence Pennsylvania," *Journal of American History* 87 (December 2000): 857–61, 876–77, quotation, 866.

14 Ibid., 878–82.

15 Stanley Elkins and Eric McKitrick, *The Age of Federalism: The Early American Republic, 1788–1800* (New York: Oxford University Press, 1993), 469–73, quotation, 472. The authors consider initially the case made by some historians that the whiskey tax was not an economic burden but conclude that it was on its own and part of a larger pattern of grievances: "It *was* a popular movement" (ibid., 467–68, quotation, 473).

16 I have relied on the standard study, Thomas P. Slaughter, *The Whiskey Rebellion: Fron-*

tier Epilogue to the American Revolution (New York: Oxford University Press, 1986), 3, 109–17, 179–83, 186–89, 206; regarding the "rural mob," see ibid., 187; as "a frontier-wide movement," see ibid., 5. See also Roger V. Gould, "Patron-Client Ties, State Centralization, and the Whiskey Rebellion," American Journal of Sociology 102 (September 1996): 409–11, quotation, 410. Gould points out that "serious armed resistance" did not begin until federal officers delivered summonses to delinquent distillers to appear in federal courts in distant Philadelphia, necessitating not only a long, expensive trip but removal from the protective influence of local influentials and judges (Gould, "Patron-Client Ties," 411).

17  Slaughter, Whiskey Rebellion, 109, 117, 165, 169–70, 206; see also Elkins and McKitrick, Age of Federalism, 469. As Jeffrey J. Crow has argued, "Not only was it difficult to collect the excise west of the Appalachians, but in vast areas of cis-Appalachia—notably North Carolina—internal taxes were resisted and ignored with impunity. . . . The law was so abhorrent to North Carolinians that it was virtually unenforceable" (Jeffrey J. Crow, "The Whiskey Rebellion in North Carolina," North Carolina Historical Review 66 [January 1989]: 28).

18  Elkins and McKitrick, Age of Federalism, 467, 470–71; Jacob E. Cooke, "The Whiskey Insurrection: A Re-Evaluation," Pennsylvania History 30 (July 1963): 336–41. Cooke calls into question the legitimacy of the westerners' complaints but points to Neville's role as critical: "If one man was responsible for the whiskey insurrection it was General John Neville" (Cooke, "Whiskey Insurrection," 336). One of Cooke's most provocative arguments is that economic grievances did not play so prominent a part in (his reading of) the westerners' remonstrances; rather, "excise taxes were inimical to the freedom which should characterize a free society" (Cooke, "Whiskey Insurrection," 335). This point brings to mind what David Hackett Fischer characterizes as the "backcountry idea of natural liberty" or "natural freedom" that derived in large part from the British border country (Fischer, Albion's Seed: Four British Folkways in America [New York: Oxford University Press, 1989], 777).

19  Bouton, "Road Closed," 884–85; regarding the "Shaysites" accusation, see William Findley, History of the Insurrection in the Four Western Counties of Pennsylvania (Philadelphia: Samuel Harrison Smith, 1796), 35; Mary K. Bonsteel Tachau, "A New Look at the Whiskey Rebellion," in The Whiskey Rebellion: Past and Present Perspectives, ed. Steven R. Boyd (Westport, Conn.: Greenwood Press, 1985), 98, 110, 111; Crow, "Whiskey Rebellion in North Carolina," 19. Regarding Kentucky, see Saul Cornell, The Other Founders: Anti-Federalism and the Dissenting Tradition in America, 1788–1828 (Chapel Hill: University of North Carolina Press, 1999), 212–13.

20  Steven R. Boyd, "Afterword," in Whiskey Rebellion, ed. Boyd, 184–85; Cornell, Other Founders, 212–13. Slaughter, Whiskey Rebellion, 194–204, argues that just before the federal army marched, moderates had regained control of resistance in western Pennsylvania.

21  Roy F. Nichols, The Invention of the American Political Parties (New York: Macmillan, 1967), 174–77; Elkins and McKitrick, Age of Federalism, 282–88. Although it is not clear how many citizens were paying attention in the early 1790s, "after 1791 or 1792 Republican journalism was always a formidable threat to the party in power" (Donald H. Stewart, The Opposition Press of the Federalist Period [Albany: State University

of New York Press, 1969], 31). Stewart's bibliography of all newspapers, along with their often indeterminate political identifications, indicates that very few Republican papers existed before 1796 (Stewart, *Opposition Press*, 869–93).

22  It is necessary, however, to keep in mind the low level of voters' engagement. Joyce Appleby has referred to Jefferson's and Madison's attempts in the mid-1790s to alert the "largely inert political community of voters about the undemocratic tendencies of the Washington administration" in "E Pluribus Unum: The Ideological Imperative in Revolutionary America," in *Articulating America: Fashioning a National Political Culture in Early America: Essays in Honor of J. R. Pole*, ed. Rebecca Starr (Lanham, Md.: Rowman and Littlefield, 2000), 162.

23  Eugene Perry Link, *Democratic-Republican Societies, 1790–1800* (New York: Columbia University Press, 1942); Elkins and McKitrick, *Age of Federalism*, 451–88. Elkins and McKitrick observe that in the mid-1790s "a 'populist impulse' became discernible" but add that it "had not quite been there before," a view at odds with the one expressed previously here (Elkins and McKitrick, *Age of Federalism*, 451).

24  Link, *Democratic-Republican Societies*, 6–15, 71–85; Elkins and McKitrick, *Age of Federalism*, 457–58, 460, quotation, 457. The latter disagree with Link that the "lower orders" were well represented in the societies and argue that they were led especially by "men of considerable substance" (Elkins and McKitrick, *Age of Federalism*, 458); at the same time they hold that the societies "never did have a great degree of popular support" (Elkins and McKitrick, *Age of Federalism*, 461). There may well have been more than the forty-odd societies counted originally by Link. Forrest McDonald has contended that research by his students uncovered nearly a dozen societies in New England missed by Link (McDonald, *The Presidency of George Washington* [Lawrence: University Press of Kansas, 1974], 130 [n. 3]).

25  Elkins and McKitrick, *Age of Federalism*, 461. Link argued against earlier scholarship that the societies' roots were American; Elkins and McKitrick point to the Jacobin clubs of France, in 1793 not yet in great disfavor in the United States, as immediate models for the societies. See Link, *Democratic-Republican Societies*, 461; Elkins and McKitrick, *Age of Federalism*, 456.

26  Philip S. Foner, ed., *Democratic-Republican Societies, 1790–1800: A Documentary Sourcebook of Constitutions, Declarations, Addresses, Resolutions, and Toasts* (Westport, Conn.: Greenwood Press, 1976), 53, 348, 151. Other assertions of the people's sovereignty came from, for example, the German Republican Society of Pennsylvania; the Republican Society of the Town of Newark, New Jersey; the Republican Society in Portland, Maine; the Democratic Society in the County of Addison, Vermont; and the Democratic Society of the Borough of Norfolk (ibid., 57, 95, 147, 269, 275, 348). In his introduction Foner describes the societies' members as "a coalition of merchants, political leaders, landowners, slaveowners, professionals, small tradesmen, mechanics, seamen, and laborers" (ibid., 9). While he concludes that most members were mechanics, Foner emphasizes the presence of public officials, merchants, and professionals more than Link (ibid., 7–8). Link, as a champion of the societies, argues that their dominant virtue was that they sought to translate the doctrine of popular sovereignty "into actual political life" (Link, *Democratic-Republican Societies*, 124). Their purpose, says David Waldstreicher, was to show that the government

and "the people" were distinct, that the government did not necessarily speak for the people (Waldstreicher, *In the Midst of Perpetual Fetes: The Making of American Nationalism, 1776–1820* [Chapel Hill: University of North Carolina Press, 1997], 131–33, 136).

27 Foner, *Democratic-Republican Societies*, 257; Vermonter quotation, Link, *Democratic-Republican Societies*, 106 (n. 23). The emphasis here is not at odds with the view that the societies expressed traditional republican fears and concerns and also constituted "a democratic and egalitarian uprising not against, but on behalf of, key strands of classical politics" (Matthew Schoenbachler, "Republicanism in the Age of Democratic Revolution: The Democratic-Republican Societies of the 1790s," *Journal of the Early Republic* 18 [Spring 1998]: 241).

28 First quotations, John L. Brooke, "Ancient Lodges and Self-Created Societies: Voluntary Association and the Public Sphere in the Early Republic," in *Launching the "Extended Republic": The Federalist Era*, ed. Ronald Hoffman and Peter J. Albert (Charlottesville: University Press of Virginia, 1996), 309–10; Albert Koschnik, "The Democratic Societies of Philadelphia and the Limits of the American Public Sphere, circa 1793–1795," *William and Mary Quarterly*, 3d ser., 68 (July 2001): 617–18; *Gazette* quotation, Elkins and McKitrick, *Age of Federalism*, 460.

29 Quotation, Link, *Democratic-Republican Societies*, 189; Koschnik, "Democratic Societies of Philadelphia," 635–36; Foner, *Democratic-Republican Societies*, 40; and see, generally, Richard Hofstadter, *The Idea of a Party System: The Rise of Legitimate Opposition in the United States, 1780–1840* (Berkeley: University of California Press, 1969).

30 Quotations, James Thomas Flexner, *George Washington: Anguish and Farewell (1793–1799)* (Boston: Little, Brown and Co., 1969), 183–84; see also Elkins and McKitrick, *Age of Federalism*, 484–85.

31 Elkins and McKitrick, *Age of Federalism*, 485; Link, *Democratic-Republican Societies*, 145–48.

32 Brooke, "Ancient Lodges and Self-Created Societies," 316–23, Jefferson quotation, 323; Foner, *Democratic-Republican Societies*, 35; Koschnik, "Democratic Societies of Philadelphia," 624–25; Link, *Democratic-Republican Societies*, 188–202.

33 Hamilton quotation, Cooke, "Whiskey Insurrection," 336; congressman quotation, Richard A. Kohn, *Eagle and Sword: The Federalists and the Creation of a Military Establishment in America, 1783–1802* (New York: Free Press, 1975), 202; Madison quotation, Elkins and McKitrick, *Age of Federalism*, 486–87; last quotation, Link, *Democratic-Republican Societies*, 206. Brooke has characterized the Republican shift as moving away from the "revolutionary Enlightenment" to the "moderate Enlightenment" (Brooke, "Ancient Lodges and Self-Created Societies," 327).

34 Cornell, *Other Founders*, 200–213, quotations, 217–18. For a similar point regarding Republican leaders' distancing themselves from unlawful actions, see Johann N. Neem, "Freedom of Association in the Early Republic: The Republican Party, the Whiskey Rebellion, and the Philadelphia and New York Cordwainers' Cases," *Pennsylvania Magazine of History and Biography* 127 (July 2003): 268–78. William Findley, for example, wrote shortly afterward, "The great error among the people was an opinion, that an immoral law might be opposed and yet the government respected,

and all other laws obeyed, and they firmly believed that the excise law was an immoral one" (Findley, *History of the Insurrection*, 300).

35 Paul Douglas Newman, *Fries's Rebellion: The Enduring Struggle for the American Revolution* (Philadelphia: University of Pennsylvania Press, 2004), ix–x, 2.

36 Ibid., ix–x.

37 *The Two Trials of John Fries on an Indictment for Treason* (Philadelphia: William W. Woodward, 1800), 17, 81. Fries admitted taking papers from an assessor at Quakertown "but without force; perhaps under the awe and terror of the numbers who demanded them" (ibid., 81).

38 Anne Lombard, "Manhood and Citizenship during the Quasi-War with France, 1797 to 1799," 9, 10, paper delivered at the annual meeting of the Organization of American Historians, March 31, 2005, San Jose, Calif. I am indebted to Professor Lombard for sharing this paper with me.

39 Newman, *Fries's Rebellion*, 38, xi, xii.

40 Ibid., 11, 38.

41 Elkins and McKitrick view the resolutions not "as expositions of constitutional theory but as a powerful piece of party propaganda" (Elkins and McKitrick, *Age of Federalism*, 721). In Kentucky, county conventions called by leading Jeffersonians had replaced the Democratic societies of 1794; see Joan Wells Coward, *Kentucky in the New Republic: The Process of Constitution Making* (Lexington: University Press of Kentucky, 1979), 110.

42 Jefferson and Madison quotations, Elkins and McKitrick, *Age of Federalism*, 723, 724, 724–25; final quotation, of political scientist Stein Rokkan, Formisano, *Transformation of Political Culture*, 7.

43 Brooke, "Ancient Lodges and Self-Created Societies," 316–27, quotation, 313; Hofstadter, *Idea of a Party System*.

44 Taylor, *Liberty Men and Great Proprietors*, 3, 13–21; quotation, Alan Taylor, "'Stopping the Progres [sic] of Rogues and Deceivers': A White Indian Recruiting Notice of 1808," *William and Mary Quarterly*, 3d ser., 42 (January 1985): 91.

45 Taylor, *Liberty Men and Great Proprietors*, 118–21, 184, 189, 192, 268–79. Similarly, in the 1790s the Pennsylvania farmers who resisted tax collectors and revenue officers "blackened their faces and dressed as Indians—or clad themselves in women's clothing" (Bouton, "Road Closed," 882).

46 Taylor, *Liberty Men and Great Proprietors*, 183, 186–88, 195–203.

47 For description of the Republicans' emergence and co-optation of the settler cause, see ibid., 206–7, 209–22, quotations, 216, 222.

48 Ibid., 230, 231–32; Alan Taylor, *William Cooper's Town: Power and Persuasion on the Frontier of the Early American Republic* (New York: Alfred A. Knopf, 1995), 256–87. The tempering of the Jeffersonians, as noted above, began with the Federalist reaction to the Democratic-Republican societies and the Whiskey Rebellion. Seth Cotlar has pointed out that the Federalists' "cultural offensive" of 1798, embodied in the Alien and Sedition Acts but also accompanied by oral and printed attacks on radical democrats as bloodthirsty, atheistic Jacobins, caused established Jeffersonians to distance themselves from radical democrats in their coalition and also tarnished

"what was once an inspirational vision of 'the people' reconstituting their political institutions in order to more literally govern themselves" (Seth Cotlar, "The Federalists' Transatlantic Cultural Offensive of 1798 and the Moderation of American Democratic Discourse," in *Beyond the Founders: New Approaches to the Political History of the Early American Republic*, ed. Jeffrey L. Pasley, Andrew W. Robertson, and David Waldstreicher [Chapel Hill: University of North Carolina Press, 2004], 276–93, quotation, 291).

49 Formisano, "State Development in the Early Republic," 18–19.


CHAPTER FOUR

1 James D. Richardson, *A Compilation of the Messages and Papers of the Presidents, 1789–1897*, 10 vols. (New York: Bureau of the National Literature, 1897), 1:43–46, 130, 218–22, 309–12, 366–70, 451–53, 509–11, 2:509–11.

2 Noble E. Cunningham Jr., *The Presidency of James Monroe* (Lawrence: University Press of Kansas, 1996), 36, 112; Richardson, *Compilation*, 2:573–79, quotations, 2:575–76.

3 Richardson, *Compilation*, 2:655–63, quotations, 2:662, 663.

4 Ibid., 860 65, quotations, 862; Lynn Hudson Parsons, *John Quincy Adams* (Madison, Wis.: Madison House, 1998), 176.

5 George Dangerfield, *The Awakening of American Nationalism: 1815–1828* (New York: Harper and Row, 1965), 231; Richardson, *Compilation*, 2:865–83, quotations, 2:882, 883. "Few presidential programs have been summed up with such cogency; few have offered such evidence of careful thought, keen intelligence, and lofty vision; and few have betrayed so strange an inattention to the known susceptibilities of its audience" (Dangerfield, *Awakening of American Nationalism*, 232).

6 Richardson, *Compilation*, 3:999–1001, 1222–24, 4:1530–37, quotations, 4:1534–35; Marvin Meyers, *The Jacksonian Persuasion: Politics and Belief* (1957; New York: Vintage, 1960), 18–19.

7 "Speech of Mr. Webster, of Massachusetts [January 26 and 27, 1830]," in Herman Belz, ed., *The Webster-Hayne Debate on the Nature of the Union: Selected Documents* (Indianapolis: Liberty Fund, 2000), 125–26 (emphasis added). Regarding the appeal to the majesty, wisdom, and will of the people, see also Daniel T. Rodgers, *Contested Truths: Keywords in American Politics since Independence* (New York: Basic Books, 1987), 89.

8 In his study of "pre-industrial" popular movements in France and England, George Rudé chooses the 1840s as an admittedly "arbitrary" point dividing them from "political demonstrations" of the industrial era (George Rudé, *The Crowd in History, 1730–1848* [New York: John Wiley and Sons, 1964], 5). For an argument that a barter economy persisted as the market developed, see James A. Henretta, "The 'Market' in the Early Republic," *Journal of the Early Republic* 18 (Summer 1998): 289–304.

9 For an introduction to debates regarding the market revolution, see "A Symposium on Charles Sellers, *The Market Revolution: Jacksonian America, 1815–1846*," *Journal of the Early Republic* 12 (Winter 1992): 445–76; and Melvyn Stokes and Stephen Conway, eds., *The Market Revolution in America: Social, Political, and Religious Expressions* (Char-

lottesville: University Press of Virginia, 1996). A perceptive analysis of this literature, along with a mediating argument, can be found in Naomi R. Lamoreaux, "Re-
thinking the Transition to Capitalism in the Early American Northeast," *Journal of
American History* 90 (September 2003): 437–61.

10   George Rogers Taylor, *The Transportation Revolution, 1815–1860* (New York: Rinehart,
     1951); Allan R. Pred, *Urban Growth and the Circulation of Information: The United States
     System of Cities, 1790–1840* (Cambridge, Mass.: Harvard University Press, 1973); quo-
     tation, Ronald P. Formisano, *The Transformation of Political Culture: Massachusetts Parties,
     1780s–1840s* (New York: Oxford University Press, 1983), 176.

11   Bruce Laurie, *Artisans into Workers: Labor in Nineteenth-Century America* (New York: Far-
     rar, Straus and Giroux, 1989), 15–46, quotations, 28, 46.

12   Ava Baron, "Acquiring Manly Competence: The Demise of Apprenticeship and
     the Remasculinization of Printers' Work," in *Meanings for Manhood: Constructions of
     Masculinity in Victorian America*, ed. Mark C. Carnes and Clyde Griffen (Chicago: Uni-
     versity of Chicago Press, 1990), 152–53, quotation, 153; Mary P. Ryan, *Cradle of the
     Middle Class: The Family in Oneida County, New York, 1790–1865* (New York: Cambridge
     University Press, 1981), 155, 178–84, 210, 236, 238; Jeanne Boydston, "The Woman
     Who Wasn't There: Women's Market Labor and the Transition to Capitalism in the
     United States," *Journal of the Early Republic* 16 (Summer 1996): 191, 199–200. French
     tailors resisted the putting-out system and denied employers' claims that home-
     based work strengthened the family. Rather, said the tailors, all work should be
     done at the shops "in a regular and equitable manner," and apprentices could be
     trained as workers and into manhood; otherwise, "honorable craftsmen" would
     be reduced to "miserable *appièceurs*," piece workers used sporadically and having
     status as low as at-home women workers. See Joan Wallach Scott, "Work Identi-
     ties for Men and Women: The Politics of Work and Family in the Parisian Garment
     Trades in 1848," *Gender and the Politics of History* (rev. ed.; New York: Columbia Univer-
     sity Press, 1999), 96–100, quotations, 96, 97.

13   First quotation, Ava Baron, "Questions of Gender: Deskilling and Demasculiniza-
     tion in the U.S. Printing Industry, 1830–1915," *Gender and History* 1 (Summer 1989):
     181; second quotation, David Leverenz, *Manhood and the American Renaissance* (Ithaca,
     N.Y.: Cornell University Press, 1989), 72–74.

14   Quotations, Bruce Dorsey, *Reforming Men and Women: Gender in the Antebellum City*
     (Ithaca, N.Y.: Cornell University Press, 2002), 18; Robert E. Shalhope, *A Tale of New
     England: The Diaries of Hiram Harwood, Vermont Farmer, 1810–1837* (Baltimore: Johns
     Hopkins University Press, 2003), 23, 277 (n. 6). None of the foregoing is meant
     to suggest that "the male-centered workplace" was the only "locus from which the
     identity, behavior, social relations and consciousness" of working men emanated,
     though I would argue that for the threatened artisans described here it was the
     major influence. See Alice Kessler-Harris, "Treating the Male as 'Other': Redefining
     the Parameters of Labor History," *Labor History* 34 (Spring/Summer 1993): 195.

15   Murray N. Rothbard, *The Panic of 1819: Reactions and Policies* (New York: Columbia Uni-
     versity Press, 1962), 14; Samuel Rezneck, "The Depression of 1819–1822: A Social
     History," *American Historical Review* 39 (October 1933): 28, 30–33, Monroe and Adams

quotations, 39. For a detailed account of the impact of the panic on one city, see Vincent F. Bonelli, "The Response of Public and Private Philanthropy to the Panic of 1819 in New York City" (Ph.D. diss., Fordham University, 1976), 19–31.

16  Rothbard, *Panic of 1819*, 7–8, 11, first quotation, 12; Malcolm J. Rohrbough, *The Land Office Business: The Settlement and Administration of American Public Lands, 1789–1837* (New York: Oxford University Press, 1968), 137–38; regarding the Bank of the United States and the treasury secretary's role, see Peter Temin, *The Jacksonian Economy* (New York: W. W. Norton, 1969), 46–48, quotation, 48; Benton quotation, Rezneck, "Depression of 1819–1822," 33.

17  Robert M. Blackson, "Pennsylvania Banks and the Panic of 1819: A Reinterpretation," *Journal of the Early Republic* 9 (Autumn 1989): 341–42. Blackson's article defends the bankers from accusations that they were irresponsible.

18  On the rise of a "middling" populist rhetoric in the 1820s and 1830s, see Kenneth Cmiel, *Democratic Eloquence: The Fight over Popular Speech in Nineteenth-Century America* (Berkeley: University of California Press, 1990), 57–66. For an episode involving white racial populism in the 1820s, see James Simeone, *Democracy and Slavery in Frontier Illinois: The Bottomland Republic* (DeKalb: Northern Illinois University Press, 2000).

19  Rothbard, *Panic of 1819*, 26; Rezneck, "Depression of 1819–1822," 42.

20  Rothbard, *Panic of 1819*, 56; Rezneck, "Depression of 1819–1822," 45–46. For details on the replevin laws considered or passed, see Rothbard, *Panic of 1819*, 32–42. These laws provoked hotly contested political battles in some states. After vigorous campaigns for and against relief, Missouri's legislature in special session passed "one of the most comprehensive programs of relief," providing a two-and-a-half-year moratorium on executions of land debts (there had been extensive buying of land), a strong minimal appraisal law, reduction of penalties for imprisonment for debt, and exemption of various personal necessities from auction sales. By 1822, however, after a court decision overturning the laws and a victory by antirelief forces in elections, the state legislature repealed the entire program. Louisiana's legislature in 1821, without much opposition, passed a stay law suspending execution sales for two and a half years and imposed a floor on the personal property that could be retained by the debtor. See Rothbard, *Panic of 1819*, 42–47, quotation, 42. North Carolina passed a stay law targeted only at buyers who had bought formerly Cherokee land from the state.

21  Rothbard, *Panic of 1819*, 43, 45, 49–50, quotation, 46. In discussing conflicts over monetary expansion between inflationists (paper money) and hard-money advocates, Rothbard concludes that such conflicts "cut sharply across regional, geographic, wealth, and occupational boundaries" (ibid., 187). Although Rothbard discusses proposals and state action regarding monetary expansion separately from relief schemes (ibid., 57–111), they often were tied closely together, as in Kentucky. New York, Massachusetts, and Virginia considered minimal appraisal laws but rejected them.

22  Charles G. Sellers Jr., "Banking and Politics in Jackson's Tennessee, 1817–1827," *Mississippi Valley Historical Review* 41 (June 1954): 62–66.

23  Ibid., 66–70, quotations, 69, 70; on wealthy debtors being prorelief, see Rothbard,

*Panic of 1819*, 49–50. The *Nashville Clarion* boasted that several wealthy men had taken the lead in calling for a special session of the legislature to act on relief measures (Rothbard, *Panic of 1819*, 48).

24 Rothbard, *Panic of 1819*, 47–52; Sellers, "Banking and Politics in Jackson's Tennessee," 70–74, quotation, 73. Sellers concludes that the voters of Tennessee had demanded "a government that would be responsive to the popular will and that would preserve the Jeffersonian ideal of equal opportunity" (Sellers, "Banking and Politics in Jackson's Tennessee," 61).

25 Rothbard, *Panic of 1819*, 52–53; Arndt M. Stickles, *The Critical Court Struggle in Kentucky, 1819–1829* (n.p.: Indiana University Graduate Council, 1929), 17. The depression came early to the previously prosperous Bluegrass region and Lexington; see Stephen Aron, *How the West Was Lost: The Transformation of Kentucky from Daniel Boone to Henry Clay* (Baltimore: Johns Hopkins University Press, 1996), 141–42; Sandra F. VanBurkleo, "'The Paws of Banks': The Origins and Significance of Kentucky's Decision to Tax Federal Bankers, 1818–1820," *Journal of the Early Republic* 9 (Winter 1989): 462; and Matthew Gerard Schoenbachler, "The Origins of Jacksonian Politics: Central Kentucky, 1790–1840" (Ph.D. diss., University of Kentucky, 1996), 124–34, 144–46, 171–74. The "political text" of one relief candidate was that "the will of the majority of the people, fairly expressed, if not contrary to the law of God is the law of the land" (Schoenbachler, "Origins of Jacksonian Politics," 172). State elections were held every August over a three-day period, voting irregularities were common, and militia companies played significant roles. See Richard P. McCormick, *The Second American Party System: Party Formation in the Jacksonian Era* (Chapel Hill: University of North Carolina Press, 1966), 211–12.

26 VanBurkleo, "'Paws of Banks,'" 466–80, quotations, 466, 467, 468, 480; Rothbard, *Panic of 1819*, 102; Kendall quotations, Schoenbachler, "Origins of Jacksonian Politics," 146. On the early bank mania, see Stickles, *Critical Court Struggle in Kentucky*, 9–11.

27 Quotation, VanBurkleo, "'Paws of Banks,'" 483; Stickles, *Critical Court Struggle in Kentucky*, 22. During 1819, various citizens' meetings had called for suspension of specie payments and "moderate paper [money] issue," stirring controversy within the state and as far away as New York City, but the legislature decided to focus on a stay law (Rothbard, *Panic of 1819*, 98–100).

28 Schoenbachler, "Origins of Jacksonian Politics," 157–63, quotations, 157, 168, 169. Clay went from being a critic of the BUS to a champion of the Kentucky Insurance Company and then "legislative midwife" to the Second Bank (1816), subsequently naming ten of the first thirteen directors of its Lexington branch (Aron, *How the West Was Lost*, 136–39, quotation, 137). Clay did not publicly oppose relief.

29 Schoenbachler, "Origins of Jacksonian Politics," 174–82; Rothbard, *Panic of 1819*, 53–55, 102.

30 "The presumption is, always, that the minority is wrong," and it can escape its situation only by enlarging itself and becoming a majority (Schoenbachler, "Origins of Jacksonian Politics," 187–91, 195–98, quotations, 195, 196). For arguments by old and new court legislative champions, see Stickles, *Critical Court Struggle in Kentucky*, 45–57, quotation regarding legislature, 44.

31  Frank F. Mathias, "The Relief and Court Struggle: Half-Way House to Populism," *Register of the Kentucky Historical Society* 71 (April 1973): 163, 165; Donald B. Cole, *A Jackson Man: Amos Kendall and the Rise of American Democracy* (Baton Rouge: Louisiana State University Press, 2004), 81–84; Stickles, *Critical Court Struggle in Kentucky*, 70–71.

32  Lynn Marshall argues that relief voters, as well as several leaders, by 1828 had become Jackson voters, although "no direct popular vote was . . . ever taken on a relief issue" (Lynn Marshall, "The Genesis of Grass-Roots Democracy in Kentucky," *Mid-America* 47 [October 1965]: 281). VanBurkleo, however, comes to a different conclusion: "Few straight lines can be drawn from 1818 to 1821, much less to 1828" (VanBurkleo, "'Paws of Banks,'" 485). It is difficult to tie relief voting to support for Jackson given that in the August 1824 state election nearly 65,000 votes were cast in a relief victory, but in the November presidential election, with little more than one-third the turnout, Clay prevailed with 70 percent of the vote (McCormick, *Second American Party System*, 215).

33  The account that follows is based on the excellent recent study by Matthew H. Crocker, *The Magic of the Many: Josiah Quincy and the Rise of Mass Politics in Boston, 1800–1830* (Amherst: University of Massachusetts Press, 1999); and my earlier research on the episode as reported in Formisano, *Transformation of Political Culture*, 181–87. Other accounts include Robert A. McCaughey, *Josiah Quincy, 1772–1864: The Last Federalist* (Cambridge, Mass.: Harvard University Press, 1974), 100–106; and Samuel Eliot Morison, *Harrison Gray Otis, 1765–1848: Urbane Federalist* (Boston: Houghton Mifflin, 1969), 436–37. On the prevalence of independent, nonpartisan local political movements later on in the nineteenth century, see Ronald P. Formisano, "The Party Period Revisited," *Journal of American History* 86 (June 1999): 100–102. The term "Middle Interest" was used as early as December 5, 1787, in the *Massachusetts Centinel*, quoted in Woody Holton, "An 'Excess of Democracy'—Or a Shortage? The Federalists' Earliest Adversaries," *Journal of the Early Republic* 25 (Fall 2005): 375 (n. 43).

34  Crocker, *Magic of the Many*, 2–4, 24–26; Formisano, *Transformation of Political Culture*, 188–89, 426 (n. 57–58); Brooks quotation, Andrew R. L. Cayton, "The Fragmentation of 'a Great Family': The Panic of 1819 and the Rise of the Middling Interest in Boston, 1818–1822," *Journal of the Early Republic* 2 (Summer 1982): 146.

35  Cayton, "Fragmentation of 'a Great Family,'" 148–52.

36  Crocker, *Magic of the Many*, 27, 32, 45–47, meeting quotation, 47.

37  Ibid., 49–55, *New England Galaxy* and Adams quotations, 49, 55; Tudor quotation, Cayton, "Fragmentation of 'a Great Family,'" 157; Formisano, *Transformation of Political Culture*, 183, 138–39, Otis quotation, 139.

38  Crocker, *Magic of the Many*, 55–59, quotation, 59.

39  Ibid., 64–72; Formisano, *Transformation of Political Culture*, 183–84.

40  Crocker, *Magic of the Many*, 70–73, *Galaxy* quotation, 70; Formisano, *Transformation of Political Culture*, 184–85. Otis advised that the old-line Federalists could not "prevent the triumph of the revolutionary movement manifested in the new city" (Cayton, "Fragmentation of 'a Great Family,'" 162).

41  Crocker, *Magic of the Many*, 80–85; Formisano, *Transformation of Political Culture*, 185; McCaughey, *Josiah Quincy*, 104–5.

42 An Exposition of the Principles and Views of the Middling Interest: In the City of Boston (Boston, 1822), 4, 5, 7; A Defense of the Exposition of the Middling Interest (Boston, 1822); Formisano, Transformation of Political Culture, 185; Crocker, Magic of the Many, 79.

43 Crocker, Magic of the Many, 81–94, 128–30.

44 Ibid., 73–75, Wayland quotation, 74.

45 Cayton sees the Middling Interest as a "vehicle of political and ideological transition" between the Federalist-Republican era and the Democratic-Whig period, wherein traditional communal politics gave way to more flexible modes allowing for conflicts of interest (Cayton, "Fragmentation of 'a Great Family,'" 166). On the Revolution's legacy, see James L. Huston, "The American Revolutionaries, the Political Economy of Aristocracy, and the American Concept of the Distribution of Wealth, 1765–1900," American Historical Review 98 (October 1993): 1079–1105.

46 Craig Calhoun, The Question of Class Struggle: Social Foundations of Popular Radicalism during the Industrial Revolution (Chicago: University of Chicago Press, 1982), vii, xi, xii, 60–94. See also the discussion of Chartism of the 1830s and 1840s in England as combining traditional ideals with demands spawned by the new industrial age in Rudé, Crowd in History, 179, 180, 183.

47 Calhoun, Question of Class Struggle, 8.

48 Ibid., 96–97, 99–100, Cobbett quotation, 101.

49 Spokesmen for workers' organizations and parties used the terms "Workingmen" and "Working Men" variously, and that will be the case here.

50 Alan Fox, History and Heritage: The Social Origins of the British Industrial Relations System (London: George Allen and Unwin, 1985), 70, 82, 87; A. E. Musson, British Trade Unions, 1800–1875 (London: Macmillan, 1972), 17, 22–23, 26–30; Keith Laybourn, A History of British Trade Unionism, c. 1770–1990 (Phoenix Mill, U.K.: Sutton Publishing Limited, 1992), 19, 22–28, 31–32; Edward P. Thompson, The Making of the English Working Class (rev. ed.; Harmondsworth, U.K.: Penguin, 1968); G. D. H. Cole, A Short History of the British Working Class Movement (New York: Macmillan, 1927), 57, 59–63, 67, 70–74, 79–80, 91–92, 105. In 1802 Parliament passed the first Factory Act regulating the use of pauper children in textile factories, but the law had little effect. See B. L. Hutchins and A. Harrison, A History of Factory Legislation (Westminster: P. S. King & Son, 1903), 44–45.

51 Edward Pessen, Most Uncommon Jacksonians: The Radical Leaders of the Early Labor Movement (Albany: State University of New York Press, 1967), 66, 72, 80. "English radicals and reformers of the early nineteenth century could base almost every call for change in the interests of the laboring poor on the theory of natural rights," Pessen argues. "Their Jacksonian labor brethren took note" (ibid., 104).

52 Laurie, Artisans into Workers, 74, 81; Pessen, Most Uncommon Jacksonians, 14; Sean Wilentz, Chants Democratic: New York City and the Rise of the American Working Class, 1788–1850 (New York: Oxford University Press, 1984), 191–204.

53 First quotation, Laurie, Artisans into Workers, 74; for the names, Pessen, Most Uncommon Jacksonians, 10. Though a Workingmen's party seems not to have been organized, newspapers in Rochester, New York, began to air the grievances of artisans, mechanics, and debtors in 1829, and from 1830 "labor newspapers," some short-lived, began publishing for the next few years. See Rochester Craftsman, February 24,

1829; and Whitney A. Cross, "Creating a City: Rochester, 1824–1834" (M.S. thesis, University of Rochester, 1936), 149–50, 242.

54 Laurie, *Artisans into Workers*, 81. For a discussion of the complexity of determining authenticity, see Pessen, *Most Uncommon Jacksonians*, 18–28. For an example of the use of Working Men's rhetoric as a political strategy by a competing elite, see Marc Ferris, "The Workingmen's Party of Hampshire County, 1811–1835," *Historical Journal of Massachusetts* 18 (Winter 1990): 37–60.

55 Quotations, Pessen, *Most Uncommon Jacksonians*, 28, 32, 21.

56 Ibid., 38, 202.

57 Samuel Whitcomb Jr., *Address before the Working Men's Society of Dedham, September 7, 1831* (Dedham, Mass., 1831), 14.

58 Formisano, *Transformation of Political Culture*, 223–24.

59 Michael Kimmel, *Manhood in America: A Cultural History* (New York: Free Press, 1996), 31, 32; last quotation, Gregory L. Kaster, "Labour's True Man: Organised Working-men and the Language of Manliness in the USA, 1827–1877," *Gender and History* 13 (April 2001): 26. Although New York City's Workingmen's factions held different versions of parental manhood, according to Joshua R. Greenberg, all used heavily gendered rhetoric. See Greenberg, "'Powerful—Very Powerful Is the Parental Feel-ing': Fatherhood, Domestic Politics, and the New York City Workingmen's Party," *Early American Studies* 2 (Spring 2004): 193, 198–99.

60 William H. Lofton, "Abolition and Labor: Appeal of the Abolitionists to the North-ern Working Classes," *Journal of Negro History* 33 (July 1948): 261–67. With the ad-vent of the Mexican War and the controversy over the Wilmot Proviso (the extension of slavery into the new territories), Workingmen's spokesmen became more anti-southern and antislavery. See Joseph G. Rayback, "The American Workingman and the Antislavery Crusade," *Journal of Economic History* 3 (November 1943): 160–63; and Lofton, "Abolition and Labor," 280–81. Regarding Garrison, see Herman Schluter, *Lincoln, Labor, and Slavery: A Chapter from the Social History of America* (1913; New York: Russell and Russell, 1965), 40. Michael Kazin describes the producer ethic of early labor radicals as male and white in *The Populist Persuasion: An American History* (2d ed.; Ithaca, N.Y.: Cornell University Press, 1998), 13–14.

61 First quotation, Wilentz, *Chants Democratic*, 266; second quotation, Lofton, "Aboli-tion and Labor," 274. On the "first wave" of penny dailies in New York, several of which had artisan editors who came out of the urban radical republican tradition, see Alexander Saxton, *The Rise and Fall of the White Republic: Class Politics and Mass Cul-ture in Nineteenth-Century America* (New York: Verso, 1990), 96–105. Saxton points out that the *Workingmen's Advocate* and the penny dailies suffered no ambiguity regarding the racial inferiority of American Indians or for the necessity of removing them for white expansion (Saxton, *Rise and Fall of the White Republic*, 102–3).

62 Formisano, *Transformation of Political Culture*, 327–28; Phillips quotation, Lofton, "Abolition and Labor," 273; Leonard L. Richards, *"Gentlemen of Property and Standing": Anti-Abolition Mobs in Jacksonian America* (New York: Oxford University Press, 1970).

63 Lofton, "Abolition and Labor," 277–78. In New York City "artisans as a group" did not endorse abolition, but a minority of artisans formed a significant core of an-tislavery support. See John Barkley Jentz, "Artisans, Evangelicals, and the City: A

Social History of Abolition and Labor Reform in Jacksonian New York" (Ph.D. diss., City University of New York, 1977), 203, 169–70, 192–95, 202; and Wilentz, *Chants Democratic*, 263 (n. 16). Regarding Massachusetts, see John L. Brooke, *The Heart of the Commonwealth: Society and Political Culture in Worcester County, Massachusetts, 1713–1861* (New York: Cambridge University Press, 1989), 362–75; and Bruce Laurie, *Beyond Garrison: Antislavery and Social Reform* (New York: Cambridge University Press, 2005), 7–8, 73, 135–38. Regarding factory workers and mechanics in antislavery societies in Rhode Island, see Deborah Bingham Van Broekhoven, *The Devotion of These Women: Rhode Island in the Antislavery Network* (Amherst: University of Massachusetts Press, 2002), 41–43. Laurie makes a strong case for the interrelatedness of labor reform and abolition in Massachusetts in the 1840s (Laurie, *Beyond Garrison*, 125–51). In the town of Lynn, according to Paul Faler, journeyman shoemakers tended to be hostile to abolitionism; however, Faler argues, while racism was widespread in Lynn among cordwainers, their hostility to antislavery stemmed from the presence of certain moralist manufacturers in the movement and because of the failure of most abolitionists to condemn the "wage slavery" of the North (Paul G. Faler, *Mechanics and Manufacturers in the Early Industrial Revolution: Lynn, Massachusetts, 1780–1860* [Albany: State University of New York Press, 1981], 211–14). Although not as strong as racism and antiabolitionism, nativism also was a significant strain among unionists in New York in the 1830s; see Wilentz, *Chants Democratic*, 266–70.

64 Formisano, *Transformation of Political Culture*, 232.

65 Ibid., 239.

66 Artisan quotation, ibid., 233; last quotation, Laurie, *Artisans into Workers*, 56.


CHAPTER FIVE

1 William Leete Stone, *Letters on Masonry and Antimasonry* (New York: O. Halsted, 1832), 5.

2 Representative works viewing Anti-Masonry as irrational (or opportunist) include David Brion Davis, "Some Themes of Counter-Subversion: An Analysis of Anti-Masonic, Anti-Catholic, and Anti-Mormon Literature," *Mississippi Valley Historical Review* 47 (September 1960): 205–24; Richard Hofstadter, *The Paranoid Style in American Politics* (New York: Knopf, 1965), 6; Edward Pessen, *Jacksonian America: Society, Personality, Politics* (rev. ed.; Homewood, Ill.: Dorsey, 1978), 261–69; and David Brion Davis, ed., *The Fear of Conspiracy: Images of Un-American Subversion from the Revolution to the Present* (Ithaca, N.Y.: Cornell University Press, 1971), xiv. Among treatments of Anti-Masonry that take a neutral or positive view are Lee Benson, *The Concept of Jacksonian Democracy: New York as a Test Case* (Princeton, N.J.: Princeton University Press, 1961), 15–17; and Michael F. Holt, "The Antimasonic and Know Nothing Parties," in *History of U.S. Political Parties*, ed. Arthur M. Schlesinger Jr., 4 vols. (New York: Chelsea House, 1973), 1:575–620. For discussion of other interpretations, see Ronald P. Formisano and Kathleen Smith Kutolowski, "Antimasonry and Masonry: The Genesis of Protest, 1826–1827," *American Quarterly* 29 (Summer 1977): 140–42.

3 Paul Goodman, *Towards a Christian Republic: Antimasonry and the Great Transition in New England, 1826–1836* (New York: Oxford University Press, 1988), 34–53, quotation, 38.

In Goodman's account, even evangelical Christians who saw Masonry as incompatible with their ideal of a Christian republic, and who were engaged in manufacturing or commerce, were, in attacking Masonry, responding to unsettling socioeconomic change.

4 Ibid., 21, 7. Goodman grants that in its origin "there was reason" for suspecting that Masonry had set itself above the law "and constituted a conspiracy at odds with republican government and Christian morality," but Anti-Masonry's growth and spread resulted from psychic anxiety caused by economic, social, cultural, and demographic change (ibid., 5).

5 The analysis here seeks to avoid a common tendency in explanations of social movements to overemphasize "psychic factors" and "non-rational motivations" while neglecting "situational conditions" (quotations, Rudolf Heberle, "Types and Functions of Social Movements," *International Encyclopedia of the Social Sciences* [New York: Macmillan and Free Press, 1968], 14:441).

6 Darrett B. Rutman, "Myths, Moralities, and Mega Theories: The Case of the Antebellum American South," in *Small Worlds, Large Questions: Explorations in Early American Social History, 1600–1850*, ed. Darrett B. Rutman and Anita H. Rutman (Charlottesville: University Press of Virginia, 1994), 281–86, quotations, 283, 285–86. Mark C. Carnes has interpreted the relationship of Masonic fraternalism to capitalism very differently from Goodman: "The fascination for fraternal ritual suggests that even as the emerging middle classes were embracing capitalism and bourgeois sensibilities, they were simultaneously creating rituals whose message was largely antithetical to those relationships and values" (Carnes, "Middle-Class Men and the Solace of Fraternal Ritual," in *Meanings for Manhood: Constructions of Masculinity in Victorian America*, ed. Mark C. Carnes and Clyde Griffen [Chicago: University of Chicago Press, 1990], 51).

7 Steven C. Bullock, *Revolutionary Brotherhood: Freemasonry and the Transformation of the American Social Order, 1730–1840* (Chapel Hill: University of North Carolina Press, 1996), 99–101, 163, 188, 247 (Virginia); 171 (Maryland); 228, 230 (North Carolina); 230, 234–35, 237 (Kentucky); 240, 252 (Tennessee); 240, 311 (South Carolina); 178 (Louisiana); 311 (Alabama); 178 (Louisiana); 252 (Delaware, Missouri); 282 (regarding the decline). In the late eighteenth century Masonic lodges were more numerous in the South than in the North relative to the white population; moreover, Brooke has extensive data regarding the importance of Masonry in southern politics in the 1790s and the fusion thereafter of the Republican political establishment and Masonry. See John L. Brooke, "Ancient Lodges and Self-Created Societies: Voluntary Association and the Public Sphere in the Early Republic," in *Launching the "Extended Republic": The Federalist Era*, ed. Ronald Hoffman and Peter J. Albert (Charlottesville: University Press of Virginia, 1996), 283, 327–29, 339–49, 362–66.

8 Ronald P. Formisano, "Antimasons and Masons: Massachusetts and New York," paper delivered at the annual meeting of the American Historical Association, December 28, 1978, San Francisco, Calif.; Formisano, *The Transformation of Political Culture: Massachusetts Parties, 1780s–1840s* (New York: Oxford University Press, 1983), 217, 219. Several Anti-Masonic leaders promoted railroads as ardently as their opponents and differed mainly in their enthusiasm for moral "improvement" in addition

to economic; see also John L. Brooke, *The Heart of the Commonwealth: Society and Political Culture in Worcester County, Massachusetts, 1713–1861* (New York: Cambridge University Press, 1989), 322, 327–28, 332–33. Richard J. Carwardine has observed that, given the later political migration of most Anti-Masonic voters to the modernizing, commercial Whig Party, their "religious concerns [were] more profound and more durable than their economic anxieties" (Carwardine, *Evangelicals and Politics in Antebellum America* [New Haven, Conn.: Yale University Press, 1993], 359 [n. 27]).

9  Kathleen Smith Kutolowski, "Antimasonry Reexamined: Social Bases of the Grass-Roots Party," *Journal of American History* 71 (September 1984): 274–76, 281, 283, 292–93. Surprisingly, most Anti-Masonic leaders were, like Masons, Episcopalian, though denominational responses were otherwise unpredictable; Anti-Masonry seems to have divided most the Baptist rank and file. The best religious predictor of Anti-Masonry was a "high degree of religious organization and activity . . . and the degree of revival activity" (ibid., 278–79, 283).

10  Robert H. Abzug, *Cosmos Crumbling: American Reform and the Religious Imagination* (New York: Oxford University Press, 1994), 19–29.

11  William Gribben, "Antimasonry, Religious Radicalism, and the Paranoid Style of the 1820s," *History Teacher* 7 (February 1974): 239–54; William Gamson, "Rancorous Conflict in Community Politics," *American Sociological Review* 31 (February 1966): 71–81; Bullock, *Revolutionary Brotherhood*, 285–87.

12  William G. McLoughlin, *New England Dissent, 1630–1883: The Baptists and the Separation of Church and State*, 2 vols. (Cambridge, Mass.: Harvard University Press, 1971), 2:759–60, 829; Bullock, *Revolutionary Brotherhood*. See also Dorothy Ann Lipson, *Freemasonry in Federalist Connecticut, 1789–1835* (Princeton, N.J.: Princeton University Press, 1977).

13  Robert Freke Gould, *The Concise History of Freemasonry* (New York: Macoy Publishing and Masonic Supply Co., 1924), 449–50; Ossian Lang, *History of Freemasonry in the State of New York* (New York: Grand Lodge of New York, 1922), 100–107; Edgar Ewing Brandon, *A Pilgrimage of Liberty: A Contemporary Account of the Triumphal Tour of General Lafayette* (Athens, Ohio: Lawhead Press, 1944), 404, 410, 413, 478–82; Kathleen Smith Kutolowski, "The Janus Face of New York's Local Parties: Genesee County, 1821–1827," *New York History* 59 (April 1978): 159. In newly settled Genesee County there were seventeen Masonic lodges and three Royal Arch chapters in twenty-two towns by the 1820s (Kutolowski, "Antimasonry Reexamined," 276).

14  The terms "counterculture" and "pseudo-aristocratic" are from Lipson, *Freemasonry in Federalist Connecticut*, 228–66; Kathleen Smith Kutolowski, "Freemasonry and Community in the Early Republic: The Case for Antimasonic Anxieties," *American Quarterly* 34 (Winter 1982): 551–53, 559, quotation, 552; Goodman, *Towards a Christian Republic*, 39–42; last quotation, Richard D. Brown, "The Emergence of Voluntary Associations in Massachusetts, 1760–1830," *Journal of Voluntary Action Research* 2 (April 1973): 66, 67–69.

15  Formisano and Kutolowski, "Antimasonry and Masonry," 142–43; Formisano, *Transformation of Political Culture*, 198–200; quotation, William F. Brainard, *Masonic Lecture, Spoken before the Brethren of Union Lodge, New-London, on the Nativity of St. John the Baptist, June 24, A.L. 5825* (New London, Conn., 1825), 4–5.

16 Bullock, *Revolutionary Brotherhood*, 220–25, 228; Kutolowski, "Freemasonry and Community," 544, 547, 555–58. Kutolowski notes a similar pattern found by Lipson in Windham County, Connecticut (Lipson, *Freemasonry in Federalist Connecticut*, 560). In North Carolina the fraternity "helped regulate the election of the governor," and the state had eighteen governors who were Masons during the early republican period (Bullock, *Revolutionary Brotherhood*, 230).

17 Bullock, *Revolutionary Brotherhood*, 246–52, 260–73. Bullock was the first to explain that the Anti-Masonic attack "expressed discontent primarily over the dramatic changes in the fraternity during the years following the Revolution" (ibid., 315).

18 Lipson, *Freemasonry in Federalist Connecticut*, 278–85; Formisano and Kutolowski, "Antimasonry and Masonry," 144–46; Formisano, *Transformation of Political Culture*, 207–10; Bullock, *Revolutionary Brotherhood*, 273. "Its [Masonry's] high-handed actions catalyzed a dramatic revaluation of post-Revolutionary Masonry" (Bullock, *Revolutionary Brotherhood*, 278). A contemporary New York historian guessed that a majority of officeholders owed allegiance to the Craft: "Legislative, judicial and executive officers, from presidents to governors to deputy marshals and constables . . . reverend senator to the town meeting orator, were, I religiously believe, a majority of them free masons" (Jabez D. Hammond, *The History of Political Parties in the State of New York*, 2 vols. [Cooperstown, N.Y.: H. and E. Phinney, 1846], 2:237–38). For an Anti-Masonic clergyman's response to Masonic character assassination, see Ray Potter, "Letter to Lorenzo Dow," Pawtucket, June 4, 1829, appended to Potter, *Memoirs of the Life and Religious Experience of Ray Potter, Minister of the Gospel, Pawtucket* (Providence, R.I.: H. H. Brown, 1829), 5–7.

19 For a full account of the origins of Anti-Masonry, see Formisano and Kutolowski, "Antimasonry and Masonry," 139–45; see also William Preston Vaughn, *The Antimasonic Party in the United States, 1826–1843* (Lexington: University Press of Kentucky, 1983), 1–9; and James S. Chase, *Emergence of the Presidential Nominating Convention* (Urbana: University of Illinois Press, 1973), 122–55. Even Chase refers to Anti-Masonry as a "virus" (Chase, *Emergence of the Presidential Nominating Convention*, 138).

20 Samuel D. Greene, *The Broken Seal; or, Personal Reminiscences of the Morgan Abduction and Murder* (Boston: Published for the author by H. H. and T. W. Carter, 1870), 35.

21 These paragraphs are based heavily on Formisano and Kutolowski, "Antimasonry and Masonry," 147–49. Formisano and Kutolowski rely primarily on writings by Masons to reconstruct the kidnapping: Erik McKinley Erickson and J. Hugo Tatsch, "The Morgan Affair," *The Builder* 12 (September 1926): 257–64, 283; unsigned article, *Masonic Standard*, July 29, 1899, reprinted in Richard Addison Searing, *History of Monroe Commandery No. 12, R. T., Stationed at Rochester, New York, 1826–1912* (Rochester, N.Y.: Geneva Press, 1913), 212–15; and the best account by a Mason, Clarence O. Lewis, "The Morgan Affair," 1966 typescript, Niagara County Historical Society and Lockport Public Library, Lockport, N.Y.

22 For more details regarding Genesee and other counties, see Formisano and Kutolowski, "Antimasonry and Masonry," 154–56. Regarding the guilty pleas, see Stone, *Letters*, 214–15, 218–19. Frederick Whittlesey, a Rochester editor who was at first hesitant about Anti-Masonry, later recalled Masons not aiding the investigation; ridiculing and justifying the crime; boasting of their influence with judges,

sheriffs, jurors, and witnesses; and taunting investigators' inability to punish any-one. See "Political Antimasonry," in Hammond, *History of Political Parties*, 2:373.

23  Stone, *Letters*, 226–27, 263–65, 535–37, quotation, 537. The "Introduction" to the Anti-Masons' printing of *The Trial of James Lackey, Isaac Everton, Chauncey H. Coe . . . [et al.] for Kidnapping Capt. William Morgan. At the Ontario General Sessions, Held at Canandaigua, Ontario County, Aug. 22, 1827* (New York, 1827), 4, mentions the comforts provided "imprisoned conspirators."

24  Formisano and Kutolowski, "Antimasonry and Masonry," 151–52, Spencer quotation, 152. Regarding the widespread belief in Morgan's murder by December 1826, see the report of comments of the judge of Common Pleas Court for Monroe County, in *Geneva Gazette and General Advertiser*, December 13, 1826, American Antiquarian Society, Worcester, Mass. In 1827 the thirty-nine-year-old Spencer had been appointed with two other lawyers to revise the statutes of New York. In 1831 when Alexis de Tocqueville and his friend Gustave de Beaumont visited Spencer at his Canandaigua Lake home, de Beaumont wrote that he found Spencer "the most distinguished man yet I have met in America." See Elizabeth Bruchholtz Haigh, "New York Antimasons, 1826–1833" (Ph.D. diss., University of Rochester, 1980), 252, 295. Haigh's is an exceptionally useful dissertation.

25  Formisano and Kutolowski, "Antimasonry and Masonry," 156–57. Anti-Masons told the legislature that while New York law harshly punished the kidnapping of blacks, with a fine of up to $2,000 and up to fourteen years' hard labor, no real punishment existed for kidnapping whites. The 1827 law made kidnapping a felony punishable by three to fourteen years' hard labor (Haigh, "New York Antimasons," 172–73, 184).

26  *Batavia Republican Advocate*, September 15, 22, October 6, 20, 1826. Regarding the Rochester committee, see *Batavia Republican Advocate*, December 29, 1826; and Frederick Whittlesey, "Book of Clippings and Handwritten Items Regarding the Morgan Abduction," Local History, Rochester Public Library, Rochester, N.Y. For various reported meetings in the region see *Batavia Republican Advocate*, October 18, December 8, 1826, January 5, 14, 17, 19, March 2, 30, 1827. Bullock, *Revolutionary Brotherhood*, 280, 294, agrees that protests did not begin as an attempt to overthrow Masonry and that Masonic intransigence led to a broader movement against it.

27  Regarding a February 21 meeting in Middlebury, Genesee County, see Henry Brown, *A Narrative of the Excitement in Western New York* (Batavia, N.Y.: Adams and McCleary, 1829), 116–17; for other meetings, see ibid., 117–18; *Batavia Republican Advocate*, June 29, July 20, August 3, 31, September 7, 14, 1827; and *Rochester Album*, July 31, 1827. The failure of Masonic moderates is revealed by the fate of Rochester's "Morgan Committee," formed in December. The non-Masons on the committee soon learned that the Masonic members were relaying confidential discussions to the Rochester-area lodges (Formisano and Kutolowski, "Antimasonry and Masonry," 161).

28  Benson, *Concept of Jacksonian Democracy*, 22, 21; *Rochester Balance*, October 1, 1827.

29  Benson, *Concept of Jacksonian Democracy*, 9; Robert O. Rupp, "Social Tensions and Political Mobilization in Jacksonian Society: A Case Study of the Antimasonic Party in New York, Pennsylvania, and Vermont, 1827–1840" (Ph.D. diss., Syracuse University, 1983), 41–42, 46–48.

30  Benson, *Concept of Jacksonian Democracy*, 9–10. For reaction against the Bucktails as "the party," see Albert Haller Tracy to Thurlow Weed, November 29, 1825, Weed Papers, Rush Rhees Library, University of Rochester, Rochester, N.Y.

31  Hanyan and Hanyan point out that the 1823 People's Party New York City candidates tended to be lawyers, merchants, and involved in finance more than their Bucktail opponents. They describe the Clintonian-People's coalition as commercially oriented and standing as much for economic development and enterprise as against "a political party, controlled by a cabal of aspiring and desperate politicians" (Craig Hanyan with Mary L. Hanyan, *DeWitt Clinton and the Rise of the People's Men* [Montreal: McGill-Queen's University Press, 1996], 217–18, quotation, 241, and 118–48, 172, 184, 213, 242–46). See also Kutolowski, "Janus Face of New York's Local Parties," 151–54. One skeptical supporter of the People's Party observed decades later that "love of rights of 'the people' were secondary affairs, and this was well understood by the Regency" (Oren Follett letter of 1881, quoted in Harriet A. Weed, ed., *Autobiography of Thurlow Weed*, 2 vols. [Boston: Houghton Mifflin and Co., 1883], 1:131).

32  Vaughn, *Antimasonic Party*, 21–22; Lorman Alfred Ratner, "Antimasonry in New York State: A Study in Pre–Civil War Reform" (M.A. thesis, Cornell University, 1958), 1–73.

33  Thompson received 38.5 percent and Southwick 12.1 percent. Vaughn, *Antimasonic Party*, 27–31; Alvin Kass, *Politics in New York State, 1800–1830* (Syracuse, N.Y.: Syracuse University Press, 1965), 125–26. The phrase "visionary and unsound" originated with Whittlesey (Hammond, *History of Political Parties*, 2:389); Hammond added that most Anti-Masons looked on Southwick's candidacy "as an abortion" (Hammond, *History of Political Parties*, 2:390). Weed later described Southwick as "blinded by his credulity and enthusiasm" (Weed, *Autobiography*, 1:86). For Weed's negative view of Southwick at the time, see Thurlow Weed, Rochester, to George M. Boughton, March 29, 1829, Weed Papers. Whittlesey complained to Weed that "many have been deterred from examining the subject [Masonic crimes] by the rant and fustian of Southwick" (Whittlesey, Rochester, to Thurlow Weed, March 1830 [no day], Weed Papers). Some Anti-Masons even believed that Southwick's nomination was "a project of the Jackson folks" (Philo C. Fuller quoted in Haigh, "New York Antimasons," 153). While that suspicion came easily to the Weed-Seward group (Haigh, "New York Antimasons," 156–58, 160, 194), the depiction by some historians of Southwick as not only an "ultra" but also a "pure" Anti-Mason overlooks Southwick's long and somewhat checkered political career, his sudden conversion to both intense Christianity and Anti-Masonry, and his alleged leaking of confidential information that hurt the prosecution of Masons; he was more willing than the republican Anti-Masons to blur the line between church and state (Haigh, "New York Antimasons," 124, 127–30, 132–33, 145–46, 165, 166–70). Regarding Southwick's well-established reputation as "eccentric," see Chase, *Emergence of the Presidential Nominating Convention*, 133.

34  First quotation, Vaughn, *Antimasonic Party*, 29; second quotation, a contemporary favorable reference to supporters of Clinton, Charles G. Hanes to Thurlow Weed, September 4, 1824, Weed Papers.

35  Kutolowski, "Antimasonry Reexamined," 285. Seward's biographer observes that charges of opportunism in regard to his embrace of Anti-Masonry "roused in him

a fury of indignation" (Glyndon G. Van Deusen, *William Henry Seward* [New York: Oxford University Press, 1967], 26). The author of a careful dissertation (directed by Christopher Lasch), after working through the manuscript collections of several Anti-Masonic leaders, has concluded that it would be "impossible to overestimate" the depth of these lawyers' and editors' beliefs in republican institutions (Haigh, "New York Antimasons," 323). For the Weed-Seward-Whittlesey group, indeed, Anti-Masonry was "primarily . . . a civic movement" (Haigh, "New York Antimasons," 50).

36 Frederick Whittlesey to Thurlow Weed, April 7, 1831, Weed Papers. Other letters in this vein to Weed include Robert H. Backus, Peterboro, September 10, 1828; Heman Norton, Albany, January 3, 1829, and February 2, 1829 (regarding his excitement at Anti-Masonic members of the senate and assembly *calling themselves* Anti-Masons and preparing to caucus); Frederick Whittlesey, January 6, 1830; F. F. Backus, Rochester, January 21, 1830; William L. Bishop, Rochester, April 10, 1830; William Leete Stone, Saratoga Springs, August 5, 1830; Francis Granger, Canandaigua, August 9, 1830; and George H. Boughton, Lockport, March 15, 1831. Similarly, see Thurlow Weed, Albany, to William Henry Seward, November 3, 1831; Albert H. Tracy, Albany, to Seward, November 19 and 26, 1831; Salmon G. Grover, Springwater, to Seward, November 12, 1831; and Seth Hunt, Keene, to Seward, November 21, 1831; all in William Henry Seward Papers, Rush Rhees Library, University of Rochester, Rochester, N.Y. See also Seward's description of Weed as politician and friend in a letter dated January 12, 1831, quoted in Frederick W. Seward, *William Henry Seward: An Autobiography from 1801 to 1834* (New York: Derby and Miller, 1891), 166. Weed saw himself as acting "honestly and honorably" (Thurlow Weed, Rochester, to George M. Boughton, March 31, 1829, Weed Papers). Vaughn regards Seward's Anti-Masonry as "genuine" and Weed's as "reasonably sincere" (Vaughn, *Antimasonic Party*, 49).

37 Granger was the son of Gideon Granger of Connecticut, postmaster general during the Jefferson and Madison administrations.

38 Vaughn, *Antimasonic Party*, 32–39; Benson, *Concept of Jacksonian Democracy*, 34. "We cannot conceal it from ourselves that Anti-Masonry is not alone powerful enough to triumph but operated with all the other materials of opposition to the present administration, it will succeed; and antimasonry will receive universally the credit of victory" (Frederick Whittlesey, Rochester, to Thurlow Weed, July 30, 1830, Weed Papers). In discussing Rochester Jacksonians' efforts to adopt at the next election "the banner of the working men," Whittlesey mocked the Jackson men and asked, "Who are the real *working-men* here—all of them almost Anti Masons—who are the farmers & mechanics—all of them Anti Masons" (Whittlesey to Weed, April 9, 1830, Weed Papers).

39 Benson, *Concept of Jacksonian Democracy*, 34–35; Haigh, "New York Antimasons," 171, 198, 210–12, 218–19; Samuel G. Andrews, Rochester, to Thurlow Weed, January 23, 1830, Weed Papers; *Rochester Anti-Masonic Enquirer*, February 23, 1830; Antimasonic Legislators Address to Constituents, April 20, 1830, in *Anti-Masonic Enquirer*, May 4, 1830.

40 Van Deusen, *William Henry Seward*, 19–20; "Farmers of Genesee! Look at This! E. T. Throop, the *Masonic* candidate for *Governor*, recommends levying, as a DIRECT TAX,

upon your property, to support *Masonic* aristocrats, the enormous sum of 300.000 DOLLARS!" (Antimasonic Broadside, [1830], No. 118, Olin Library, Cornell University, Ithaca, N.Y.). Regarding canal tolls, see Frederick Whittlesey, Rochester, to Thurlow Weed, April 9, 10, and 11, 1830, Weed Papers. The 1830 mechanics' lien law applied to New York City and County; see *Laws of the State of New York, Passed at the Fifty-Third Session of the Legislature, 1830* (Albany: E. Croswell, 1830), 412–13.

41  Charles E. Brooks, *Frontier Settlement and Market Revolution: The Holland Land Purchase* (Ithaca, N.Y.: Cornell University Press, 1996), 143–75; Kass, *Politics in New York State,* 104–9. "The political success of a host of local factions and parties in the Holland Purchase from the Clintonian Republicans to the Antimasons to the Whigs turned on their ability to stand publically against the 'aristocrats' who beguiled and exploited the majority" (Brooks, *Frontier Settlement and Market Revolution,* 221).

42  Brooks, *Frontier Settlement and Market Revolution,* 176–95, quotations, 186; Kutolowski, "Antimasonry Reexamined," 276–77. For presentations of the Anti-Masons simply as champions of the debtor farmers, see Kass, *Politics in New York State,* 104–9; and Benson, *Concept of Jacksonian Democracy,* 26 (n. 16). Regarding Wayne County, see Antimasonic Broadside, [1830], No. 2113, Olin Library, Cornell University, Ithaca, N.Y. One of Weed's correspondents wrote that the Holland Land Company agent controlled "a debt of more than seven millions of dollars against the settlers" in several counties and was using all his power against "our party, in order to subserve the views of Van Buren and the Masons" (George Washington Lay, Batavia, to Thurlow Weed, February 6, 1829, Weed Papers). Lay urged Weed in his editorials to assail "Monied Aristocracies of every description."

43  Nevertheless, Seward, as governor in 1840, confronting the beginnings of more serious tenant discontent on the great semifeudal manors of eastern New York, called for thoroughgoing land reform. He thereby angered the conservative wing of his party, leading Weed to complain to him privately of too many Whigs governing only for the rich and retaining automatic hostility to every measure that would put "the protecting aegis of the law around the rights and happiness of the lower classes." See Charles W. McCurdy, *The Anti-Rent Era in New York Law and Politics: 1839–1865* (Chapel Hill: University of North Carolina Press, 2001), 32–33, 67–68, Weed quotation, 68; and Brooks, *Frontier Settlement and Market Revolution,* 185–86.

44  Benson, *Concept of Jacksonian Democracy,* 44; Arthur M. Schlesinger Jr., *The Age of Jackson* (Boston: Little, Brown and Co., 1945), 134; *Anti-Masonic Enquirer,* May 4, 1830; Seward, *Autobiography,* 84. Fillmore drafted the bill with the help of the more experienced John Spencer; see Robert C. Schelin, "Millard Fillmore: Anti-Mason to Know-Nothing: A Moderate in New York Politics, 1828–1856" (Ph.D. diss., State University of New York at Binghamton, 1975), 31–33. For a self-serving but inside account of how Whittlesey outflanked the opposition at a Rochester meeting regarding imprisonment for debt, see Frederick Whittlesey, Rochester, to Thurlow Weed, January 26, 1830, Weed Papers.

45  Vaughn, *Antimasonic Party,* 40, 42–43. Henry Clay would not repudiate Masonry and eventually issued a criticism of Anti-Masonry. He and other National Republican leaders regarded the "egalitarian populism" of Anti-Masonry as dangerous. See

Michael F. Holt, *The Rise and Fall of the American Whig Party: Jacksonian Politics and the Onset of the Civil War* (New York: Oxford University Press, 1999), 14.

46 Vaughn, *Antimasonic Party*, 46–48; Weed quotation, Van Deusen, *William Henry Seward*, 26.

47 Vaughn, *Antimasonic Party*, 52, and Benson, *Concept of Jacksonian Democracy*, 36, give slightly varying figures regarding Masonry's decline but agree on Anti-Masonry's devastating impact west and north of the Hudson.

48 Lawrence Goodwyn, *Democratic Promise: The Populist Moment in America* (New York: Oxford University Press, 1976).

49 Vaughn, *Antimasonic Party*, 26–27; David Paul Nord, *Faith in Reading: Religious Publishing and the Birth of Mass Media in America* (New York: Oxford University Press, 2004), 6, 89–111; Candy Gunther Brown, *The Word in the World: Evangelical Writing, Publishing, and Reading in America, 1789–1880* (Chapel Hill: University of North Carolina Press, 2004), 1–2, 7, 12, quotation, 27. On the similar fixation of the temperance movement with "facts," see Abzug, *Cosmos Crumbling*, 93–94.

50 Alexis de Tocqueville, *Journey to America*, ed. J. P. Mayer, trans. George Lawrence (New Haven, Conn.: Yale University Press, 1960), 16, 29.

51 Richard Ray Lansing, Utica, to Thurlow Weed, March 23, 1829, Weed Papers; Heman Norton, Albany, to Thurlow Weed, February 2, 1829, Weed Papers; A. W. Foster, Greensburgh [Pa.], to Thurlow Weed, July 21, 1829, Weed Papers. Anti-Masons also distributed literature in Pennsylvania printed in German; see Haigh, "New York Antimasons," 309 (n. 166). "Ward's review" was Henry Dana Ward's *Antimasonic Review* (New York); "Stearns book" referred to Elder John G. Stearns, a Baptist clergyman, who had renounced Masonry before Morgan's disappearance in July 1826 and then in September published *A Inquiry into the Nature and Tendency of Speculative Masonry.* "Parkers sermon" was likely Joel Parker, *The Signs of the Times: A Sermon, Delivered in Rochester, December 4, 1828, Being the Day of Publick Thanksgiving* (Rochester: E. Peck, 1828). Parker was pastor of the Third Presbyterian Church. Regarding the circulation of books and pamphlets by agents in Oneida County, see Richard Ray Lansing, Utica, to Thurlow Weed, March 12, 1829, Weed Papers. Lansing believed that "newspaper information is not received so favorably as that contained in a book." See also *Greenfield Franklin Freeman*, January 7, 1833, American Antiquarian Society.

52 Frederick Whittlesey to Thurlow Weed, February 1, 1830, Weed Papers; Harvey Ely, Rochester, to Weed, February 20, 1830, Weed Papers; Whittlesey, Rochester, to Weed, August 4, 1830, Weed Papers. Once he took the plunge and allied himself with the Anti-Masons, Spencer himself shared the view that printed information and its dissemination would gain converts. He wrote to Seward that the Anti-Masons' 1831 legislative address "[on] the canal boat . . . was the subject of much conversation." "All we have to desire," he continued, "is that people will talk about such things and will read for themselves" (quoted in Haigh, "New York Antimasons," 294 [n. 126]).

53 Timothy Childs to Thurlow Weed, Rochester, July 14, 1830, Weed Papers. From Rhode Island came requests to Weed for all information and "facts" regarding Masonic oaths and penalties, and of any connection of New York Masonry with Rhode Island lodges; see William Sprague, Providence, to Thurlow Weed, November 22,

1831, Weed Papers; and Benjamin F. Hallett to Thurlow Weed, November 24, 1831, Weed Papers. Michael Holt has offered a political explanation for the spread of the Anti-Masonic party, attributing it to the weakness of two-party competition in particular states. See Holt, *Political Parties and American Political Development from the Age of Jackson to the Age of Lincoln* (Baton Rouge: Louisiana State University Press, 1992), 5–6. The focus here, however, is on the spread of Anti-Masonic sentiment and the movement.

54 Timothy Childs to Thurlow Weed, July 14, 1830, Weed Papers; Formisano, *Transformation of Political Culture*, 203; *Antimasonic Review* 2, no. 1 (1830): 28–30. Although presented in hyperbolic rhetoric, even the archetypical "ultraist" Anti-Mason Solomon Southwick, in his speech to the formative 1829 New York state convention, rehearsed in great detail events of 1826 before and after the kidnapping, evidence from the trials, inquiries, and seceders, regarding both the outrages and the protection of the guilty from punishment. *Speech of Solomon Southwick at the Opening of the New-York Anti-Masonic State Convention, at the Capitol, in Albany, February 19th, 1829* (Albany, N.Y.: D. B. Packard and Co., 1829).

55 *Proceedings of the Antimasonic Republican Convention of the State of Maine, 1834* (Hallowell, Maine: Herrick and Rice, 1834), 10, 21.

56 Ibid., 23.

57 John L. Brooke, "To Be 'Read by the Whole People': Press, Party, and Public Sphere in the United States, 1789–1840" (Worcester, Mass.: American Antiquarian Society, 2002), 85. See also Milton W. Hamilton, "Anti-Masonic Newspapers," *Papers of the Bibliographical Society of America* 32 (1938): 74–75, 77. Regarding Masonic pressure on editors and newspapers, see Haigh, "New York Antimasons," 60, 209; and Bullock, *Revolutionary Brotherhood*, 286. At an Anti-Masonic meeting in the town of Gates in Monroe County, Anti-Masons raised fifty dollars for "free circulation" of the *Antimasonic Enquirer* in that town; see Frederick Whittlesey, Rochester, to Thurlow Weed, January 21, 1830, Weed Papers.

58 Bullock has noted that "most" newspapers, only one-eighth of which were Anti-Masonic, refused to publicize Anti-Masonic activities and had been silent regarding the "outrages" (Bullock, *Revolutionary Brotherhood*, 284).

59 William Henry Seward to Thurlow Weed, November 14, 1832, Weed Papers. This important letter is further evidence of Seward's commitment to Anti-Masonry, filled as it is with reasons and exhortation to keep fighting, though it also contains hints of ambivalence. Seward also emphasized the distraction of the contest between Jackson and Clay, among other causes of Anti-Masonry's failure to gain politically. It corroborates the letters cited in note 36 above. On the absence of newspaper attention to "the abduction of Morgan and the great Stir at the West" in the New York City area, see Hosea L. Grover, Springwater, N.Y., to W. H. Seward, Seward Papers.

60 Richard D. Brown, *Knowledge Is Power: The Diffusion of Information in Early America, 1700–1865* (New York: Oxford University Press, 1989), 272, 296. Bullock termed print "the heart of the Antimasonic movement" (Bullock, *Revolutionary Brotherhood*, 284).

61 Richard R. John, *Spreading the News: The American Postal System from Franklin to Morse* (Cambridge, Mass.: Harvard University Press, 1995), 31, 37–38, 53–57.

62 Brooke, "To Be 'Read by the Whole People,'" 55, 61, 72.

63 William J. Gilmore, *Reading Becomes a Necessity of Life: Material and Cultural Life in Rural New England, 1780–1835* (Knoxville: University of Tennessee Press, 1989), 354–59; Andrew W. Robertson, "Voting 'Rites': The Implications of Deference in Virginia Electioneering Ritual, 1780–1820," in *Articulating America: Fashioning a National Political Culture in Early America: Essays in Honor of J. R. Pole*, ed. Rebecca Starr (Lanham, Md.: Rowman and Littlefield, 2000), 149–51; Nathan O. Hatch, *The Democratization of American Christianity* (New Haven, Conn.: Yale University Press, 1989), 11. Jack Larkin differs with Gilmore: Americans were for a rural people "strikingly literate, surpassing most of the nations of Western Europe," but most did not read very much (Larkin, *The Reshaping of Everyday Life, 1790–1840* [New York: Harper and Row, 1988], 35–36).

64 Benson, *Concept of Jacksonian Democracy*, 20, 18. Benson notes that the relationships between internal improvements, economic expansion, religious revivals, Anti-Masonry, and benevolent movements had been traced in Whitney R. Cross, *The Burned-Over District: The Social and Intellectual History of Enthusiastic Religion in Western New York, 1800–1850* (Ithaca, N.Y.: Cornell University Press, 1950), 55–137. On western New York's "economic boom," see Neil Adams McNall, *An Agricultural History of the Genesee Valley, 1790–1860* (Philadelphia: University of Pennsylvania Press, 1952), 178–81; and Ronald E. Shaw, *Erie Water West: A History of the Erie Canal, 1792–1854* (Lexington: University of Kentucky Press, 1966), 260–67.

65 *Batavia Republican Advocate*, October 15, 1826.

66 Hammond, *History of Political Parties*, 2:379; Seward, *Autobiography*, 71–72; *Proceedings of the Anti-Masonic Republican Convention of the County of Cayuga* (Auburn, N.Y.: Thomas M. Skinner, 1830), 19; *Anti-Masonic Enquirer*, March 3, 1830; Frederick Whittlesey, Rochester, to Thurlow Weed, July 13, 1830, Weed Papers; and see note 36, above. The sense that association with Anti-Masonry could tarnish a rising politician's career was expressed in a friend of Seward's warning him in 1829 to "be *moderate*" (William Kent, New York, to W. H. Seward, November 27, 1829, Seward Papers). Regarding Anti-Masonic local elite status, Kutolowski has commented: "Historians ought not to be surprised. . . . Like other political parties and factions of the early republic, Antimasons turned to established local professionals and businessmen—that is, to men with means, time, knowledge, and channels of communication—to organize their electoral efforts. Such had been the pattern of New York's Bucktails and Clintonians before them. . . . But that is no reason to deny the Antimasonic leaders an ideological base; theirs was characteristically a marriage of pure and pragmatic Antimasonry" (Kutolowski, "Antimasonry Reexamined," 286).

67 Stone, *Letters on Masonry and Antimasonry*, 167; Elizur Wright, *Myron Holley and What He Did for Liberty* (Boston: Published by the author, 1882), 17, 295–96; Vaughn, *Antimasonic Party*, 46. Although he worked closely with the pragmatists, Holley held on longer to Anti-Masonry and moved on to Connecticut, where as late as 1834 he edited an Anti-Masonic newspaper (Goodman, *Towards a Christian Republic*, 229). Regarding his radical egalitarianism, see Goodman, *Towards a Christian Republic*, 229–30.

68 Historians previously have called attention to this dimension of Anti-Masonry: see, for example, Cross, *Burned-Over District*; David M. Ludlum, *Social Ferment in Vermont*,

1791–1850 (New York: Columbia University Press, 1939); Benson, *Concept of Jacksonian Democracy*; and Formisano, *Transformation of Political Culture*. Goodman's *Towards a Christian Republic* is full of evidence of class and social resentment suffusing Anti-Masonry, but he views it as displaced anger/anxiety over a class structure more sharply defined because of economic change.

69 Adams quotation, Formisano, *Transformation of Political Culture*, 220–21; Benjamin S. Snider, *A New Year's Address, Delivered to the Citizens of Centerville, Allegany Co., N.Y., January 1, 1828; Comprising the Origin, Titles, and Attributes of Speculative Free Masonry* (Geneseo, N.Y., 1828), 21.

70 Benson, *Concept of Jacksonian Democracy*, 22, 23.

71 Bullock, *Revolutionary Brotherhood*, 295–97, 304, 307, quotations, 297, 304. The Anti-Masons' emphasis on spreading facts through printed and other media, together with their exaltation of public opinion, put them on the side of the idea of an informed citizenry, the historian of which asserts that it triumphed in the decade of the 1820s. See Richard D. Brown, *The Strength of a People: The Idea of an Informed Citizenry in America, 1650–1870* (Chapel Hill: University of North Carolina Press, 1996), 114–20.

CHAPTER SIX

1 For invocations of the Revolution, see Moses Thacher, *An Address Delivered before the Members of the Anti-Masonic State Convention: Assembled at Augusta, Maine, July 4, 1832* (Hallowell, Maine: Herrick and Farwell, 1832), 3–6; Richard Rush, *A Letter on Freemasonry by the Hon. Richard Rush, to the Committee of the Citizens of York County, Pennsylvania* (Boston: John Marsh and Co., 1831), 13; Amasa Walker to Pliny Merrick, February 9, 1830, Merrick Papers, American Antiquarian Society, Worcester, Mass.

2 Kathleen Smith Kutolowski, "Antimasonry Reexamined: Social Bases of the Grass-Roots Party," *Journal of American History* 71 (September 1984): 280; Dorothy Ann Lipson, *Freemasonry in Federalist Connecticut, 1789–1835* (Princeton, N.J.: Princeton University Press, 1977), 337; Paul Goodman, *Towards a Christian Republic: Antimasonry and the Great Transition in New England, 1826–1836* (New York: Oxford University Press, 1988), 94. Inquiry into church records may reveal the activities of women. See, for example, the actions taken by a Baptist church in Wayne County, New York, in 1828 and 1829, in First Baptist Church of Marion Records, 1804–1904, Collection Number 6063, Cornell University Library, Ithaca, N.Y. Regarding women's central role in evangelical religion and revivalism in the period, see Curtis D. Johnson, *Islands of Holiness: Rural Religion in Upstate New York, 1790–1860* (Ithaca, N.Y.: Cornell University Press, 1989), 9, 53–66, 167–68.

3 *Batavia Republican Advocate*, December 8, 1826. William Leete Stone's contemporary description of Anti-Masonry's disruption of churches and denominational associations in western New York and of large meetings of "professors of religion . . . repeatedly held" must have involved women at least indirectly (William Leete Stone, *Letters on Masonry and Antimasonry* [New York: O. Halsted, 1832], 229–30, 391–96, quotation, 396). The *Rochester Craftsman*, a Masonic paper, lightly mocked women's involvement over two years after the Wheatland meeting, May 26, 1829, while in

1827 a conservative legislative opponent of Anti-Masonry criticized excited women who "hold their meetings and pass resolutions, among others, that their daughters shall not marry Free-masons" (quotation, Elizabeth Bruchholtz Haigh, "New York Antimasons, 1826–1833" [Ph.D. diss., University of Rochester, 1980], 179). "Mrs. Lucinda Morgan" had testified at an early trial of Masons; see *The Trial of James Lackey, Isaac Everton, Chauncey H. Coe . . . [et al.] for Kidnapping Capt. William Morgan. At the Ontario General Sessions, Held at Canandaigua, Ontario County, Aug. 22, 1827* (New York, 1827), 3. This was an Anti-Masonic publication, with an epigram on the title page: "Nor wife, nor children more shall behold—Nor friends, nor sacred home."

4 Mary Ann Clawson, *Constructing Brotherhood: Class, Gender, and Fraternalism* (Princeton, N.J.: Princeton University Press, 1989), 156, 161–62; Bruce Dorsey, *Reforming Men and Women: Gender in the Antebellum City* (Ithaca, N.Y.: Cornell University Press, 2002), 105–6, quotation, 124. See also Elaine Frantz Parsons, *Manhood Lost: Fallen Drunkards and Redeeming Women in the Nineteenth-Century United States* (Baltimore: Johns Hopkins University Press, 2003), 53–74. Robert H. Abzug describes the women's entry into reform through revivals, their participation in great numbers, and their sometimes wielding "enormous if often informal and uncelebrated influence; they distributed pamphlets, circulated petitions, solicited contributions, and administered local societies" (Abzug, *Cosmos Crumbling: American Reform and the Religious Imagination* [New York: Oxford University Press, 1994], 184, and 185, 188, 190). With many unsupervised young men moving into cities, concern also arose over a masculine youth culture all too attracted to licentious behavior. See Patricia Cline Cohen, *The Murder of Helen Jewett: The Life and Death of a Prostitute in Nineteenth-Century New York* (New York: Vintage, 1999), 11, 230–47.

5 Clawson, *Constructing Brotherhood*, 15, 17, 185–87, quotations, 185, 186. "In opposition to the claims of an evangelical religion increasingly associated with women, Freemasonry offered men an institution that provided not only solidarity but an explicit defense of male secularism and moral autonomy" (ibid., 187).

6 Goodman, *Towards a Christian Republic*, 80–96, 102, quotation, 86. Bullock departs from the view presented here by describing "a correspondence" between lodge and home, rather than seeing the former as taking away from the latter; see Steven C. Bullock, *Revolutionary Brotherhood: Freemasonry and the Transformation of the American Social Order, 1730–1840* (Chapel Hill: University of North Carolina Press, 1996), 259. Within marriages and sexual relations, according to Charles Rosenberg, the male ideal of the "Christian gentleman" competed with the traditional male role of "aggressive masculinity"; see Charles Rosenberg, "Sexuality, Class, and Role in 19th-Century America," *American Quarterly* 35 (May 1973): 139, 140.

7 Abzug describes evangelical reform as turning to topics concerning the social and educational order, and he identifies temperance, Sabbatarianism, and manual labor as three such areas that shared a new militancy that "broached questions of ritual and symbolic order on society and the individual," but he never mentions their contemporary movement, Anti-Masonry. But it, too, could be described as a strategy for "reestablishing the sacred essence of society" (Abzug, *Cosmos Crumbling*, 80).

8 At the installation of a new lodge in Monroe County, Rush township, a Masonic procession with a band was joined by ladies for "solemnities" in a nearby grove;

see *Rochester Telegraph*, August 15, 1826. On Masonic rhetoric and literature, see Lipson, *Freemasonry in Federalist Connecticut*, 191–97; Kathleen Smith Kutolowski, "Freemasonry in the Early Republic: The Case for Antimasonic Anxieties," *American Quarterly* 34 (March 1982): 549; and Goodman, *Towards a Christian Republic*, 87.

9 *Speech of Solomon Southwick, at the Opening of the New-York Anti-Masonic State Convention, at the Capitol, in Albany, February 19th, 1829* (Albany, N.Y.: D. B. Packard and Co., 1829), 15; Bullock, *Revolutionary Brotherhood*, 180–82. The controversy over female moral reform in the late 1830s in Utica, New York, also was implicitly a collision between competing versions of manhood. See Mary P. Ryan, *Cradle of the Middle Class: The Family in Oneida County, New York, 1790–1865* (New York: Cambridge University Press, 1981), 12–13, 124–27.

10 Timothy Fuller, *An Oration, Delivered at Faneuil Hall, Boston, July 11, 1831* (Boston: Suffolk Anti-Masonic Committee, 1831), 6; Middlesex address in *Greenfield (Mass.) Franklin Freeman*, March 11, 1833; Pliny Merrick, *Col. Merrick's Letter on Speculative Free Masonry* (Worcester, Mass.: Dorr and Howland, 1829), 9, 12. Deerfield's Anti-Masonic legislator introduced a resolution (not adopted) to inquire "how far the practice of using refreshments at Massachusetts Lodges has tended to create and confirm habits of intemperance" (*Greenfield Franklin Freeman*, February 11, 1833).

11 *Speech of Solomon Southwick*, 13.

12 For the maneuvering attending the Wirt nomination and Wirt's ambivalence, see William Preston Vaughn, *The Antimasonic Party in the United States, 1826–1843* (Lexington: University Press of Kentucky, 1983), 55–69, quotation, 65.

13 Anya Jabour, *Marriage in the Early Republic: Elizabeth and William Wirt and the Companionate Ideal* (Baltimore: Johns Hopkins University Press, 1998), 11–12, 4–7, 53–54, quotations, 4, 6. Goodman, *Towards a Christian Republic*, 96, emphasizes the child-rearing aspect of republican motherhood. Wirt also gave completely conventional advice to his daughter regarding the best way to "make yourself pleasing to others" by using "the witchcraft of woman"; see John P. Kennedy, *Memoirs of the Life of William Wirt*, 2 vols. (Philadelphia: Blanchard and Lea, 1856), 2:97. Despite the fact that for a long time in the early republic "judicial patriarchy" defined women as lacking civic capacity and under the principle of *feme covert* as subject to their husband's status, at times an alternate vision, "also written by men," broke through to conceive of women as independent, politicized citizens. See Linda K. Kerber, "The Paradox of Women's Citizenship in the Early Republic: The Case of Martin *vs.* Massachusetts, 1805," *American Historical Review* 97 (April 1992): 371–75, 378.

14 Goodman, *Towards a Christian Republic*, 94–95; Joan von Mehren, *Minerva and the Muse: A Life of Margaret Fuller* (Amherst: University of Massachusetts Press, 1994), 19–20, 22; quotation, Ann Douglas, "Margaret Fuller and the Search for History: A Biographical Study," *Women's Studies* 4 (1976): 44. While Timothy Fuller "took pride in her [his daughter's] precocious abilities, and enjoyed her companionship in his favorite studies," he was not "tender, wise considerate"; "in the Fuller household the whole punctuation was masculine" (Thomas Wentworth Higginson, *Margaret Fuller Ossoli* [1890; New York: Greenwood Press, 1968], 27, 28–29).

15 Goodman, *Towards a Christian Republic*, 95–96, Walker quotation, 96. Goodman views Fuller and Walker as socially marginal men, whereas the interpretation here stresses

their progressivism, as well as their being enmeshed in a web of associations and soul-satisfying benevolent activity.

16 Elizur Wright, *Myron Holley and What He Did for Liberty* (Boston: Published by the author, 1882), 29, 31, 156, quotation, 161; Goodman, *Towards a Christian Republic*, 229–30.

17 Wright, *Myron Holley*, 177, 306–7.

18 Ibid., 175–76.

19 Ibid., 168–69, 174, 180.

20 Blanche Glassman Hersh, *The Slavery of Sex: Feminist-Abolitionists in America* (Urbana: University of Illinois Press, 1978), ix. The strongest statement of the connection between abolition and feminism is Keith E. Melder, *Beginnings of Sisterhood: The American Woman's Rights Movement, 1800–1850* (New York: Schocken Books, 1977), 77–159; see also Judith Wellman, *The Road to Seneca Falls: Elizabeth Cady Stanton and the First Woman's Rights Convention* (Urbana: University of Illinois Press, 2004), 49–154. Julie Roy Jeffrey pays but slight attention to women's rights in *The Great Silent Army of Abolitionism: Ordinary Women in the Antislavery Movement* (Chapel Hill: University of North Carolina Press, 1998), 162–63, 165.

21 First quotation, Nancy Isenberg, *Sex and Citizenship in Antebellum America* (Chapel Hill: University of North Carolina Press, 1998), xvii; second quotation, Nancy Hewitt, *Women's Activism and Social Change: Rochester, New York, 1822–1872* (Ithaca, N.Y.: Cornell University Press, 1984), 254.

22 Deborah Bingham Van Broekhoven, *The Devotion of These Women: Rhode Island in the Antislavery Network* (Amherst: University of Massachusetts Press, 2002), 149. While acknowledging that a few of the women abolitionists she studied did develop concerns regarding women's rights, Van Broekhoven emphasizes that most of them did not raise broader concerns; they did not see their extensive petitioning activity as a step toward voting but rather as a way to preserve the family and Christianity (motives similar to those of Anti-Masonic women) (ibid., 30–31, 50, 68–69, 150). Similarly, "While female activism implicitly challenged the tenets of domesticity and submission . . . many female activists sought to work within rather than challenge these bonds of womanhood" (Hewitt, *Women's Activism and Social Change*, 39). For another interpretation that emphasizes that a majority of abolitionist women did not become feminists, see Beth A. Salerno, *Sister Societies: Women's Antislavery Organizations in Antebellum America* (DeKalb: Northern Illinois University Press, 2005), 118, 125, 149, 158.

23 Janet L. Coryell, "Superseding Gender: The Role of the Woman Politico in Antebellum Partisan Politics," in *Women and the Unstable State in Nineteenth-Century America*, ed. Alison M. Parker and Stephanie Cole (College Station: Texas A&M University Press, 2000), 84–112; Christopher J. Olsen, "'Molly Pitcher of the Mississippi Whigs': The Editorial Career of Mrs. Harriet N. Prewett," *Journal of Mississippi History* 58 (Fall 1996): 237–54.

24 Michael D. Pierson, aware of the conventional view that abolitionism influenced feminism, has argued for a significant impact stemming from the women's rights movement to abolition in forging a critique of southern slavery's patriarchal ideals; see Pierson, "'Slavery Cannot Be Covered Up with a Broadcloth or a Bandanna': The

Evolution of White Abolitionist Attacks on the Patriarchal Institution," *Journal of the Early Republic* 25 (Fall 2005): 387, 400, 406. Pierson has asserted also that antislavery men and women held more egalitarian views of marriage than their contemporaries; see Pierson, *Free Hearts and Free Homes: Gender and American Antislavery Politics* (Chapel Hill: University of North Carolina Press, 2003), 15, 18–19.

25 First quotation, David M. Ludlum, *Social Ferment in Vermont, 1791–1850* (New York: Columbia University Press, 1939), 97; second quotation, *Proceedings of the Anti-Masonic State Convention, Holden at Montpelier, Vt. June 26 and 27, 1833* (Montpelier, Vt.: Knapp and Jewett Printers, 1833), 4. "The Ballot box is the great reservoir of public sentiment. It is the herald of the people, that makes known their decisions, and proclaims their will" (*Proceedings of the Anti-Masonic State Convention, Holden at Montpelier, Vt.*, 5).

26 Vaughn, *Antimasonic Party*, 71–72, 75–79. In August 1829 Anti-Masons gathered at Montpelier for the first political convention ever held in the state. Previously, parties had nominated candidates by legislative caucuses, but the Anti-Masons, as a grassroots movement, had no representatives in the legislature (Ludlum, *Social Ferment in Vermont*, 116–17).

27 Vaughn, *Antimasonic Party*, 75–80; Goodman, *Towards a Christian Republic*, 140.

28 Anti-Masonic counties also had been in the forefront of the populist insurgency against New York and New Hampshire land claims in the 1770s and 1780s (see chapter 2). Vaughn, *Antimasonic Party*, 71–72; Goodman, *Towards a Christian Republic*, 123, 130–31, 134, 136–37; Randolph A. Roth, *The Democratic Dilemma: Religion, Reform, and the Social Order in the Connecticut River Valley of Vermont, 1791–1850* (New York: Cambridge University Press, 1987), 156–58; Ludlum, *Social Ferment in Vermont*, 102, 104–6, 108, 156–58. There are discrepancies in these accounts regarding the degree of support for Anti-Masonry in various denominations. However, there tends to be agreement that within each denomination the more evangelical and Calvinist elements gravitated to Anti-Masonry. Regarding early hostility among Baptists to Masonry, see William G. McLoughlin, *New England Dissent, 1630–1883: The Baptists and the Separation of Church and State*, 2 vols. (Cambridge, Mass.: Harvard University Press, 1971), 2:829. Regarding the "heartland of Vermont's democratic revolution," where Anti-Masonic newspapers and voting flourished, see Randolph A. Roth, "The Other Masonic Outrage: The Death and Transfiguration of Joseph Burnham," *Journal of the Early Republic* 14 (Spring 1994): 60–62, quotation, 62.

29 Roth, *Democratic Dilemma*, 117–41, 153–56, quotations, 117, 156–57.

30 First quotations, Ludlum, *Social Ferment in Vermont*, 90; last quotation, Goodman, *Towards a Christian Republic*, 139–40, also 128. On Masonic militance, see Vaughn, *Antimasonic Party*, 86–87. "Each attack on Masonry heightened the resistance of the adherents of the institution; *two reservoirs of moral sentiment had been rapidly created and neither could be drained off.* . . . The Grand Lodge was hardly in the mood to renounce the fraternity" (Ludlum, *Social Ferment in Vermont*, 121, italics mine).

31 Roth, *Democratic Dilemma*, 154.

32 Goodman, *Towards a Christian Republic*, 141–42; quotations, Frank M. Bryan, *Yankee Politics in Rural Vermont* (Hanover, N.H.: University Press of New England, 1974), 12,

19. Some Anti-Masonic activists acted in the manner of unscrupulous politicians beginning in 1829 when they began to exploit unfounded rumors that officials at the Vermont state prisons, all Masons, had faked the death of an inmate and brother to help him escape serving time for rape. The accusations gained traction in part because of notorious abuses at the prison. When Anti-Masons took over the executive branch, they did administer the prison, and other state institutions, with "new men—Christian, benevolent, egalitarian—[in their eyes] the antithesis of the archetypal Mason" (Roth, "Other Masonic Outrage," 56–69, quotation, 62).

33 John L. Brooke, *The Heart of the Commonwealth: Society and Political Culture in Worcester County, Massachusetts, 1713–1861* (New York: Cambridge University Press, 1989), 344–52.

34 Ronald P. Formisano, *The Transformation of Political Culture: Massachusetts Parties, 1780s–1840s* (New York: Oxford University Press, 1983), 201–10. The *Boston Anti-Masonic Free Press* printed full reports of the western New York trials of Freemasons who had gotten off with light or no sentences; see, for example, June 12, 1829, and January 22, 1830.

35 Formisano, *Transformation of Political Culture*, 211–14; regarding Anti-Masons' antipolitical and antiparty attitudes, see ibid., 204, 220. Adams had read William Leete Stone's *Letters on Masonry and Antimasonry* (New York: O. Halsted, 1832), and after hearing a July 11, 1831, reading at Faneuil Hall of Richard Rush's letter regarding Masonry's offenses, Adams wrote in his diary that "the most stirring passage in Rush's letter is the statement that not one of the men convicted in the State of New York of agency in the kidnapping of Morgan had been expelled from the lodge to which he belongs" (Charles Francis Adams, ed., *Memoirs of John Quincy Adams: Comprising Portions of His Diary from 1795 to 1848*, 12 vols. [Philadelphia: J. B. Lippincott and Co., 1874–77], 8:379). For Adams see also Daniel Walker Howe, *The Political Culture of the American Whigs* (Chicago: University of Chicago Press, 1979), 43–68. A key theme of Rush's letter was the inability to execute "the laws of the land . . . upon the authors of an audacious and bloody conspiracy" (Richard Rush, *A Letter on Freemasonry, by the Hon. Richard Rush, to the Committee of the Citizens of York County, Pennsylvania* [Boston: John Marsh and Co., 1831], 6).

36 Formisano, *Transformation of Political Culture*, 202, 207–8, Dean quotation, 208–9; last quotations, Brooke, *Heart of the Commonwealth*, 311, 328. The Anti-Masonic *Greenfield Franklin Freeman* had agitated for militia reform; see, for example, May 27, 1833. From 1830 to 1834 the Grand Lodge also built a costly new hall in Boston. On the strength of Masonry in Boston, see Benjamin V. French, Boston, to Thurlow Weed, January 7, 1832, Weed Papers, Rush Rhees Library, University of Rochester, Rochester, N.Y. French claimed that the Anti-Masonic newspaper, now a daily, had a subscription of "about 280 in the city, 100 in the legislature."

37 Formisano, *Transformation of Political Culture*, 154–56, 218–19; Goodman, *Towards a Christian Republic*, 163–64. Regarding Trinitarians, see McLoughlin, *New England Dissent*, 2:1222–23.

38 Formisano, *Transformation of Political Culture*, 217–18.

39 First quotation, Seth Hunt, Keene, N.H., to William H. Seward, September 19,

1831, Seward Papers, Rush Rhees Library, University of Rochester, Rochester, N.Y.; Adams quotation, Formisano, *Transformation of Political Culture*, 220. See also Seth Hunt, Boston, to W. H. Seward, August 6, 1831, Seward Papers.

40  Vaughn, *Antimasonic Party*, 161–63; Lipson, *Freemasonry in Federalist Connecticut*, 270–71, 280, 293, 296, 307–14; Goodman, *Towards a Christian Republic*, 215–21, 227–31, quotations, 220, 221. A study using number of churches per town found a relationship between Anti-Masonry and Congregationalists, Baptists, and Methodists. Meanwhile, elite Episcopalians, Masonry, and opposition to Anti-Masonry were closely associated according to that and other evidence. See Thomas E. Cavanagh, "The Antimasonic Party in Connecticut," unpublished paper in my possession. Both Masons and Anti-Masons had contact with their counterparts in New York, and Connecticut Masons may have been involved in the Morgan affair; see Lipson, *Freemasonry in Federalist Connecticut*, 272–73.

41  Lipson, *Freemasonry in Federalist Connecticut*, 329–35, quotation, 329.

42  Patrick T. Conley, *Democracy in Decline: Rhode Island's Constitutional Development, 1776–1841* (Providence: Rhode Island Historical Society, 1977), xiv, 219–20, 223.

43  Vaughn, *Antimasonic Party*, 134–36; Goodman, *Towards a Christian Republic*, 196–97. The denominations generally most receptive to Anti-Masonry, though they were often divided, were the Baptists, Free Will Baptists, Quakers, and Orthodox Congregationalists, while Universalists often defended Masonry (Goodman, *Towards and Christian Republic*, 202–7).

44  Vaughn, *Antimasonic Party*, 136–38, quotation, 137.

45  Goodman, *Towards a Christian Republic*, 207–8; Vaughn, *Antimasonic Party*, 140–45.

46  Vaughn, *Antimasonic Party*, 134, 138–39; Goodman, *Towards a Christian Republic*, 213–14.

47  Conley, *Democracy in Decline*, 219–22, 225, 234–35, 237–38, quotation, 277. On Sprague, see Goodman, *Towards a Christian Republic*, 207. Regarding Anti-Masons' coalition politics with Jacksonian Republican antisuffragists, see Vaughn, *Antimasonic Party*, 135, 140–43, 147, 149.

48  Conley, *Democracy in Decline*, 246, 252–53, 272–73; Goodman, *Towards a Christian Republic*, 201, 205, 207–11. Some Anti-Masons opposed suffrage reform; see Conley, *Democracy in Decline*, 246.

49  Quotation, Philip Shriver Klein, *Pennsylvania Politics, 1817–1832: A Game without Rules* (Philadelphia: Historical Society of Pennsylvania, 1940), 14; Robert O. Rupp, "Social Tension and Political Mobilization in Jacksonian Society: A Case Study of the Antimasonic Party in New York, Pennsylvania, and Vermont, 1827–1840" (Ph.D. diss., Syracuse University, 1983), 89, 126.

50  Regarding Ely and the Anti-Masonic convention, see Lee Benson, *The Concept of Jacksonian Democracy: New York as a Test Case* (Princeton, N.J.: Princeton University Press, 1961), 194–95; and Vaughn, *Antimasonic Party*, 92. Amos Ellmaker, former state attorney general from Lancaster County and the Anti-Masons' nominee for vice president in 1832, described the republican character and Anti-Masonic tendencies of the pietist Germans in Amos Ellmaker to William H. Seward, October 25, 1831, Seward Papers.

51  Vaughn, *Antimasonic Party*, 90, 92–93; Charles McCool Snyder, *The Jacksonian Heritage:*

*Pennsylvania Politics, 1833–1848* (Harrisburg: Pennsylvania Historical and Museum Commission, 1958), 28, 71–72; Klein, *Pennsylvania Politics*, 241. On the lack of Anti-Masonic leadership and organization in Pennsylvania in 1831, see Philo Case Fuller, Geneseo, to Thurlow Weed, July 25, 1831, Weed Papers.

52 First quotation, Rupp, "Social Tension and Political Mobilization in Jacksonian Society," 127; Klein, *Pennsylvania Politics*, 14, 281, 326; Vaughn, *Antimasonic Party*, 91–92, 94–98. Anti-Masons also appealed to rural pietist republicans by denouncing Philadelphia as "overwhelming, arrogant, dictatorial" (Vaughn, *Antimasonic Party*, 92). "Masonry is *proved* to be political," declared the *Anti-Masonic Sun Almanac, 1832*, by Avery Allen (Philadelphia, 1832), 2, Olin Library, Cornell University, Ithaca, N.Y.

53 Vaughn, *Antimasonic Party*, 98–110.

54 Snyder, *Jacksonian Heritage*, 66. Ralph Korngold attributed Stevens's Anti-Masonry to the prevalence of Quaker, Mennonite, Dunker, Amish, Dutch Reformed, and Scotch Presbyterian religionists in his district, as well as to his egalitarian instincts honed by youthful humiliations resulting from his poverty; see Korngold, *Thaddeus Stevens: A Being Darkly Wise and Rudely Great* (New York: Harcourt, Brace, 1955), 25–26.

55 Fawn M. Brodie, *Thaddeus Stevens: Scourge of the South* (New York: W. W. Norton, 1959), 22, 24, quotations, 40–41. Brodie depicts Anti-Masonry as originating in genuine grievances but then turning into a hysterical "witch-hunt" and "frenzy" soon put to political uses by opportunist politicians (ibid., 39, 47, 59).

56 Ibid., 17–62, quotations, 51, 26.

57 Ibid., 56, 59–60, quotation, 59; Snyder, *Jacksonian Heritage*, 51, 52. Wolf was as unselfish as Stevens since his support of the school law split his party and led to Ritner's victory.

58 Brodie, *Thaddeus Stevens*, 60–61, quotation, 61. One-half of the votes for repeal in the House came from predominantly German districts. The Anti-Masons were more divided against repeal than the other parties, voting 15 to 12 against it, while Jacksonian Republicans voted 33 to 19 against and Whigs 9 to 2 (Snyder, *Jacksonian Heritage*, 52–53). Philadelphia and Carlisle already had tax-supported schools.

59 Frank Gerrity, "The Masons, the Antimasons, and the Pennsylvania Legislature, 1834–1836," *Pennsylvania Magazine of History and Biography* 99 (April 1975): 189–96; Snyder, *Jacksonian Heritage*, 81. From 1832 on, nearly all Pennsylvania lodges "suspended their work on account of the prevailing excitement" (Alfred Creigh, *Masonry and Antimasonry: A History of Masonry in Pennsylvania since 1792* [Philadelphia: Lippincott, Grambo and Co., 1854], 84). Vaughn reports that from 113 chartered lodges in 1827, only 45 remained "in good standing" by 1839 (Vaughn, *Antimasonic Party*, 109–10, 113).

60 In Maine an Anti-Masonic candidate for governor received 2,384 votes in 1833, whereas over 60,000 ballots had been cast the year before in the presidential election, only 844 for Wirt (Vaughn, *Antimasonic Party*, 164–65). See also *Proceedings of the Antimasonic Republican Convention of the State of Maine, 1834* (Hallowell: Herrick and Rice, 1834); Vaughn, *Antimasonic Party*, 165–67; and Herbert Ershkowitz, *The Origin of the Whig and Democratic Parties: New Jersey Politics, 1820–1837* (Washington, D.C.: University Press of America, 1982), 106–7, 155–57. In 1826 thirty-one lodges had sent representatives to New Jersey's grand lodge "communication," but in 1834 only four did so.

61 Masons continued to hold public processions in various places, including a June 1832 celebration of St. John's Day in Cincinnati. See Vaughn, *Antimasonic Party*, 153–60; Donald J. Ratcliffe, *The Politics of Long Division: The Birth of the Second Party System in Ohio, 1818–1828* (Columbus: Ohio State University Press, 2000), 256, 316. In two Western Reserve counties Anti-Masons exploited resentments against "Village Aristocracy" (Ratcliffe, *Politics of Long Division*, 269).

62 Ronald P. Formisano, *The Birth of Mass Political Parties: Michigan, 1827–1861* (Princeton, N.J.: Princeton University Press, 1971), 60–67, 103–25. Historians have not found significant Anti-Masonic political activity in most of the Old Northwest and border states. Illinois, Indiana, Kentucky, and Missouri experienced no significant Anti-Masonic organization. Yet chartered lodges and Masonic activity all declined in these areas, again testifying to the strength of Anti-Masonry's impact as a (yet undocumented) social movement on public opinion in those areas and in the South. See Vaughn, *Antimasonic Party*, 169–71.

63 On Anti-Masons' moving on to antislavery/abolition, see Ludlum, *Social Ferment in Vermont*, 133. Richard J. Carwardine has asserted that Anti-Masons were often Sabbatarians and hence strongly opposed to the Jackson administration, which frustrated efforts to stop Sunday mails (Carwardine, *Evangelicals and Politics in Antebellum America* [New Haven, Conn.: Yale University Press, 1993], 100). In contrast, Donald J. Ratcliffe has asserted that "significant portions of the Antimasonic press [in Ohio] categorically opposed restrictions on the transportation of the mail on Sundays" (Ratcliffe, "Antimasonry and Partisanship in Greater New England, 1826–1836," *Journal of the Early Republic* 15 [Summer 1995]: 208–9).

64 For Masonic anti-Catholicism, see *Boston Masonic Mirror*, January 18, 1832. On links between Anti-Masons and abolition, see Formisano, *Transformation of Political Culture*, 327.

65 This is not to say that those who presently identify themselves as progressives, liberals, conservatives, or reactionaries always hold political positions that are ideologically consistent.

66 William Leete Stone addressed his balanced and well-researched account of the New York "outrages" and subsequent events to both Masons and Anti-Masons in the hope of quieting the controversy; while presenting a full account of the obstruction of justice by Masonic sheriffs and juries, he nevertheless believed it unreasonable for Anti-Masons to exclude Masons from the jury box elsewhere (Stone, *Letters on Masonry and Antimasonry*, 247, 253, 464–64, 389–90). Yet Stone described a controversy in Washington County, New York, in a case not related to the Morgan trials but growing out of the "outrages," in which Masonic jurors, with a Mason on trial, had held their Masonic ties higher than civil law (ibid., 471–72).

67 For Bruce's actions, see Ronald P. Formisano and Kathleen Smith Kutolowski, "Antimasonry and Masonry: The Genesis of a Protest, 1826–1827," *American Quarterly* 29 (Summer 1977): 155. This account of the trial of Bruce, Orsamus Turner, and Jared Darrow has relied on Stone's extensive account in *Letters on Masonry and Antimasonry*, 341–44, quotations, 342, 344.

68 Stone himself found some of the testimony regarding Giddings's beliefs "questionable," but, and this was the judgment of a learned and otherwise secular-minded

man of letters, he found the court "clearly right in rejecting him, both by the principles of the constitution and the common law." Stone believed that "*belief in the existence of a Supreme Being, and a future state of rewards and punishments,*" was an "indispensable requirement" for court testimony (Stone, *Letters on Masonry and Antimasonry*, 348, 349).

69  Quotations, Ratcliffe, "Antimasonry and Partisanship in Greater New England," 219. Ratcliffe endorses the Masonic position. For *Jackson v. Gridley* see *Jackson v. Gridley* 18 Johns 98 (N.Y. 1820). In subsequent cases, one in the state supreme court (1823) and another in a circuit court (1824), judges had stretched their understanding of the law to mean that those who believed in punishment in this world, as was known to be the case with some Universalists, could be held to be competent witnesses.

70  Haigh, "New York Antimasons," 198; Stone, *Letters on Masonry and Antimasonry*, 484–500.

71  Haigh, "New York Antimasons," 198, 218–19.

72  Robert C. Schelin, "Millard Fillmore: Anti-Mason to Know-Nothing: A Moderate in New York Politics, 1828–1856" (Ph.D. diss., State University of New York at Binghamton, 1975), 33, quotation, 38; Juridicus [Millard Fillmore], *An Examination of the Question, "Is It Right to Require any Religious Test as a Qualification to be a Witness in a Court of Justice?"* (Buffalo, N.Y., 1832), reprinted in Frank H. Severance, ed., *Millard Fillmore Papers*, 2 vols. (Buffalo, N.Y.: Buffalo Historical Society, 1907), 1:71, 72–75, quotations, 72, 75. Fillmore wrote, "The honest, honorable, upright man, who would not tell an untruth to save his right arm, whether under oath or not; when questioned as to his belief, though it varies from the common standard, freely, candidly and fearlessly confesses it, and is rejected; while the dishonest lying hypocrite denies what his real sentiments are, tells a falsehood, and is admitted to testify" (Juridicus, *Examination of the Question*, 80).

73  *Atwood v. Weldon*, 7 Conn. 66, 85, 86 (1828); Jarvis Means Morse, *A Neglected Period of Connecticut's History, 1818–1850* (New Haven, Conn.: Yale University Press, 1933), 101–2. The original Universalists believed in universal salvation and rejected a future state of rewards and punishments. One branch of the church believed in punishment for sins in this life and another branch, in some punishment, not eternal, in the afterlife. Some judges in the antebellum period required that a competent witness believe in a future state of punishment, while more courts allowed individuals to testify who believed in present or limited future retribution. Atheists and nonbelievers in a Supreme Being had little chance of testifying. See "A Reconsideration of the Sworn Testimony Requirement: Securing Truth in the Twentieth Century," *Michigan Law Review* 75 (August 1977): 1681–89. For Universalist beliefs, see McLoughlin, *New England Dissent*, 1:654–55, 2:1235–37; and Ernest Cassara, *Universalism in America: A Documentary History* (Boston: Beacon Press, 1971).

74  Morse, *Neglected Period of Connecticut's History*, 104–5; Lipson, *Freemasonry in Federalist Connecticut*, 299–300.

75  Goodman, *Towards a Christian Republic*, 141–42; Ann Lee Bressler, *The Universalist Movement in America, 1770–1880* (New York: Oxford University Press, 2001), 78–79, quotation, 78. Bressler attributes Vermont Universalists' opposition to Masonry to

their having become a "well-established and influential" denomination in Vermont, with fifty-seven societies in 1831; elsewhere, Universalists tended to be a minority and were "more open to Masonry's deliberately transconfessional appeal" (Bressler, *Universalist Movement*, 79–80). According to Goodman, eight of ten Universalist clergymen were Anti-Masons (Goodman, *Towards a Christian Republic*, 131).

CHAPTER SEVEN

1 Robert H. Wiebe, *The Opening of American Society: From the Adoption of the Constitution to the Eve of Disunion* (New York: Knopf, 1984), 130, refers to a "popular revolution in choices" that occurred during the 1820s; see also Tom Coens, "The Formation of the Jackson Party, 1822–1825" (Ph.D. diss., Harvard University, 2004).

2 M. J. Heale, *The Making of American Politics: 1750–1850* (London: Longman, 1977), 116, 122–23, quotation, 122. "An exuberant celebration of democracy and a populistic suspicion of entrenched political elites played a part in breaking down those political practices which could not be readily accommodated to the principles of popular sovereignty" (ibid., 128).

3 Bertram Wyatt-Brown, "Prelude to Abolitionism: Sabbatarian Politics and the Rise of the Second Party System," *Journal of American History* 58 (September 1971): 316–41; Richard R. John, "Taking Sabbatarianism Seriously: The Postal System, the Sabbath, and the Transformation of American Political Culture," *Journal of the Early Republic* 10 (Winter 1990): 517–67; Ronald P. Formisano, *The Transformation of Political Culture: Massachusetts Parties, 1780s–1840s* (New York: Oxford University Press, 1983), 173–96.

4 Michael F. Holt, *The Rise and Fall of the American Whig Party: Jacksonian Politics and the Onset of the Civil War* (New York: Oxford University Press, 1999), 8, 9, 112–15; Robert V. Remini, *The Election of Andrew Jackson* (Philadelphia: Lippincott, 1963); Richard P. McCormick, "New Perspectives on Jacksonian Politics," *American Historical Review* 65 (January 1960): 288–301; Richard P. McCormick, *The Presidential Game: The Origins of American Presidential Politics* (New York: Oxford University Press, 1982), 177–78. For an emphasis on the role of professional politicians in the 1828 Jackson campaign, see Heale, *Making of American Politics*, 130, 143–47.

5 Kathleen Smith Kutolowski, "Antimasonry Reexamined: Social Bases of the Grass-Roots Party," *Journal of American History* 71 (September 1984): 286–88, quotation, 288. For disagreement regarding Anti-Masonry's mobilizing capacity, see Donald J. Ratcliffe, "Antimasonry and Partisanship in Greater New England, 1826–1836," *Journal of the Early Republic* 15 (Summer 1995): 199–239.

6 Daniel Walker Howe, "The Evangelical Movement and Political Culture in the North during the Second Party System," *Journal of American History* 77 (March 1991): 1216–17; Formisano, *Transformation of Political Culture*, 173–81, 196–98. "The Antimasonic critique explored and popularized the powerful ideals of conscience, public opinion, and purified religion that reinforced the growing cultural dominance of democracy and evangelicalism" (Steven C. Bullock, *Revolutionary Brotherhood: Freemasonry and the Transformation of the American Social Order, 1730–1840* [Chapel Hill: University of North Carolina Press, 1996], 279).

7  On the development of a (more populist) blend of demonstrative and deliberative discourse in both oral and print communication during the first decades of the nineteenth century and after Jackson's election, see Andrew W. Robertson, *Political Rhetoric in the United States and Britain, 1790–1900* (Ithaca, N.Y.: Cornell University Press, 1995), 6, 69–81.

8  Donald B. Cole, *Jacksonian Democracy in New Hampshire, 1800–1851* (Cambridge, Mass.: Harvard University Press, 1970), 108–24; Robert V. Remini, *Andrew Jackson and the Bank War: A Study in the Growth of Presidential Power* (New York: Norton, 1967), 55–64; Formisano, *Transformation of Political Culture*, 251–52.

9  Holt, *Rise and Fall of the American Whig Party*, 15–16; Heale, *Making of American Politics*, 168–69. "The people's president thus resorted to the new politics of democracy . . . for while the veto message was formally addressed to Congress it was really directed to the American people, reaching out to them in language suited to the hustings" (Heale, *Making of American Politics*, 169).

10  Holt, *Rise and Fall of the American Whig Party*, quotations, 16; Jackson quotations, Arthur M. Schlesinger Jr., *The Age of Jackson* (Boston: Little, Brown, 1945), 90.

11  Lee Benson, *The Concept of Jacksonian Democracy: New York as a Test Case* (Princeton, N.J.: Princeton University Press, 1961), 47–48, 51–54, 90–92, quotation, 48; Holt, *Rise and Fall of the American Whig Party*, 16–17; Francis Granger, Canandaigua, to Thurlow Weed, October 6, 1830, Weed Papers, Rush Rhees Library, University of Rochester, Rochester, N.Y. Other letters to Weed show Anti-Masonic hostility toward the state banks: see Walter Cunningham, Poughkeepsie, to Thurlow Weed, February 16 and March 6, 1830, and James K. Livingston, Rochester, to Thurlow Weed, March 10, 1830, both in Weed Papers.

12  Benson, *Concept of Jacksonian Democracy*, 49–50, *Advocate* quotation, 50; second quotation, John C. Spencer, Canandaigua, to Thurlow Weed, May 24, 1831, Weed Papers. Regarding prominent Anti-Masons' acquiring stock in a new Buffalo bank, see Albert H. Tracy, Buffalo, to William H. Seward, June 2, 1831, Seward Papers, Rush Rhees Library, University of Rochester, Rochester, N.Y.

13  Benson, *Concept of Jacksonian Democracy*, 55.

14  Holt, *Rise and Fall of the American Whig Party*, 17–18; Charles S. Sydnor, *The Development of Southern Sectionalism, 1819–1848* (Baton Rouge: Louisiana State University Press, 1948), 205–6. Clay received about 37 percent of the popular vote.

15  Frank Otto Gatell, "Spoils of the Bank War: Political Bias in the Selection of Pet Banks," *American Historical Review* 70 (October 1964): 35–58; James Roger Sharp, *The Jacksonians versus the Banks: Politics in the States after the Panic of 1837* (New York: Columbia University Press, 1970); Holt, *Rise and Fall of the American Whig Party*, 23–30.

16  Benson, *Concept of Jacksonian Democracy*, 57–63; first Clay quotation, Heale, *Making of American Politics*, 181; Holt, *Rise and Fall of the American Whig Party*, 24–28, second Clay quotation and last quotation, 27, 28. For an illustration of the impact of the veto and Jackson's actions against the bank on one voter in Vermont, a former Jeffersonian Democrat who had been a Jackson supporter, see Robert Shalhope, *A Tale of New England: The Diaries of Hiram Harwood, Vermont Farmer, 1810–1837* (Baltimore: Johns Hopkins University Press, 2003), 185–86 (this comes within a most illuminating chapter, "Birth of a Whig," 168–93).

17 Holt, *Rise and Fall of the American Whig Party*, 28, 29.

18 Ibid., 29–30.

19 Ibid., 30.

20 Formisano, *Transformation of Political Culture*, 252–55, quotation, 252.

21 Ibid., 253.

22 Ibid., 254.

23 Ibid., 255–56; William Preston Vaughn, *The Antimasonic Party in the United States, 1826–1843* (Lexington: University Press of Kentucky, 1983), 186–87. Goodman's estimates regarding New England's Anti-Masonic voters' subsequent partisan affiliations differ. Though many became Whigs, in some states, he asserts, as many or more became Democrats, while at the same time many former Anti-Masons, harboring "demanding moral standards and persisting antipartisan sentiments," refused to vote for Democrats or Whigs (Paul Goodman, *Towards a Christian Republic: Antimasonry and the Great Transition in New England, 1826–1836* [New York: Oxford University Press, 1988], 238).

24 Quotations, Formisano, *Transformation of Political Culture*, 256–57. The 1835 platform constituted "the high-water mark of Democratic social criticism" (ibid., 257).

25 Ibid., 256–57. Several more years would pass before the Massachusetts Democrats endorsed a ten-hour day. The radical populist appeal of 1835 coincided with internal reform of the party's power structure and demotion of a clique of Boston officeholders that enhanced the party's electoral appeal (ibid., 257).

26 Goodman, *Towards a Christian Republic*, 238, estimates that rather large proportions of Anti-Masonic voters in Massachusetts, Vermont, and Maine did not vote in 1836.

27 Vaughn, *Antimasonic Party*, 81–82, 84–86, 127–31, 148–49, 151, 162–63; Daniel Wells, Greenfield [Mass.], to George Bliss, March 31, 1835, Bliss Papers, Massachusetts Historical Society, Boston, Mass.; Holt, *Rise and Fall of the American Whig Party*, 36–38, last quotation, 39.

28 Vaughn, *Antimasonic Party*, 172–78, quotation, 173; Holt, *Rise and Fall of the American Whig Party*, 97–101; John J. Reed, "Battleground: Pennsylvania Antimasons and the Emergence of the National Nominating Convention," *Pennsylvania Magazine of History and Biography* 122 (January/April 1998): 108–15. "In Lancaster County, Pennsylvania, once the most Antimasonic jurisdiction in the United States, the Harrison-Granger electors won over the Democratic ticket by a 2,115 vote majority (6,250 to 4,145), although Van Buren carried the Keystone State by 4,200 votes" (Vaughn, *Antimasonic Party*, 179).

29 See Hiram Harwood's reaction to the moralist strain of Whig leaders who were prominent in Bennington, Vermont, before 1837, in Shalhope, *Tale of New England*, 186–87, 192.

30 First quotation, Vaughn, *Antimasonic Party*, 186; Kutolowski, "Antimasonry Reexamined," 290–92, quotations, 290, 291.

31 Vaughn describes the Weed-Seward wing of Whiggery as "the most progressive faction in an essentially conservative party" (Vaughn, *Antimasonic Party*, 49).

32 Ibid., 180–82, 187.

33 Ronald P. Formisano, *The Birth of Mass Political Parties: Michigan, 1827–1861* (Princeton, N.J.: Princeton University Press, 1971), 133–36; Formisano, "The New Political

History and the Election of 1840," *Journal of Interdisciplinary History* 23 (Spring 1993): 661–82.

34 Regarding the populist rhetoric of the parties, especially the Democrats, see Joel H. Silbey, "'To One or Another of These Parties Every Man Belongs': The American Political Experience from Andrew Jackson to the Civil War," in *Contesting Democracy: Substance and Structure in American Political History, 1775–2000*, ed. Byron E. Shafer and Anthony J. Badger (Lawrence: University Press of Kansas, 2001), 73–75. Regarding partisan hyperbole, see Formisano, *Transformation of Political Culture*, 325–26; and Holt, *Rise and Fall of the American Whig Party*, 107. Glenn C. Altschuler and Stuart M. Blumin express skepticism regarding the intensity of party loyalty and the actual extent of popular participation in party-related activities. They also assert that the 1840 election was not "a massive referendum on significant public issues in a time of crisis"; rather, historians "have long recognized the reductionist sloganeering of the log-cabin and hard-cider campaign as a means of stirring up popular support without engaging policy issues, indeed, by avoiding them as much as possible." Even Blumin and Altschuler concede, however, that 1840 was the "first truly massive campaign and election," though they also argue that the great majority of citizens in one town were "not so much enthused as harassed by the campaign" (Altschuler and Blumin, *Rude Republic: Americans and Their Politics in the Nineteenth Century* [Princeton, N.J.: Princeton University Press, 2000], 34–35, 27, 33). Holt's meticulous description of the 1840 campaign emphasizes that despite the seeming lack of substance in all the hoopla and ballyhoo, the Whigs' primary focus on the economic condition of the country was crucial, and that the "the salvation of liberty and republican self-government constituted the Whigs' second most important theme" (Holt, *Rise and Fall of the American Whig Party*, 89–90, 105–13, quotation, 109).

35 Richard J. Carwardine, *Evangelicals and Politics in Antebellum America* (New Haven, Conn.: Yale University Press, 1993), 58, 59. Carwardine points repeatedly to evangelicals' having been Anti-Masons and then Whigs (ibid., 58, 62, 64, 100, 109) and also challenges the assertions of Goodman and others that Anti-Masons were redirecting anxiety over the changing economy and modernization against Masons. If that were true, asks Carwardine, why did Anti-Masons move on in such large numbers to a party favoring state-sponsored economic improvement to expand a market economy? (ibid., 359 [n. 27]). Regarding the Whigs' emphasis on protecting the morals of the people from irreligious Democrats and involving women in their campaign events "to testify to the party's family-oriented respectability," see Holt, *Rise and Fall of the American Whig Party*, 109.

36 Vaughn, *Antimasonic Party*, 187; Carwardine, *Evangelicals and Politics*, 64, 65. Regarding Anti-Masons and the power of conscience in politics, see also Bullock, *Revolutionary Brotherhood*, 298–302. Regarding the continuation of Anti-Masonry in the evangelical wing of the Whig Party, and the Whigs as a more secularized version of the "Christian Party," see Formisano, *Birth of Mass Political Parties*, 104. In the 1850s the Republican Party became more of a Protestant party than the Whigs had ever been (Formisano, *Birth of Mass Political Parties*, 324).

37 Vaughn, *Antimasonic Party*, 182–83; *Historical Statistics of the United States: Colonial Times to 1970* (Washington, D.C.: U.S. Bureau of the Census, 1975), Part II, 1072, 1076;

William Nisbet Chambers, "Election of 1840," in *History of American Presidential Elections, 1789–1965*, ed. Arthur M. Schlesinger Jr. (New York: Chelsea House Publishers, 1971), 643–744; Formisano, "New Political History and the Election of 1840," 161–82. The Anti-Masons hoped for significant patronage in Harrison's administration, but the only high post awarded to an Anti-Mason was the appointment of Francis Granger, the Anti-Masons' former candidate for New York governor, as postmaster general (Vaughn, *Antimasonic Party*, 183).

38  Carwardine, *Evangelicals and Politics*, 278. "The sabbatarian and Antimasonic crusades, though narrowly based, demonstrated evangelicals' potential for mobilizing pious voters behind a program of political purification. The significance of this lesson was not lost on the organizers of the heterogeneous amalgam of anti-Jacksonians that made up the Whig party. Not all sabbatarians and Antimasons would necessarily become enthusiastic Whigs, but a doctrine of moral improvement gave the party an ideological glue, and this, along with Whiggery's emphasis on social and economic modernization, ensured the adherence to the party of more than its fair share of postmillennialists" (ibid., 320). See also Daniel Walker Howe, "Religion and Politics in the Antebellum North," in *Religion and American Politics: From the Colonial Period to the 1980s*, ed. Mark A. Noll (New York: Oxford University Press, 1990), 133–35. In Ohio after 1840 the Whig Party "became more obviously the party of the morally concerned" (Donald J. Ratcliffe, *The Politics of Long Division: The Birth of the Second Party System in Ohio, 1818–1828* [Columbus: Ohio State University Press, 2000], 327).

39  Martin B. Duberman, *Antislavery Vanguard: New Essays on the Abolitionists* (Princeton, N.J.: Princeton University Press, 1965), 403–4 (n. 5); Goodman, *Towards a Christian Republic*, 239. The following paragraphs draw heavily on Goodman's analysis of the "affinities of ideology, organization, and leadership" between Anti-Masonry and abolitionism.

40  Benson, *Concept of Jacksonian Democracy*, 113; Gerrit Smith to Thurlow Weed, Peterboro, June 14, 1831, Weed Papers. Smith wrote that the Clay folks had made him a delegate to their national convention and that "I am a good deal of a Clay man, but still more of an Antimason." On the transition from Anti-Masonry to antislavery and antisouthernism, see Leonard L. Richards, *The Slave Power: The Free North and Southern Domination, 1780–1860* (Baton Rouge: Louisiana State University Press, 2000), 6–7.

41  Goodman, *Towards a Christian Republic*, 239; *Rochester Daily Advertiser*, November 25 and 27, 1828; *Rochester Rights of Man*, May 24, 1834; Slade quotation, Dumas Malone, ed., *Dictionary of American Biography* (New York: Charles Scribner's Sons, 1964), 9:203–4; David M. Ludlum, *Social Ferment in Vermont, 1791–1850* (New York: Columbia University Press, 1939), 125, 135. For other indications of antislavery orientation among Anti-Masons, see *Greenfield (Mass.) Franklin Freeman*, July 1, 1832; and Elizabeth Bruchholtz Haigh, "New York Antimasons, 1826–1833" (Ph.D. diss., University of Rochester, 1980), 116.

42  Garrison quotation, Formisano, *Transformation of Political Culture*, 327.

43  Goodman, *Towards a Christian Republic*, 239–40.

44  Ibid., 240–41.

45 On the fears of elites, see Leonard L. Richards, *"Gentlemen of Property and Standing"*: *Anti-Abolitionist Mobs in Jacksonian America* (New York: Oxford University Press, 1970); quotations and emphasis on the threat to the Union, David Grimsted, *American Mobbing, 1828–1861: Toward Civil War* (New York: Oxford University Press, 1998), 7, 18, 7–32. During the worst year of antiabolitionist violence, 1835, many other riots and mobs (147 in all) disturbed the country, but two-fifths of the 109 riots between July and October were related to blacks, slave or free (Grimsted, *American Mobbing*, 4, 12).

46 Regarding Garrison in Boston, see Formisano, *Transformation of Political Culture*, 327–28, 477 (n. 20). Paul A. Gilje has interpreted the 1834 New York City riot against blacks and abolitionists as motivated primarily by racial hatred (Gilje, *The Road to Mobocracy: Popular Disorder in New York City, 1763–1834* [Chapel Hill: University of North Carolina Press, 1987], 162–69). On the increasing prevalence of racial themes in political discourse in the 1820s and 1830s, see David Waldstreicher, "The Nationalization and Racialization of American Politics: Before, Beneath, and Between Parties, 1790–1840," in *Contesting Democracy*, ed. Shafer and Badger, 37–63.

47 Harriet Martineau, *Society in America*, 2 vols. (London: Saunders and Otley, 1837), 1:168–69, quotation, 178; Formisano, *Transformation of Political Culture*, 328–29. For violence against abolitionists generally, see Beth A. Solerno, *Sister Societies: Women's Antislavery Organizations in Antebellum America* (DeKalb: Northern Illinois University Press, 2005), 42–45, 85–89.

48 Edward Pessen, *Jacksonian America: Society, Personality, Politics* (Homewood, Ill.: Dorsey Press, 1978), 301–2; quotation, Grimsted, *American Mobbing*, 17. Richard R. John has reinterpreted the suppression of abolitionist mails as a response of slaveholders and their northern antiabolition allies to the spread of the postal system itself, to reverse the tendency of the postal system to strengthen the bonds of union (John, *Spreading the News: The American Postal System from Franklin to Morse* [Cambridge, Mass.: Harvard University Press, 1995], 257–82).

49 Julie Roy Jeffrey, *The Great Silent Army of Abolitionism: Ordinary Women in the Antislavery Movement* (Chapel Hill: University of North Carolina Press, 1998), 49–51, 94, quotations, 49, 50. Women also were subjected to sexual ridicule (Solerno, *Sister Societies*, 90–92).

50 On the pressure brought to bear by antislavery activists and the Liberty Party on northern congressmen who had voted reliably with the South into the 1840s, see Holt, *Rise and Fall of the American Whig Party*, 155–57; and Richards, *Slave Power*, 137–59. Holt points to the Liberty Party's achieving a balance of power in several states, but he argues that the party caused fewer Whig losses in congressional elections than did redistricting (Holt, *Rise and Fall of the American Whig Party*, 157).

51 For a different view, see Robert W. Fogel, *Without Consent or Contract: The Rise and Fall of American Slavery* (New York: W. W. Norton, 1989). While the Free Soil Party contained "many dedicated idealists," its leaders differed little from those of the major parties, and the movement was "not characterized by a groundswell of popular support but was dominated by a few at the top" (Frederick J. Blue, *The Free Soilers: Third Party Politics, 1848–1854* [Urbana: University of Illinois Press, 1973], x). For the reform and populist elements in Massachusetts's Free Soil Party, see Bruce Laurie, *Beyond*

*Garrison: Antislavery and Social Reform* (New York: Cambridge University Press, 2005), 273–75. In the South, while no antislavery movement existed, critics of slavery "on behalf of whites" did use populist arguments (Carl N. Degler, *The Other South: Southern Dissenters in the Nineteenth Century* [New York: Harper and Row, 1974], 47–96).

52 "The social sources of abolitionism are complex and require fresh empirical study, but historians who locate them in the northern evangelical churches must explain why a majority of evangelicals rejected [antislavery] immediatism" (Goodman, *Towards a Christian Republic*, 242).

CHAPTER EIGHT

1 Robert Wiebe, *The Opening of American Society: From the Adoption of the Constitution to the Eve of Disunion* (New York: Random House, 1984), quotations, 155. In the 1840s "the sovereign people seemed everywhere on the march" (Daniel T. Rodgers, *Contested Truths: Keywords in American Politics since Independence* [New York: Basic Books, 1987], 101).

2 Wiebe, *Opening of American Society*, 156, quotation, 349; see also Gerald Leonard, *The Invention of Party Politics: Federalism, Popular Sovereignty, and Constitutional Development in Jacksonian Illinois* (Chapel Hill: University of North Carolina Press, 2002).

3 Mark Voss-Hubbard, "The 'Third Party Tradition' Reconsidered: Third Parties and American Public Life, 1830–1900," *Journal of American History* 86 (June 1999): 121–50.

4 Wiebe, *Opening of American Society*, xii–xiii, xv, last quotation, 252; Michael F. Holt, *Political Parties and American Political Development: From the Age of Jackson to the Age of Lincoln* (Baton Rouge: Louisiana State University Press, 1992), 27. See also Sean Wilentz, *The Rise of American Democracy: Jefferson to Lincoln* (New York: W. W. Norton, 2005).

5 First quotations, Wiebe, *Opening of American Society*, 321; Lee Benson, *The Concept of Jacksonian Democracy: New York as a Test Case* (Princeton, N.J.: Princeton University Press, 1961), 336; last quotation, M. J. Heale, *The Making of American Politics: 1750–1850* (London: Longman, 1977), 177; Edward Pessen, "The Egalitarian Myth and American Social Reality: Wealth, Mobility, and Equality in the 'Era of the Common Man,'" *American Historical Review* 76 (October 1971): 989–1034.

6 Heale, *Making of American Politics*, 229.

7 The principal studies of the episode are Marvin E. Gettleman, *The Dorr Rebellion: A Study in American Radicalism, 1833–1849* (New York: Random House, 1973); and George M. Dennison, *The Dorr War: Republicanism on Trial, 1831–1861* (Lexington: University Press of Kentucky, 1976); but Patrick T. Conley, *Democracy in Decline: Rhode Island's Constitutional Development, 1776–1841* (Providence: Rhode Island Historical Society, 1977), is indispensable. Also useful are Chilton Williamson, "Rhode Island Suffrage since the Dorr War," *New England Quarterly* 28 (March 1955): 34–50; Chilton Williamson, *American Suffrage: From Property to Democracy, 1760–1860* (Princeton, N.J.: Princeton University Press, 1960); and Arthur May Mowry, *The Dorr War; or, The Constitutional Struggle in Rhode Island* (1901; New York: Chelsea House, 1970).

8 U.S. House, *Interference of the Executive in Affairs of Rhode Island*, 28th Cong., 1st sess., 1844, House Report No. 546 (a large compilation of primary documents, also

known as *Burke's Report*, after Edmund Burke, the reform Democratic congressman who headed the committee that investigated events in Rhode Island); Dan King, *The Life and Times of Thomas Wilson Dorr* (Boston: Published by the author, 1859), 26–27; Williamson, *American Suffrage*, 243–46; Peter J. Coleman, *The Transformation of Rhode Island, 1790–1860* (Providence: Rhode Island Historical Society, 1983), 255–57. *Burke's Report* presented its material from a Dorrite-Democratic point of view to help elect James K. Polk in 1844, and while "still the most valuable published source on the Dorr Rebellion, [it] was also a political campaign document" (Conley, *Democracy in Decline*, 359).

9   I am indebted for this framing of the "Dorr War" to Christian G. Fritz, "Recovering the Lost Worlds of America's Written Constitutions," *Albany Law Review* 68, no. 2 (2005): 261–93, quotation, 273. See also Fritz, "Fallacies of American Constitutionalism," *Rutgers Law Journal* 35 (Summer 2004): 1350–56, 1366–68. Fritz demonstrates the vitality throughout the nation of the unconstrained view of the people's sovereignty from the Revolution to the 1840s in a forthcoming book, *American Sovereigns: The Constitutional Legacy of the People's Sovereignty before the Civil War* (Cambridge University Press). See also Forrest McDonald, *States' Rights and the Union: Imperium in Imperio, 1776–1876* (Lawrence: University Press of Kansas, 2000).

10  Fritz, "Recovering the Lost Worlds," 267–68, quotations, 268.

11  John L. Brooke, "Exhibition Review: Right and Might: The Dorr Rebellion and the Struggle for Equal Rights," review of an exhibition and catalog by the Rhode Island Historical Society, *Journal of American History* 80 (June 1993): 197.

12  Mowry, *Dorr War*, 1. The estimates are from Mowry, who concluded that the "rival figures make it certain that the 10,000 or more actual freemen were scarcely half of the possible voters" (ibid., 75–76). On "out of doors" republicanism the standard source is Gordon S. Wood, *The Creation of the American Republic, 1776–1787* (Chapel Hill: University of North Carolina Press, 1969); see also Robert Shalhope, *The Roots of Democracy: American Thought and Culture, 1760–1800* (Boston: Twayne, 1990).

13  Conley, *Democracy in Decline*, 243–45, 277, 294.

14  Coleman, *Transformation of Rhode Island*, viii–ix, 83–133, 219–20, 228; Conley, *Democracy in Decline*, 145–61. Paul Goodman also stresses the oligarchic character of the state's outwardly republican polity, though he concedes that "many independent electors . . . added a popular and unpredictable element" (Goodman, *Towards a Christian Republic: Antimasonry and the Transformation of New England* [New York: Oxford University Press, 1988], 195.) For emphasis on the independence of artisans and operatives, see Gary Kulick, "Pawtucket Village and the Strike of 1824: The Origins of Class Conflict in Rhode Island," *Radical History Review* 17 (Spring 1978): 6–9, 12–19.

15  Coleman, *Transformation of Rhode Island*, 268. Impressive testimony to the openness of voting may be found in the lists of South Kingston voters in the papers of Democratic leader and landowner Elisha R. Potter, Potter Collection, Rhode Island Historical Society, Providence, R.I. (RIHS); see, for example, "Vote for 1st Rep., Aug. 1837," and "Vote for 2nd Rep., Aug. 1837." Also see the 1842 circular letter of the Providence Central Committee, Law and Order Party, March 1842, Broadsides Collection, John Hay Library, Brown University (JHL). Regarding open voting generally in the nineteenth century, see Paul Bourke and Donald A. DeBats, "The Structure

of Political Involvement in the Nineteenth Century: A Frontier Case," *Perspectives in American History*, new ser., 3 (1986): 207–38.

16  Abuses described in testimony of Aaron White Jr., in *Burke's Report*, 277; last quotation, Elisha R. Potter to Dutee J. Pearce, December 20, 1841, Pearce Papers, RIHS.

17  First quotation, C. Allen, Centreville, to John B. Francis, March 25, 1842, Francis Papers, RIHS; second quotation, *Address to the Freemen of the Agricultural and Manufacturing Interests of Rhode Island* (Providence: Republican Herald, 1829), 8. See also John B. Francis to Elisha R. Potter, July 4, 1842, Potter Collection; and William G. Goddard, *An Address to the People of Rhode Island, on the Occasion of the Change in the Civil Government of Rhode-Island* (Providence: Knowles and Vose, 1843), 56–57. Regarding the complexities of Rhode Island's "agrarian" interest, see James L. Marsis, "Agrarian Politics in Rhode Island, 1800–1860," *Rhode Island History* 34 (February 1975): 12–21.

18  Coleman, *Transformation of Rhode Island*, 264–66; Conley, *Democracy in Decline*, 237–39, 263; Jacob Frieze, *Concise History of the Efforts to Obtain an Extension of Suffrage in Rhode Island from the Years 1811 to 1842* (Providence: Benjamin F. Moore, 1842), 22–23.

19  Though not a member of an antislavery society, Dorr also favored abolition of the slave trade in Washington, D.C. The "Address to the People of Rhode Island, from the Convention Assembled at Providence on the 22nd day of February, and again on the 12th day of March, 1834, to Promote the Establishment of a State Constitution" was written largely by Dorr (printed in *Burke's Report*, 151–85). See also Frieze, *Concise History*, 27; Gettleman, *Dorr Rebellion*, 12–15, 17–18; Conley, *Democracy in Decline*, 249–52, 258–77, 278–80, 283–85; and Dennison, *Dorr War*, 18–21. Regarding Dorr's focus on other issues, see Thomas W. Dorr to Alexander H. Everett, January 27, 1840, and Dorr to Robert Rantoul, February 1, 1840, Dorr Papers, JHL. A clipping of a September 25, 1839, communication of Dorr's to the *Providence Journal* in the Dorr Papers, RIHS, also reveals the broad range of Dorr's reform interests.

20  Conley, *Democracy in Decline*, 292–97; Frieze, *Concise History*, 29; King, *Life and Times*, 82; Gettleman, *Dorr Rebellion*, 34; Williamson, *American Suffrage*, 250; quotations, Thomas A. Jenckes, "Record of the Proceedings of the Governor and Council under the Resolutions of the Assembly referring to them sundry petitions indicted and imprisoned for offences against the state," 1843, Dorr Papers, RIHS; Charles T. Congdon, *Reminiscences of a Journalist* (Boston: J. R. Osgood and Co., 1880), 106. For various contemporary publications dealing with events in the early 1840s, see John Russell Bartlett, *Bibliography of Rhode Island* (Providence: Alfred Anthony, 1864), 82–106. Among many accounts of the 1840 campaign, see Robert J. Dinkin, *Campaigning in America: A History of Election Practices* (New York: Greenwood Press, 1989), 49–53.

21  Dr. John A. Brown, a Providence brewer and physician, founded the paper. Regarding the suffrage association's origins, see Frances H. Whipple McDougall, *Might and Right* (Providence: A. H. Stillwell, 1844), 70–71; *Burke's Report*, 247–48; Conley, *Democracy in Decline*, 287, 292–93, 299; and Dennison, *Dorr War*, 30. McDougall is also cited as Frances H. Whipple Green.

22  Conley, *Democracy in Decline*, 299–300; Frieze, *Concise History*, 30–32; Coleman, *Transformation of Rhode Island*, 273; quotations, Elisha R. Potter, *Considerations on the Questions of the Adoption of a Constitution, and Extension of the Suffrage in Rhode Island* (Boston:

T. H. Webb and Co., 1842), 15, 16. On Democratic conversions to suffrage reform, see C. M. Marsh to Thomas W. Dorr, November 11, 1840, Dorr Papers, JHL. Mowry, *Dorr War*, 52–53, insists that the renewed reform movement originated with neither the Whig nor the Democratic Party.

23 Conley, *Democracy in Decline*, 300–303; Gettleman, *Dorr Rebellion*, 37–40; "'Convention Quick Step,' Composed and Respectfully Dedicated to the Rhode Island Suffrage Association by Henry S. Cartee. Performed by the American Brass Band, April 17, 1841" (Boston, 1841), Newberry Library, Chicago. This sheet music displays a lithograph of a huge procession of some 3,000 participants and festivities on a plain above the city with beer, roasted ox, calf, and hog. See Conley, *Democracy in Decline*, 302.

24 Conley, *Democracy in Decline*, 309–13; Deborah Bingham Van Broekhoven, *The Devotion of These Women: Rhode Island and the Anti-Slavery Network* (Amherst: University of Massachusetts Press, 2002), 45. The abolitionists ended up with the worst of both worlds, deeply resented by suffragists and attacked by Whigs "as though they were Dorrites. Law-and-Order Whigs accused antislavery society members of furnishing arms and money to Dorrites" (Van Broekhoven, *Devotion of These Women*, 45).

25 Welcome Arnold Greene, *The Providence Plantations: City of Providence* (Providence: J. A. & R. A. Reid, 1886), 81–82; Dennison, *Dorr War*, 51–52; Coleman, *Transformation of Rhode Island*, 274–75; Conley, *Democracy in Decline*, 151–56, 315.

26 Conley, *Democracy in Decline*, 316.

27 Gettleman, *Dorr Rebellion*, 61–62; and especially Conley, *Democracy in Decline*, 320 (n. 20) (on the "great ideological and substantive differences" between the competing constitutions). Both constitutions are printed in *Burke's Report*. A rising temperance reform influenced negative attitudes toward Irish Catholics; see Marsis, "Agrarian Politics in Rhode Island," 18–21.

28 Conley, *Democracy in Decline*, 317. Regarding the Irish influx that began in the 1840s, see Robert A. Wheeler, "Fifth Ward Irish-Immigrant Mobility in Providence, 1850–1870," *Rhode Island History* 32 (May 1973): 53.

29 The constitutions are reprinted also in Mowry, *Dorr War*, quotations, 323, 349.

30 Conley, *Democracy in Decline*, 317–18.

31 Ibid., 319–23; Joshua B. Rathbun, Tiverton, to Thomas W. Dorr, March 25, 1842, Dorr Papers, JHL; William Emmons to Dutee J. Pearce, March 18, 1842, Pearce Papers. See also "Native American Citizens! Read and Take Warning!" (March 1842) and "No Right to Make Any Difference Between Native and Naturalized Citizens!" (March 1842), Broadsides Collection, JHL; William Wiecek, "Popular Sovereignty in the Dorr War: Conservative Counterblast," *Rhode Island History* 32 (May 1973): 35–51; and Joyce M. Botelho, *The Power of the People: Constitutions in Conflict*, book 2 of *Right and Might: The Dorr Rebellion and the Struggle for Equal Rights* (Providence: Rhode Island Historical Society, 1992), 39.

32 Dorr quoted in King, *Life and Times*, 92. Frieze, a critic of Dorr, made a similar point. He had been a suffrage association member until July 1840 and voted for the People's Constitution, but he "felt perfectly free" to vote for any other constitution (Frieze, *Concise History*, 127–28). Also regarding fluidity of opinion in the middle, see John H. Clarke, Providence, to Elisha R. Potter, February 24, 1842, Potter Collection. Issues

having nothing to do with constitutional reform also influenced the vote on the Freeholders' Constitution, notably a clause pertaining to shore and fishery rights that antagonized many on both sides. See John B. Francis to Elisha R. Potter, March 25, 1842, Potter Collection; and "Rights of Fishery" (March 1842), Broadsides Collection, JHL.

33 Greene, *Providence Plantations*, 82; Conley, *Democracy in Decline*, 325–27, Tyler quotation, 325; Mowry, *Dorr War*, 123. "The threat of interference [by Tyler] was . . . equivalent to the actual presence of the troops" (Elias Smith, Boston, to Thomas W. Dorr, August 15, 1842, Dorr Papers, JHL). Dorr's parents wrote to him on April 8 to plead with him to change course (Gettleman, *Dorr Rebellion*, 86). Dorr initially took the Algerine Law lightly, as something "meant merely to frighten the common sort of folks" (Thomas W. Dorr to Aaron White, April 4, 1842, Dorr Papers, JHL).

34 King, *Life and Times*, 99; Thomas Wilson Bicknell, *The History of the State of Rhode Island and Providence Plantations*, 6 vols. (New York: American Historical Society, 1920), 2:796; McDougall, *Might and Right*, 236–37; Conley, *Democracy in Decline*, 327–29. Because of the suffragists' paralyzing scruples, "the cause was defeated," said Dorr in 1843, "if not lost" (*Burke's Report*, 738).

35 This statement is based on a partial search of town and county histories. Jeremiah Sheldon and George H. Brown of the Democratic and suffrage stronghold of Glocester became prominent in town affairs; see Elizabeth A. Perry, *A Brief History of the Town of Glocester, Rhode Island* (Providence: Providence Press Company, 1886), 122–26. More impressive still were local notables who supported the People's Constitution in strongly Charterite southern and western towns, such as Joseph Gavitt of Charlestown (William Franklin Tucker, *Historical Sketch of the Town of Charlestown, Rhode Island, 1636 to 1876* [Westerly, R.I.: G. B. & J. II. Utter, 1877], 59–61), Silas Weaver of Kent (J. R. Cole, *History of Washington and Kent Counties, Rhode Island*, 2 vols. [New York: W. W. Preston & Co., 1889], 2:1139), and Wager Weeden of South Kingstown (Cole, *History of Washington and Kent Counties*, 2:369–70). William P. Arnold, a representative from Westerly, in 1846 bought the woolen mills at the village of Shattuck's Weir and renamed the place "Dorrville." He later leased and sold the property to fellow Dorrite Wager Weeden. See Frederick Denison, *Westerly (Rhode Island) and Its Witnesses, 1636–1876* (Westerly, R.I.: J. A. & R. A. Reid, 1878), 184. Nathaniel C. Smith of Barrington was thirty years old in 1842 and later served many years on the school committee and town council (Thomas Williams Bicknell, *A History of Barrington, Rhode Island* [Providence: Snow & Farnham, 1898], 587). Bicknell noted that while Barrington was strongly Charterite, "family ties were broken by the strain of partisanship" (Bicknell, *History of Barrington*, 495). William Goodell observed that Charterite writers who described suffrage men as "low rabble" had nevertheless made some remarkable admissions: "Dr. Tucker . . . says:—'The evil has infected the churches'—'Sad divisions have taken place—friend has been strayed against friend, brother against brother—lines of alienation have run through families and firms of business.'—And Dr. [Francis] Wayland says their movements 'have been fostered and abetted, in some instances, by the civil magistrates, and yet more . . . by men who have been nurtured among us, who have sat at our tables, and been warmed by our fire-sides.'" See William Goodell, *The Rights and Wrongs of Rhode Island*

(Whitesboro, N.Y.: Press of the Oneida Institute, 1842), 8; John Brown Francis to Elisha R. Potter, April 20, 1842, Potter Collection. The list of Foundry legislators is in *Burke's Report*, 451–52, 71–73.

36 Conley, *Democracy in Decline*, 333–38; Gettleman, *Dorr Rebellion*, 107–18; quotation, David Grimsted, *American Mobbing, 1828–1861: Toward Civil War* (New York: Oxford University Press, 1998), 214, 336 (n. 43 and 44). Regarding the New Yorkers' misleading Dorr, see also Mowry, *Dorr War*, 166–79. Mowry recorded the conflicting recollections of several witnesses who heard Dorr's speech and concluded that whatever the exact words, they were inflammatory (Mowry, *Dorr War*, 176–78). Conley notes that "Dorr spoke of military actions mainly in defensive terms" (Conley, *Democracy in Decline*, 336).

37 Conley, *Democracy in Decline*, 337–41, quotation, 340; Congdon, *Reminiscences*, 110; Dennison, *Dorr War*, 85–86. The best account of the faulty cannon and faint-heartedness of some of Dorr's "troops" is in *Burke's Report*, 907–8.

38 State officials exaggerated the military threat posed by suffragists, though President Tyler was well informed regarding the hysteria of Governor King and his advisors. See Gettleman, *Dorr Rebellion*, 127; Conley, *Democracy in Decline*, 343; and *Burke's Report*, 685–87, 699. The phrase "fear of prisons" was used by the Dorrite shoemaker Luther Martin of Warren in an 1844 letter from jail to Dorr, quoted in Peter C. Magrath, "Optimistic Democrat: Thomas W. Dorr and the Case of *Luther vs. Borden*," *Rhode Island History* 29 (August/November 1970): 99.

39 Conley, *Democracy in Decline*, 344–45; Gettleman, *Dorr Rebellion*, 128–30; Elisha R. Potter, Kingston, to John Tyler, June 10, 1842, Potter Collection. For an example of "no force" suffragism on the part of a Baptist minister critical of the state government, see untitled manuscript in James McKenzie Papers, 1812–1873, RIHS. "A Horrible Plot *Discovered*!!" (1842), Broadsides Collection, JHL, purported to expose a "most foul and ferocious plot" by Dorr and a few of his desperate followers to bring to Providence "armed ruffians from the city of New-York to butcher their fellow-citizens."

40 Frieze, *Concise History*, 112–15; Gettleman, *Dorr Rebellion*, 131–41; Dennison, *Dorr War*, 87–95; Conley, *Democracy in Decline*, 344–51. For optimistic advice to Dorr regarding potential military support before Chepachet, see John S. Harris to Dorr, June 12, 1842, Charles E. Newell to Dorr, June 13, 1842, William J. Miller to Dorr, June 15, 1842, J. Sprague, Chepachet, to Dorr, June 15, 1842, and Burrington Anthony to Dorr, June 17, 1842, all Dorr Papers, JHL. For contrary advice see Aaron White, Woonsocket, to Dorr, June 12, 1842, Dorr Papers, JHL; but compare Aaron White to Dorr, June 18, 1842, Dorr Papers, JHL. Some of Dorr's closest friends opposed his return to Chepachet: see Benjamin Albro, W. S. Burgess, et al., "Remonstrance against the proceedings at Chepachet by several suffrage men," June 25, 1842, Dorr Papers, JHL. Dorr replied to Burgess, angrily asking if "the brave men who have acted in support of the constitution by all necessary means" were simply to be "given up" to the Algerines (Thomas W. Dorr, Glocester, to W. S. Burgess, June 27, 1842, Dorr Papers, JHL). A letter of apology written by Burgess several months later is revealing of the pressures on Dorr at Chepachet (Burgess to Dorr, October 30, 1842, Dorr Papers, JHL).

41 The first two quoted phrases are from Elisha R. Potter to John Tyler, July 6, 1842, draft copy, and Elisha R. Potter to John Tyler, June 10, 1842, draft copy, Potter Collection; see also John B. Francis to Elisha R. Potter, June 7, 1842, Potter Collection. The Potter Collection, the Thomas F. Carpenter Papers (RIHS), and the Dorr Papers (JHL) contain much information regarding Law and Order repression. See especially Elisha R. Potter to John Tyler, July 6, 1842, Potter Collection; W. S. Burgess to Thomas W. Dorr, May 9, 1842, Aaron White, New Boston, Conn., to Dorr, September 1, 1842, and C. R. Williams to Dorr, November 2, 1842, Dorr Papers, JHL; Thomas F. Carpenter to Albert C. Green, attorney general, September 19, 1842, Carpenter Papers. "The Algerines . . . are endeavoring to induce landlords to turn their tenants out of their houses, who bore arms in defense of the people's rights. . . . They also discharge every man from employment on the same ground" (David Parmenter, Providence, to Thomas W. Dorr, May 10, 1842; in a similar vein, John S. Harris to Dorr, June 2, 1842, Dorr Papers, JHL).

42 Conley, *Democracy in Decline*, 351, 372–73; quotation, David Parmenter to Thomas W. Dorr, September 30, 1842, Dorr Papers, JHL; Coleman, *Transformation of Rhode Island*, 284–85. Natives also needed $134 worth of personal property to vote in town financial affairs. For the ratification vote the Law and Order party mobilized its supporters throughout the state; see circular letter from Providence Central Committee, "Gentlemen— . . ." [1842], Broadsides Collection, JHL. Regarding African American enfranchisement, see Conley, *Democracy in Decline*, 345, 372. Nevertheless, some suffragists were willing to accept a "tolerable" constitution. See Abby H. Lord, Providence, to Thomas W. Dorr, October 2, 1842, Dorr Papers, JHL.

43 Conley, *Democracy in Decline*, 354; Dorr quotation, *Burke's Report*, 759. The names and occupations of many Dorrites appeared in *Burke's Report*, with artisans most commonly mentioned; men identified as "yeoman," "husbandman," or "farmer" were fewer but persistently present (*Burke's Report*, 332–40, 756, 790, 792, 794, 795, 798, 804, 811, 814). Some Dorrite leaders owned substantial property (*Burke's Report*, 107); men persecuted by the Law and Order militia included a minister, farmer, Providence brewer, and "very respectable" innkeeper (*Burke's Report*, 135, 156, 175–81). Frieze also noted divisions among freeholders and non-freeholders and claimed that many non-freeholders defended the Charter government (Frieze, *Concise History*, 129–30). Similarly, the militia companies on both sides consisted of many middling and lower-class men. For a characterization of the Law and Order militia as lower class, see John S. Harris to Thomas W. Dorr, September 12, 1842, Dorr Papers, JHL; for a contrary view see William M. Bailey, Waterville, Maine, to Thomas W. Dorr, June 14, 1842, William M. Bailey Papers, RIHS. A loyalist militia party that invaded the home of Dorrite shoemaker Martin Luther in Warren, leading to the court case *Luther vs. Borden*, consisted of three master mariners, a cooper, a carpenter, a tailor, a customhouse officer, a merchant, and a seaman (*Burke's Report*, 358).

44 Quotation, McDougall, *Might and Right*, 16 (the author herself a member of a founding family); Coleman, *Transformation of Rhode Island*, 244, 262; Benjamin Knight, *History of the Sprague Families of Rhode Island, Cotton Manufacturers and Calico Printers from William I to William IV* (Santa Cruz: H. Coffin, 1881), 14–15, 23–29; Goodman, *Towards a Christian Republic*, 208–12. The wealthy reportedly gave large sums to the

Law and Order party; see Almon D. Hodges Jr., ed., *Almon Danforth Hodges and His Neighbors: An Autobiographical Sketch of a Typical Old New Englander* (Boston: T. R. Marvin & Son, 1909), 194. The grandson of a Providence bookstore owner who supported the People's Constitution said that a "handful of men among the property-owning class" joined the reform movement and were "ostracised, villified, and denounced as traitors to their class" (Margaret Bingham Stillwell, "A Man Who Dared to Stand Alone: A Sidelight on the Dorr Rebellion 1842–1844," *Rhode Island History* 36 [May 1977]: 35). Dr. Metcalf Marsh, a "manufacturer" of Slatersville, was a prominent Dorrite (Walter A. Nebiker, *The History of North Smithfield* [North Smithfield, R.I.: North Smithfield Bicentennial Commission, 1976], 128–29).

45  Dexter Randall, *Democracy Vindicated, and Dorrism Unveiled* (Providence: H. H. Brown, 1846), 38; Conley, *Democracy in Decline*, 246, 259, 272; Goodman, *Towards a Christian Republic*, 201.

46  Robert J. Cottrol, *The Afro-Yankees: Providence's Black Community in the Antebellum Era* (Westport, Conn.: Greenwood Press, 1982), 72–74, 76–77, 85; J. Stanley Lemons and Michael A. McKenna, "Re-enfranchisement of Rhode Island Negroes," *Rhode Island History* 30 (February 1971): 7–10; Conley, *Democracy in Decline*, 311–12, Potter quotation, 345; Goodell, *Rights and Wrongs*, 5–6; McDougall, *Might and Right*, 294. At first some abolitionists campaigned against the People's Constitution because of black exclusion, but some abolitionist men and women became some of Dorr's staunchest supporters. Blacks voted in the November 1842 ratification of the Law and Order Constitution. It, too, included a separate referendum on black suffrage, which passed 3,357 to 1,004.

47  Conley, *Democracy in Decline*, 350, 373; Dorr quotation, *Burke's Report*, 765; "half and half" from Wilkins Updike to Elisha R. Potter, April 6, 1842, Potter Collection; *History of the Kentish Guards* (n.p., n.d.), 14, 16; East Greenwich, R.I., *Proceedings of the Citizens of East Greenwich and Vicinity* (Providence, 1842), 10; John J. Richards, "History of the Collapse of Compulsory Military Service in Rhode Island, 1836–1842," manuscript, ca. 1930, RIHS, 66, 79–84. For a suffragist racist cartoon, see "Governor King's Extra," in *The Broadsides of the Dorr Rebellion*, comp. Russell J. De Simone and Daniel C. Schofield (Providence: Rhode Island Supreme Court Historical Society, 1992), 55. "Foreign Voters! [1845 or 1846]," Broadsides Collection, JHL, detailed the threat to the state's agricultural and industrial interests from a growing population of Irish Catholic workers, nine-tenths of whom "uniformly vote the ultra-radical ticket" and were all Dorrites. "To the Hon. General Assembly of the State of Rhode Island, at their May Session, A.D. 1846," Broadsides Collection, JHL, complained of the stigma attached to naturalized citizens by the colored population's exercising the right of suffrage as freely as white native citizens, "thereby degrading naturalized citizens below the colored population." The petitioners claimed not "to envy the colored population," but, "as the impression is abroad, that the colored population is inferior to the white and shaded population, the insult is more piercing."

48  Potter's memorandum labeled "1837 Town Meeting Bill" included payment for fourteen decanters of liquor and of twenty-three cents each to forty individuals; quotations, J. S. Harris to Elisha R. Potter, August 22, 1837, John B. Francis to Elisha R. Potter, April 1838, and George D. Cross, Westerly, to Elisha R. Potter, March 26,

1842, all in Potter Collection. See also Elisha R. Potter to J. B. Francis, March 25, 1842, Francis Papers; and John R. Waterman to Elisha R. Potter, March 19, 1838, Potter Collection. Regarding Democrats pressuring blacks, see William J. Brown, *The Life of William J. Brown of Providence, R.I.* (Providence: Angell and Co., 1883), 160–62.

49   *Providence Journal*, April 18, 1843; Walter S. Burgess to Thomas W. Dorr, April 6, 1843, in Sidney S. Rider, "The Development of Constitutional Government in Rhode Island," Manuscript in 27 Scrapbooks, vol. 22, RIHS (this manuscript contains extensive quotations from letters to Dorr).

50   Ariel Ballou to Thomas W. Dorr, November 2, 1842, Dorr Papers, JHL; circular letter from Democratic and Equal Rights Committee, Anson Potter, Thomas F. Carpenter, et al., January 10, 1843, Broadsides Collection, JHL; details of economic pressure in Providence in letters to Thomas W. Dorr from Frederick I. Beckford, April 10, 1843, and Philip B. Stiness, April 14, 1843, quoted in Rider, "Development of Constitutional Government," RIHS; Hill quoted in Conley, *Democracy in Decline*, 354–55 (n. 84). See also McDougall, *Right and Might*, 308–9. Political pressure also came to bear in loyalist militia companies; see "To the Members of the Kentish Guards," Bristol, April 7, 1843, [no signature], Allen Papers, RIHS.

51   See chapter 9.

52   Gettleman, *Dorr Rebellion*, 162–73; Dennison, *Dorr War*, 106–8; Conley, *Democracy in Decline*, 366–71 (superb on events after 1843). Dorr noted his pardon in his diary thusly: "T. W. Dorr restored to full political and civil rights, by General Assembly, May 9, '51[.] No special oath of allegiance—no oath taken. Algerines backed out. A proof of the efficacy of never giving up in a good cause" (Dorr Diary, Dorr Papers, JHL).

53   First quotation, William M. Bailey to Jane Keeley, Waterville, Maine, June 14, 1842, Bailey Papers; Catherine R. Williams, Keene, N.H., to Thomas W. Dorr, October 9, 1842, Dorr Papers, JHL (regarding unreal fears held by the Charterite affluent); organizer quotation, Paul Buhle, Scott Molloy, and Gail Sansbury, eds., *A History of Rhode Island Working People* (Providence: Institute for Labor Studies and Research, 1983), 10, 11. Conservative hyperbole was delivered also from the pulpit; see, for example, Francis Wayland, *The Affairs of Rhode Island. A Discourse Delivered in the Meeting-House of the First Baptist Church, Providence, May 22, 1842* (Boston: William D. Ticknor, 1842); and Mark Tucker, *A Discourse Preached on Thanksgiving Day, in the Beneficent Congregational Meeting House, Providence, July 21, 1842* (Providence: Benjamin F. Moore printer, 1842).

54   Van Broekhoven, *Devotion of These Women*, 27–53. Although many abolitionists later supported the suffragists during the Algerine persecutions, in attacking the People's Constitution earlier they had alienated the disenfranchised artisans, mechanics, and shopkeepers in factory villages who had been receptive to the antislavery message (ibid., 41–43).

55   Mowry, *Dorr War*, 3. This and the following paragraphs rely heavily on Ronald P. Formisano, "The Role of Women in the Dorr Rebellion," *Rhode Island History* 51 (August 1993): 89–104.

56   For invocations of the Revolution, see McDougall, *Right and Might*, 313; and Susan H. Graham, "'Call Me a Female Politician, I Glory in the Name!': Women Dorrites and

Rhode Island's 1842 Suffrage Crisis" (Ph.D. diss., University of Minnesota, 2006), 109–25.

57 Formisano, "Role of Women," 91–96; quotation, Harriet Bailey to Jane Keeley, June 14, 1842, Bailey Papers. Writer Catherine R. Williams, one of Dorr's strongest supporters, had published a book earlier claiming for women prominent participation in the American Revolution; see Williams, *Tales National and Revolutionary* (Providence: H. H. Brown Printers, 1830). Charterite women greeted the Providence militia returning from Chepachet with a "shower of flowers" (Elisha Dyer, "Reminiscences of Rhode Island in 1842 as Connected with the Dorr Rebellion," *Narragansett Historical Register* 6 [1888]: 185).

58 Formisano, "Role of Women," 95; Catherine R. Williams to Thomas W. Dorr, November 2, 1842, Dorr Papers, JHL. Regarding Williams, see Sidney S. Rider, *Bibliographical Memoirs of Three Rhode Island Authors: Joseph K. Angell, Frances H. (Whipple) McDougall and Catherine R. Williams*, Rhode Island Historical Tracts, no. 11 (Providence: S. S. Rider, 1880), 51–61. Graham, "'Call Me a Female Politician,'" develops some of these same points.

59 Formisano, "Role of Women," 97–99; Catherine Williams to Thomas W. Dorr, November 2, 1842, Dorr Papers, JHL.

60 Van Broekhoven, *Devotion of These Women*, 30–34. See also Lori D. Ginzberg's brilliant discussion of the relationship between religion and women's citizenship and activism: "The conflation of respectable womanhood with restricted religious and sexual practices pervaded antebellum claims to the rights of citizens—and to the denial of those rights" (Ginzberg, *Untidy Origins: A Story of Woman's Rights in Antebellum New York* [Chapel Hill: University of North Carolina Press, 2005], 39–44, quotation, 43).

61 Formisano, "Role of Women," 101. One suffragist woman, Lidea Rodgers, reportedly accompanied Dorr's men on their ill-fated siege of the arsenal and served them coffee and refreshments (Graham, "'Call Me a Female Politician,'" 265). Henry B. Anthony, editor of the *Providence Journal* and a fierce critic of the People's movement, published a long satirical poem in January 1843, "The Dorriad," mocking the alleged incompetence and cowardice of suffrage men in the attack on the arsenal (Mowry, *Dorr War*, 390–94). Anthony was and continued to be one of the state's leading nativists (Conley, *Democracy in Decline*, 276–77).

62 At least two suffragist women later joined the struggle for woman suffrage (Graham, "'Call Me a Female Politician,'" 298).

63 Wiebe, *Opening of American Society*, 251; Joel H. Silbey, *The American Political Nation, 1838–1893* (Stanford, Calif.: Stanford University Press, 1991), 177. The basic work on this process in fact deals with New York State: L. Ray Gunn, *The Decline of Authority: Public Economic Policy and Political Development in New York, 1800–1860* (Ithaca, N.Y.: Cornell University Press, 1988). See also Jennifer Nedelsky, *Private Property and the Limits of American Constitutionalism: The Madisonian Framework and Its Legacy* (Chicago: University of Chicago Press, 1990). Both Whigs and Democrats "represented coalitions of state machines," and the Jacksonians' introduction of the "spoils" system "reinforced the pattern of decentralization and led to the degradation of the government, particularly the bureaucracy" (William G. Shade, "'Revolutions May Go

Backwards': The American Civil War and the Problem of Political Development," *Social Science Quarterly* 55 [December 1974]: 756). For the corrosive impact of the Jacksonians' patronage practices on the post office, see Richard R. John, *Spreading the News: The American Postal System from Franklin to Morse* (Cambridge, Mass.: Harvard University Press, 1995), 206–56.

64 Rowland Berthoff and John M. Murrin, "Feudalism, Communalism, and the Yeoman Freeholder: The American Revolution Considered as a Social Accident," in *Essays on the American Revolution*, ed. Stephen G. Kurtz and James H. Hutson (Chapel Hill: University of North Carolina Press, 1971), 267–68. "The feudal revival was as divisive as it was profitable," Berthoff and Murrin continue, "provoking more social violence after 1745 than perhaps any other problem." Regarding the republican ideal, see Robert E. Shalhope, "Republicanism and Early American Historiography," *William and Mary Quarterly*, 3d ser., 39 (April 1982): 347.

65 Quotation, Charles W. McCurdy, *The Anti-Rent Era in New York Law and Politics, 1839–1865* (Chapel Hill: University of North Carolina Press, 2001), xiii. I have relied primarily on two recent and exhaustive secondary studies of the Anti-Rent Wars: Reeve Huston, *Land and Freedom: Rural Society, Popular Protest, and Party Politics in Antebellum New York* (New York: Oxford University Press, 2000); and McCurdy, *Anti-Rent Era*; as well as David Maldwyn Ellis, *Landlords and Farmers in the Hudson-Mohawk Region, 1790–1850* (New York: Octagon Books, 1967); and the useful Henry Christman, *Tin Horns and Calico: A Decisive Episode in the Emergence of Democracy* (New York: Henry Holt and Co., 1945). Huston and McCurdy, equally valuable, reach somewhat different conclusions regarding the episode.

66 McCurdy, *Anti-Rent Era*, quotations, 1, 93; Huston, *Land and Freedom*, 24–27; Ellis, *Landlords and Farmers*, 226–30. Huston observes that landlords' titles were "notoriously weak" with some "founded in outright fraud" (Huston, *Land and Freedom*, 19–20). Under New York law in the 1840s, however, that history did nothing for the tenants.

67 Rensselaerwyck rents had been paid originally in wheat, but by the 1830s changes in soil fertility and wheat-growing expansion elsewhere had forced most tenant farmers, especially in hill towns, to switch to dairying and livestock. Regarding changes in agriculture and landlord-tenant relations, see Ellis, *Landlords and Farmers*, 229–30; Huston, *Land and Freedom*, 44–55, 77–84; and McCurdy, *Anti-Rent Era*, 12–13; regarding political changes, see Huston, *Land and Freedom*, 57, 60, 75. On landlords and Van Buren Democrats, see also John L. Brooke, *Columbia: Civil Life in the Middle Hudson, 1776–1821*, chap. 9 (forthcoming).

68 Ellis, *Landlords and Farmers*, 235–36; McCurdy, *Anti-Rent Era*, 16–17; Huston, *Land and Freedom*, 85, 88–90, quotation, 88. Huston provides the most detailed account of the encounter.

69 On "Rent Day" typically the farmers stood in the cold outside the manor office waiting for their names to be called, then paid their "rates" through a porthole window and received their receipts and their orders for their obligatory day's labor. A tenant farmer later recalled his resentment of the tenant's treatment on such days: "I have been in several different courts where criminals have been arraigned . . . where

they had more liberty and more privilege allowed them than the honest and hard-working yeomanry in that office" (Christman, *Tin Horns and Calico*, 12).

70  Ellis, *Landlords and Farmers*, 237–38; McCurdy, *Anti-Rent Era*, 17–22; Huston, *Land and Freedom*, 90–92, quotations, 94.

71  Quotations, McCurdy, *Anti-Rent Era*, 18, 37; Albany County farmer also quoted in Christman, *Tin Horns and Calico*, 23.

72  McCurdy, *Anti-Rent Era*, 43–58, quotation, 58; Huston, *Land and Freedom*, 98–100. Huston comments on "rhetorical support and policy inaction" (Huston, *Land and Freedom*, 98).

73  Ellis, *Landlords and Farmers*, 240–42. The tenants' new defiance also signified their "disenchantment with the Whig Party" (McCurdy, *Anti-Rent Era*, 69). The descriptive phrases and Boughton's words are from Christman, *Tin Horns and Calico*, 41, 73–75. White "Indians" had engaged in vigilantism against landlords for decades: in 1791 "Indians" resisting a sale in Columbia County had killed a county sheriff (Alfred F. Young, *The Democratic Republicans of New York: The Origins, 1763–1797* [Chapel Hill: University of North Carolina Press, 1967], 204–5).

74  On the spread of the movement, see Ellis, *Landlords and Farmers*, 242–43; and McCurdy, *Anti-Rent Era*, 95–97. There had been Anti-Rent violence in April 1842 on the Livingston estate in Schoharie County (Ellis, *Landlords and Farmers*, 243). The exemption bill applied primarily to perpetual leases and much of Rensselaerwyck Manor, prompting petitions to flow into the legislature from other manors where the leases were in lives (McCurdy, *Anti-Rent Era*, 87–89). Stephen Van Rensselaer IV did not attempt to collect rent for nearly three years after his largest creditor, Daniel Dewey Barnard, a conservative Whig political leader, gave him more of a grace period in the interest of helping the Whig Party (McCurdy, *Anti-Rent Era*, 74–76).

75  McCurdy, *Anti-Rent Era*, 100–103; Huston, *Land and Freedom*, 100–101.

76  Huston, *Land and Freedom*, 101–2. The decisions were *Bronson v. Kinzie* (1843), dealing with two Illinois statutes, and in New York, *Taylor v. Porter* (1843). In the former, according to McCurdy, "the Court [said it] knew violations of the Contract Clause when it saw them" (McCurdy, *Anti-Rent Era*, 107–8, quotation, 108); and in *Taylor* the New York judges said the legislature could not allow a landlocked freeholder to appropriate a right-of-way across a neighbor's property whether to vote, serve on juries, or meet any "essential duties of citizenship" because when "one man wants the property of another . . . the legislature cannot aid him in making the acquisition" (McCurdy, *Anti-Rent Era*, 107–9, 111–12). "Neither opinion fixed a clear boundary between the conflicting principles at hand" (McCurdy, *Anti-Rent Era*, 115). Regarding the Whigs' "unscrupulous manipulation," see McCurdy, *Anti-Rent Era*, 139.

77  Ellis, *Landlords and Farmers*, 244–45, quotation, 244; Huston, *Land and Freedom*, 101–3; regarding the New York Supreme Court case *Quackenbush v. Danks* (1844), see McCurdy, *Anti-Rent Era*, 151–52.

78  Ellis, *Landlords and Farmers*, 245, 258; first quotation, Huston, *Land and Freedom*, 104; McCurdy, *Anti-Rent Era*, 148–49, 156–62, second quotation, 151. Ellis originally pointed out that Anti-Renters imitated the methods of political parties, an observation elaborated on by Huston, who also notes the example and training ground of

reform societies (Ellis, *Landlords and Farmers*, 246–48; Huston, *Land and Freedom*, 63). These excellent accounts of the spread of Anti-Rentism do not indicate the relative weight of various events or actions by supporters or opponents in the huge expansion of 1844, but it seems likely that what McCurdy describes as the "sensation" among tenants regarding the new "evidence" of the fraudulence of landlords' titles was crucial. By the end of 1843, McCurdy observes, "very few inhabitants of the [Van Rensselaer] manor believed that the proprietors had a valid title" (McCurdy, *Anti-Rent Era*, 99, 100).

79 Huston, *Land and Freedom*, 147–48; McCurdy, *Anti-Rent Era*, 165–70; Ellis, *Landlords and Farmers*, 252, 260–61.

80 Huston, *Land and Freedom*, 107–11, 152, quotation, 107; McCurdy, *Anti-Rent Era*, 206, 214. Before the *Freeholder*, other short-lived Anti-Rent papers appeared: the *Helderberg Advocate* (1840) and *Guardian of the Soil* (1843); later the *Voice of the People* appeared in Delaware County (Ellis, *Landlords and Farmers*, 251–52). Thomas A. Devyr, editor of the *National Reformer*, a Long Island monthly, became involved with Anti-Rent as early as 1842, became editor of the *Freeholder* when it began in 1844, was fired in 1845, and began his own Albany paper, the *Albany Anti-Renter*, which lasted until November 1846 (McCurdy, *Anti-Rent Era*, 173–74, 201, 215, 267–68). Like Anti-Masonry, Anti-Rent struggled to get a favorable hearing in most established newspapers.

81 McCurdy, *Anti-Rent Era*, 172–73, 206, 212–15; Huston, *Land and Freedom*, 158–59. Regarding the excessive focus of Whig/Anti-Rent leaders on the title test bill, see McCurdy, *Anti-Rent Era*, 202–4. McCurdy stops short of accusing the principal Whig/Anti-Rent leaders of opportunism, but he views the strategy as first benefiting the Whig Party. Regarding the National Reform Association, see Mark A. Lause, *Young America: Land, Labor, and the Republican Community* (Urbana: University of Illinois Press, 2005).

82 Huston, *Land and Freedom*, 149–50, quotation, 150; McCurdy, *Anti-Rent Era*, 215–22, 232–33; Ellis, *Landlords and Farmers*, 265–67.

83 Huston, *Land and Freedom*, 155–57; McCurdy, *Anti-Rent Era*, 235, 251, 254, 258, quotation, 258. On the November 1845 elections, see McCurdy, *Anti-Rent Era*, 222. Huston comments that the distress bill actually worked to the landlords' advantage by making "reentry" easier (Huston, *Land and Freedom*, 157).

84 Huston, *Land and Freedom*, 159–61; McCurdy, *Anti-Rent Era*, 126. McCurdy refers to the "pathetic constitutional amendments" dealing with landholdings that "spoke to the future" (McCurdy, *Anti-Rent Era*, 261). See also Gunn, *Decline of Authority*, 170–97.

85 McCurdy, *Anti-Rent Era*, 234–59, esp. 258–59; James C. N. Paul, *Rift in the Democracy* (Philadelphia: University of Pennsylvania Press, 1957); William W. Freehling, *The Road to Disunion: Secessionists at Bay, 1770–1854* (New York: Oxford University Press, 1990), 411–52; Leonard L. Richards, *The Slave Power: The Free North and Southern Domination, 1780–1860* (Baton Rouge: Louisiana State University Press, 2000), 134–89.

86 Herbert D. A. Donovan, *The Barnburners: A Study of the Internal Movements in the Political History of New York State, 1830–1852* (New York: New York University Press, 1925; reprint, Philadelphia: Porcupine Press, 1974), 75–79; McCurdy, *Anti-Rent Era*, 268–70.

87  McCurdy, *Anti-Rent Era*, 270–72, 281–86; Huston, *Land and Freedom*, 175–80. Huston describes Young's proposal as "cynical" and aimed not at relief for tenants but "at *appearing to do so*" (Huston, *Land and Freedom*, 180). During the late 1840s "anti-renters learned with dramatic finality the limits to popular power under the second party system" (Huston, *Land and Freedom*, 175).

88  McCurdy, *Anti-Rent Era*, 249–55, 283–84, 273 (regarding "land rush"). Huston points out that buyouts also resulted from tenants' improved access to credit, markets, and new machinery (Huston, *Land and Freedom*, 191–92). Regarding National Reformers and Free Soil, see Huston, *Land and Freedom*, 170–72. By 1850 almost four-fifths of the Livingston lands had been sold. In December 1853 the New York Court of Appeals "finally quashed the government assault on landlord titles" (McCurdy, *Anti-Rent Era*, 286).

89  Huston, *Land and Freedom*, 170–73, 183–87. Whig and Democratic Anti-Rent leaders "endorsed many tenants' commitment to the principle that each man had a 'natural right to the land' and made it safe for vested rights and for capitalism. They did so by placing the existing distribution of land out of the bounds of discussion and by focusing their constituents' attention on the public lands. Dividing these lands among working farmers would encroach upon nobody's property rights—except for those of the Indians, who, as every anti-renter knew, were destined to disappear at the approach of white settlers" (ibid., 73).

90  Huston, *Land and Freedom*, 186–88, 193. As late as 1850 the Anti-Rent vote was still punishing Democrats in the state election (Donovan, *Barnburners*, 115). The best chance for a compromise worked out by the legislature came in 1850, after a rare court decision went against a landlord, but once again the focus on title invalidation caused Anti-Rent leaders to ignore it. Ironically, an 1858 state supreme court decision protecting yet once again the lease in fee was decided by Ira Harris, a former legislative darling of the Anti-Renters. On the Rensselaer manor, rent strikes and resistance continued up to and, briefly, after the Civil War, until in 1865 a disciplined force of militia marched into the Helderbergs and ejected the last tenant strikers (McCurdy, *Anti-Rent Era*, 288–330).

91  Huston, *Land and Freedom*, 111–14, 132, quotation, 132. The comparison with the Regulators, Anti-Masons, and others is mine; I also see the Anti-Renters' notions of "popular sovereignty" as far less "Jacksonian" than Huston does and much more rooted in traditions of the people's sovereignty reaching back to the Revolution and before, as described here in previous chapters.

92  While Huston and McCurdy are essential to understanding the political, social, and legal dimensions of the Anti-Rent Wars, Christman's account more clearly reflects the Anti-Renters' positioning themselves in the Revolutionary legacy; see Christman, *Tin Horns and Calico*, 56, 65, 74, 76, 135, 147, 151, 159, 162, 251, quotation, 151.

93  *New-York Weekly Tribune*, September 8, 1845, quoted in Ellis, *Landlords and Farmers*, 231–32; for a longer excerpt, see McCurdy, *Anti-Rent Era*, 225. McCurdy extensively analyzes Whig and Democratic competition for Anti-Rent votes and defends the routine operation of Democratic Party politics as not "demagoguery" and instead faults the parties for their unwillingness to have a solution if it meant their oppo-

nents received credit (McCurdy, *Anti-Rent Era*, 332–33). Perhaps, then, the operative word is hypocrisy, or opportunism. Daniel Dewey Barnard, Whig politician, lawyer, and creditor and friend of Van Rensselaer, believed that the Anti-Rent movement had been changed from a local and temporary outburst to dangerous "popular licentiousness" by those who had "patronized and advocated, or at least encouraged because not condemned, by those who, by their position in society, their calling and their associations, command public attention, possess in some degree, the public confidence, and exercise, therefore, a strong influence over public opinion" (McCurdy, *Anti-Rent Era*, 229).

94 Huston, *Land and Freedom*, 88–89, 108–9, 116–18, quotation, 88; see also Ellis, *Landlords and Farmers*, 249–50. Many Anti-Renters were former Democratic or Whig activists, or had experience in reform societies, and included "substantial farmers, merchants, manufacturers, and professionals" (Huston, *Land and Freedom*, 110).

95 Huston, *Land and Freedom*, 38–39, 64, 125–29.

96 Anti-Rent counties previously voted reliably Democratic, and that party tended to be the defender of patriarchal norms far more than the Whigs or after them the Republicans, thus reinforcing Huston's point. On the Democrats as defenders of patriarchy, see Michael D. Pierson, *Free Hearts and Free Homes: Gender and American Antislavery Politics* (Chapel Hill: University of North Carolina Press, 2003), 97, 100–114.

97 Huston, *Land and Freedom*, 116–24.

98 Greeley quotation, McCurdy, *Anti-Rent Era*, 224. Greeley continued: "He ponders on his difficulties and perplexities, calculates the gross amount of rent which his ancestors and he have paid, and the question will force itself upon him — 'For what should I pay this rent?'"

99 Christman, *Tin Horns and Calico*, 74, 192–93.

100 Ibid., 74, 275.

101 McCurdy, *Anti-Rent Era*, 334. McCurdy usefully points out that most of those "agents," — i.e., governors, legislators, judges, and members of the 1846 constitutional convention — "were lawyers. Training and experience inclined them to take seriously the constitutional restraints that Anti-Rent leaders assailed as mere landlord talismans" (ibid., 335).

CHAPTER NINE

1 William E. Nelson, *Americanization of the Common Law: The Impact of Legal Change on Massachusetts Society, 1760–1830* (Cambridge, Mass.: Harvard University Press, 1975), 90–92; Morton J. Horowitz, *The Transformation of American Law, 1780–1860* (Cambridge, Mass.: Harvard University Press, 1977), 19–22.

2 First quotation, Patrick T. Conley, *Democracy in Decline: Rhode Island's Constitutional Development, 1776–1841* (Providence: Rhode Island Historical Society, 1977), 357; second quotation, David Grimsted, *American Mobbing, 1828–1861: Toward Civil War* (New York: Oxford University Press, 1998), 217; Christian G. Fritz, "Recovering the Lost Worlds of America's Written Constitutions," *Albany Law Review* 68, no. 2 (2005): 261–93.

3 Conley, *Democracy in Decline*, 375; Fritz, "Recovering the Lost Worlds," 286. A sym-

pathetic Boston lawyer, a Democrat, published a book accusing the Rhode Island charter government of rebelling "against the clearly expressed will of the people" and argued that the issue at stake was "the sovereign right of the people to create, change, abolish government, as they deem their interest to require" ([John Augustus Bolles], *"The Affairs of Rhode Island": Being a Review of President Wayland's "Discourse"* [Boston: Benjamin B. Mussey, 1842], 4, 7).

4 Fritz, "Recovering the Lost Worlds," 287–89.

5 A. Clark Hagensick, "Revolution or Reform in 1836: Maryland's Preface to the Dorr Rebellion," *Maryland Historical Magazine* 57 (December 1962): 347–49; population figures from Bernard C. Steiner, "The Electoral College for the Senate of Maryland and the Nineteen Van Buren Electors," *Annual Report of the American Historical Association, 1895* (Washington, D.C.: Government Printing Office, 1896), 138–39.

6 W. Wayne Smith, *Anti-Jacksonian Politics along the Chesapeake* (New York: Garland, 1989), 120, 123. Regarding "oligarchies in rural society," see Whitman H. Ridgway, *Community Leadership in Maryland, 1790–1840: A Comparative Analysis of Power in Society* (Chapel Hill: University of North Carolina Press, 1979), 20–43.

7 Hagensick, "Revolution or Reform," 349–52; Ridgway, *Community Leadership in Maryland*, 65–66, 113–14.

8 Hagensick, "Revolution or Reform," 352–57; Smith, *Anti-Jacksonian Politics along the Chesapeake*, 118, 124–29, 132–33; on the bipartisan reaction, see Steiner, "Electoral College," 140–54, quotations, 140, 141–42, 143, 146. The Whigs also charged that the Democrats' real objective was less democratic reform and more gaining the state for Van Buren in the coming presidential election.

9 Smith, *Anti-Jacksonian Politics along the Chesapeake*, 134–38; Jean H. Baker, *The Politics of Continuity: Maryland Political Parties from 1858 to 1870* (Baltimore: Johns Hopkins University Press, 1973), 1–3.

10 Peter C. Magrath, "Optimistic Democrat: Thomas W. Dorr and the Case of *Luther vs. Borden*," *Rhode Island History* 29 (August/November 1970): 110–11.

11 Ibid., 111. Woodbury observed that large majorities usually attained their goals peacefully, but when resisted "by those in power . . . the popular movement will generally succeed, though it only be a use of physical and moral strength" (ibid.).

12 Conley, *Democracy in Decline*, 366, 374–76 (n. 115), 376–77.

13 William G. Shade, "Political Pluralism and Party Development: The Creation of a Modern Party System, 1815–1852," in Paul Kleppner et al., *The Evolution of American Electoral Systems* (New York: Greenwood Press, 1981), 78–79; Robin L. Einhorn, *Property Rules: Political Economy in Chicago, 1833–1872* (Chicago: University of Chicago Press, 1991); Michael H. Frisch, *Town into City: Springfield, Massachusetts, and the Meaning of Community, 1840–1860* (Cambridge, Mass.: Harvard University Press, 1972); Kenneth Winkle, *The Politics of Community: Migration and Politics in Antebellum Ohio* (New York: Cambridge University Press, 1988). Historians have for a long time recognized that the wealthy tended to withdraw from elective office after 1800, but for the argument that "upper-class political values" persisted, see R. A. Burchell, "The Role of the Upper Class in the Formation of American Culture," in *The End of Anglo-America: Historical Essays in the Study of Cultural Divergence*, ed. R. A. Burchell (Manchester, U.K.: Manchester University Press, 1991), 190–92. For a severe view of voting as compro-

mised by illegal voting, bribery, intimidation, and legal voters being turned away, see Richard Franklin Bensel, *The American Ballot Box in the Mid-Nineteenth Century* (New York: Cambridge University Press, 2004). Bensel's study focuses on contested elections between 1850 and 1868.

14 For skepticism regarding citizen engagement and counterarguments, see Glenn C. Altschuler and Stuart M. Blumin, "Limits of Political Engagement in Antebellum America: A New Look at the Golden Age of Participatory Democracy," *Journal of American History* 84 (December 1997): 855–85; Harry L. Watson, "Humbug? Bah! Altschuler and Blumin and the Riddle of the Antebellum Electorate," ibid., 886–93; Jean Harvey Baker, "Politics, Paradigms, and Public Culture," ibid., 894–99; Norma Basch, "A Challenge to the Story of Popular Politics," ibid., 900–909; and Altschuler and Blumin, *Rude Republic: Americans and Their Politics in the Nineteenth Century* (Princeton, N.J.: Princeton University Press, 2000). Alexander Keyssar has described the period from 1790 to 1850 first as one of liberalization, in which states removed property requirements while local practice undermined taxpaying qualification and municipalities broadened their franchises and loosened residency requirements. At the same time, states passed laws that also narrowed passage to the ballot box and excluded several specific kinds of persons who had earlier possessed the right to vote. Among conservatives and the upper classes, apprehensions regarding a mass democratic electorate remained widespread (Keyssar, *The Right to Vote: The Contested History of Democracy in America* [New York: Basic Books, 2000], 29–33, 53–67). Keyssar presents the Dorr "War" as exemplifying widespread reluctance to enfranchise "a large, urban proletariat" (Keyssar, *Right to Vote*, 69).

15 Ronald P. Formisano, "The 'Party Period' Revisited," *Journal of American History* 86 (June 1999): 93–120; Mark Voss-Hubbard, "The 'Third Party Tradition' Reconsidered: Third Parties and American Public Life, 1830–1900," ibid., 121–50.

16 Among other episodes, see Tracy Campbell, *The Politics of Despair: Power and Resistance in the Tobacco Wars* (Lexington: University Press of Kentucky, 1993). Catherine McNicol Stock, *Rural Radicals: Righteous Rage in the American Grain* (Ithaca, N.Y.: Cornell University Press, 1996), conflates Regulators and their descendants with later mob violence, vigilantism, lynching, and the like.

17 Kermit L. Hall, "The Judiciary on Trial: State Constitutional Reform and the Rise of an Elected Judiciary, 1846–1860," *Historian* 45 (May 1983): 347; Horowitz, *Transformation of American Law*, 259, 260–61. Horowitz does not connect these decisions to Anti-Rent, but see above, chapter 8.

18 By 1855 thirteen states from Maine to Delaware to Iowa had passed the equivalent of a "Maine Law." On prohibition in the 1853 elections, see Michael F. Holt, *The Rise and Fall of the American Whig Party: Jacksonian Politics and the Onset of the Civil War* (New York: Oxford University Press, 1999), 778–86, 788, 790–92, 799–800. On the "Maine Law" in that state's realignment, see Richard D. Wescott, *New Men, New Issues: The Formation of the Republican Party in Maine* (Portland: Maine Historical Society, 1986), 95–97, 107–9, 113, 115. In 1851 the activity of Michigan's temperance movement was at a "nadir," but after the passage of the Maine Law, popular enthusiasm for prohibitory legislation built up rapidly. See John W. Quist, *Restless Visionaries: The Social Roots*

*of Antebellum Reform in Alabama and Michigan* (Baton Rouge: Louisiana State University Press, 1998), 266–72, quotation, 266.

19  On the Catholic hierarchy's blunders and rising anti-Catholicism, see Ray Allen Billington, *The Protestant Crusade, 1800–1860: A Study in the Origins of American Nativism* (New York: Macmillan, 1938), 267–80, 289–314; regarding Catholic "attacks . . . on our free school system," see Thomas R. Whitney, *A Defence of the American Policy* (New York: De Witt and Davenport, 1856), quotation, 66, 277–78. Catholic-Protestant conflict over schools began in 1851 in Baltimore; see Frank Towers, *The Urban South and the Coming of the Civil War* (Charlottesville: University of Virginia Press, 2004), 86–87; also Erik B. Alexander, "'The Democracy Must Prepare for Battle': Know-Nothingism in Alabama and Southern Politics, 1851–1859," *Southern Historian* 27 (Spring 2006): 29.

20  Holt, *Rise and Fall of the American Whig Party*, 741–46, 774–75, 779–80, 845. Pierce was trying to placate Pennsylvania's Democratic Catholics who had been infuriated when Campbell had been the only Democrat on the party's statewide ticket to lose in 1852, blaming their own party's Protestant voters for "cutting" Campbell (Michael F. Holt, *The Political Crisis of the 1850s* [New York: John Wiley and Sons, 1978], 124, and generally 120–27). It is important to note that Protestant immigrants, especially British, tended to vote anti-Democratic and were attracted to the Know-Nothings. See William E. Gienapp, *The Origins of the Republican Party, 1852–1856* (New York: Oxford University Press, 1987), 145–46, 423–24. The role of Protestant Irish ("Orangemen") is a neglected dimension of Know-Nothingism. Though not numerous, the Protestant Irish had been involved in native American parties in the 1840s, as well as in street battles with the Catholic Irish. See Lee Benson, *The Concept of Jacksonian Democracy: New York as a Test Case* (Princeton, N.J.: Princeton University Press, 1961), 167–68; Billington, *Protestant Crusade*, 195–96; Paul Kleppner, *The Cross of Culture: A Social Analysis of Midwestern Politics, 1850–1900* (New York: Free Press, 1970), 77; and Michael A. Gordon, *The Orange Riots: Irish Political Violence in New York City, 1870 and 1871* (Ithaca, N.Y.: Cornell University Press, 1993), 12–13, 22.

21  Michael F. Holt, *The Fate of Their Country: Politicians, Slavery Extension, and the Coming of the Civil War* (New York: Hill and Wang, 2004), 114–15.

22  Ronald P. Formisano, *The Birth of Mass Political Parties: Michigan, 1827–1861* (Princeton, N.J.: Princeton University Press, 1971), 247–53; William E. Gienapp, "Nativism and the Creation of a Republican Majority in the North before the Civil War," *Journal of American History* 72 (December 1985): 530–31. For the role of Know-Nothings in the 1854 Ohio election, won by the "People's Party," which "rested on the twin pillars of anti-Nebraskaism and anti-Catholicism," see William E. Gienapp, *The Origins of the Republican Party, 1852–1856* (New York: Oxford University Press, 1987), 113–21, quotation, 121. In Maine, the Fusion or People's Party that preceded the Republican Party combined "antiliquor, antislavery extension, and antiforeign" elements in its platform; see Wescott, *New Men, New Issues*, 132. For New Hampshire, see Richard H. Sewell, *John P. Hale and the Politics of Abolition* (Cambridge, Mass.: Harvard University Press, 1965), 157–60.

23  Towers, *Urban South*, 73, 99, 117.

24  Tyler Anbinder, *Nativism and Slavery: The Northern Know Nothings and the Politics of the 1850s* (New York: Oxford University Press, 1992), 3–4.

25  Robert William Fogel, *Without Consent or Contract: The Rise and Fall of American Slavery* (New York: W. W. Norton, 1989), 354–75, quotations, 354, 356; Ronald P. Formisano, *The Transformation of Political Culture: Massachusetts Parties, 1780s–1840s* (New York: Oxford University Press, 1983), 331–40. Fogel has provided perhaps the most multicausal account of the populist insurgencies of the mid-1850s (Fogel, *Without Consent or Contract*, 320–80). He, too, emphasizes the local issues that emerged in cities, such as defense of public schools against Catholic encroachment, reform of local police to enforce laws against drunkenness and prostitution and to control elections, passage of mechanics' lien laws, abolition of imprisonment for debt, and halting corruption in the distribution of licenses for business and in city patronage (Fogel, *Without Consent or Contract*, 367). Regarding the schools, Catholics, and Know-Nothingism in Cincinnati, where German Protestants rallied to anti-Catholic candidates, see Gienapp, *Origins of the Republican Party*, 121.

26  Holt, *Political Crisis of the 1850s*. In this and earlier works Holt stresses also the shock of economic change and immigration; see, for example, Holt, "The Politics of Impatience: The Origins of Know Nothingism," *Journal of American History* 60 (1973): 309–31. Alexander Keyssar emphasizes that Know-Nothingism was at its core political (Keyssar, *Right to Vote*, 84). Even Fogel asserts that if any single idea united native workers, "it was that politicians of both major parties were corrupt, concerned primarily with lining their own pockets and in maintaining their grip on offices"; and the worst aspect of their corruption was toadying to immigrants and illegal voting (Fogel, *Without Consent or Contract*, 367).

27  Mark W. Summers, *The Plundering Generation: Corruption and the Crisis of the Union, 1849–1861* (New York: Oxford University Press, 1987), quotation, 66, also 35–36. Know-Nothings in Charleston, South Carolina, proclaimed themselves the "true opponents of bribery and corruption in elections" (James Marchio, "Nativism in the Old South: Know-Nothingism in Antebellum South Carolina," *Southern Historian* 8 [Spring 1987]: 49–50). A recent study of the movement in Massachusetts, Connecticut, and Pennsylvania concludes that in its initial phase "antiparty self-representation and commitment was the central organizing principle of northern Know Nothingism" (Mark Voss-Hubbard, *Beyond Party: Cultures of Antipartisanship in Northern Politics before the Civil War* [Baltimore: Johns Hopkins University Press, 2002], 11). See also Anthony Gene Carey, *Politics, Slavery and the Union in Antebellum Georgia* (Athens: University of Georgia Press, 1997), 188.

28  Formisano, *Transformation of Political Culture*, 136–48 (for the first decades of the nineteenth century), 337–38 (for the 1850s). For a recent discussion, see Bruce Laurie, *Beyond Garrison: Antislavery and Social Reform* (New York: Cambridge University Press, 2005), 201–2, 213–25.

29  Anbinder, *Nativism and Slavery*, 60; Fogel, *Without Consent or Contract*, 365; William J. Evitts, *A Matter of Allegiances: Maryland from 1850 to 1861* (Baltimore: Johns Hopkins University Press, 1974), 65–66, 70. For Know-Nothing antipartyism and secrecy in Mississippi, see Christopher J. Olsen, *Political Culture in Mississippi: Masculinity, Honor,*

and the Antiparty Tradition, 1830–1860 (New York: Oxford University Press, 2000), 64, 151–52, 157. A Know-Nothing lodge in Worcester, Massachusetts, practiced secrecy to guard against infiltration and tried to keep out lawyers, who, it was feared, would do all the talking and silence mechanics and artisans (Elizabeth Phelps Brengle, "Worcester's Know Nothings," seminar paper, Clark University, 1977, in my possession). On how seriously another Massachusetts lodge took violation of the secrecy oath, see Voss-Hubbard, Beyond Party, 121–22.

30 Formisano, Transformation of Political Culture, 336–40. See also Lawrence M. Lipin, Producers, Proletarians, and Politicians: Workers and Party Politics in Evansville and New Albany, Indiana, 1850–87 (Urbana: University of Illinois Press, 1994), 44–60.

31 The Coalition passed a general incorporation law, homestead exemption, mechanics' lien law, and regulations of railroads and financial institutions; increased funding for public schools and for asylums for the blind and "insane"; and shifted election of Harvard College overseers away from a self-elected board that had perpetuated Unitarian control and to the legislature. While the impetus for the "Maine Law" contained implicit antiforeign and anti-Catholic animus, the Free Soilers in the Coalition struck directly at the huge influx of needy immigrants coming after the Irish famine of the late 1840s by sponsoring a draconian set of "poor laws" and a Pauper Removal Act, resulting in the sending of hundreds of indigents to northern New England states, to workhouses in rural Massachusetts, or back to their country of origin. See Laurie, Beyond Garrison, 210–11, 273–75.

32 Hearkening back to the rural Regulators' resentment of eastern rule in the 1780s, the Coalition would have moved the state capital forty miles west from Boston to Worcester.

33 Formisano, Transformation of Political Culture, 333; John R. Mulkern, The Know-Nothing Party in Massachusetts: The Rise and Fall of a People's Movement (Boston: Northeastern University Press, 1990), 102–4. In 1857 the Republicans placated the Know-Nothings they had absorbed into their ranks by passing a constitutional amendment making the ability to read the state constitution in English and to write one's name necessary to vote. In 1859, similarly, the Republicans required naturalized citizens to wait two additional years to vote.

34 Laurie, Beyond Garrison, quotations, 279, 280–81; Mulkern, Know-Nothing Party, 104. Abolitionist Theodore Parker described the 1855 nativist legislature as "the strongest antislavery body that had ever assembled in the country" (Laurie, Beyond Garrison, 279). Mulkern has said it "outperformed all its predecessors combined in its response to territorial and slavery issues." The Know-Nothing governor vetoed the Personal Liberty Law, but the legislature overrode his veto a second time; the governor also prevented the legislature from removing the state probate judge who had returned Anthony Burns to South Carolina (Mulkern, Know-Nothing Party, 104–5). For an early study that described the reform dimensions of nativism, see Oscar Handlin, Boston's Immigrants, 1790–1880: A Study in Acculturation (Cambridge, Mass.: Harvard University Press, 1941).

35 Mulkern, Know-Nothing Party, 101.

36 Ibid., 111, quotation, 107. In contrast to Mulkern, Voss-Hubbard stresses the Know-

Nothings' resemblance to traditional parties in also legislating to promote economic development, though he credits them with achieving a balance between regulation and promotion of business interests (Voss-Hubbard, *Beyond Party*, 162).

37  Formisano, *Transformation of Political Culture*, 334, 479 (n. 37); Mulkern, *Know-Nothing Party*, 105–6. Historians have paid relatively little attention to Know-Nothing governance at the city and town level, but in Massachusetts the nativists expanded local infrastructures to provide public facilities, such as baths and concert venues, and authorized localities to lay gas and water mains and to construct highways, bridges, wharves, and other improvements. Municipalities with Know-Nothing leadership upgraded police and fire protection to new levels (after firing foreigners), and the legislature reached into public markets to answer ancient complaints about cheating to establish uniform weights and measures for necessities such as coal, milk, and grains. See Mulkern, *Know-Nothing Party*, 108–9. Frank Towers has argued that Baltimore Know-Nothings expanded city payrolls to strengthen their electoral machinery and dominate at the polls in "Violence as a Tool of Party Dominance: Election Riots and the Baltimore Know Nothings, 1854–1860," *Maryland Historical Magazine* 95 (Spring 1998): 9.

38  Regarding various nativist laws, see Anbinder, *Nativism and Slavery*, 136–42.

39  Billington, *Protestant Crusade*, 295–300; Formisano, *Birth of Mass Political Parties*, 218, 234, 256–57; Dale B. Light, *Rome and the New Republic: Conflict and Continuity in Philadelphia Catholicism between the Revolution and the Civil War* (Notre Dame, Ind.: University of Notre Dame Press, 1996), 316–25. The influence of Know-Nothings in the 1855 Michigan legislature registered in a 50 to 9 vote for the "Act Concerning Churches," while it voted for a Personal Liberty Law 40 to 28 (Formisano, *Birth of Mass Political Parties*, 257). Billington notes that the church "suffered less" from the church property laws "than from the controversies that inspired them" (Billington, *Protestant Crusade*, 300).

40  Quotation, Gienapp, *Origins of the Republican Party*, 196; Anbinder, *Nativism and Slavery*, 135–36. Because they did not want to alienate German Protestant voters, the Ohioans also supported equal rights for all foreign-born citizens who were Americanized and owed no allegiance to any authority higher than the Constitution. Nativists did indeed see themselves as defenders of religious freedom and toleration against the Roman priesthood (Whitney, *Defense of the American Policy*, 52–103).

41  Anbinder, *Nativism and Slavery*, 142–45, quotation, 142. In Chicago "police and fire department reform were closely linked with . . . the prohibition of liquor" (Einhorn, *Property Rules*, 151).

42  Anbinder, *Nativism and Slavery*, 142–45.

43  Bensel, *American Ballot Box*, 11 (for the "voting window"), 13–14, 20–22 (for control of polling places). Regarding nativist incivility and violence in Cincinnati against German voters, see Gienapp, *Origins of the Republican Party*, 196–97. As noted earlier, Bensel's view of nineteenth-century voting stresses large imperfections in the conduct of elections, as well as low voter issue information. Even Michael Schudson's upbeat account of U.S. political development, however, echoes Bensel in his description of Gilded Age voting and elections (Schudson, *The Good Citizen: A History of American Civic Life* [Cambridge, Mass.: Harvard University Press, 1998], 162–65).

44 Bensel, *American Ballot Box*, 168–85, quotation, 183; Evitts, *Matter of Allegiances*, 98, 105–17. Towers describes the Know-Nothings' self-justifying rationale for violence as "enlightened partisanship," one they used in Baltimore and elsewhere in the urban South. Purifying politics of what they regarded as its general corruption "did not entail an end to traditional practices so much as it required an extra effort by Know-Nothing leaders to use the potentially corrupt means of party politics for virtuous republican ends" (Towers, *Urban South*, 99, 107). Towers also holds that Know-Nothings "intensified" the violence and succeeded in enlarging their probable majorities by reducing the opposition vote through intimidation (Towers, "Violence as a Tool of Party Dominance," 9, 18–25).

45 Leon Cyprian Soulé, *The Know Nothing Party in New Orleans: A Reappraisal* (Baton Rouge: Louisiana Historical Association, 1961), 39–113, especially 53–60, 62–75. Regarding control of the police, see Towers, *Urban South*, 122. Soulé's excellent and neglected study revises the notion that the Know-Nothings of New Orleans were not anti-Catholic (they were from their inception), and it is invaluable for its focus on the struggle for control of polling places. The Know-Nothings maintained control of the city through 1860 despite the state Democrats' efforts to remove control of the city election machinery to a state board and the rise of an Independent movement disgusted with what American control had become. By 1858 the wealthy citizens who had been part of the nativist coalition had dropped out and control had shifted to labor organizers, and by 1861 the party had substantially changed its character.

46 Peyton Hurt, *The Rise and Fall of the "Know Nothings" in California* (n.p., 1946?), reprinted from the *Quarterly Journal of the California Historical Society* 9 (March and June 1930): 24–26, quotation, 26; Philip J. Ethington, *The Public City: The Political Construction of Urban Life in San Francisco, 1850–1900* (New York: Cambridge University Press, 1994), quotation, 115–16. According to Ethington, San Francisco's Know-Nothings held less interest in nativism and temperance than their counterparts elsewhere and arose from "a political crisis with political causes," namely, reaction to "caucus corruption" and election frauds. The Vigilante-People's Party that succeeded them took up the cause of electoral purity even more strenuously—"The ballot box was the supreme icon of the Vigilante movement" (Ethington, *Public City*, 112–24, 133–34, quotations, 113, 122).

47 Towers, *Urban South*, 87–89, 93–94, 96–97, 100, 110–12. The American Party benefited also from "Protestant radicals'" tirades against Catholics, though the relationship between evangelicals and Know-Nothings was mixed (ibid., 105–6, 108).

48 Laurie, *Beyond Garrison*, 219; see also the testimony involving appeals to would-be voters' "manhood and strength" in Baltimore's tumultuous 1859 election, in Bensel, *American Ballot Box*, 21 (n. 36). When southern nationalists (Democrats) attacked Know-Nothing manhood by charging that the nativists were really antislavery, the Know-Nothings returned the accusations in kind. See Towers, *Urban South*, 96–98. On the centrality of masculine assertiveness to Know-Nothing and rival gangs, see Elliott J. Gorn, "'Good-Bye Boys, I Die a True American': Homicide, Nativism, and Working-Class Culture in Antebellum New York City," *Journal of American History* 74 (September 1987): 397, 403–7. Gorn's suggestion that nativism encompassed the

street-brawling masculine ideal, as well as that of the evangelical, bourgeois ideal (seen here earlier in Anti-Masonry), has not been explored.

49  These insights are from Voss-Hubbard, *Beyond Party*, 117–20, quotations, 118, 120. Voting itself, as Bensel has pointed out, took place in many places such as saloons and livery stables where respectable women would not be found. But even at other polling places, such as grist mills, private homes, or even schoolhouses, voting was an all-male enterprise, where liquor flowed freely and drunken men were common (Bensel, *American Ballot Box*, 20). For an extensive discussion of the connections between gangs, clubs, and violent elections in Baltimore, see Towers, *Urban South*, 127–43.

50  Quotation, Jean Gould Hale, "'Co-Laborers in the Cause': Women in the Antebellum Nativist Movement," *Civil War History* 25 (June 1979): 119; Janet L. Coryell, "Superseding Gender: The Role of the Woman Politico in Antebellum Partisan Politics," in *Women and the Unstable State in Nineteenth-Century America*, ed. Alison M. Parker and Stephanie Cole (College Station: Texas A&M University Press, 2000), 84–112; Christopher J. Olsen, "'Molly Pitcher' of the Mississippi Whigs: The Editorial Career of Mrs. Harriet N. Prewett," *Journal of Mississippi History* 58 (Fall 1996): 237–54, and "Respecting 'the Wise Allotment of Our Sphere': White Women and Politics in Mississippi," *Journal of Women's History* 11 (Autumn 1999): 104–25; Alice Taylor, "From Petitions to Partyism: Antislavery and the Domestication of Maine Politics in the 1840s and 1850s," *New England Quarterly* 77 (March 2004): 71–72, 85 (n. 32). See also Lori Ginzberg, "'Moral Suasion Is Moral Balderdash': Women, Politics, and Social Activism in the 1850s," *Journal of American History* 73 (December 1986): 601–22; and Voss-Hubbard, *Beyond Party*, 79, 92. In the 1880s one of the most enlightened human beings of the nineteenth century, Elizabeth Cady Stanton, regarded "'ignorant' black and naturalized voters who opposed [woman] suffrage" as unworthy of the vote, and would erect literacy as a standard for men and women, for all races, and for native-born and naturalized voters (Jean H. Baker, *Sisters: The Lives of America's Suffragists* [New York: Hill and Wang, 2005], 122).

51  Regarding labor legislation and women, see Voss-Hubbard, *Beyond Party*, 155–61; and Paula Baker, "The Domestication of Politics: Women and American Political Society, 1780–1920," *American Historical Review* 89 (June 1984): 620–47. In the three states he studied Voss-Hubbard found just one public display mounted by nativist women and regarded them as more often serving as accessories (Voss-Hubbard, *Beyond Party*, 115). See also C. Kay Larson, *Great Necessities: The Life, Times, and Writing of Anna Ella Carroll, 1815–1894* (New York: Xlibris Corporation, 2004), 109–10. Unfortunately, Larson's account contains no information on nativist women other than Carroll, but it does corroborate themes developed here and in Towers's description of Know-Nothingism in Maryland (Larson, *Great Necessities*, 120–26). As elsewhere, "the Republicans were able to take up the corruption issue, capitalize on it, and as a result draw off Know Nothing support" (Larson, *Great Necessities*, 140).

52  Formisano, *Transformation of Political Culture*, 332–33; Mulkern, *Know-Nothing Party*, 111; Voss-Hubbard, *Beyond Party*, 153; Norma Basch, *In the Eyes of the Law: Women, Marriage, and Property in Nineteenth-Century New York* (Ithaca, N.Y.: Cornell University Press, 1982); Paul Bourke and Donald DeBats, *Washington County: Politics and Com-*

munity in Antebellum America (Baltimore: Johns Hopkins University Press, 1995), 117–20, 124, 138, 140–45. Regarding lip service to separate spheres, see Olsen, "Mrs. Harriet N. Prewett."

53 According to Michael D. Pierson, the 1856 election marked the "high point of antebellum women's political activism" (Pierson, *Free Hearts and Free Homes: Gender and American Antislavery Politics* [Chapel Hill: University of North Carolina Press, 2003], 22). On Republican antipartyism in Massachusetts, Connecticut, and Pennsylvania, see Voss-Hubbard, *Beyond Party*, 179, 214–16; and in Michigan, see Formisano, *Birth of Mass Political Parties*, 264, 327–28.

54 For example, see Eric Foner, *Free Soil, Free Labor, Free Men: The Ideology of the Republican Party before the Civil War* (New York: Oxford University Press, 1970); Richard H. Sewell, *Ballots for Freedom: Antislavery Politics in the United States, 1837–1860* (New York: Oxford University Press, 1976); Dale Baum, *The Civil War Party System: The Case of Massachusetts, 1848–1876* (Chapel Hill: University of North Carolina Press, 1984); and Anbinder, *Nativism and Slavery*. For a different version of this approach, emphasizing New York City Know-Nothingism as deriving from conservative Whiggery and class concerns, see Bruce Levine, "Conservatism, Nativism, and Slavery: Thomas R. Whitney and the Origins of the Know-Nothing Party," *Journal of American History* 88 (September 2001): 455–88.

55 For example, see Gienapp, "Nativism and the Creation of the Republican Majority" and *Origins of the Republican Party*; Fogel, *Without Consent or Contract*; Mulkern, *Know-Nothing Party*; Holt, *Rise and Fall of the American Whig Party*; Voss-Hubbard, *Beyond Party*; and Laurie, *Beyond Garrison*. For an excellent discussion of divergent interpretations, see Laurie, *Beyond Garrison*, 272–87. Older studies with similar interpretations include Michael F. Holt, *Forging a Majority: The Formation of the Republican Party in Pittsburgh* (New Haven, Conn.: Yale University Press, 1969); Formisano, *Birth of Mass Political Parties*; and Joel H. Silbey, " 'The Undisguised Connection': Know Nothings into Republicans: New York as a Test Case," in Silbey, *The Partisan Imperative: The Dynamics of American Politics before the Civil War* (New York: Oxford University Press, 1985), 127–65. Although the shape of Know-Nothing "reform" in rural Washington County, Oregon, differed from that, say, in eastern or midwestern cities, its ideology and "sentiments . . . continued and were wholly absorbed after 1858 into . . . the Republican Party" (Bourke and DeBats, *Washington County*, 165, and 159–64).

56 This issue lies at the heart of the debate regarding the degree to which Know-Nothingism, nativism, and anti-Catholicism shaped the Republican Party.

57 A similar process of "ideological representation" was imposed on the Molly Maguires, Irish labor unionists who engaged in collective violence and assassination in the anthracite coal fields of Pennsylvania in the 1860s and 1870s, wherein "the violence in which the Molly Maguires undoubtedly engaged was put to all sorts of uses by contemporaries, most effectively by those who were opposed to Irish immigrants and organized labor." See Kevin Kenny, *Making Sense of the Molly Maguires* (New York: Oxford University Press, 1998), 6, 3–12 (this is not to suggest that the Molly Maguires were a populist movement). For a brief, penetrating comment regarding the reproduction of "elite bias that underestimates the insurgents' grievances and popular support," as well as exaggerates the "radical" aspirations of insurgents, see Alan

Taylor, "'Stopping the Progress of Rogues and Deceivers': A White Indian Recruiting Notice of 1808," *William and Mary Quarterly*, 3d ser., 42 (January 1985): 95–96. In a related vein, R. Laurence Moore has criticized the "typecasting" of outsiders in American history "as heroes, villains, or victims" to serve ideological or political purposes; see Moore, "Insiders and Outsiders in American Historical Narrative and American History," *American Historical Review* 87 (April 1982): 396. Moore raises questions regarding the difficulty for historians of defining which groups or individuals stood inside or outside the mainstream of American experience.

# Index

Blumin, Stuart M., 271 (n. 34)

Boston: antiabolitionists in, 156; Anti-Masonry in, 109, 128; legacy of Revolution in, 44; Middling Interest in, 77–82; Tea Party in, 186; Working Men's party in, 84–85

*Boston Artisan*, 88

*Boston Debtor's Journal*, 78

*Bostonian and Mechanics' Journal*, 77, 82

*Boston Independent Chronicle*, 51

*Boston Masonic Mirror*, 155

Boston Tea Party, 44, 181, 186

Bottom-up movements, 15

Boughton, Smith, 181, 186, 188

Bowdoin, James, 28, 31, 40–41

Bressler, Lee, 267–68 (n. 75)

Bribery: in voting, 172–73

Brinkley, Alan, 6–7, 8

Britain. *See* England

Brodie, Fawn M., 265 (n. 55)

*Bronson v. Kinzie*, 285 (n. 76)

Brooke, John L., 228 (n. 29), 229–30 (n. 39), 238 (n. 33)

*Brooklyn Eagle*, 188

Brooks, Charles E., 254 (n. 41)

Brooks, James, 78

Brown, George H., 278 (n. 35)

Brown, Richard D., 111

Brown, Richard Maxwell, 226 (n. 19)

Bruce, Eli, 136

Bryan, William Jennings, 8, 10

Bucktail Republicans, 101–2, 106

Bullock, Steven C., 114, 250 (nn. 16–18), 256 (n. 58), 268 (n. 6)

Burgess, W. S., 279 (n. 40)

*Burke's Report*, 275 (n. 8), 280 (n. 43)

Burns, Anthony, 205

Burr, Aaron, 53

BUS. *See* Bank of the United States, Second

Bushman, Richard L., 232 (n. 62)

Calhoun, Craig, 83

California, 209–10

Calvinism, 126

Campbell, James, 201

Canals, 69, 102, 122

Canovan, Margaret, 10

Carnes, Mark C., 248 (n. 6)

Carpenter, Thomas F., 168, 170, 171

Carroll, William, 74

Carwardine, Richard J., 153, 154, 249 (n. 8), 266 (n. 63), 271 (n. 35), 272 (n. 38)

Catholicism: and Anti-Masonry, 135; church property in, 200–201, 207; in "Dorr War," 166, 167, 195; Know-Nothings' opposition to, 198, 199–201, 204, 205, 207; in political culture, 212–13

Cato (pseudonym), 40

Cayton, Andrew R. L., 245 (n. 45)

Centinel (pseudonym), 39–40, 233 (n. 68)

Centralized power: American Revolution's opposition to, 7, 21; in Constitution, 36, 38; populist fear of, 7, 10

Charterites, 166–76

Chepachet, R.I., 169, 170

Child labor, 245 (n. 50)

Christian communalism, 8

Christian manhood: in abolitionism, 158; in Anti-Masonry, 118–19, 126; in Know-Nothingism, 211; in temperance movement, 199

Christian republicanism, 92–95, 118–19, 126, 127, 158

Churches: disestablishment of, 45–46, 234–35 (n. 6); property of, 200–201, 207. *See also* Religion

Cincinnati, 87

Citizenship: limitations of, 21–22, 37; Working Men's parties on, 86

Civic nationalism, 13

Civility, norms of, 13

Civil rights movement, 2, 7

Civil War, 213

Clanton, Gene, 5

Class, social: in antibank movement, 72; in Anti-Masonry, 113–14; in "Dorr War,"

172; in Middling Interest, 77–82; and popular sovereignty, 160. *See also* Elites

Clawson, Mary Ann, 259 (n. 5)

Clay, Henry: on Anti-Masonry, 254 (n. 45); in Bank War, 143, 145, 146; labor movement on, 88; in presidential elections, 145, 150, 151, 152; on relief laws, 75, 77, 243 (n. 28)

Clinton, DeWitt, 69, 100, 101, 102, 122

Clintonians, 101–2, 105

Coalitions, political, 104–5, 204

Cobbett, William, 83

Cold War, 1

*Columbian Centinel*, 80

Commercialization, 68–69

Communalism, 8

Communications revolution, 68–69, 111, 219 (n. 16)

Congregational churches, 46

Congress, U.S.: on alcohol taxes, 47, 48; in Bank War, 143–44; on Democratic-Republican societies, 56, 57; in "Dorr War," 194; and economic depression, 72; elite versus the people in, 38; Hamilton's policies opposed in, 51; on Missouri Compromise, 198; rise of partisanship in, 51, 52

Conley, Patrick, 166, 169, 279 (n. 36)

Connecticut, 45, 129, 138–39

Conservatives: in American Revolution, 19; under Articles of Confederation, 24; on popular sovereignty, 161; populist rhetoric used by, 2

Conspiracies, 12, 13–14

Constitution, U.S.: Anti-Federalist influence on, 37, 41; centralized power in, 36, 38; contracts clause of, 181; masculinity and, 39–40; ratification of, 37, 39, 41; in relief wars, 75–76; strict-constructionist view of, 60. *See also* Anti-Federalists; Federalists

Constitutions, state. *See* State constitutions

Continental Congress, 23

Contract law: in Anti-Rent Wars, 181, 182

*Contrast, The* (Tyler), 33–34, 39, 230 (n. 48)

Cooke, Jacob E., 236 (n. 18)

Cornell, Saul, 37–38, 57, 232 (n. 60), 233 (n. 68)

Corruption: Know-Nothings on, 200, 203, 214

Cotlar, Seth, 239–40 (n. 48)

Coughlin, Charles, 6–7

Council of Censors, 192

Countryman, Edward, 230 (n. 39)

Country thought, 21, 72

Court party, 13, 53, 54, 76–77

Courts: Anti-Masonry and, 136–39; in Anti-Rent Wars, 181, 182, 185, 197–98; in Middling Interest, 78–79; popular election of judges and, 197; on relief laws, 74–77; religious tests for witnesses in, 136–39. *See also* Supreme Court, U.S.

Credit: in economic depression, 71–77; in Middling Interest, 78; in relief wars, 72–77; in Whiskey Rebellion, 47–48

Crow, Jeffrey J., 236 (n. 17)

Cultural populism, 8, 10, 220 (n. 24)

Culture, political: American Revolution's shaping of, 21; Anti-Masonry's influence on, 141–42; centrality of populism in, 3; of early republic, 46–47; movement from center to right in, 61; nativism and anti-Catholicism in, 212–13; popular sovereignty in, 21, 159–60; role of opposition in, 55, 57; status of democratic culture in 1820s, 195–96

Daggett, David, 139

Dangerfield, George, 240 (n. 5)

Davis, John, 127–28, 148

Day, Luke, 29

Dean, Paul, 128

Debt. *See* Credit

Decisionmaking: and popular sovereignty, 222 (n. 45)

Declaration of Independence, 20

Deferential-participant political culture, 46

De La Torre, Carlos, 220 (n. 26)

Democracy: advance of in 1820s and 1830s, 195–96; and Anti-Federalists and Federalists, 38; as concept, 3

Democrat: evolution of meaning of term, 46

Democratic Party: on abolitionism, 155, 201; in Anti-Rent Wars, 182, 183–84, 186, 198; in "Dorr War," 162, 164, 169, 171, 172, 173, 191; Know-Nothings' opposition to, 201–2, 209; in Maryland's electoral system, 193–94; on popular sovereignty, 159; and Working Men's parties, 88–89

Democratic Republicans (Democrats): Anti-Masons as, 147, 150; Bank War and, 147; emergence of, 143, 148–49; platform of, 149; in presidential elections, 152; Whig Party's opposition to, 149–53

Democratic-Republican societies, 53–57

Democratic Society of Norfolk, 54

Democratic Society of Pennsylvania, 53

Democratic Society of Philadelphia, 56

Democratic Society of the City of New York, 54

Dependence: versus masculinity, 69–70

Depression of 1819, 70–72, 78

Devyr, Thomas A., 286 (n. 80)

Direct democracy, 2

Direct Tax of 1798, 58

Disestablishment, 45–46, 234–35 (n. 6)

Distress bills, 183–84

Domesticity, 119, 120, 124

Domestic policy, 44, 46

Dorr, Thomas Wilson, 163, 165, 167–76, 191–92

"Dorr War," 160–76; Charterites' opposition to, 166–76; in 1844 presidential election, 191; legacy of, 173–76, 191–92, 195; origins of, 160–64; People's Constitution in, 159, 165–67, 171; People's government in, 168–70; Supreme Court on, 194–95; views of popular sovereignty in, 161, 165, 166, 191; women in, 174–76

Douglass, Elisha P., 225 (n. 13)

Douglass, Frederick, 165

Dual sovereignty, 36

Durfee, Job, 167, 174

Economic populism, 8, 10, 11

Economy: and Anti-Masonry, 112; under Articles of Confederation, 23–24; depression of 1819–22 in, 70–77; downturn of 1783–85 in, 23–24; early nineteenth-century changes in, 68–70; government power in, 177; Hamilton's policies on, 41, 51; and Know-Nothingism, 202, 206; and Middling Interest, 78; and Panic of 1819, 63, 78

Education: Anti-Masons on, 121–22, 134; Know-Nothingism on public education, 200, 205, 206, 207; women's, 121–22

Egalitarianism: in political culture, 46

Ekirch, A. Roger, 227 (nn. 23–24)

Elections: Anti-Masonry in, 100–101, 103–7; Working Men's party in, 84–89. *See also* Gubernatorial elections; Judicial elections; Local elections; Presidential elections; State elections

Electoral college, 192–94

Elite Anti-Federalists, 38–39, 57

Elites: in American Revolution, 20, 22; in antibank sentiment, 72; Anti-Masonry on, 93, 113–14; in Bank War, 143–44; concept of popular sovereignty created by, 17, 222 (n. 42); concept of the people among, 20–21; divisions among, 44–45; Federalists on rule by, 35; knowledge versus business, 220 (n. 23); Middling Interest on, 77–82; popular protest repressed by, 27, 44; rhetoric against, 22; role of, in democracy, 4; views of, on popular sovereignty, 20–21; in Whiskey Rebellion, 49

Elkins, Stanley, 235 (n. 15), 237 (nn. 23–25), 239 (n. 41)

Ellmaker, Amos, 264 (n. 50)

Ely, Ezra Stiles, 132, 153

Eminent domain, 180, 185, 197

Empire: ideas of, in American Revolution, 22

Energy, political, 4

England: concept of the people in, 20; labor radicalism in, 82–84; Levellers in, 17–18; popular sovereignty in, 17–18, 21; rhetoric in, 2; trade barriers established by, 23–24; U.S. relations with, 52

Erie Canal, 69, 102, 122

Ethington, Philip J., 295 (n. 46)

Ethnic nationalism, 12–13

Europe: recent populist movements in, 1, 9, 12

Evangelical wing of Whig Party, 149–53

Evans, George Henry, 183

Everett, Edward, 148

Executive tyranny, 146–47

Exemption Act of 1842 (New York), 182

Extremism: populism associated with, 1

Factory Act of 1802 (Britain), 245 (n. 50)

Faler, Paul, 247 (n. 63)

Faneuil Hall (Boston), 79, 128

Federalist Central Committee, 78, 79, 80

Federalists: versus Anti-Federalists, 35; decline of, 60–61; on Democratic-Republican societies, 54, 56; and economic development, 24; on elite rule, 35; establishment as party, 44; on "Fries's Rebellion," 58; masculinity of, 39–40; Middling Interest and, 77–81; in movement of center to right, 61; origin of name, 37; paranoia among, 13–14; popular protest repressed by, 43–44; in ratification process, 37; Shaysism used by, 30, 36; use of term, 235 (n. 11); on Whiskey Rebellion, 49–51, 56

Federal power: and Anti-Rent Wars, 177

Feminism: Anti-Masonry and, 124–25; Know-Nothingism and, 211; in progressive populist movements, 11

Fenner, James, 130, 171

Feudal revival, 177

Fifteen Gallon Law (Massachusetts), 151

Fillmore, Millard, 103, 137–38

Findley, William, 238–39 (n. 34)

Fischer, David Hackett, 236 (n. 18)

Fogel, Robert William, 292 (nn. 25–26)

Foner, Philip S., 237 (n. 26)

Foreign policy, 44, 46

Foster, William, 148

France: Democratic-Republican societies on, 53; concept of the people in, 20; U.S. relations with, 52

Francis, John Brown, 130, 172–73

*Frankfort Argus of Western America*, 75

Freeholders Committee of Safety, 182

Freeholders' Constitution (Rhode Island), 166–67

Freemasonry. *See* Masonry

Free Soil Party: abolitionism in, 157–58; Anti-Masons in, 123; Anti-Rent Wars and, 183, 185; and Know-Nothings, 204–5

French Revolution (1789), 13, 52, 53

Freneau, Philip, 51

Friends of Free Suffrage, 175

Fries, Jacob, 58, 59, 239 (n. 37)

"Fries's Rebellion" (1799–1800), 57–59

Frieze, Jacob, 277 (n. 32), 280 (n. 43)

Fritz, Christian G., 161, 191, 192

Fugitive Slave Law of 1850, 205

Fuller, Margaret, 121–22

Fuller, Philo, 105

Fuller, Timothy, 117, 120, 121–22

Fusion candidates, 201

Gamble, Elizabeth, 121

Garrison, William Lloyd, 87, 154–55, 156, 165

*Gazette of the United States*, 51

Gellner, Ernest, 1

Gender: and Constitution, 36–37; in populist movements, 11, 12, 32–34, 39–40. *See also* Masculinity; Women

*General Advertiser*, 51

Genesee County (New York): Anti-Masonry in, 93, 102, 106, 118, 142; Masonry in, 96–99

Genet, Edmond, 52

Gentlemen: in antiabolitionism, 87; Jeffersonian Republican, 52–53; masculinity of, 32–34; Regulators fight, 26; versus yeomen, 32–33

Georgia, 49, 93

German Americans, 58, 59, 132, 134

German Republican Society of Philadelphia, 53, 54

Giddings, Edward, 136–37

Ginzberg, Lori D., 283 (n. 60)

Goodell, William, 172, 278 (n. 35)

Goodman, Paul, 92–94, 118, 119, 139, 248 (nn. 3–4), 258 (n. 68), 270 (n. 23), 274 (n. 52), 275 (n. 14)

Gould, Roger V., 236 (n. 16)

Government: power of, and Anti-Rent Wars, 177; separation of church and, 45–46

Governors. See Gubernatorial elections

Granger, Francis, 104–5, 107, 144, 272 (n. 37)

Granger, Gideon, 253 (n. 37)

Great Awakening, Second, 92, 123

Great Proprietors, 61

Greece, ancient, 4

Greeley, Horace, 186, 187

Green Mountain Boys, 25

Gubernatorial elections: antibanking sentiment in, 74, 75; Anti-Masonry in, 104–5, 107, 125–28, 130, 132; in Anti-Rent Wars, 184; in "Dorr War," 168; modern, 2; Regulators and, 41; Whig Party in, 148; Working Men's parties in, 88

Hamilton, Alexander: economic policies of, 41, 51; on English relations, 52; opposition to policies of, 13, 51; in Whiskey Rebellion, 47–50, 56

Hampshire, Mass., 28

Hancock, John, 41

Handicrafts, 69

Hard cider campaign, 152–53, 164

Harlequins, 122

Harrison, William Henry, 150, 151, 152–53, 272 (n. 37)

Hart, Vivien, 218 (n. 8)

Hatch, Nathan O., 45, 112, 234 (n. 5)

Hayne, Robert Y., 67–68

Heale, M. J., 268 (n. 2), 269 (n. 9)

Henry, Patrick, 121

Hertzke, Allen D., 8, 10, 217–18 (n. 8), 220 (nn. 23–24)

Hewitt, Nancy, 261 (n. 22)

Hill, Hiram, 173

Hofstadter, Richard, 13, 218 (n. 12)

Holland Land Company, 105, 106

Holley, Myron, 113, 122–23, 125, 129, 154

Holt, Michael F., 143, 146, 147, 201, 202, 271 (n. 34), 273 (n. 50)

Holton, Woody, 230 (n. 40)

Homestead Act, National, 183

Hudson River valley, 24–25

Hunkers, 184

Huston, Reeve, 187, 287 (n. 89)

Hutson, James H., 221–22 (n. 39)

Ideology: as concept, 3

Immigration, 202; in contemporary Europe, 9

Inaugural addresses, 65–67, 91

Independence: in masculinity, 69–70

Indians: Anti-Renters pose as, 180–83, 186–89; Whiskey Rebels pose as, 48; Working Men's parties on, 246 (n. 61)

Industrial revolution, 68, 82–84, 161–62

Inequality: and popular sovereignty, 159–60

Information: elite monopoly on, 44–45

Innovation, 12

Institutions: progressive views of, 11

Insurgencies, popular: before American Revolution, 6, 24–27; in early republic, 47; goals of, 6; Jefferson on, 41–42; legitimacy of, 19; after War of 1812, 6. See also specific events and groups

Intolerance, 7–8, 12–13

Inventing the People (Morgan), 17

Rent Wars, 177–85; in "Dorr War," 160–76; in "Fries's Rebellion," 58; Jeffersonian Republicans on, 62–63; in Maine insurgency, 61–62; pre-Revolutionary riots over, 24–26, 226 (n. 17); in relief wars, 74–75; speculation on, 25–26, 63, 71. *See also* Property qualifications

Lansing, Richard Ray, 255 (n. 51)

Larkin, Jack, 257 (n. 63)

Larson, C. Kay, 296 (n. 51)

Lasch, Christopher, 7–8, 15

Lathrop, Samuel, 127

Latin America, 8–10

Laurie, Bruce, 69

Law and Order constitution (Rhode Island), 169–71

Law and Order party, 169–73

Leasehold system, 177–85

Lee, Henry, 50

Left-wing populist movements. *See* Progressive populist movements

Legislatures. *See* Congress, U.S.; State legislatures

Lenin, Vladimir, 7, 219 (n. 21)

Levellers, 17–18

*Lexington Public Advertiser*, 76

Liberalism, classical, 7–8

*Liberator, The*, 87, 154, 155

Liberty: in American Revolution, 19, 21; Constitution on, 36

Liberty Men, 61–62

Liberty Party, 123, 154, 157

Lincoln, Abraham, 1

Lincoln, Benjamin, 29, 33

Lincoln, Levi, 127

Lincoln, William, 229 (n. 37)

Link, Eugene Perry, 237 (nn. 24, 26)

Lipson, Dorothy Ann, 118

Livingston family, 24

Local elections: Anti-Masonry in, 100–101, 104, 106; Know-Nothingism in, 200, 208–10; Middling Interest movement in, 77–82; Working Men's parties in, 85

Localism, 10, 38–39

Long, Huey, 6–7

Louisiana, 242 (n. 20)

Lower middle class, 7–8

Luther, Martin, 279 (n. 38), 280 (n. 43)

Luther, Seth, 163

*Luther v. Borden*, 194–95, 280 (n. 43)

Lynd, Staughton, 226 (n. 17)

Lyons, Matthew N., 218 (n. 13)

Madison, James: on Alien and Sedition Acts, 60; on congressional districts, 38; and Democratic-Republican societies, 53, 56–57; on French relations, 52; Hamilton's policies opposed by, 51; on the people, 65; on ratification, 37; Virginia Resolution by, 60; Washington administration on, 13

Main, Jackson Turner, 35

Maine: Anti-Masonry in, 109–10, 134; disestablishment in, 45; popular insurgency in, 61–62; prohibition in, 199, 208, 211

Maine Law, 199, 204, 208

Majority, tyranny of, 114

*Man, The* (newspaper), 86

Manning, William, 43

Manufacturing growth, 69

Marcy, William M., 107

Market revolution, 68, 92, 93, 111, 219 (n. 16)

Marriage, companionate, 121

Marshall, Lynn, 244 (n. 32)

Martineau, Harriet, 156

Maryland: electoral system in, 192–94; Know-Nothings in, 208–9, 210; whiskey tax in, 49

Masculinity: in abolitionism, 158; in Anti-Federalist rhetoric, 39–40; Anti-Masonic ideal of, 118–20, 126; in Anti-Rent Wars, 187; apprenticeship and, 69–70; community and, 32; in Know-Nothingism, 210; in reactionary movements, 12; of Regulators versus gentlemen, 32–34; in republicanism, 21–22; in Working Men's rhetoric, 86,

War," 166, 167, 172, 195; of Know-Nothings, 198, 199–200, 202, 204, 205, 208; in political culture, 212–13; in Republican Party, 212

Negative advertising, 15

Nelson, Dana, 40

Neopopulist parties, 9, 12

Neville, John, 49, 50, 56, 236 (n. 18)

*New Age and Constitutional Advocate*, 164

New England Association of Farmers, Mechanics, and Other Workingmen, 87, 88

*New England Galaxy*, 79, 80

New Hampshire: Anti-Masonry in, 134; disestablishment in, 45; popular insurgencies in, 25, 227 (n. 25)

New Jersey: Anti-Masonry in, 134; constitution of, 23; suffrage in, 23

New Orleans, 209

Newspapers: Anti-Masonic, 110–11; Anti-Rent, 183; on Democratic-Republican societies, 54–55, 56; Federalist, 37, 39, 55; on Hamilton's policies, 51; Masonic, 110–11; opposition, 51, 55; in postal system, 111; Working Men's, 86, 87. *See also specific papers*

New York: abolitionism in, 154; Anti-Masonry in, 93–95, 98–115, 136–38; Anti-Rent Wars in, 176–89; Bank War in, 144–45; constitution of, 184; Democratic Party in, 182, 183–84, 186; judicial review in, 197; Masonry in, 96–101, 107; party divisions in, 184; party emergence in, 101–2; pre-Revolutionary insurgencies in, 24–25; ratification by, 39; religious tests for witnesses in, 136–38; suffrage in, 142, 225 (n. 12); Whig Party in, 151, 180–85, 186; Working Men's party in, 85, 87, 246 (n. 59)

New York City, 85, 87, 246 (n. 59)

*New York Daily Gazette*, 54–55

*New York Evening Post*, 101

*New York Herald*, 188

*New York Journal*, 39, 51

*New York Tribune*, 186

*New York Working Man's Advocate*, 145, 183

*Niles' Register*, 70–71

"No rent" movement, 25

North: Know-Nothingism in, 201

Northampton, Mass., 28

Northampton County, Pa., 58–59

North Carolina: under Articles of Confederation, 24; property requirements in, 225 (n. 12); Regulators in, 25–27; whiskey tax in, 49

Ohio, 87, 135, 207

Onuf, Peter S., 231 (n. 52)

Open voting, 162–63, 203–4

Opposition, political: by Democratic-Republican societies, 53–57; legitimacy of, 53–55; rise of, 51–53

Order of the Star Spangled Banner, 199–200

Oregon, 211

Orthodox Trinitarian Congregationalists, 128

Otis, Harrison Gray, 78, 79, 80, 244 (n. 40)

Outwork system, 69, 241 (n. 12)

Palmer, R. R., 222 (n. 41)

Pamphlets, 81, 138, 167

Panic of 1819, 63, 78

Paranoia, 13–15; in American Revolution, 13–14, 221–22 (n. 39); in Anti-Masonry, 14–15, 92; connotations of term, 222 (n. 39); in progressive versus reactionary movements, 12, 13

Parker, Joel, 255 (n. 51)

Parker, Richard D., 4, 5, 218 (n. 12)

Parliament, 17–18, 84, 245 (n. 50)

Parlin, Ann, 175–76

Partisanship: in Anti-Rent Wars, 214; Know-Nothings' opposition to, 200–201, 203, 210, 214; rise of, 44, 51, 52; in Whig Party, 153; Working Men's parties' opposition to, 86

Paternalism, 21–22

Patriarchy, 36–37

Pelham, Mass., 32

Pennsylvania: antibank sentiment in, 72; Anti-Masonry in, 131–34; constitution of, 22, 48, 192; Democratic-Republican societies in, 53, 54, 56; popular insurgencies in, 227 (n. 25); Working Men's party in, 84, 85–86. *See also* "Fries's Rebellion"; Whiskey Rebellion

Pennsylvania Gazette, 51

"People, the," 3, 17, 19, 20–21, 37, 43, 47, 54, 57–68

People's Constitution (Rhode Island), 159, 165–67, 171

People's Party (1820s New York), 102, 141

People's (Populist) Party (1890s), 5–6, 7, 12

People's sovereignty, 17–18, 19–21, 43, 141, 159–60, 191–92, 196, 197; Anti-Masonry on, 114–15; and Democratic Republican societies, 54–55; and "Dorr War," 161, 166; in presidential inaugurals, 65–68; procedural versus nonprocedural, 191–95

*People the Best Gove[r]nors, The* (anonymous), 19, 23, 225 (n. 13)

Perkins, Thomas H., 78

Perot, Ross, 2

Pessen, Edward, 85, 86, 245 (n. 51)

Pet banks, 146

Peterloo Massacre (1819), 84

Philadelphia: Anti-Masonry in, 132; Democratic-Republican societies in, 53, 54; Working Men's party in, 84, 85–86

Philadelphia Convention (1787), 36

Philadelphiensis (pseudonym), 40

Philips family, 25

Phillips, John, 81

Phillips, Kevin, 21

Phillips, Wendell, 87

Piedmont, 25–26, 226–27 (n. 21)

Pierce, Franklin, 201, 205

Pierson, Michael D., 261–62 (n. 24)

Pitman, John, 166–67

Pittsburgh, 49, 56

Plebian Anti-Federalists, 38–39, 41, 57

Police forces, 208, 209

Political opposition. *See* Opposition, political

Political participation: Anti-Masonry's influence on, 142; Democratic-Republican societies on, 54; in 1840 presidential election, 152; and voter turnout, 142, 153

Pollack, Norman, 5

Popular sovereignty. *See* People's sovereignty

Populism, 1, 3, 6, 7–8, 35, 45; Anti-Masonic populism, 112–15; of Anti-Rent movement, 185–89; of Middling Interest, 77–82; populist sensibility, 4, 5; populist style, 2; religious populism, 45–46, 81–82, 111–12; rise of populist rhetoric, 143–49, 176–77

*Populism: Its Meaning and National Characteristics* (Ionescu and Gellner), 1

Populist movements: analytical framework for, 1–16; in 1840s, 196; in eighteenth century, 24, 43, 47; progressive and reactionary, 9–16

*Populist Persuasion, The* (Kazin), 2

Postal system, 111, 156, 201

Post Office Act of 1792, 111

Post Office Act of 1836, 156

Potter, Elisha, 164, 169, 172–73

Poverty, 113

Pragmatists: in Anti-Masonry, 94, 103–4, 107

Presidential elections: of 1800, 59–60; of 1824, 66; of 1828, 67, 101, 103, 142; of 1832, 88, 107, 120–21, 125–26, 145; of 1836, 150–51; of 1840, 152–53, 157; of 1844, 191; of 1852, 201; of 1928, 213; of 1992, 2

Press. *See* Newspapers

Press, freedom of, 39

Printing industry, 69–70

Progressive populist movements: Anti-Masonry as, 117–39; challenges of studying, 3, 5; civic nationalism of, 13; common features of, 11–12; Know-

Nothingism as, 199, 204, 206–7, 213; leadership of, 11; localist defense in, 10; reactionary features of, 10, 16

Prohibition: in Know-Nothingism, 199, 204, 205, 207–8, 211

Property of Catholic church, 200–201, 207

Property qualifications: in "Dorr War," 160–76, 195; end of, 195–96; in state constitutions, 22, 23, 142, 225 (n. 12)

Protest, popular: in American culture, 6–7; before American Revolution, 24–27; under Articles of Confederation, 24; elites' repression of, 27, 44; legitimacy of, 19; Republicans on legality of, 57; as template in American Revolution, 19, 43–44. See also specific events and groups

Protestant farmers, 26

Providence Journal, 167

Public affairs: churches' role in, 45–46

Publications, 81, 108–11, 138, 167

Public opinion, 114–15

Public sphere, 38–39, 41, 44–45, 91, 111; Anti-Federalist and Federalist views of, 39, 54; and Democratic Republican societies, 54–55

Pulteney estates, 106

Quincy, Josiah, 80–81

Racism, 86–87, 156, 165

Railroads, 69, 111

Ramsay, David, 22

Ratcliffe, Donald J., 266 (n. 63)

Ratification, 37, 39, 41

Reactionary populist movements: anti-abolitionism as, 157; Anti-Masonry as, 117, 125–39; challenges of studying, 3, 5; common features of, 12–13; Know-Nothingism as, 199, 204, 206–7, 213; labor movement as, 83; localist defense in, 10; progressive features of, 10, 16

Reform movements, 123, 199; and public sphere, 142–43

Registry voters, 171, 173, 195

Regulators: in The Contrast (play), 33–34;

definition of, 25, 228 (n. 28); "Fries's Rebellion" and, 58, 59; interpretations of, 214; leadership of, 30, 31; in Massachusetts, 27–32, 40–41, 214; members of, 31–32, 227 (n. 23); in North Carolina, 25–27; origins of term, 25; progressive populism of, 10; in South Carolina, 25; women in, 32

Relief laws, 72–77

Relief/new court party, 76–77

Religion: in Anti-Masonry, 92–95, 102–3, 118–19, 137; disestablishment of, 45–46, 234–35 (n. 6); freedom of, 46, 137; in Know-Nothingism, 200; in Masonry, 95, 96; in Middling Interest, 81–82; publications promote, 111–12; in Regulations, 27; and temperance, 199; tests of, of witnesses, 136–39; in Whig Party, 149–53; women's role in, 123; in Working Men's parties, 88

Religious populism, 45

Rensselaerwyck, Manor of, 177–78, 179–80

Rent. See Anti-Rent Wars

Replevin laws, 73, 75

Republicanism, 7, 8, 21–22; artisan, 183; and "Fries's Rebellion," 59

Republican Party: emergence of, 212

Republicans: and Democratic-Republican societies, 56, 57; establishment as party, 44; in Middling Interest, 78–82; organization of party, 57; paranoia among, 13–14; post-Revolutionary insurgencies' influence on, 47; on Whiskey Rebellion, 57

Resentment, 7, 15

Restorationism, 12

Revivalism, 92, 95, 152

Revolutionary War. See American Revolution

Rhetoric, populist: anti-elite, 22; of Anti-Federalists, 39–40; of Anti-Masonry, 94–95, 102, 158; in Anti-Rent Wars, 176–77, 186; in Bank War, 143–47; class resentment in, 72; conservative

ment in, 72; economic depression and, 70–72; Middling Interest in, 77–82; relief wars and, 72–77; and rhetoric on the people, 65–68; socioeconomic context for, 68–70; Working Men's parties in, 82–89

Shays's Rebellion, 30; in Whiskey Rebellion, 47, 49–51, 55
Washington Society, 56
Wayland, Francis, 81–82
Webster, Daniel, 65, 67–68, 150
Weed, Thurlow: and Anti-Mason publications, 108, 109; in Anti-Masonry, 103–7; in Bank War, 146; newspaper of, 104, 110; on the people, 113
Wellstone, Paul, 217 (n. 4)
Wheatland, N.Y., 118
Wheeler, Adam, 31
Whig Party: on abolitionism, 155; Anti-Masons in, 107, 123, 135, 145, 147, 149–53; in Anti-Rent Wars, 180–86, 198; and Bank War, 145–46, 147; Catholic voters in, 201; and "Dorr War," 162, 164, 167, 171, 172–73; emergence and rise of, 145–48, 150; evangelical wing of, 149–53; Know-Nothings' opposition to, 201–2, 204–5; in Maryland's electoral system, 193–94; National Republicans and, 147; origin of name, 146; on popular sovereignty, 159; in presidential elections, 150–51, 152–53; principles of, 146–47; traditional interpretations of, 146
Whigs: in Revolution, 14, 20, 27
Whiskey Rebellion (1794), 47–51; Anti-Federalists on, 57; defeat of, 50–51; Democratic-Republican societies in, 55–57; Federalists on, 49–51, 56; interpretations of, 47, 50–51; leadership of, 49–50; origins of, 47–49; political protest in, 48–49; violent protest in, 49
"White Indians," 61–62, 196–97
White men's republic, 36, 231 (n. 54)
Whiting, William, 29–30, 228 (n. 32)
Whitman, Walt, 188–89
Whittlesey, Frederick, 104, 107, 109, 113, 250–51 (n. 22), 252 (n. 33)

Wiebe, Robert, 159–60, 177
Wilentz, Sean, 222 (n. 43)
Wilkinson, Smith, 129, 130
Wilkinson family, 171
Williams, Catherine R., 175–76
Wilson, Henry, 205
Wirt, William, 107, 120–21, 125–26
Witnesses: religious tests for, 136–39
Wolf, George, 132, 134
Wollstonecraft, Mary, 121
Women: in abolitionism, 123–25, 158; in Anti-Masonry, 117–25, 126–27; in Anti-Rent Wars, 187; Constitution on, 36–37; in "Dorr War," 174–76; education for, 121–22; in 1840 presidential election, 152; in Know-Nothingism, 210–12; in progressive movements, 11; in reactionary movements, 12; in Regulations, 32; in Republican Party, 212; suffrage for, 23, 176
Women's rights. See Feminism
Wood, Gordon, 14, 230–31 (n. 51)
Woodbury, Levi, 194
Worchester, Mass., 31, 32
Working Men's parties, 82–89; Anti-Masons working with, 104–5; in electoral politics, 84–89; emergence of, 83, 84; ideology of, 83–84, 85–86; use of term, 245 (n. 49); and Whig Party, 147–48
World War II, 2
Wright, Silas, 183, 188

Yeoman persuasion, 32–33
Young, Alfred F., 232 (n. 58)
Young, John, 184–85
*Young America*, 183

Zagarri, Rosemarie, 231 (n. 55)